Property
(V)

LAW OF COMMONS AND OF TOWN AND VILLAGE GREENS

Second Edition

LAW OF COMMONS AND OF TOWN AND VILLAGE GREENS

Second Edition

Navjit Ubhi

Barry Denyer-Green

Published by
Jordan Publishing Limited
21 St Thomas Street
Bristol BS1 6JS

British Library Cataloguing-in-Publication Data
A catalogue record for this book is available from the British Library.

ISBN 1 84661 044 3

Typeset by Etica Press Limited, Malvern, Worcestershire
Printed in Great Britain by Antony Rowe Limited, Chippenham, Wilts

PREFACE

There have been two principal developments since the publication of the first edition of this book. The Commons Act 2006 covers four principal matters: a more efficient and useful registration system for rights of commons and town or village greens, changes to the definition of Class c town or village greens to make the registration of these greens easier, the creation of commons councils concerned with the management of commons, and improved procedures for protecting commons from unlawful works. The other development is the decision of the House of Lords in the 'Trap Grounds' case clarifying the procedures and criteria for the registration of a town or village green under the Commons Registration Act 1965, a decision that will also have some relevance under the 2006 Act.

We have tried to state the law as at 19 September 2006.

Navjit Ubhi
Barry Denyer-Green
September 2006

CONTENTS

TABLE OF CASES

References are to paragraph numbers

TABLE OF STATUTES

References are to paragraph number

TABLE OF STATUTORY INSTRUMENTS AND GUIDANCE

References are to paragraph numbers

GLOSSARY

Abatement

A self-help remedy enabling commoners to remove obstructions to the exercise of their rights, the abatement of a nuisance.

Amerciaments

A punishment by which the offender stood in the court of his lord and was at his mercy.

Appendant rights

Rights that were attached to land by operation of law such as rights of common of pasture attached to arable land that was granted by the lord of the manor before 1290 (or possibly 1189).

Approvement

The lord of the manor or owner of the soil had the right to inclose the land not required for the commoners.

Appurtenant

Rights attached to land by express deed of grant or by prescription not being rights attached by operation of law.

Award

The formal document made under an Act of Inclosure setting out the terms of inclosure of land or the regulation of the common lands.

Beastgates

A right to graze a fixed number of animals. See Stint.

Bookland

An Anglo-Saxon form of land ownership of ecclesiastical origin.

Bote

A Saxon word for the products of the soil in the form of wood or timber.

Bridle path

A public highway over which the public have rights to pass on horse, cycle or foot.

Bylaws

Local laws made under delegated law-making powers.

Cart-bote

Wood required for making and repairing agricultural implements.

Cattlegates

See Stint.

Chief rents

Rents payable in respect of land held from the lord of the manor.

Common fen

Fens and marshes in eastern England were often subject to rights of common.

Common land	Has various meanings according to the statutory context but generally means land subject to rights of common.
Common of shack	Right to put animals in common in a common field after harvest to pick up the fallen ears of corn.
Common fields	Originally large fields, strips of which were separately owned, but over the whole of which the several owners had rights in common to graze animals after the removal of arable crops.
Commonable lands	Has various meanings but confined in this work to land divided into separate strips over which all the several owners have rights of common grazing after harvest or in fallow years.
Commoners	Persons having rights of common over common land.
Cone-burrow	See Coney-burrow.
Coney-burrow	A type of warren where rabbits are bred.
Copyhold	A form of land ownership by which the owner held title to land within a manor and according to its customs subject to the will of the lord: abolished in 1922.
Court Baron	Manorial court dealing with the rights of copyholders.
Court Leet	Manorial court of criminal jurisdiction.
Cowgrasses	See Stint.
Cow-leaze	See Stint.
Curtilage	The immediate court yard or land surrounding a dwelling.
Custom	A right, obligation, or privilege having the force of law.
Customary Court	One of the manorial courts.
Customary freeholders	A form of copyhold by which the owner held title according to the custom of the manor and not at the will of the lord.
Customary rights	See Custom.
Damages	In litigation a sum awarded for compensation from a wrongdoer.

Deed	Document satisfying certain formalities and which is used for the creation and transfer of land and interests in land, amongst other matters.
Deed of dedication	A formal undertaking by the maker having legal consequences, such as the dedication of land for public access under section 193 of the Law of Property Act 1925.
DEFRA	The Government Department for Environment, Food and Rural Affairs.
Demesne	Land within a manor owned and occupied by the lord for his own purposes.
Demise	The grant of a lease.
Depasture	To bring to an end the rights of pasture.
Dominant tenement	Land having the benefit of rights, such as the rights of common.
Driving the common	The rounding up of animals on a common to remove strays and those in excess of individual rights.
Easement	A right attached to land exercisable over other land in a different ownership, such as a right of way.
Enclosure	See Inclosure.
Enfeoff	To make a person the owner of land by means of a feoffment. See Feoffment.
Equitable right	An interest in land enforceable under the rules of equity and generally only, against persons having notice of the same.
Estate	An interest in land. Since 1925 the only legal estates are the fee simple absolute in possession (freehold) or the term of years absolute (leasehold).
Estovers	Produce of the land in the form of wood or timber.
Express grant	The grant of an interest in land by way of an actual deed of grant.
Extinguishment	The bringing to an end of a right or interest in land.
Fallow land	Land resting between arable crops and usually down to grass.
Fee simple absolute	One of the two estates in land. See Estate.
Fen	Marshy tracks of land in east England.
Fence month	Period during which a royal forest was closed for the protection of deer.

Feoffment	Originally a public ceremony by which a person acquired an interest in land.
Feudal system	The form of society under which the manor was the principal unit, the lord of the manor providing protection for his serfs and his tenants and they in turn owing him service or payments.
Foldage	The right of the lord of the manor to require his tenants to put their sheep on his demesne.
Folkland	Anglo-Saxon land ownership where the owners cultivated land under a open or common field system.
Footpath	A public highway over which the public have the right to pass on foot.
Franchises	A liberty or privilege, such as the right to hold a market, existing at common law or as a custom as an interest in land.
Frankpledge	The means of preserving the peace by which men where pledged in groups of ten with each member providing surety for the others.
Free warren	Right to keep and kill hares and rabbits within a specified area.
Freehold	One of two legal estates in land amounting, in effect, to absolute ownership. See Estate.
Furzes	Small bushes cut for fodder or bedding.
Gated pasture	See Beastgate.
Glebe	Land belonging to the parish priest.
Grant	As in the grant of some right or interest in land to another, usually by deed.
Grantee	The person to whom a grant is made.
Grantor	The person making the grant.
Half year land	Land cultivated by its several owners for half a year and subject to grazing in common for the remainder. See also Lammas land.
Hay-bote	A right to take wood or timber to repair fences.
Herbage	The produce of land that can be cut or grazed by animals.
Hereditament	Interest in land capable of passing, originally to an heir; corporeal hereditaments are tangible objects such as land and buildings and incorporeal

hereditaments are intangible objects such as *profits à prendre.*

Heriots   In relation to copyhold the customary right of the lord of the manor to take the best beast of a tenant upon the latter's death.

House-bote   The right to take wood or timber to repair buildings.

Husbandry   The activity of farming.

Implied grant   In relation to a *profit à prendre*, arising by implication from long user ("prescription") rather then by express grant.

In gross   A *profit à prendre* existing independently of the ownership of any land.

Inclosure   The process of extinguishing rights of common and converting common land to land free of such rights.

Inclosure award   See inclosure and award.

Incorporeal hereditament   See hereditament.

Injurious affection In relation to compulsory purchase compensation, the diminution in value caused by public works to land retained by a claimant.

Intercommoning   In relation to common fields, the rights of the owners of the field strips to graze the whole in common after the removal of the arable crops.

Lammas Day   1 August (New Calendar), land opened on Lammas Day for grazing in common, usually land used for hay crops.

Lammas land   See Lammas Day.

Laneland or Lænland Anglo-Saxon form of ownership having commercial basis.

Leasehold   One of two legal estates in land by which a tenant holds land for a defined period. See Estate.

Legal memory   The Coronation of Richard I 1189.

Levant and *couchant* A qualification of the extent of rights of common of pasture limited to the number of animals that can 'get up and lie down' on the dominant tenement during winter.

Licence   Permission or consent to be on land not amounting to a legal interest.

Licensee   The person to whom a licence is given.

Licensor	The person who grants a licence.
Limitation	A statutory bar on bringing legal proceedings after a specified period of time.
Lord of the manor	The person owning the Norman unit of land ownership known as the manor, the manor remaining a property right the owner of which retains this descriptive title.
Lost modern grant	A legal fiction arising where an easement or *profit à prendre* is claimed by prescription; the law assumes that the legal interest was granted by deed, and the deed has been lost.
Lot meadow	Commonable land owned in severalty usually used as hay meadows where owners draw lots to determine the individual strips to be cut for hay by each owner.
Manor	See Lord of the manor.
Manorial court	See Courts Baron, Leet and Customary.
Manorial waste	See waste land of a manor.
Meadow land	Land down to grass and usually used for grazing and hay.
Memorandum	A clause or document noting the particulars of some transaction or matter.
Mean high water mark	The average of the high tide water levels; below which the land is owned by the Crown
Metes	Measurement
Metes and bounds	By measurements and boundaries.
Metropolitan commons	Usually a common within the metropolitan police district on the 10 August 1866.
National parks	Areas of land identified for special scenic protection under the National Parks and Access to the Countryside Act 1949.
Nuisance	A tort or legal wrong.
Open field system	An agricultural practice by which a large field was held in strips by separate owners who together grazed their animals over the whole after the removal of the arable crops.
Pannage	A right to put swine to woodlands to forage for acorns and beech mast.

Part performance	A legal doctrine by which a lack of formality can be overcome where one party partly performs his legal obligations.
Pasturage	A right of pasturage is a right to use land for grazing.
Piscary	A right to take fish.
Prescription	Legal doctrine by which easements and *profits à prendre* can be acquired by long user.
Profit à prendre	A legal interest in land consisting of a right to take the produce or part of the soil of another, such as rights of common.
Pur cause de vicinage	The right to inter-common as between adjoining commons; actually a defence to an action in trespass where animals stray off the 'home' common.
Quia Emptores	Statute of Edward I 1290.
Quit rents	Dealing with the transfer of interests in land.
Reeves	An official supervising, eg, the management and stocking of a common.
Registered land	Land whose ownership is registered under the Land Registration Acts 1925–2002.
Regulated pasture	Pasture regulated by an inclosure award and owned by the graziers in undivided shares.
Reservation	An area of land or some interest in land kept back out of a conveyance or other deed by the vendor.
Right in gross	Such as a *profits à prendre* where the right is held without being annexed to any land
Right of way	An easement and a legal interest in land entitling the grantee to pass and re-pass over another's land.
Rights of common	Has various definitions under different statutes, but generally rights exercised by commoners in common with the owner of the soil such as rights to graze.
Seigniorial	Associated with a feudal lord.
Servient land	Land over which an easement or a *profit à prendre* is exercised.
Servient tenement	See servient land.
Several vesture	A right to all the products of the soil of another exercisable by several or separate persons.
Several	See Severalty.

Severalty	Where a property or interest in property is held by two or more persons, it is held in severalty where each has a distinct and ascertained share as apposed to joint ownership (or tenancy).
Severance compensation	Compulsory purchase compensation where land is severed.
Shack	See common of shack.
Sheep heaves	An area of land where a hefted flock of sheep graze, hefting means that the sheep have learnt and keep to the boundaries of that land.
Sheepheaf	See Sheep heaves.
Sheepwalk	See Sheep heaves.
Sites of special scientific interest	An area of nature conservation notified under the Wildlife and Countryside Act 1981.
Sole pasture	A right to graze usually held by a single person, or where held by more, each holding a stint of equal size.
Sole profit	A *profit à prendre* where the owner of land has granted to another person or persons the whole and exclusive right such as a right to pasture, and retains no such right himself.
Sole vesture	See a sole profit, a sole vesture is the right to all the produce of the land excluding timber.
Stint	A distinct and equal share in a right such as a right of pasture normally entitling a stint holder to a fixed number of animals.
Stint holders	See Stint.
Stinted pasture	See Stint, there are various other names such as Cattlegate, Beastgate, Cowgrasses, Beastgrasses, Cow-leaze and Pasturegate.
Strays	Animals found on a common not belonging to any of the commoners.
Surcharging	Animals found on a common in excess of the numbers permitted to be present.
Tenancy	See leasehold.
Tenants in common	Form of co-ownership by which the individuals hold distinct shares.
Tenement	Land capable of being owned by a tenure, such as a freehold or leasehold.

Term of years absolute	One of two legal estates in land, see leasehold.
Time immemorial	See Legal memory.
Turbary	Right to take peat or turves for fuel.
Vesture	Right to take all the produce of the land excluding timber.
Vicinage	See *pur cause de vicinage*.
Villeins	The inhabitants of a feudal manor required to work for the lord.
Warrens	A free warren is a right to keep beasts and birds, namely, hare, rabbit, pheasant, partridge and wild duck.
Waste land of the manor	The uninclosed lands of a manor that may or may not be subject to rights of common.
Wayleaves	A statutory right to lay a pipe or cable across private land.

Chapter 1

BACKGROUND

1.1   INTRODUCTION

The Commons Registration Act 1965 made provision for the registration of commons and town and village greens, and of rights of common. The Commons Act 2006 contains new improved provisions for the maintenance of registers of commons, greens and rights of commons; it also provides for the repeal of the 1965 Act, and for the future management of commons. There are strong arguments in favour of dealing with the registration requirements and provisions of the 1965 and 2006 Acts in a book on commons before anything else. The difficulty with that approach is that the reader may not understand the legal and historical context in which the two Acts came to apply, or the terms and definitions that were, and to a lesser extent, are now, relevant. In this book we therefore first deal with the historical and legal context of commons, and explain a number of legal concepts and principles, before examining in detail the effect of the 1965 and 2006 Acts.

1.2   WHAT IS COMMON LAND?

Aside from any statutory definitions, common land is that land over which commoners are entitled to exercise rights of common, such as grazing their animals; most of it is privately owned land. The rights are exercisable together with, or to use the technical expression, *in common* with, others.[1] All or part of the open uninclosed waste area of the unit of land ownership known since the Norman conquest as 'the manor', would have been common land. The owner of the manor and, therefore, of the common land, was the lord of the manor.[2]

However, some lands were known as *commonable lands*. Although their origin and purpose are discussed elsewhere in this book,

---

[1]   The expression 'common land' has particular meanings under different statutes. The definition of 'common land' under the Commons Registration Act 1965 is considered later in this chapter. The Commons Act 2006 does not define common land, as such.

[2]   However, the position is not always so clear: see Chapter 5.

commonable lands were generally arable lands that were cropped in strips by individuals but which were, as a whole, subject to rights of common, usually grazing, when the crops had been removed and during the fallow year.[1] Under the Commons Registration Act 1965, commonable lands fell within the definition of *common land* for registration purposes.[2]

It was originally a popular misconception that common land belongs to everyone and that the public have rights of access over all common land. Prior to October 2005, rights of access were largely restricted to metropolitan commons and certain other commons to which s 193 of the Law of Property Act 1925 had been applied. Generally, there was no public right of access to rural commons, such as those in the upland and hill areas that are still used for grazing purposes. But since October 2005, when the Countryside and Rights of Way Act (CROW Act) 2000 came fully into force, there has been a general public right of access on foot over all registered common land.[3]

The meaning of 'common land' can actually be much more complicated than the introductory explanation set out above. There has been much legislation concerning common land and the expression may have slightly different meanings under different Acts and for different purposes. For most purposes, common land is any land registered as such under the Commons Registration Act 1965 and the Commons Act 2006.

1.3   WHAT ARE RIGHTS OF COMMON?

In the case of the uninclosed land in a manor, rights of common were originally held by the freehold (and copyhold) tenants of the lord of the manor.[4] They were local people who lived and worked within the manor and were often referred to as *commoners*. Rights of common were also held by the owners of commonable lands. As the author of one treatise put it:[5]

---

[1]   See Chapters 2 and 3.

[2]   Section 22(1).

[3]   Registered common land is that registered under the Commons Registration Act 1965.

[4]   Prior to 1926 interests in land included freeholds and copyholds. Strictly, only freeholders held *rights* of common, as incidences of their grants; copyhold tenants had *rights* as part of the custom of the appropriate manor.

[5]   Woolrych *A Treatise on the Law of Rights of Common* (1824), at p 13.

'A Right of Common is an incorporeal hereditament, and may be said to exist where two or more, by virtue of a grant, prescription, or custom, take, in common with each other, from the soil of a third person, a part of the natural profits thence produced.'

The more usual rights of common are:

– grazing or pasturage;
– pannage: to put pigs in woodland to graze on acorns and beech mast;
– piscary: to take fish;
– turbary: to take peat turves for fuel;
– estovers: the Saxon word was bote; it consisted of wood and timber and was expressed as house-bote (firewood, and wood for repairing a house), plough or cart-bote (making and repairing agricultural implements) and hay-bote (for repairing fences);
– rights in the soil: right to take sand, gravel, stone, marl and other minerals.

Today, the principal legal interests that can exist in land are the two legal estates (freehold and leasehold) and legal interests such as easements and *profits à prendre*.[1] *Profits à prendre* are rights to take something from another's land and therefore include rights of common. Rights of common are therefore capable of being legal interests in land today.[2]

1.4 WHAT ARE TOWN AND VILLAGE GREENS?

A town or village green is usually that part of the local common that lies within or immediately around the centre of a town (in reality, and in most cases, an expanded village) or village and, accordingly, would have been subject to rights of common. However, town and village greens are often used for a wide range of recreational, leisure and husbandry purposes, and therefore may not necessarily be subject to rights of common.

Because of their recreational and leisure value, town and village greens have been accorded more and more legislative protection and

---

1 Law of Property Act 1925, s 1; under Commonhold and Leasehold Reform Act 2000, s 2, an application can be made to register a freehold estate in land as a freehold estate in commonhold land. This is likely to be restricted to blocks of flats.

2 Rights of common are more fully explained in Chapters 3 and 4.

management control.[1] As such, they were registrable under the Commons Registration Act 1965,[2] and remain registrable under the Commons Act 2006.

1.5   FACTUAL BACKGROUND

Common land comprises some 550,000 hectares – about 4% of the total land area in England and Wales. There are some 367,000 hectares in England (about 3% of the total land area), of which nearly 50% (180,000 hectares) is either wholly or partially designated as Sites of Special Scientific Interest. In England, over 48% of common land lies mainly within National Parks, and 31% is wholly or partially within Areas of Outstanding Natural Beauty. Surprisingly, just over 51% of all registered commons in England are less than 1 hectare in area, and only 1.3% are 1,000 hectares or more in area. Just over half of England's common land is in Cumbria and North Yorkshire.[3]

1.6   HISTORICAL BACKGROUND

Common land has had a significant role in the agricultural life of England and Wales. However, during the eighteenth and nineteenth centuries substantial areas of common land were inclosed and apportioned out to the larger landowners in the locality. The effect of inclosure was to end the commoners' rights and to divide up the inclosed land among the larger landowners. That was especially true of the more agriculturally fertile land. However, by the mid-nineteenth century there was increasing concern about the role that common land provided or could provide for wider recreational purposes. Thus, legislation in that century made provision for rights of public access for recreational purposes in relation to, for example, commons in metropolitan areas.

The role of common land in the agricultural economy of any locality originally operated within a legal context of manorial courts and the freehold and copyhold tenants of the manor. That legal framework was partially dismantled by the reforms of property law in 1922–1925

---

[1]   See Chapter 9.

[2]   Section 1(1)(a), for example by custom or use as of right for 20 years: *R v Oxfordshire County Council, ex parte Sunningwell Parish Council* [2000] AC 335.

[3]   These facts and figures are taken in part from the website of the Department of Food and Rural Affairs (Defra): www.defra.gov.uk.

when copyholds were abolished.[1] After 1925 most of the principal purposes of the manorial courts no longer existed and the management of common land and the regulation of the rights of the commoners through the manorial courts virtually ceased to take place. In any event, the role of common land in agricultural practices became significantly less important in the lowland and more densely populated areas of the country. It was against that background that a Royal Commission produced a report in 1958.[2]

The Commission's principal recommendations were the creation of a statutory register of common land, its ownership and the rights of commoners, the creation of public rights of access over all commons, and provisions for the regulation and management of commons primarily with regard to the changing expectations of the general public that common land had an important role to play in the future. Parliament enacted the Commons Registration Act 1965 to give effect to the first of these recommendations. But it was not until the CROW Act 2000 that Parliament enacted legislation that will give the public a right of access on foot to all registered common land where such a right did not already exist.

1.7   COMMONS REGISTRATION ACT 1965

The Commons Registration Act 1965 required the registration of all common land, town and village greens, the ownerships of common land and of rights of commons.[3] The 1965 Act contained its own, and rather wide, definition of *common land* that was relevant for registration purposes:[4]

'In this Act, unless the context otherwise requires, –

"common land" means –
(a)   land subject to rights of common (as defined in this Act) whether those rights are exercisable at all times or only during limited periods;
(b)   waste land of a manor not subject to rights of common;

---

[1]   Law of Property Act 1922.

[2]   *Royal Commission Report on Common Land.*

[3]   See Chapter 8.

[4]   Section 22(1).

but does not include a town or village green or any land which forms part of a highway. '

'Rights of common' were defined as including:[1]

'… cattlegates or beastgates (by whatever name known) and rights of sole or several vesture or herbage or of sole or several pasture, but does not include rights held for a term of years or from year to year.'

This definition of common land is considered in more detail later in this book, but it is wider than the initial working definition adopted at the commencement of this chapter as it includes both commonable land and waste land of the manor not subject to rights of common.

Of 7,039 common land units in England, only 34.6% have registered rights of common and these commons account for nearly 88% of the total area of common land. Of the commons with registered rights, 65% have five registered rights or less and 13.7% have 20 rights or more. Rights to graze cattle were registered on 20% of commons, sheep on 16%, horses and ponies on 13% and estovers (the right to take wood for certain purposes) on 10%. There are approximately 24,157 rights entries on the registers, although this represents a complex situation because of duplication of rights and cross-referencing between adjacent commons. In relation to the ownership of commons, some 1,900 commons had no known owners. At the time of registration, 1,787 commons were in private ownership, 679 had private owners for parts of the land, 1,230 were owned by parish and other councils and 431 were owned by a variety of organisations including charities and trusts.[2]

1.8   RECENT DEVELOPMENTS: THE COMMONS ACT 2006

1.8.1   Background to the Act

In November 2000, in the *Rural White Paper*,[3] the Government stated that it was committed to legislate on common land as soon as Parliamentary time allowed. Its objective was:

---

1   Commons Registration Act 1965, s 22(1).

2   See the Defra website: www.defra.gov.uk.

3   *Rural White Paper: Our Countryside: The Future – A Fair Deal for Rural England* (Defra, 2000).

'to provide for the protection of all commons for the benefit of future generations; ... we want to increase our ability to tackle over-grazing wherever it occurs and to provide fairer and more effective systems of registration and management. We will also look to improve the arrangements for town and village greens.'

In 2002 the Government published its *Common Land Policy Statement*. The Statement contained proposals for future legislation with a view to securing the future of common land and village greens, and to protect the features and characteristics that make such land so valuable. The 2006 Act gives effect to the recommendations in this Statement, and makes a number of other detailed changes. It will be brought into effect in stages between 2006 and 2008. The promoting government department is the Department of the Environment, Food and Rural Affairs (Defra).

1.8.2   Registration

Part 1 of the Act will replace and improve the registration system using the registers under the Commons Registration Act 1965. The registers will then be amended and errors and mistakes corrected more easily. It will also place limitations on the grant of rights of common to ensure the affected land can sustain the burden of the rights. Defra will consult on Part 1, and the proposed regulations, early in 2007 with a view of introducing the new rules in stages, starting with a few registration authorities, from late 2007 onwards.[1] However, one provision is already in force: the severance of a registered right of common from any land to which it is attached is now prohibited subject to certain limitations.

1.8.3   Management

Part 2 contains powers enabling the appropriate national authority in England and Wales to establish commons councils with functions related to the management of agricultural activities, vegetation and the exercise of rights of common on common land or on town or village greens where rights of common exist over such land. There are also powers to modify or remove existing statutory schemes of management that might conflict with functions given to a new commons council. Defra will consult on the implementation of this

---

[1]   The Defra website (www.defra.gov.uk) should be consulted on the last position.

Part, and the necessary regulations, in early 2008 with the first commons council being set up in 2008.[1]

1.8.4   Protection

Section 194 of the Law of Property Act 1925 prohibited, without the consent of the Secretary of State, the erection of fencing and other works on land that was subject to rights of common on 1 January 1926. That provision will be repealed by the Act, and certain other enactments amended. Part 3 of the Act contains new powers to prohibit works on common land. There is a new and improved consent procedure. This Part of the 2006 Act, together with the necessary regulations, is likely to be in force in late 2007.

1.8.5   Town and village greens

In relation to town and village greens, the 2006 Act makes a number of detailed but important changes to the registration of greens.[2] Where an application is made for registration of land as a town or village green, on the basis of at least 20 years' qualifying use by the public, difficulties can arise where that use ceases for a period of time prior to the application, or construction works are carried out on the land under the benefit of planning permission. These and other problems are addressed in the new registration requirements. These provisions are likely to be in force by mid-2007.

---

[1]   The Defra website (www.defra.gov.uk) should be consulted on the last position.

[2]   Section 15.

Chapter 2

HISTORICAL DEVELOPMENT

2.1   INTRODUCTION

This chapter sets out a brief outline of the historical development of common land and common rights. The following extract from the *Royal Commission Report on Common Land* sets the scene:[1]

> 'The common lands of England and Wales are in general of immemorial antiquity. In certain cases they may be of comparatively recent origin, but in the main they are, in England, as old as English society. In Wales their origin is not less ancient. Just as the Port Meadow at Oxford is the oldest surviving institution in that city, older by centuries than the University, so the common lands of England and Wales are generally the most ancient institution we now possess; older by far than Parliament, older even than the manor within whose organisation and control they subsequently fell.'

2.2   PRE-1066

2.2.1   The importance of agricultural practices

The law of commons has never been an abstract set of rules devised by law-makers of long ago. Rather it was agricultural practices, centuries old, that gave rise to customs and practices that, in due course, came to shape the law of commons. Although many of the terms associated with the law of commons now appear archaic, and some of the legal concepts may seem somewhat opaque, they developed to give structure and form to the prevalent agriculture systems of the day. Accordingly, the law of commons cannot be understood without some knowledge of those agricultural practices that came to shape and influence the form of the law.

---

[1]   WG Hoskins *History of Common Land and Common Rights*, Appendix II, at para 1.

(a)   The rural economy

There are two aspects of the development of the law of commons that need to be recognised. First, the importance of agriculture in the economy of England and Wales. It was the largest sector of the economy and the principal employer until well into the nineteenth century. Not only was agriculture important for obvious reasons of human survival, there were periods in English history when the export of agricultural products was a considerable contributor to the generation of national wealth, the wool industry during the Elizabethan period being a prime example. The second feature in the association of agriculture with the development of the law of commons was the changing nature of agricultural practices. In the earliest periods of the agricultural history considered below, the efficient use of land and the nature of the agriculture practised, demanded the co-operation of those working the land – the farmers and smallholders; sharing the use of fallow land for grazing purposes was in everyone's best interests.[1] Similarly, sharing the use of unploughed or uncultivated land, and the resources it provided, was both necessary and sensible for the efficient continuation of rural communities. People needed wood for heating and cooking, the construction of buildings and tools, and for making fences and repairing hedges. But uncultivated land provided other resources, such as grazing for animals, acorns or beech mast for pigs, and gravel, stone, clay and sand for making roads and, importantly, constructing buildings.

There is a further important factor that shaped the customs and practices associated with agriculture. Most of the country consisted of agricultural communities and the transport infrastructure was, generally, rudimentary. Accordingly the movement of resources between one community and another was quite often extremely difficult, especially during the winter months. High value, low weight, resources might be moved from one part of the country to another, but low value, bulky and heavy resources, such as sand, stone, hay, straw, wood or timber, were far less likely to be transported over large distances between agricultural communities. A high degree of co-operation was necessary to maintain the self-sufficiency of agricultural communities in respect of the commonly consumed resources.

---

[1]   The fallow land was the land put down to grass and resting between crop rotations.

(b)   The open-field systems

An important contribution made to the development of rights of common was the open-field system of agriculture. This was a system of farming that was predominantly arable but required additional tracts of pasture (meadows for hay and other permanent pasture for grazing). Although the open-field system was largely confined to the arable areas of England, it did exist elsewhere. Under this system, individuals would till strips of land within the open field to grow crops. After the crops were harvested, the whole of the open field would be thrown open to all for the grazing of animals. However, the open-field system also required meadow land to grow grass for hay and, although this too was cut on an individual basis, the whole of the common meadow would be thrown open for grazing purposes once the hay crop had been taken. Arable cropping was carried out on a strict rotation basis so that every third or fourth year was a fallow year when only a grass crop, which took few nutrients from the soil, would be grown. During a fallow year animals would graze the fallow land and dung it at the same time.

(c)   Royal Commission Report on Common Land

The *Royal Commission Report on Common Land* assists our understanding in the use of the wilder and uninclosed parts of England and Wales:[1]

> 'Extensive common lands existed not only in the original woods of pre-Conquest England, or on the open moorlands of northern and western England and Celtic Wales, but also in the widespread marches and fens that border the coasts of this country. Of this type the fens and marshes that surrounded the Wash, in Lincolnshire, Norfolk and Cambridgeshire, furnish perhaps the best documented example, though they may be regarded – like the woods of Kent or the uplands of Devon – as typical of their class in any part of the country.
>
> Here we find, too, inter-commoning over a wide area of country. The great wastes of the fens, much of them drying out in the summer months, were managed by groups of villages adjacent to them. Sometimes the group was determined by geographical proximity, sometimes by ancient administrative arrangements of which only echoes may now survive; but whichever the arrangement these groups

---

[1]   WG Hoskins *History of Common Land and Common Rights*, Appendix II.

and their rights were sharply defined and clear differentiated. At first these wastes were treated as common fen, and the group of villages was the managing authority. At a later date, when the partition of the common fen among the individual villages and its appropriation by manorial lords took effect, the villages claimed that their right to inter-common in the fen had existed from time out of mind. Once again we see that common rights are older than the manor, and once again the inference is, as in Kent and elsewhere, that they go back to the earliest days of the Old English settlement.'

2.2.2　The Celts

Although this section deals with the position pre-1066, it is difficult to identify any useful or relevant starting date. Crop rotation and the efficient use of fallow and uncultivated land are the features that form the genesis of the development of customs that later became more formalised as the law of commons. It is believed that, in Celtic times, crop rotation was practised. There was probably a 4-year crop rotation so that each year one of four fields would be kept fallow and uncultivated. Continuously cropping land soon exhausts its manurial value, therefore, allowing an area to lie fallow each year enabled the nutrients to be restored. Apart from any natural rebalancing of soil nutrients, in the absence of an intensively grown crop, the fallow land would be grazed by animals. The dung from these animals and that collected from farmsteads would be used to fertilise the soil. Celtic people were tribal and survival of a tribe depended upon co-operation. One can assume that tribal customs and practices dictated the form of crop rotation and regulated the use of the fallow land, and the cropped land during the winter, by animals belonging to the tribe and its members.

The Roman Invasion placed substantial demands upon agriculture, but also brought with it a number of improvements. Although the invaders required greater quantities of grain, farm implements were much improved, as well as storage methods. However, the system of crop rotation, as such, remained. Even the Romans found that you cannot grow a cereal or any other crop in the same field year after year without yields beginning to deteriorate; fallow land was still required, and cropped land was still available for pasturing animals after a crop was harvested.

2.2.3 Anglo-Saxon period

With the withdrawal of the Romans one might assume that no substantial change in the pattern of agricultural activities would have occurred, other than those changes consequential to changes in the nature of the market for produce and the loss of regularisation that the Romans had no doubt imposed. However, the Anglo-Saxon period leading up to the Norman Invasion was probably the most influential in shaping and refining those agricultural practices that influenced the development of what we now call the law of commons. During the Anglo-Saxon period the method of cultivation was that of the common or open-field system. The cultivated land of each community was divided up into two or three open and uninclosed fields. Each field was divided into a number of strips; a strip was about an acre in size. It was usually a furlong (40 rods) in length, and 4 rods in breadth.[1] A member of a community would own strips scattered between the open fields. In accordance with the custom and practice of the community, at least one open field would be required to remain fallow every year. After the crops were harvested each year and during its fallow year, all members of the community were entitled to allow their cattle to pasture this field as it was, during its fallow year, a 'common' field and the members of the community had common rights of grazing over it.

Land within a common field, or other land, on the fringes of a village, which was not suitable for cultivation of crops, was used as common pasture over which, again, the villagers had common rights. Also, stretching out beyond the common fields, and probably to the boundaries with the next community, were the waste lands over which all had rights to graze their animals and take resources, such as timber. In some cases adjoining communities might share common rights over such waste land.

Such farming practices, associated with the open or common field system, with the use of crop rotation and the common use of fallow and waste lands, continued up to the sixteenth and seventeenth centuries in most parts of the country.

Anglo-Saxon land ownership was generally of three kinds: Folkland, Bookland or Laneland. Those who owned Folkland were free men

---

[1] See Seebohm *Village Community*, at chapter 1 and Holdsworth *A History of English Law* (2nd edn) vol II, at pp 56–78.

owning land that was kept within the family and which was subject to the customs of the locality. These individuals were the cultivators, owning land that they cultivated under the open or common field system. Bookland was originally of ecclesiastical origin, and the incidence of such ownership was governed by the book; it was often a superior form of tenure.[1] Accordingly Folkland held by the cultivators might also be Bookland held by some superior chief, or the Church. It is this form of ownership which probably formed the basis of the titles held by the lords of manorships after the Norman Invasion. Laneland was land held by way of a temporary loan or gift for a period of time, usually for a term of three lives. Whilst Bookland was usually land granted by the King, Laneland represented more of a commercial arrangement within lower levels of land ownership.[2]

What is significant about these forms of land ownership is that they illustrate a more communal, co-operative form of ownership at one end, namely Folkland, to more individual notions of private ownership and rights in the form of both Bookland and Laneland.[3] If the origins of the law of commons are to be found anywhere, the open or common field system and the form of that ownership known as Folkland are the most likely candidates.

Again the *Royal Commission Report on Common Land* helps us to understand the refinement and articulation of common rights:[4]

'The history of common rights in England ... may be viewed as that of an increasing limitation of rights to more sharply defined classes of user. This limitation arose naturally from the pressure of a growing population upon a fixed supply of land throughout historic times. The degree of pressure, and hence the chronology of the limitation of common rights, varied according to local circumstances. But whatever the local variations, the general picture is clear.

At first there was abundant land for everyone, and too few people to colonise or farm it. Common rights had no need of definition and therefore could hardly be said to exist. The first limitation we detect is a

---

[1] 'The book' is the law to which the land was subject: see Holdsworth *A History of English Law* (2nd edn) vol II, at p 68.

[2] Ibid, at pp 56–78.

[3] See Holdsworth *A History of English Law* (2nd edn) vol II.

[4] WG Hoskins *History of Common Land and Common Rights*, Appendix II, at paras 7, 8 and 9.

restriction of these ancient customary practices in a given area to the men of one particular shire. It is at this point that we may speak of the origin of common rights. Where there is no limitation, there can be no rights. Before this date we ought to speak of customary practices rather than of rights; and these might well go back to the earliest generations of pastoral farming in Britain. We next observe a limitation of common rights to a particular *region* in a county. Examples from Kent are the woodland region of the Chart, and the marshes subject to Wye. As late as 1086 Doomsday Book refers to a pasture in Suffolk which is common to all the men of the hundred of Coleness and to no-one else.

The process of limitation of common rights had generally gone much farther than this by the time of the Norman Conquest. In a great number of places common pastures and other common rights were now limited or appropriated to particular manors, or particular vills, or particular boroughs ...

The process of limitation and appropriation continued over several centuries. Common rights often, perhaps generally, became restricted to a particular class of inhabitant within a borough, or a vill, or a manor. The last stage of limitation was reached when even this restriction had to be narrowed by introducing the conception of a *stint* for every right in the common pasture. Instead of each commoner of the borough, manor or vill being free to pasture as many beasts as he liked, the growing shortage of pasture compelled each commoner to agree to a quota according, generally, to the size of his farm.'

2.3 NORMAN CONQUEST

Following the Norman Conquest in 1066, William I divided up the land as he saw fit. He rewarded his followers, and those Anglo-Saxons who came over to him, with grants of land. By such grants, his followers held the lands upon certain conditions of homage and services. William I was the overlord; his followers held land from him as his chief tenants.[1] The structure of the so-called feudal system so imposed was as follows. The chief tenants owed obligations to the King but, in turn, were entitled to rely on the obligations owed to them by their tenants and villains. The principal unit was the manor

---

[1] See Harpum et al, ed, *Megarry & Wade: The Law of Real Property* (6th edn, Sweet & Maxwell), at para 2–002.

and the lord of the manor was usually a chief tenant of the King.[1] Within the manor would be one or more villages. One must bear in mind that the imposition of the structure of the manorship upon Anglo-Saxon village communities encountered a number of difficulties. First, there would have been a language difficulty with the lord of the manor generally speaking only Norman-French, and the villains only Anglo-Saxon. Secondly, any significant interference with the system of agricultural practices, described above, would have been likely to bring chaos and even starvation to the communities. Thirdly, many holders of a manorship would frequently have been away on business with the King, or providing military service for him and they would have left in charge their stewards to manage their affairs in their absences.

The profound effect of the imposition of the manorial system on the previous system of villages is explained in the *Royal Commission Report on Common Land*:[2]

> 'There can be little doubt that originally common land was common property. Outside the valuable arable and meadows of the villages and towns there was for several centuries no need or incentive to appropriate the wild wastes of the moors, heaths, fens, marshes, and woods, into private hands. Customary practices of grazing animals, of taking turf ... and wood for fuel and building ..., of fishing ..., of taking the fruits of Nature, developed unchecked and unchallenged in that large and ample world where there was more than enough for all. The appropriation of these common lands into private ownership is one of the profoundest and at the same time most obscure changes in English history. We see it developing as early as the ninth century; and it was probably the general result of the imposition of manorial system upon an original village communal system. The process of appropriating common land into private ownership was still far from complete at the making of Doomsday Book (1086). But in general common lands and wastes ... had passed into the private ownership of manorial lords by the early thirteenth century, leaving to the peasantry only their customary rights over the surface. Even these surface rights were not safe from the growing claims of many lords, and the agrarian history of the thirteenth century is full of battles between lords and peasants over

---

[1]   The idea of a manor was not completely new as the seigniorial concept was known to the Anglo-Saxons.

[2]   WG Hoskins *History of Common Land and Common Rights*, Appendix II, at para 14.

questions of common rights. Common rights were the mere shadow (though a valuable shadow) of the substance that had once been; but even the shadow had to be fought for and jealously guarded.'

Against that background the agricultural practices and customs of a village were merely absorbed into the manorial system. The lord would often have to conform to the communal system of agriculture, and conform to the rules that governed the use of the uninclosed or waste lands. These rules were asserted against him by his freehold tenants as well as the whole community.[1] The manor was a source of wealth and services for the lord of the manor. Where agricultural practices could be developed, such as by drainage or the cultivation of waste or uncultivated land, the lord of the manor would have a powerful incentive to advance such matters. He derived additional income from higher rents, but his own freehold and other tenants derived obvious benefits as well.[2]

2.3.1 Manorial courts

With the advent of the manor came courts that regulated various aspects of manorial life. Manorial courts were the institutions through which the lord of the manor was able to regulate and resolve land ownership problems, deal with the obligations to provide services and also deal with issues arising from customs of the agricultural practices. Formerly there were three separate courts: the Court Leet; the Court Baron; and the Customary Court. In the Court Leet local by-laws could be made to control animals grazing on the fallow land in the system of open fields, whereas in the Customary Court, by-laws could be made and enforced to control animals on the manorial waste. These courts were normally presided over by the lord's steward, who acted as judge and kept the records. The customary tenants were required to appear and acted like a jury in deciding whether or not a practice was a custom of the manor.

The Court Baron was concerned with the wider enforcement of law and order within the manor. It also recorded the names of new tenants and their heirs. The steward acted as a clerk and kept the records, and the beadle kept order.[3]

---

[1]   See Holdsworth *History of English Law* (2nd edn) vol 7, at p 146.

[2]   For a general background, see H S Bennett *Life on the English Manor* (1948).

[3]   See Jessel *The Law of the Manor* (1998), at chapter 13.

2.3.2   Approvement

One of the common issues between the lord of the manor and his tenants was whether he could approve the common or waste land of the manor without their consent. The word 'approve' meant enclose and bring into cultivation the common land. This would be of commercial advantage to the lord of the manor if he could add it to the land that he held or occupied himself – the lord's demesne. It could also be indirectly to his advantage in that he could let such approved land and derive rents from it. However, it was not necessarily to the advantage of all of the manor's tenants. Because of the uncertainty as to whether the lord of the manor could approve without consent, the Statute of Merton (1235–1236) was enacted to clarify the position and to provide that a lord could approve the common or waste land of the manor without his tenants' consent provided that he left them a sufficiency of common for their purposes. A further Commons Act was passed in 1285 to extend the right of approvement where commoners had rights of common across the commons of two adjoining manors; this Act also prohibited legal actions against a person who had erected a windmill, sheepcote or cowshed, or made necessary enlargements of his curtilage on the common or waste land.

Between 1086 (Doomsday Book) and 1348 (the Black Death) the population of England and Wales trebled.[1] The increase in the population, and the demands it put on agriculture, resulted in the approvement or inclosure of large tracts of the open waste lands which contributed to the disappearance of what had hitherto been common land. The approvement or inclosure of waste lands was in the interests of both the lord of the manor and the more important of his tenants who were agriculturally more productive, and many thousands of farms were created during this period.

The Commons Act 1285 was repealed by the Commons Act 2006; any power of approvement of a common that subsisted at common law was abolished.

---

[1]   Royal Commission on Common Land, Appendix II, at para 18.

2.4   INCLOSURE MOVEMENTS

2.4.1   Changes in agricultural practices

Changes in agricultural practices were to alter the significance of the manor and hastened the inclosure of the common lands. The open-field system with its strict crop rotation and its regulated grazing of the fallow land, was much shaped by the use of the ox as the principal means of ploughing land. In time the ox was replaced by the horse which meant that land could be ploughed more efficiently. However, the horse was less suited to grazing the fallow lands and required large quantities of hay during the winter.[1] The increased use of the horse, and the decline in the use of oxen, altered the balance in the need for open uninclosed land as against cultivated land, and changed the practice of using the fallow land for communal grazing purposes in favour of the cutting of hay that could only be done on an individual, rather than a communal basis. A further factor was the rise in sheep farming during the fifteenth and sixteenth centuries. The open fields, the strip fields and other areas that had been used for arable crops, and customary grazing of the intervening fallow areas, were much more profitably used by sheep for grazing purposes. Indeed many villages were cleared and destroyed in order to facilitate sheep farming.[2]

By the seventeenth and eighteenth centuries further developments in agricultural machinery enabled the less productive areas of common land to be reclaimed, cultivated and used for arable cropping or higher quality pasturage. Inclosure of common land proceeded at a great pace during this period,[3] however, serious concerns were being expressed about the consequences of inclosing common land. As it was put in the *Royal Commission Report on Common Land*:[4]

> 'The disappearance of millions of acres of common lands caused great local hardships. It was not only the economic loss to the commoner, fatal though that often was. The disappearance of a familiar and perhaps beautiful part of the ancient peasant world often caused the deeper pain. ...

---

[1]   See Jessel, *The Law of the Manor* (1998), at chapter 3.

[2]   Ibid.

[3]   The legislation is considered at Chapter 7.

[4]   WG Hoskins *History of Common Land and Common Rights*, Appendix II, at para 50.

Much of the inclosed common land was ploughed up for corn, especially in eastern England, and it was generally believed that the total food production of the nation had thereby increased. But many honest observers in their own localities thought quite otherwise, and William Cobbett said so most pungently of all. Horton Heath was a common of 150 acres. Cobbett reckoned that

> "the cottagers produced from their little bits, in food, for themselves, and in things to be sold at market, more than any neighbouring farm of 200 acres ... I learnt to hate a system that could lead English gentlemen to disregard matters like these! That could induce them to tear up 'wastes' and sweep away occupiers like those I have described! Wastes indeed! Give a dog an ill name. Was Horton Heath a waste? Was it a 'waste' when a hundred, perhaps, of healthy boys and girls were playing there on a Sunday, instead of creeping about covered with filth in the alleys of a town?"[1]

Quite aside from the process of approvement and inclosure was the refinement and restriction on the exercise of customary rights or rights of common. In most cases these became necessary because of pressures on the use of land, hence the regulation imposed by the stint, and the restriction on the numbers of animals that could be placed on the common.[2]

2.5   LEISURE AND RECREATION

The development and growth of the towns and cities in England during the nineteenth century brought an increased demand for land for recreational and leisure purposes.[3] Indeed the growth was so rapid that many areas of uninclosed common land and other wastes became surrounded by urban development. The legislation passed in the nineteenth century was therefore primarily directed to restricting the inclosure of common land, and to providing, in certain cases, public rights of access to certain urban commons for recreational purposes.[4] Thus, in the Inclosure Act 1845, common land in the

---

[1]   See William Reitzel (ed) *The Progress of a Plough Boy to a Seat in Parliament.*

[2]   See Chapter 3.

[3]   See G Shaw Lefevre *English Commons and Forests* (1894) for a description of the battles to protect commons for recreational purposes.

[4]   This is considered in more detail in Chapter 10.

neighbourhood of a town could not be inclosed except by order, and no town or village green could be inclosed under the Act. The Act also made provision for the appropriation of areas for the purposes of exercise and recreation for the inhabitants of a neighbourhood.

By the twentieth century the exercise of commoners' rights had largely died out in many parts of the country. Although grazing rights in the hill and upland areas of England and Wales remain important even today, most of the common land in the lowland areas was rarely used by the commoners in exercise of their rights. The most recent legislation has been concerned with protecting common land by requiring registration,[1] creating public rights of access on foot over registered commons,[2] and providing for the future management of commons and rights of common.[3]

---

[1]   Commons Registration Act 1965.

[2]   CROW Act 2000.

[3]   Commons Act 2006.

Chapter 3

CLASSIFICATION OF COMMON LANDS

3.1   INTRODUCTION

This chapter describes the different types of land that have been, or can be, subject to rights of common. Not all such land was manorial waste of the manor. Rights of common were exercised over commonable lands at the appropriate times of the year (between reaping and sowing), and in fallow years. Woodlands and forests have been subject to special rights of common. In particular parts of the country, what were originally local customs have resulted in lands being subject to, what was called, common of shack and gated or stinted pastures.

3.2   MANORIAL WASTE

In *Potter v North (Sir Henry)*, in an argument put by the Attorney-General to the Court of King's Bench, it was said that:[1]

> 'Upon the creation of manors, the lords took as much as was for their own use into their demesnes, they distributed as much as was convenient amongst their tenants; what was left was called the lord's waste, which was neglected by the lord because he had before taken into his demesnes what he had need of.'

That needs to be put in context. Within a manor, the lands fell into three broad categories: first the lord's demesne land, namely the land that he occupied and had cultivated for his use and that of his household; secondly, land held by the other freeholders within the manor and the copyhold tenants; thirdly, the waste land of the manor as described above, this land was uninclosed and uncultivated land.

Not all the waste lands of a manor were necessarily subject to rights of common. Such rights depended upon any grants (express or implied) of rights of common in relation to the freehold owners, and

---

[1]   1 Ventr 383 at 395; 86 ER 245, at 252.

the custom of the manor in relation to the copyhold tenants. Where such rights did exist, the rights would have been appropriate to the nature of the waste, or the relevant part of the waste. Thus, for example, if the waste consisted entirely of land suitable for grazing purposes, one would expect rights of common of pasture, but not the other rights, such as rights to take estovers. On the other hand, waste that consisted partly or mainly of woodland, might be subject to rights of common of estovers and, possibly, rights of common of pannage but not necessarily rights of common of pasture. In any event, where the woodland part of the waste was subject to rights of common of pannage, such rights or customs were sometimes subject to restrictions.[1]

In the case of waste lands adjoining the sea, the boundary is the mean high water mark. If land is added by accretion, such land acquires the character of the land to which it is added. As Farwell J said in *Mercer v Denne*:[2]

> 'Further, the opinion of text-writers, dealing with the analogous cases of accretion to copyholds and wastes of manors ... Hall on the Sea Shore (2nd ed p 113; p 789 of Mr. Stuart Moore's edition) concludes that the land which has accreted to the lord as freehold must be subject to the copyhold interest of the tenant of the land to which it has been added, or, if waste, to the local customs, common, &c., prescribed for by the tenants in respect of such waste.'

Under the Commons Registration Act 1965, common land was defined as land subject to rights of common and waste land of a manor not subject to rights of common.[3] Accordingly, all waste land was registrable, whether or not it was subject to rights of common. Further, waste land of a manor not subject to rights of common was registrable even where the ownership of the waste land had passed to a person who does not own the manorship.[4]

---

[1]   See Chapter 4.

[2]   [1904] 2 Ch 534, at 560, *affirmed* [1905] 2 Ch 538.

[3]   Section 22(1).

[4]   See *Hampshire County Council v Milburn* [1990] 2 All ER 257.

3.3 COMMONABLE LANDS AND SIMILAR RIGHTS

3.3.1 Commonable lands

The word 'commonable' is used in different contexts and in several statutes to mean different things. It is a word often used in connection with rights of common over waste land. Therefore, it does not follow that wherever that word is found, it necessarily has the meaning now to be ascribed to it.[1] However, in general terms, commonable lands are those lands owned or held in severalty during part of the year, but which are subject to rights in common after the severalty crop has been removed and during fallow years.[2] Severalty means individual ownership of the appropriate share. It is usually associated with the original open-field system whereby individuals owned strips of the open field. The strips were cultivated for arable crops. When the crops had been removed, then the whole open field would be open to those who held rights of common to graze their animals. The persons holding such rights would either be the individual owners of the strips, that is the severalty owners, or they and other persons.

3.3.2 Lammas lands or half-year lands

Lammas lands were usually meadows used for the purposes of growing grass for taking a hay crop. These lands were the open arable and meadow lands, strips of which were owned or held in severalty during part of the year, and which were commonable to persons holding the severalty rights and to other classes of commoners when the severalty crop or hay had been removed.[3] On Lammas Day,[4] after the appropriate crops had been removed, the fields were then open to all those entitled to exercise rights in common, usually of pasturage. Jessel MR said in *Baylis v Tyssen-Amhurst*:[5]

> '... lammas lands, that is, lands which, as I understand the meaning of the term, belong to a person who is absolutely the owner in fee simple, to all intents and purposes, for half the year, and the other half of the

---

[1]   See Gadsden *The Law of Commons* (1988), at p 18, where the author recognises the inherent problems in attempting a definition.

[2]   *Halsbury's Laws of England* (4th edn) vol 6, at para 506.

[3]   Ibid, at para 517.

[4]   Lammas Day was 1 August (or 12 August under the old calendar).

[5]   (1877) 6 ChD 500 at 507.

year he is still the owner in fee simple, subject to a right of pasturage over the lands by other people. Now what that right of pasturage is, of course must be determined by usage, or, as lawyers call it, prescription, which means an implied grant by a former owner of the lammas lands to other people who have the right of pasturage.

Now, in the first place, this right of pasturage, as far as I can understand it, over lammas lands, is always a right annexed to the ownership of some other lands. I use the term "annexed" advisedly. That right, of course, must be determined on the ordinary principles of law, and those principles, as I understand them, say, that where the right is annexed to other lands, the right must have some connection with those other lands to make it what is called appurtenant; that is, there must be some relation between the enjoyment of the right and the enjoyment of those other lands. You may have various connections. The commonest of all is where the right enjoyed is with respect of the beasts which plough the land. The beasts used for ploughing are fed in winter from the land which they plough, and in the summer, in ordinary commons, they go upon the commons. Or it may be the other way, like these lammas lands, where the lands are cultivated till August, and then the beasts are driven upon them in the winter months. That is one connection. It may be the plough beasts.

There may be various other connections. You might, for instance, have a right to depasture so many beasts as are required to manure the land. You might have various other suggested connections between the beasts used on the land and the number of beasts that might depasture. You might require the beasts for various purposes on the land occupied; and those beasts, not exceeding a certain number, might be depastured on the lammas lands or the common lands, as the case may be. But in all ways there must be some connection between the occupation of the lands in respect of which the right is enjoyed and the right itself, which connection from its nature must to a certain extent limit the right enjoyed. You might say for every beast used on the land, not exceeding one beast per acre, there might be a right of common. But used in some way on the land, I think the beasts must be, to make the right appurtenant; otherwise, I do not see what the meaning of the word "appurtenant" is. It is a right appurtenant to the land.'

3.3.3   Shack

Shack is the grain from the ear of the corn that falls to the ground, usually during the harvesting process. A common of shack is similar to the rights over lammas lands in that the land may be held in severalty for part of the year, but after harvest, those persons having the common of shack may put their beasts upon the shack land so that the grain that has fallen to the ground can be consumed. The origin of the right may have arisen in the nature of *vicinage*; in other words because of the difficulties of inclosures, and for the general convenience of all concerned, it was customary to allow the beasts of all the severalty owners onto the lands of all to clean up the fallen grains.[1] The actual practice will depend upon the custom and usage of the particular locality.[2] As with lammas lands, there must be some quantity or measure of the common of shack in terms of the number of beasts. The rule of *levancy* and *couchancy* will apply in the absence of any other rule.[3] The literal meaning of this rule is that the number of beasts a person may put on the shack land is that number that could be maintained on that person's own land during the winter.[4]

In some localities, custom and usage permitted a severalty owner to enclose his own part of the open field. If he did so, then he not only brought to an end the common of shack over his severalty piece of land, but he also brought to an end his right of common of shack over the remaining uninclosed severalty pieces.[5]

3.3.4 Stinted pastures

Stinted pastures have various names, such as cattlegate, beastgate (Suffolk), cowgrasses, beastgrasses, cow-leaze (Epping Forest), and pasturegate. 'Gated' and 'stinted' mean the same thing, the terms denote the number of animals that the holder of the right is entitled to put on the common. Cattlegate is probably the most common term to describe these various rights; cattlegates are found mainly in the north of England. The lord of the manor may own the soil but subject to the right of pasture by the cattlegate owners.[6] Alternatively the

---

[1] See *Corbet's case* (1585) 7 Co Rep 5a, 77 ER 417.

[2] *Cheesman v Hardham* (1818) 1 B & Ald 706 at 711.

[3] Ibid.

[4] As explained in *Robertson v Hartopp* (1889) 43 ChD 484 at 516, a case concerning appendant rights.

[5] See *Corbet's case* (1585) 7 Co Rep 5a, 77 ER 417.

[6] *Rigg v Earl of Lonsdale* (1857) 1 H&N 923.

ownership of the soil may be held by the cattlegate owners themselves as tenants in common.[1]

Similar to cattlegates are the sheep heaves also found in the north of England. These were small plots of pasture, found in the middle of the waste land of the manor, the ownership of which belonged to a person other than the lord of the manor. However, there is doubt as to whether sheep heaves ever existed as such and, in any event, they must now be regarded as obsolete.[2]

3.3.5   Regulated pastures

Where an order of inclosure was made under the Inclosure Act 1845, this could provide for the conversion of land into a regulated pasture; the ownership of the soil would then belong to the owners of the stints as tenants in common. The rights of common were extinguished but the management of the regulated pasture was vested in the stint holders. Strictly, the land ceased to be common land.

3.3.6   Commons Registration Act 1965

Although this Act will be repealed by the Commons Act 2006, it made provision for the registration of rights of common that is continued in the 2006 Act. The wide definition of common land in the 1965 Act included land subject to rights of common 'whether those rights are exercisable at all times or only during limited periods'.[3] Accordingly, most of the rights described under this heading of commonable lands are such rights and the land over which they are exercisable was therefore common land for the purposes of the 1965 Act, and such land, and the rights of common over it, fell to be registered under the Act. In the case of regulated pastures, it is doubtful whether such rights were capable of registration under the 1965 Act as they would not, following an inclosure award, have any longer been rights of common as such.[4]

---

[1]   *R v Whixley Inhabitants* (1786) 1 Term Rep 137.

[2]   See Gadsden *the Law of Commons* (1988), at p 98.

[3]   Section 22(1).

[4]   See Gadsden *the Law of Commons* (1988), at p 38.

3.4   THE OLD ROYAL FORESTS

A 'forest' has a particular meaning. It is not necessarily woodland, but it describes an area of land that was formerly subject to 'forest law'. Forests were large areas of land over which the King had exclusive hunting rights in the exercise of his prerogative. The forest laws protected those rights.[1] The King's hunting rights and the forest laws that protected them, overlay the ownership of land by others within the forest and the rights of commoners over common land. There were special courts to enforce the laws: the Court of Attachment had summary jurisdiction and the Court of Swainmote was concerned with the more serious offences; sentence was pronounced by the Chief Justice in Eyre. The principal officers were the wardens and verderers, and below them the keepers and the reeves. The latter marked and controlled the cattle of the commoners. By the seventeenth century these special courts no longer sat. In 1829 the residual royal powers were vested in the Commissioner of His Majesty's Woods and Forests.[2]

The remnants of the original Royal forests include the New Forest in Hampshire, the Forest of Dean in Gloucestershire, Epping Forest, near London and Ashdown Forest in Sussex. There were originally 68 Royal forests but most were divided up into private ownership and wholly or partially inclosed.

Rights of common over land within a Royal forest could be acquired by prescription, even by a class of persons consisting of the inhabitants of a parish. The foundation for prescription is a grant (even though implied) and it could be assumed that the Crown could make such a grant in derogation of its forestral rights, especially as the same were oppressive upon the inhabitants.[3] Rights of common of pasture in a forest were generally limited to horses and cattle,[4] although the right to pasture sheep has been claimed.[5] In some forests there were prescriptive rights of pasture by sheep but in others the common of pannage existed. However, a common feature of all the

---

[1]   Forest laws were abolished by Wild Creatures and Forest Laws Act 1971. Forests were protected before the Norman invasion: see *the Laws of Canute*, Winchester 1016.

[2]   See WA Gordon *The Law of Forestry* (1955), at pp 66–68.

[3]   *Willingdale v Maitland* (1866) LR 3 Eq 103.

[4]   See *Leicester Forest Case* (1607) Cro Jac 155.

[5]   See WA Gordon *The Law of Forestry* (1955), at p 70.

forests was that any rights were subject to restrictions and controls in the interests of the preservation of the game for the King. For instance, in some forests there was a 'fence month' or a winter heyning. These were periods during which the forest was closed for the protection of deer either during fawning or in winter when pasture was reserved only for the deer.[1] In the Forest of Dean, rights of common have never been admitted by the Crown, and animals are only permitted by sufferance.

---

[1]   See *Halsbury's Laws of England* (4th edn) vol 6, at para 514. In the New Forest, the *fence month* was 15 days before and after midsummer day.

Chapter 4

CLASSIFICATION OF RIGHTS OF COMMON

4.1   INTRODUCTION

The right of commoners to let their animals graze on common land is the right that most readers understand as amounting to rights of common. Behind this relatively simple concept lie two formative matters. First, the history, origin and nature of agricultural practices, as explained in Chapter 2, have had a considerable effect on the legal form of rights of common. Secondly, the development of the law relating to rights of common, both the common law, and the customary law enforced in the manorial courts, has given rights of common, in their various forms, certain legal characteristics.

In this chapter, rights of common are first classified and explained according to their legal form and consequence. Later in the chapter the various kinds of rights of common are described. Although some mention may be made in this chapter of the various statutory provisions that regulate or are concerned with the registration of rights of common, this chapter is primarily concerned with the common law and customary law relating to rights of common and not with any analysis of various statutory definitions which may be relevant for specific purposes.

4.1.1   Effect of the Commons Registration Act 1965

The Commons Registration Act 1965 provided for, inter alia, the registration of rights of common, and registration will be continued by the Commons Act 2006. Whilst some explanation of the different types of rights of common, and their origin and legal development, may be interesting, the consequences of the 1965 Act renders such background of little significance today. All rights of common that existed prior to 31 July 1970 were required to be registered.[1] Further, any rights of common that existed prior to that date, but which were

---

[1]   Section 1(1).

not then registered under the Act could not any longer be exercisable.[1] However, provision was made under the 1965 Act for the registration of new rights of common created after 31 July 1970.[2] The 1965 Act also provided that where a right of common consisted of or included a right to graze animals that is not limited by number, then the right was required to be registered by reference to a stated number of animals. Indeed the right could not, after the registration had become final, be exercised in relation to more than the specified and registered number of animals.[3] The effect of that provision meant that many of the interesting and difficult problems related to stinted pastures, where the numbers of animals might have varied according to the conditions from time to time, are now only of interest for historical reasons. The basic rule under the 1965 Act was whether a particular right of common was registered and, if it was a right of grazing, what were the specified number of animals that were registered. If the right existed prior to 31 July 1970, but was not registered under the 1965 Act, it could not thereafter be exercised.

4.1.2   Effect the Commons Act 2006

This Act will replace and improve the registration system under the 1965 Act. When the relevant provisions are in force, it will also make additional changes to the registration and status of rights of common. The 2006 Act adopts the same definition of a right of common as the 1965 Act,[4] and such a right therefore includes a cattlegate or beastgate and a right of sole or several vesture or herbage or of sole or several pasture. After the commencement of the relevant provisions, the following restrictions will apply to the creation of rights of common.

A right of common cannot at any time be created over land by virtue of prescription.[5] Prescription is the acquisition of a right, such as a right of common, by actual user as of right for the minimum prescriptive period of not less than 20 years.[6]

A right of common can only be created by express grant if the land is not registered as a town or village green and the right is attached to,

---

[1]   Section 1(2)(b).

[2]   Commons Registration (New Land) Regulations 1969, SI 1969/1843.

[3]   Section 15.

[4]   See section 61(1).

[5]   Section 6(1).

[6]   See Chapter 6 below.

and therefore capable of benefiting identifiable, land.[1] The creation of a right of common only has effect if it complies with such requirements as to form and content as regulations may provide,[2] and the creation of a right of common will not operate until on an application to have the right registered in a register of common land, or if the right is over land not registered as common land, the land is registered as common land.[3] An application to register the creation of a right of common consisting of a right to graze any animal will be refused if in the opinion of the commons registration authority the land over which it is created would be unable to sustain the exercise of that right, and if the land is already registered as a common land, any other rights of common registered as exercisable over the land.[4] Although the creation of new or additional rights of common may be rare, the registration authorities will no doubt have to take expert advice about any land in issue, whether already a common or not, can support further livestock. These new rules fit in with the policy behind the provisions of the 2006 Act to better manage common land.[5]

4.1.3 Conclusions

The reader should therefore be careful with the material that follows in this chapter. Much of it would have been relevant to the process of registration under the 1965 Act where applicants were seeking to establish rights of common for the registration process, but today the material in this chapter serves only to explain those rights of common that have been registered.

4.2 CLASSIFICATION OF RIGHTS OF COMMON

In *Hampshire County Council v Milburn*,[6] Lord Templeman made reference to the manorial system which the Normans partly inherited and partly established, and identified three categories of land that were comprised in a typical manor:[7]

---

[1] Section 6(3).

[2] Section 6(4).

[3] Section 6(5).

[4] Section 6(6).

[5] See Chapter 11 below.

[6] [1990] 2 All ER 257.

[7] Ibid, at 258e.

'The demesne land belonged to the lord of the manor. The copyhold land was divided between the tenants of the lord of the manor. The remainder of the land consisted of uncultivated land, referred to as the waste of the manor. The waste was the natural source of grazing, fodder and fuel for all the inhabitants of the manor. The waste land belonged to the lord of the manor subject to the rights of the tenants to enjoy in common the fruits or some of the fruits of the soil in the manner of a "profit à prendre". The rights of the commoners varied from manor to manor. The extent of the right of any particular commoner depended on the origin of the right and might depend on the size and situation of land held by the commoner. A grant of arable land to a freeman prior to 1290 entitled him by common law to the use of the manorial waste for such purposes as were necessary for the maintenance of his husbandry. Common rights could also be acquired by grant, custom or prescription. The right of a commoner was the right "to eat the grass with the mouths of his cattle, or to take such other produce of the soil as he may be entitled to".'

4.2.1   The forms of landownership and rights of common

Lord Templeman's description of the model of the English manor may be a little too simple. Within the manor, there were three types of owners (or tenants, as they would originally have been called): freeholders; customary freeholders; and copyholders. The lord of the manor would have been a freeholder, although others might have come to acquire freeholds from the lord. Customary freeholders and copyholders were both tenants of the lord. A customary freehold was a superior type of copyhold, the freeholder holding his interest by the custom of the manor and holding a copy of the manorial court roll, the copyholder holding merely at the will of the lord.

The distinction between these different types of ownership was important in relation to the acquisition of rights of common. Only the true freeholder could acquire a right of common by grant. Customary freeholders and copyholders could only acquire such rights according to the custom of the manor, and not by prescription. Customary freeholds and copyholds were abolished in 1922.[1]

---

[1]   Law of Property Act 1922.

4.2.2   Rights of common as legal interests

There are various ways in which rights of common fall to be classified. Under English law of property, rights of common are interests in land, generally referred to as incorporeal hereditaments. Provided certain formalities are satisfied concerning their grant (or presumed grant, if acquired by prescription), they are legal interests in land.[1] Rights of common fall within that category of legal interests in land known as *profits à prendre*. As Lord Lindley in *Duke of Sutherland v Heathcote* said:[2]

> 'A *profit à prendre* is a right to take something off another person's land; such a right does not prevent the owner from taking the same sort of thing from off his own land; the first right may limit, but does not exclude, the second.'

A *profit à prendre* falls within, and shares many of the legal characteristics of, the same broad category of legal interests in land as easements. Easements are concerned with the right to use another person's land such as through the exercise of a right of way, whereas a *profit à prendre* is concerned with the right to take something from another's land. Although rights of common are *profits à prendre*, historically they came first. In *Gale on Easements*[3] the authors state that:

> 'A *profit à prendre* may be enjoyed to the exclusion of all other persons, in which case it is termed a "sole" or "several" profit. On the other hand, a profit may be enjoyed in common with one or more persons, including the owner of the servient land, when it is call a profit "in common" or right of common. Every right of common is, therefore, a *profit à prendre*, but not every *profit à prendre* is a right of common.'

This book is not concerned with those *profits à prendre* that are not rights of common. Thus, for example, the grant to a grantee that he alone to the exclusion of all others may fish a river belonging to the grantor is a *profit à prendre* 'sole' or 'several', but cannot be a right of common.

---

[1]   Law of Property Act 1925, s 1(2).

[2]   [1892] 1 Ch 475 at 484.

[3]   (17th edn), at para 1–129.

4.2.3   Rights of common classified by legal form

Turning to the legal form of rights of common, the common law has recognised the following classification:

(1)   rights of common appendant;
(2)   rights of common appurtenant;
(3)   rights of common in gross; and
(4)   rights of common *pur cause de vicinage* (by reason of vicinage).

The precise origin or classification of any right of common that was registered under the Commons Registration Act 1965 is no longer particularly relevant. Rights of common appendant can no longer be created. As they cannot be created, there is no scope for the registration of any such rights under the 1965 Act as newly created rights. The same is also probably true of rights of common *pur cause de vicinage*; all such rights would have been registered and no such new rights can now be created. The precise characteristics of rights of common appendant, and rights of common *pur cause de vicinage*, therefore, no longer have to be considered in any detail as any such rights that existed prior to 31 July 1970 have either been registered with specific numbers of animals or, if they were not registered, can no longer be exercised.[1]

What follows is, therefore, a brief explanation of the legal characteristics of each of these four categories.

(a)   Rights of common appendant

A right of common appendant is said to be annexed to land by operation of law and it probably only existed as a common of pasture.[2] Prior to the statute Quia Emptors 1290, the lord of a manor could create a new tenure, that is grant a new interest in land, by what was called subinfeudation. Where the lord of the manor granted an interest in arable land to a freeholder by subinfeudation, the freeholder obtained as appendant to the arable land the right to pasture certain animals. These were animals necessary to plough and manure the land granted to him, and no more in number. This was explained by Park B in *Dunraven (Earl) v Llewellyn*,[3] where he first sets

---

[1]   Section 1(2)(b) of the 1965 Act.

[2]   Harpum et al (eds) *Megarry & Wade: The Law of Real Property* (6th edn, Sweet & Maxwell), at para 18–083.

[3]   (1850) 15 QB 791.

out an extract from Lord Coke's Commentaries on the Statute of Merton:[1]

'By this recital [of that statute] a point of the ancient common law appeareth, that when a Lord of a manor (whereon was great waste grounds) did enfeoff others of some parts of arable land, the feoffees ad manutenend servitium socae, should have common in the said wastes of the Lord for two causes. One, as incident to the feoffment, for the feoffee could not plough, and manure his ground without beasts, and they could not be sustained without pasture, and by consequence the tenant should have common in the wastes of the Lord for his beasts, which do plough and manure his tenancy, as appendant to his tenancy, and this was the beginning of common appendant. The second reason was for maintenance and advancement of agriculture, and tillage, which was much favoured in law.'

Park B then said:

'This right, therefore, is not a common right of all tenants, but belongs only to each grantee, before the statute of quia emptores, of arable land, by virtue of his individual grant, and as an incident thereto: and it is as much a peculiar right of the grantee as one derived by express grant, or by prescription, though it differs in its extent, being limited to such cattle as are kept for ploughing and manuring them the arable land granted, and as are of a description fit for that purpose; whereas the right by grant or prescription has no such limits, and depends on the will of the grantor.'

The extent of a right of common appendant in pasture is more fully explained below.

(b)   Rights of common appurtenant

A right of common appurtenant is a right that is attached to a particular piece of land and passes to successors in title on any disposal, such as by way of sale or will. Such a right does not arise automatically by way of operation of law as in the case of a right of common appendant; a right of common appurtenant is created by grant, but if no grant can be shown, may be established by prescription. The basis for prescription is, in effect, an implied grant.

---

[1]   At p 810 referring to the statute 20 H 3, c, 4.

(c) Right of common in gross

A right of common in gross is a right that lies in either grant or prescription, but the right is not attached to the ownership of any particular piece of land. Accordingly the owner of a right of common in gross may own any particular piece of land or no land at all, and is entitled to dispose of that right independently from the disposal of any land.[1] The origin of the right of common in gross is probably to be found in those situations where the lord of the manor had more than sufficient waste to meet the needs of those commoners with rights of common appendant and or appurtenant, and therefore granted rights of common in gross to others who may or may not have held any land. Subject to the effect of the Commons Act 2006, the right may be acquired by grant or prescription.[2] Where a right of common of pasture appurtenant is held, this right can be severed from the dominant land to which it was originally attached; the right of common then becomes a right in gross.[3] On Dartmoor severance of a common of pasture appurtenant is forbidden.[4] The Commons Act 2006 prohibits the severance of a right of common unless the right is transferred to certain public bodies, it is severed temporarily for letting or leasing, or it is authorised by an order of Natural England or the Countryside Council for Wales.[5]

(d) Rights of common by reason of vicinage

There is a very simple idea behind the nature of this right of common. Where the waste lands of two separate manors adjoin, it may be difficult in practice to restrain the grazing animals of the commoners of one manor from going into the waste of the adjoining manor. The background is explained in Blackstone's *Commentaries*:[6]

> 'Common *because of vicinage*, or neighbourhood, is where the inhabitants of two townships which lie contiguous to each other, have usually intercommoned with one another; the beasts of the one straying mutually into the other's fields, without any molestation from either.

---

[1] 2 BL Com 34.

[2] *Tyrringham's Case* (1584) 4 Co Rep 36b.

[3] *Bettison v Langton* [2002] 1 AC 27, [2001] 3 All ER 417; *Bunn v Channen* (1813) 5 Taunt 244.

[4] Dartmoor Commons Act 1985, s 8.

[5] See Commons Act 2006, s 9 and Sch 1.

[6] (23rd edn, 1854), Book 2, chapter 3, at pp 34–35.

This is indeed only a permissive right, intended to excuse what in strictness is a trespass in both, and to prevent a multiplicity of suits ...'

Further, in *Jones v Robin* Parke B said:[1]

'It must be considered to be established that a common, or as it is sometimes called feeding, ... pur cause de vicinage, is not properly a right of common or profit à prendre but rather an excuse for a trespass ... Lord Coke says that the person entitled cannot put in his cattle into the adjoining waste, but they must escape into it ...'

In *Newman v Bennet* Waller LJ said:[2]

'While [a right of common by reason of vicinage] ... may be useful as a shield against trespass (and ... distress ...), it is still a right of common, though limited in character because it is determinable. It can be determined by fencing off, and however impracticable that might be ... it is a theoretical possibility.'

The limitation on the number of animals that are entitled to the benefit of a right of common by reason of vicinage was explained in *Commissioners of Sewers v Glasse* when Jessel MR said:[3]

'In common of vicinage there is a limitation of the right of this sort. Neither party can put on the commons more beasts than his own common will maintain ...'

Rights of common by reason of *vicinage* will therefore be restricted to grazing. The extent of these rights and the conditions for their existence, are considered further below.

The subject matter of rights of common, of whatever legal form, is now explained.

4.3   RIGHTS OF COMMON OF PASTURE

The right of common of pasture is the right that is, and was, most frequently encountered. In essence, it is the right of an owner of land within the manor to graze animals on the waste lands of the manor

---

1   (1847) 10 QB 620 at 632, 116 ER 235 at 240.
2   [1980] 3 All ER 449 at 454c.
3   (1874) LR 19 Eq 134, at 161.

or, in the case of the open-field system, of the owner of a strip in the open field to graze animals after crops have been taken or in the fallow year. As explained above, the right of common of pasture existed in any of the four legal forms of rights of common known to the common law. However, it is probably correct that rights of common appendant and rights by reason of *vicinage* will only involve rights of common to pasture animals. In respect of each of the rights to pasture animals, described below, it is not an incident of the right to be able to bring extra feed on to the common land, although shepherding by a vehicle over a large area would be a reasonable use if exercised with minimum interference with the landowner's rights.[1]

4.3.1   Rights of common of pasture appendant

(a)   Registration

The effect of the Commons Registration Act 1965 was to render the legal characteristics of rights of common of pasture appendant obsolete. If such rights existed prior to 31 July 1970, they were required to be registered.[2] If they were registered, and the rights were not in respect of a definite number of animals, registration required a specified number of animals to be entered.[3] If the right of common existed prior to 31 July 1970, and was not registered, the right can no longer be exercised.[4] What follows is therefore a description of the origin and legal characteristics of rights of common of pasture appendant, but there is little practical significance in the characteristics of this particular right today.

(b)   Origin and creation

It was explained above that this was a right that arose by operation of law where there was a grant of land by a lord of the manor before the statute of Quia Emptores.[5] The right only arose in respect of what was described as *anciently* arable land. Provided the land was originally arable land at the time of the grant (before 1290), the fact that later it came to be used for pasture land, or that a house was built on part of

---

1   *Besley v John* [2003] All ER D 481 (Oct), CA.

2   Section 1.

3   Section 15.

4   Section 1(2)(b).

5   1290.

it, will not change the status of *anciently* arable land for the purposes of a claim to retain the right of common of pasture appendant.[1]

Because a right of common of pasture appendant does not depend upon actual grant or prescription, it is not necessary to prove actual user of the right in order to establish a claim. Proof only that the land of the claimant was *anciently* arable land is sufficient to give rise to the existence of the right by operation of law. Accordingly, there are only two grounds for defeating a claim: first, that it can be shown that the alleged *anciently* arable lands were never granted by the lord of the manor prior to 1290; and, secondly, where the character of the land in respect of which the claim is made has so altered, by change of use or development, that no right could any longer be exercised.[2]

(c) Limitation on numbers of animals

There is a limit on the number and type of animals in respect of which a common of pasture appendant can be exercised. Although the number of animals that might originally have been turned out upon the common may have been limited to the number required, from time to time, for the proper farming of the land of the commoner, the common law came to apply the rule of *levancy* and *couchancy* which meant the number of animals that would be lying within the buildings and could be kept there throughout the winter.[3] However, in *Robertson v Hartopp* Fry LJ said that he thought the principle of *levancy* and *couchancy* was more the measure of capacity of the land than a condition to be actually and literally complied with by the cattle lying down and getting up, or by their being fed off the land.[4]

(d) Type of animals

The type of animals in respect of which the right may be exercised is also limited. Farm animals were normally referred to by the generic word 'cattle'. The right was confined to animals needed for the purposes of ploughing (horses and oxen) and animals needed to manure the arable land, such as cattle proper and sheep. Other

---

[1]   *Tyrringham's Case* (1584) 4 Co Rep 36b, where it was considered that an appendant right could not have been created after 1189.

[2]   *Carr v Lambert* (1866) LR 1 Exch 168 and *Scrutton v Stone* (1893) 9 TLR 478, affirmed (1893) 10 TLR 157.

[3]   *Scholes v Hargreaves* (1792) 5 Term Rep 46.

[4]   (1889) 43 ChD 484.

animals, such as pigs and goats, could not have been used in the exercise of a right of common appendant. It was also important that the animals turned onto the common in the exercise of a right of common appendant were those animals belonging to the commoner for the purpose of ploughing or manuring his arable land, or borrowed for that special purpose.[1]

(e)   Miscellaneous characteristics

Because a right of common of pasture appendant arises by operation of law, the normal rules of prescription do not apply. However, the right implies prescription, in the sense that the commoner is using land belonging to another (the lord of the manor) for grazing his animals. It is partly for that reason that only a freeholder within the manor acquired an appendant right. Further, the lord of the manor himself did not have *rights* of common of pasture over his own waste lands. The extent to which the lord of the manor put animals on the waste lands of the manor that were otherwise necessary for ploughing and manuring the arable land within his own demesne lands, was really an incident of his own rights as lord of the manor and owner of the soil.[2]

The right of common of pasture appendant could not arise in respect of the use of the open-field system.

4.3.2   Rights of common of pasture appurtenant

In *Bettison v Langton* Lord Nichols explained the background to rights of common of pasture appurtenant:[3]

> 'For centuries many farmers whose lands adjoin the local common have enjoyed the right to put out their sheep and cattle to graze on the common. The animals wintered on the farms, but in the summer months they were let out to graze on the open common. ... These rights have feudal origins ... Traditionally grazing rights are an adjunct of the lands of the farmers who own the rights. The rights had their origin in actual or presumed grant, usually the latter. The law assumes that long continued use must have had a lawful origin. The number of animals that a farmer was entitled to depasture on the common was limited to

---

[1]   *Rumsey v Rawson* (1669) 1 Vent 18.

[2]   *Musgrave v Inclosure Commissioners* (1874) LR 9 QB 162; *Baring v Abbingdon* (1892) 2 Ch 374.

[3]   [2001] 3 All ER 417 at 419.

the animals his land could support through the winter. The language was picturesque: the right was limited to the number of beasts "levant and couchant" ("getting up and lying down") on the farmer's holding in the winter months. These rights could be passed on or sold, but only with the farm to which they were appurtenant. They were to be enjoyed by the occupier for the time being. They could not be sold separately, or "severed", from the farm.'

(a) Customary freeholds and copyholds

Unlike a right of common of pasture appendant, which was restricted to grants of freehold land prior to 1290, rights of common of pasture appurtenant may be exercisable by freeholders whose estates were, prior to 1922, copyholds and customary freeholds.[1] Indeed, a right of common of pasture appurtenant could be claimed by a person who did not own land within the manor but came to use the waste land of the manor for grazing his animals, and who acquired a right by prescription.[2]

(b) Registration

Any right of common of pasture appurtenant that existed prior to 31 July 1970 was required to be registered, and if the right was not in respect of a definite number of animals, a definite number of animals had to be specified for registration purposes.[3] If such rights were not registered, they can no longer be exercised.[4] Rights of common of pasture appurtenant can still be created by express grant, although such creation will be subject to limitations when the relevant provisions of the Commons Act 2006 are in force.[5] Any such new rights are therefore capable of registration.[6]

4.3.3 Right of common *pur cause de vicinage*

This is a right that cannot exist alone save as an addition to some other right of common, such as a right of common appendant, appurtenant, or in gross. The primary right is exercisable by the

---

[1] *Robertson v Hartopp* (1889) 43 Ch D 484; *Hall v Byron* (1877) 4 Ch D 667.

[2] *Sacheverell v Porter* (1637) W Jo 396; *Clarkson v Woodhouse* (1782) 5 Term Rep 412n.

[3] Commons Registration Act 1965, ss 1 and 15.

[4] Ibid, s 1(2)(b).

[5] Section 6 of the Commons Act 2006 will prohibit the creation of any right of common unless certain matters can be satisfied; this is more fully considered in Chapters 6 and 8.

[6] Commons Registration (New Land) Regulations 1969.

commoner over a particular common and the additional right of *vicinage* is exercisable over an adjoining common that is contiguous with the first one. The commoner has no primary right over the neighbouring common but he does have the subsidiary and additional right of *vicinage*. The right can be terminated by the erection of a fence between the two adjoining commons.[1]

The requirement to register rights of common under the Commons Registration Act 1965 gave rise to difficulties in the case of rights of *vicinage*. Apparently some rights of this nature were registered, and others were not. The preliminary question is whether they should have been registered. That seems doubtful because a right of *vicinage* is not a substantive right of common, it is more a customary recognition that animals on adjoining commons will stray and, in effect, provide no more than a defence to trespass proceedings.[2]

4.3.4   Common of pasture in gross

This right may be without limit as to the number of animals that can be put on the common, or may be specified as to a number certain. In practice such a right is more likely to be for a number certain, especially where the right arose by prescription. That is because the prescription would have been in respect of a number certain, such as by reference to the principle of *levancy* and *couchancy*.[3] The Commons Act 2006 prohibits the severance of a right of common, which will include a right of pasture in gross, unless the right is transferred to certain public bodies, it is severed temporarily for letting or leasing, or it is authorised by an order of Natural England or the Countryside Council for Wales.[4]

4.3.5   Right of foldcourse

This right is sometimes referred to as sheepwalk or foldage, or sometimes free fold. This began as a right of the lord of the manor to have the sheep of his tenants on his land so that they would manure

---

[1]   *Gullett v Lopes* (1811) 13 East 348, 104 ER 404.

[2]   *Newman v Bennett* [1980] 3 All ER 449, a right of common limited in character.

[3]   *Mellor v Spateman* (1669) 1 Saund 339.

[4]   See Commons Act 2006, s 9 and Sch 1.

it. Although not originally a right of common, where it remains, it has acquired the characteristics of a right of common.[1]

4.4   COMMON OF TURBARY

This is the right to take turf or peat for heating purposes. It is a right that has to be appurtenant to a house or building. Turfs or peat cut can only be consumed within the house, and cannot be sold.[2] Where in the common or waste the right may be exercised depends on the custom of the particular manor.[3]

4.5   COMMON OF ESTOVERS

This is the right to take the products of the soil in the form of wood or timber. The Saxon word for estovers was bote; it consisted of wood and timber and was expressed as house-bote (firewood, and wood for repairing a house), plough or cart-bote (for making and repairing agricultural implements) and hay-bote (for repairing fences). If the right is in the form of house-bote, the right is in respect of the house or building as it existed at the date of the grant or period of prescription. Although the right is not lost if the building is rebuilt, it will not extend to enable wood or timber to be taken for the purposes of building or repairing any enlargement to the original building.[4]

Generally the right is to take underwood and trees of little value, such as birch, willow, alder or hazel.[5] Accordingly, the more valuable trees, such as oaks, are less likely objects of estovers. The right of estovers is not necessarily limited to wood or timber and may include heather or bracken as fodder or litter for cattle.[6] A right to estovers is never without limitation. It may be limited by reference to cartloads or by reference to the needs of the holding to which the right is attached.[7]

---

[1]   *Robinson v Duleep Singh* (1878) 11 ChD 798.

[2]   *Valentine v Penny* (1605) Noy 145, 74 ER 1107.

[3]   *Maxwell v Martin* (1830) 6 Bing 522, 130 ER 1382 and *Clarkson v Woodhouse* (1782) 5 Term Rep 412, 101 ER 231.

[4]   *A-G v Reynolds* [1911] 2 KB 888 and *Luttrel's Case* (1601) 4 Co Rep 84b.

[5]   *Earl de la Warr v Miles* (1881) 17 ChD 535.

[6]   *Smith v Earl Brownlow* (1870) LR 9 Eq 241; *Earl de la Warr v Miles* (1881) 17 ChD 535.

[7]   *Earl de la Warr v Miles* (1881) 17 ChD 535; *Earl Pembroke's Case* (1636) Clay 47.

4.6   COMMON OF PISCARY

A right of common of piscary is a right to fish with others in a river or water belonging to a further person. The right can either be appurtenant or in gross. It may exist in a non-navigable river but it cannot exist in a tidal navigable river as the soil of such a river is presumed to be owned by the Crown.[1] A common of piscary may be created by grant, in which case the extent of the rights granted are a matter of agreement between the parties. However, if a common of piscary is claimed by prescription, it can only be appurtenant to a house, and the fish taken are those for use in the house.[2]

4.7   COMMON IN THE SOIL

There are a wide variety of rights of common to take parts of the soil such as marl (for manuring), sand, stone or other minerals. The right may be appurtenant or held in gross and can be acquired by grant or by prescription.[3] In the case of land that was originally held as a copyhold tenement, the right can be claimed by custom, but not by prescription.[4] The characteristics of both the rights of estovers and of turbary apply, namely that the products must be used in connection with the land or building to which the right attaches. Although where the right exists in gross, it will usually be limited in some form of quantity.

4.8   COMMON IN PANNAGE

The right of common of pannage (or mast) is similar to the right of pasturage. Pannage is to put pigs into woodlands to enable them to feed on such things as acorns and beech mast. The right will usually have been limited to the appropriate times of the year when the acorns and beech mast will be on the ground.[5] In the case of Royal forests, the time of pannage began on Holy-rood Day, 15 days before Michaelmas and ended 40 days after Michaelmas.[6]

---

[1]   *Ward v Cresswell* (1741) Willes 265; *A-G for British Colombia v A-G for Canada* [1914] AC 153.

[2]   *Clayton v Corby* (1843) 5 QB 415; *Lord Chesterfield v Harris* [1908] 2 Ch 397.

[3]   *Gateward's Case* (1607) 6 Co Rep 59b.

[4]   *Rogers v Brenton* (1847) 10 QB 26; *Heath v Deane* [1905] 2 Ch 86.

[5]   *Chilton v Corporation of London* (1878) 7 ChD 562.

[6]   *Manwood's Forest Laws* (4th ed, 1717), at p 230, quoted in Gordon, *Law of Forestry* (1955), at p 70.

4.9   RIGHTS OF SOLE

4.9.1   General meaning

Where the owner of the soil retains the right to use his own land for, say, the grazing of pasture, and grants rights of pasture to others, those rights of pasture are rights of common; they may be exercised in common with the owner of the soil. However, where the owner grants to another person or persons the whole and exclusive right to pasture, and retains no such right himself, he has granted a sole profit. The distinction between rights of common and a sole right depends entirely on whether the owner of the soil has retained any right of the same nature or product that he has granted.

The words 'sole' and 'several' probably mean the same thing and are interchangeable in use in this context.[1]

A sole right (or profit) can be granted to one person. Having granted that right the owner cannot grant any more rights of the same nature in the same land. A sole right may be granted by the same grant to several persons, such as to all the tenants of a particular manor.[2] In the usual case of a grant of rights of sole in pasture, each share would be known as a stint, or beastgate or cattlegate. The shares or stints can be acquired by others – even by the owner of the soil.[3]

The owner or owners of rights of sole, say of pasture, may be able to exclude the owner of the soil from putting his own cattle on the land to take any of the pasture, but the owner of the soil may exercise any other rights of ownership, such as the taking of game.[4]

Because the definition of a right of common in the Commons Act 2006 includes a right of sole, the restrictions on the creation of new rights, discussed at the beginning of this chapter, will have application.[5]

---

[1]   Gadsden *Law of Commons*, at chapter 3.

[2]   *Hoskins v Robins* (1671) 2 Wms Saund 324, 85 ER 1123.

[3]   *Lonsdale (Earl) v Rigg* (1856) 11 Ex 654, 156 ER 992.

[4]   Ibid.

[5]   Section 6.

4.9.2   Vesture

Vesture includes all the produce of the land excluding timber. It includes corn, grass, underwood and all that can be cut by the scythe.[1] A right of vesture does not include any right to the non-agricultural products that can be dug out of the soil.[2] A right of sole vesture might be exercisable by the owner (or owners) of the sole at limited periods of the year leaving the owner of the soil to take agricultural produce, such as a hay crop outside those periods.

4.9.3   Herbage

This is a sole right to take grass by cutting or grazing.[3] The right is less than vesture but more than a right of pasture, which does not include the cutting of grass.

4.9.4   Pasture

The sole right in pasture, whether held by a single person (a single stint), or more usually by a number of persons (each holding a stint), permits such persons to take the grass only through the mouths of their cattle.[4] Where there is more than one stint in a sole pasture, each stint is of equal size. Stints may have specified numbers of animals attached to them. This right is common in the north of England and is frequently owned in gross. That means that the right is not attached to the land, if any, belonging to the owner of the right. Sole rights of pasture are assignable.[5] But the transfer of a sole right of common must satisfy the provisions of the Commons Act 2006: see Chapter 8.

4.9.5   Other sole rights

A *profit à prendre* is a right and a legal interest to take a specified product from land belonging to the owner of the soil. Such a right is not confined to vesture, herbage or pasture, but can include the right to take or dig some specified product out of the soil, such as marl or sand. However, sole *profits à prendre* that are not sole rights to vesture, herbage or pasture are not registrable under the Commons Registration Act 1965; they are not further considered in this book.

---

[1]   Co Litt 4b.

[2]   *Re Tenants of Owning* (1587) 4 Leon 43, 74 ER 718.

[3]   *Earl de la Warr v Miles* (1881) 17 ChD 535.

[4]   *Cox v Glue* (1848) 5 CB 533, at 548, 136 ER 987, at 993.

[5]   *Welcome v Upton* (1840) 6 M&W 536, 151 ER 524.

4.9.6   Commons Registration Act 1965

Chapter 8 explains the registration requirements of this Act. The registrable rights include 'cattlegates or beastgates (by whatever name known) and rights of sole or several vesture or herbage or of sole or several pasture'.[1] Sole rights of vesture, herbage and pasture were therefore registrable, and the land over which such rights are exercisable is common land under the 1965 Act.[2] The same definition is used in the Commons Act 2006.[3]

---

[1]   Sections 1(1)(b) and 22(1).

[2]   Section 22(1).

[3]   Section 61(1).

Chapter 5

OWNERSHIP OF COMMON LAND

5.1 INTRODUCTION

As discussed in Chapters 1 and 2, common land was that part of the manor that was not occupied by the copyhold tenants, nor was it part of the lord's demesne lands. It was that part of uninclosed land which was available and used by the copyhold tenants, the customary freeholders and the other freeholders in common with the lord of the manor for, principally, the grazing of animals and the taking of estovers. Therefore, originally, the owner of the common lands was the lord of the manor. The lord of the manor would have held the common lands of the manor under one of the freehold titles.

In the case of commonable lands, that is those lands subject to the open-field system or similar, such open fields were owned in strips of approximately 1 acre each by the various several owners.

Whatever may have been the origin of ownership, many commons are now owned by public bodies, such as local authorities. Save that such bodies may have additional statutory powers to manage common land, and to make schemes and by-laws, the incidents of ownership of a public body are no different from any other owner.

This chapter addresses the nature, incidents and liabilities of the ownership of the common lands. The Commons Act 2006 contains provisions for the management of commons and the creation of commons councils in that connection. Although these provisions are discussed in more detail in Chapter 11 below, they must be taken into account in considering the scope of the powers of an owner of a common.

5.2 LORD OF THE MANOR

It is necessary to explain the ownership of common lands in the wider context of the ownership of a manor in its lord. The lord of the manor normally held the manorship directly from the Crown. Under the original feudal arrangements, the manor was held upon terms by which the lord of the manor owed certain duties to the King such as of homage (or loyalty) and the provision of services (such as military). The lord of the manor was, in effect, in control of the whole of the geographical area of the manor and all who lived within it. Save for the free men within the manor, all others would originally have been serfs required to work for and provide services to the lord of the manor. Because of his legal and actual control over all that was within the boundaries of the manor, and of its inhabitants, the lord of the manor enjoyed many rights and incidents of his ownership. The extent of these rights is well illustrated by the deemed effect of a conveyance of a manor set out in s 62(3) of the Law of Property Act 1925:

'A conveyance of a manor shall be deemed to include and shall by virtue of this Act operate to convey, with the manor, all pastures, feedings, wastes, warrens, commons, mines, minerals, quarries, furzes, trees, woods, underwoods, coppices, and the ground and soil thereof, fishings, fisheries, fowlings, courts leet, courts baron, and other courts, view of frank pledge and all that to view of frank pledge doth belong, mills, mulctures, customs, tolls, duties, reliefs, heriots, fines, sums of money, amerciaments, waifs, estrays, chief-rents, quitrents, rents charge, rents seck, rents of assize, fee farm rents, services, royalties, jurisdictions, franchises, liberties, privileges, easements, profits, advantages, rights, emoluments, and hereditaments whatsoever, to the manor appertaining or reputed to appertain, or, at the time of conveyance, demised, occupied, or enjoyed with the same, or reputed or known as part, parcel, or member thereof.'[1]

These rights fall into two broad groups: corporeal hereditaments (those matters that physically exist, such as wastes, warrens, etc); and incorporeal hereditaments (those matters that cannot be physically touched, but are in the nature of rights or benefits, such as fisheries, the holding of courts and the entitlement to rents, etc). A full explanation of the nature of all the incidents of the ownership of the lord of the manor is beyond the scope of this book. What is clear is that the ownership of the wastes and commons is but one of the incidents of that ownership.

---

[1]   Many of the expressions set out above are explained in the glossary to this book.

Increasingly the ownership of a common has become severed from the ownership of the lord of the manor. Where that has taken place, the person owning the common lands, which were originally part of the manor, will generally enjoy the same characteristics of ownership of that soil, as the lord of the manor would have done so had he retained its ownership. However, such an owner would not enjoy all the other and usual incidents of the ownership of a manor.

5.3   OWNERSHIP OF THE SOIL OF COMMON LAND

The ownership of the soil of the common is capable of being held under the two legal estates in land, namely the fee simple absolute in possession (freehold) or term of years absolute (lease).[1] The normal presumption is that the owner of the soil owns everything upwards to the heavens and downwards to the centre of the earth subject only to the rights of the commoners. Subject to any statutory restrictions, the owner may use the common lands for any purposes he chooses provided he does not interfere with the commoners' rights. Thus, for example, if the common land is extensive, and the number of persons owning rights of common is limited, the common land may have spare capacity for the grazing of animals. In such circumstances the owner of the soil is entitled to grant licences to strangers to pasture animals.[2] Subject, again, to not interfering with the rights of the commoners, the owner of the soil is entitled to shoot over and take game on the common. He is therefore entitled to grant shooting rights to a third party.[3]

One of the principal characteristics of the ownership of the soil of the common is the right of the lord or owner of the soil to pasture his own animals on the common. This right was not dependent upon there being a sufficiency of common land, or pasture on it, for the commoners.[4] Indeed, in those limited cases in which a right to exclude the lord from the common arises, such a right is a sole or several pasture or herbage and is not a right of common at all. Somewhat confusingly, such rights in sole or several pasture or

---

[1]   The Law of Property Act 1925, s 1(1). The new legal estate of commonhold is not relevant to the ownership of common land.

[2]   See *Mellor v Spateman* (1669) 1 Saund 339 at 345; *Atkinson v Teesdale* (1772) 2 Wm BL 817.

[3]   *Ewart v Graham* (1859) 7 HL Cas 331.

[4]   Co Litt 122a.

herbage, are included in the definition of rights of common in the Commons Registration Act 1965,[1] and the Commons Act 2006.[2]

The expression 'the lord of the manor' may therefore be synonymous with the expression 'owner of the soil of the common'. However, care must be taken in understanding some of the earlier decided authorities as to whether the expression 'lord of the manor' means strictly that, or is simply being used to indicate the owner of the soil.

Although the established incidents of ownership of the soil of a common are discussed below, several of these may be limited by management schemes made by commons councils set up under the Commons Act 2006.[3]

5.3.1   Powers of leasing

A distinction must be made between the power of the lord of the manor to grant leases of common land and his power to grant leases of the waste land of the manor. The lord of the manor has power to grant leases of common land, although any leases so granted will be subject to the rights of the commoners. However, there is a limited power in the Inclosure Act 1773, s 15 by which the lord of the manor may, with the consent of three-quarters of persons having rights of common on the wastes and commons, grant a lease for a term not exceeding 4 years of any part not exceeding one-twelfth in area of such wastes and commons. The lease must be granted for the best and most improved yearly rent that can, by public auction, be obtained and the net rents shall then be applied in the draining, fencing or otherwise improving the residue of those wastes and commons.

In the case of the waste land of a manor that is not subject to rights of common, such land only retains that particular status for so long as it has the physical characteristics of being 'open, uncultivated and unoccupied'.[4] The effect of the lord of the manor granting any lease of any waste lands of the manor not subject to rights of common must surely mean that the land is no longer unoccupied, thus causing such land to cease to be waste land.

---

[1]   Co Litt 122a and Commons Registration Act 1965, s 22(1).

[2]   Section 61(1).

[3]   See Chapter 11 below.

[4]   See *Attorney-General v Hanmer* (1858) 27 LJ Ch 837.

5.3.2 Right to grant grazing rights

Consistent with the proposition that the owner of a common may grant leases of it, at common law the owner may grant grazing rights provided there is sufficient pasture left for the commoners.[1] However, this right will be restricted by the provisions of the Commons Act 2006. When the relevant provisions of the 2006 Act are in force, a right of common, which of course includes a right to graze animals, will only be able to be created by express grant if the land is not registered as a town or village green and the right is attached to, and therefore capable of benefiting identifiable, land.[2] The creation of such a right will only have effect if it complies with such requirements as to form and content as regulations may in due course provide,[3] and the creation of a right of grazing will not operate until on an application to have the right registered in a register of common land, or if the right is over land not registered as common land, the land is registered as common land.[4] An application to register a right to graze any animal will be refused if in the opinion of the commons registration authority the land over which it is to be created would be unable to sustain the exercise of that right, and if the land is already registered as a common land, any other rights of common registered as exercisable over the land.[5]

5.3.3 Grazing for the owner's animals

The essential characteristic of land subject to rights of common is that those rights are rights in common with the owner of the soil. Accordingly, the lord or owner of the soil has a right to pasture his own animals on the common. It is irrelevant that there may not be enough grazing for the commoners' animals.[6] As it would seem that a commons council could make rules limiting both the exercise of rights of common, and the rights to use the surplus of common land,[7] such rules could restrict an owner from grazing his own animals.

---

[1]   *Smith v Feverell* (1675) 2 Mod Rep 6, 86 ER 909; *Arlett v Ellis* (1827) 7 B&C 346.

[2]   Section 6(3).

[3]   Section 6(4).

[4]   Section 6(5).

[5]   Section 6(6).

[6]   Co Litt 122a; *Arlett v Ellis* (1827) 7 B&C 346.

[7]   Section 31(4) of the Commons Act 2006.

5.3.4   Trees, timber and woodland

The owner may plant trees on common land provided such planting does not interfere with the sufficiency of pasturage. The owner is also entitled to those trees that grow naturally on common land. Where the trees completely exclude the ability of the commoners to exercise their rights of common, the commoners may then abate the nuisance by felling the trees.[1] But if the effect of the trees is merely to prevent the commoners from enjoying their rights of common as beneficially as they are entitled to, the commoners cannot then fell the trees by way of self-abatement, and must bring legal proceedings for nuisance.[2]

5.3.5   Rights to game

The owner of the soil has a right to take game from the common land and the waste land of the manor, and may grant shooting rights to third parties.[3] The grant of such a right is a *profit à prendre*.

5.3.6   Warrens

The beasts and birds of a warren are hare, rabbit, pheasant, partridge and wild duck.[4] What is known as a 'free warren' is a right to keep beasts and birds of a warren. It is not a characteristic of the ownership of the manor, or of the soil of a common. It could have been acquired by direct grant of franchise from the Crown or by prescription (which assumes such a grant).[5] One particular type of warren was known as the cone-burrow (or coney-burrow). This was a warren used for the keeping of rabbits. Where the owner of the soil was entitled to exercise free warren, he could make or enlarge cone-burrows provided such works did not interfere with the sufficiency of grazing or other rights to which the commoners were entitled.[6]

5.3.7   Rights to minerals

In principle the lord or owner of the soil was always entitled to take minerals or other materials from the soil of the common. However,

---

[1]   *Sandgrove v Kirby* (1797) 1 Bos & P 13.

[2]   *Hope v Osborne* [1913] 2 Ch 349.

[3]   *Ewart v Graham* (1859) 7 HL Cas 331; *Wickham v Hawker* (1840) 7 M&W 63.

[4]   *Fitzhardinge (Lord) v Percell* [1908] 2 Ch 139.

[5]   2 Bl Com 38.

[6]   *Gresill v Hoddesden* (1608) Yelv 143, 80 ER 96.

the exercise of such rights must not interfere with the sufficiency of the grazing or other rights to which the commoners are entitled.[1] In practice, the biggest constraint on the extraction of minerals from common land will be the need to obtain the necessary planning permission.

5.3.8 Right to drive

The lord of the manor had the right to drive the common. This meant an entitlement to round up and collect all the animals with a view to establishing whether any animals were present that did not belong to commoners or whether any of the commoners had more than their entitlement by way of numbers of animals on the common.[2] Probably this right survives the registration and management provisions of the Commons Registration Act 1965 and the Commons Act 2006. However it is likely that the functions of commons councils, which will be set up under the 2006 Act, to make rules for the management of a commons will render this right superfluous.[3]

5.3.9 Prescription or custom

All the various rights set out above might be limited by prescription or the custom of the manor.[4]

5.3.10 Right of approvement

The Commons Acts 1236 and 1285 authorised the approvement of common land. Approvement was the right of inclosing lands subject to rights of common, provided there was no interference with the sufficiency of those rights.[5] In practice, the right of approvement had become virtually obsolete because of later legislation imposing restrictions on the inclosure of commons.[6] The Commons Act 2006 abolished powers of approvement and the Commons Act 1285 ceases to have effect.

---

[1] *Robinson v Duleep Singh* (1876) 11 Ch D 798.

[2] *Thomas v Nicholls* (1681) 3 Lev 40.

[3] Section 31 of the Commons Act 2006.

[4] *Wolstanton Ltd v Newcastle-under-Lyme Borough Council* [1940] AC 860, [1940] 3 All ER 101.

[5] *Arlett v Ellis* (1827) 7 B&C 346; *Betts v Thompson* (1871) 6 Ch App 732.

[6] See Chapter 7.

5.3.11 Wayleaves and easements

Because the lord of the manor is the owner of the soil, subject only to the rights of common, he is free to grant wayleaves. Any grant must not interfere with the rights of common. Such grants may include rights to the utility services to lay pipes and cables over or under the common. Special problems have arisen in the case of easements over common land; these are considered below.

5.4   COMMONABLE LANDS

Commonable lands include lands subject to the open-field system and also lammas lands and shack lands.[1] These lands will not necessarily have been owned by the lord of the manor. Their origin lay in the open-field system of agriculture by which individuals owned strips of the open field, of about 1 acre. They were known as several owners, because they individually owned those strips – distinct shares of the open field. After harvest, that is between reaping and sowing, the whole open field would then be thrown open to all owners (and occasionally others) to pasture their animals and manure the land. That would also have occurred during the fallow year. Accordingly, such land was subject to rights of common between reaping and sowing and, according to the custom, in the fallow years. During the time of the year when a crop was being grown, the individual owners were owners as such, and had all the rights and incidents of such ownership. In rural areas, the open field may well have been held in freehold by the lord of the manor, and the individual strips of land held by the lord's tenants under either customary freehold or copyhold. In some urban areas, the town or borough would have owned the common field for the benefit of all, and granted leases of strips to farmers. There are very few examples today of working open-field systems.[2]

5.5   EASEMENTS OVER COMMON LAND

As explained above, the owner of the soil of common land is entitled, as a matter of land law, to do as he wishes with the common provided he does not interfere with the rights of the commoners. He can therefore grant rights to shoot, or additional rights of common such as of pasture where there is an excess of sufficiency of pasture

---

[1]   Chapter 3.

[2]   Laxton, in Nottinghamshire, and Laugharne in Wales, are two examples.

for the existing commoners.[1] Both of these types of grant are grants capable of being *profits à prendre*, which, together with easements, are legal interests in land sharing certain similar legal characteristics.

However, the grant of an easement over common land, such as an easement (or right) of way, can give rise to certain problems. In the case of an *express* grant of a right of way, the grantee cannot carry out works, such as the creation of a road surface that will either interfere with the rights of the commoners or will breach a number of statutory provisions that prohibit works on commons.[2] Such works may amount to an inclosure, or may otherwise require the consent of the Secretary of State.[3] Where a common is owned by a parish or other council, such as under the Open Spaces Act 1906, it may well be a breach of the duties of such an owner, as a trustee for the benefit of the enjoyment of the public to grant such rights.[4]

Other enactments included s 193 of the Law of Property Act 1925, which made provision for public access to certain commons for air and exercise.[5] However, subsection (4) made it a criminal offence for any person, without lawful authority, to draw or drive upon any land to which the section applies any carriage, cart, caravan, truck or other vehicle.[6] By 1930 motor vehicles were seen as being in need of some control, and s 14(1) of the Road Traffic Act 1930 made it an offence for a person to drive, without lawful authority, a mechanically propelled vehicle on, to or upon any common land, moorland or other land of whatever description, not being land forming part of a road. This provision was ultimately re-enacted in s 34(1) of the Road Traffic Act 1988 with the phrase *'or other land of whatever description'* being substituted by *'or land of any other description'*.

---

[1] *Ewart v Graham* (1859) 7 HL Cas 331 (shooting rights); *Wickham v Hawker* (1840) 7 M&W 63 (rights to hawk, hunt, fish and fowl); *Smith v Feverall* (1675) 2 Mod 6, 86 ER 909. This is now subject to the restrictions imposed by s 6 of the Commons Act 2006.

[2] These are fully discussed in Chapter 11.

[3] Such as under Law of Property Act 1925, s 194 or the Commons Act 2006.

[4] Open Spaces Act 1906, s 10.

[5] It applied to metropolitan commons within the meaning of the Metropolitan Commons Act 1866 to 1898, manorial waste or common that was wholly or partly within an area that was before 1 April 1974 a borough or urban district, and, following a deed of dedication by the owner, to any other area that was at the commencement of the Act subject to rights of common: see s 193(1).

[6] The CROW Act 2000 contains powers to repeal this provision, but will grant rights of access to access land: see ss 3 and 102 and Sch 16.

5.5.1   Can easements be granted over common land and greens?

Easements are acquired by express grant from the owner of the land over which the easement is to be exercised, or by prescription, that is long user as of right. A prescriptive period of not less than 20 years is required; any 20-year period where the doctrine of lost modern grant is relied on, and the 20-year period expiring on the date when the right is put in issue by some act such as the issue of proceedings where the Prescription Act 1832 is relied. Easements may be implied in certain special circumstances.[1] In *Hanning v Top Deck Travel Group Ltd*[2] the Court of Appeal decided that an easement of way over common land could not be acquired by prescription where the conduct relied on was prohibited by public statute; s 193(4) of the 1925 Act was the relevant provision. Illegality of user negated the acquisition of an easement by prescription. That decision gave sufficient justification to the owners of unenclosed areas to charge for the grant of easements of way in relation to existing tracks.[3] Section 68 of the Countryside and Rights of Way (CROW) Act 2000 was enacted to address the problem; a compulsory conferment of an easement in accordance with the relevant regulations could be obtained, if certain requirements are satisfied, but the right had to be paid for. This is considered in more detail below.

In *Massey v Boulden*[4] the illegality principle adopted in *Hanning*, that a prescriptive right cannot be acquired by a user in breach of a criminal statute, was accepted as correct, and the Court of Appeal decided that prescriptive rights of way could not be acquired over a track on a village green as such user was contrary to s 34(1) of the Road Traffic Act 1988 (and the provisions it re-enacted, originating in the Road Traffic Act 1930); a green was *'land of any other description'*. Shortly afterwards *Hanning* was applied by the Court of Appeal in *Bakewell Management Ltd v Brandwood*,[5] a case involving the use of access tracks by some 28 houses over a common where the illegality provision in s 193(4) of the 1925 Act was relied on; the owner of the common had

---

[1]   For the details, see a more detailed work such as *Gale on Easements*.

[2]   (1993) 68 P&CR 14.

[3]   Such owners included the National Trust and public and local authorities, the latter with Treasury encouragement: see McNall, *Righting Wrongs ? Prescriptive Easements and Illegality* (2004) 68 Conv 67 at 69.

[4]   [2003] 2 All ER 87.

[5]   [2003] 1 EGLR 17.

offered to grant rights of way to the house owners upon payment of 6% of the value of their properties.

In allowing the appeal of the house owners in *Brandwood*,[1] the House of Lords overruled *Hanning*. As Lord Scott of Foscote said, the important qualification to the illegality imposed by s 193(4) was the words in the subsection '*without lawful authority*'.[2] He reasoned that the servient owner of the common was able, notwithstanding the statutory prohibition in subsection (4), to make a lawful grant of an easement; an easement acquired by prescription was founded upon the fiction of a lost grant or under s 2 of the Prescription Act 1832, and involved conduct that was illegal in the tortious sense. He therefore concluded that *Hanning* could not be justified on the footing that conduct illegal in the criminal sense was different in kind from conduct illegal in the tortious sense, particularly where the conduct was only criminal where the landowner had given no authority.[3] In agreeing, Lord Walker of Gestingthorpe said that in the ordinary case of prescription, the prior authority of the landowner is presumed or inferred from long user, even though every act of user during the prescriptive period takes place without his actual prior authority and is tortious. He did not see that any public interest would be served by holding that the absence of the landowner's actual prior authority should produce a different result in cases where s 193(4) come into play.[4]

Although the House of Lords decision in *Brandwood* is characterised by discussion of what is called the *illegality principle*, this overlooks the more general proposition underlying the prescriptive acquisition of easements.[5] That proposition is that as prescription is founded upon the notion or fiction of a grant by the servient owner, if the servient owner could not at the time have made an express grant, what can be called the *competency* question, a grant cannot be acquired by prescription.[6]

---

[1]   [2004] UKHL 14.

[2]   Ibid para 24.

[3]   Ibid para 46.

[4]   Ibid para 59.

[5]   Prescriptive acquisition in this paper includes acquisition under the doctrine of lost modern grant.

[6]   *Barker v Richardson* (1821) 4 B&Ad 579; *Mill v Commission of the New Forest* (1856) 18 CB 60; *Oakley v Boston* [1976] QB 270.

The *Brandwood* decision throws up three issues. First, if the illegality principle is not the only restriction on the prescriptive acquisition of easements, and the competency question must also be considered, are there any aspects of competency that would affect the ability of an owner of a common or town or village green to grant easements of way that may affect the rights of the commoners or local inhabitants? In particular, does the fact that many owners of such unenclosed areas are local authorities or similar bodies restricted by statutory powers and having fiduciary or similar responsibilities have a bearing on competency? Second, the relaxation of the illegality principle adopted in *Brandwood* raises issues as to how far that relaxation will apply in relation to other legislation or rules of law that make conduct on unenclosed areas criminal. For example, will the relaxation apply to both limbs of s 34(1) of the Road Traffic Act 1988, to the public statutes that protect greens and the additional protection conferred by the Commons Act 2006? Third, although the relaxation of the illegality principle in *Brandwood* would appear to restrict the scope for the statutory acquisition of easements under s 68 of the CROW Act 2000, was this provision more limited than might otherwise appear? The latter provision will be repealed in late 2006 by the Commons Act 2006 in any event.

5.5.2   Prescriptive acquisition of easements and competent grantors

Lack of competence to make an express grant will prevent the prescriptive acquisition of an easement. That lack of competence may arise because a landowner cannot make a effective grant that would amount to public nuisance, or because the landowner is in a position of a fiduciary and could not make a valid grant unless certain conditions are satisfied, such as under the Open Spaces Act 1906. The competence of owners of commons and greens (unenclosed areas) to expressly grant easements of way has two aspects. First, competence in the sense of the landowner having sufficient residual interest to grant the rights in issue having regard to the rights already granted and affecting the area, such as the rights of the commoners: a *residual right* to grant. Second, and somewhat related, competence in the sense of having power to create and grant the rights in issue: the *power* to grant. As a prescriptive grant presupposes an express grant, the competence of an owner of an unenclosed area to make a grant affecting a common or a green in either sense is relevant.[1]

In respect of commons or greens subject to rights of common, the landowner has all the rights of a freeholder to grant easements subject to those rights; but the landowner cannot grant a right in respect of a subject-matter that has already been granted away. Thus if a common has sufficiency only to provide for the commoners having rights of common, there is no sufficiency left in the ownership of the servient owner that could be the subject of rights that might be granted by that owner.[2] In *Barker v Richardson* a prescriptive acquisition of an easement failed because the owner at the time was a tenant for life and, not having an estate of inheritance, would not have had the power to make an express grant of the easement.[3] Accordingly, a grant cannot be made if the owner does not enjoy a sufficiency of the rights to enable him to make a grant of or out of them.

An owner's lack of competency to grant rights over land already dedicated as a public highway has been treated both in terms of lack of rights to make a grant and also in terms of public nuisance. Thus in *Sheringham Urban District Council v Holsey* a claim to use a public footpath by vehicles failed on two grounds. First, because as the owner himself could not use the way for vehicles, he did not have the right or the power to dedicate the same for vehicular use. Second, because such conduct would have been a public nuisance and the owner had no power to grant rights that would have amounted to a public nuisance.[4] The position must be the same in connection with greens. In the case of a green, the right of the local inhabitants to access the area for recreational purposes will be founded on one or other of the three classes of greens, either registered or registrable

---

[1] Competence or capacity to make a grant was considered in *Angus & Co v Dalton* (1877) 3 QBD 85 and *Tehidy Minerals Ltd v Norman* [1971] 2 QB 528 at p 552. See also *Oakley v Boston* [1976] QB 270.

[2] *Doe d. Lowes v Davidson* (1813) 2 M&S 175 at p 184; *Arlett v Ellis* (1827) 7 B&C 346 at p 362.

[3] (1821) 4 B&Ad 579.

[4] (1904) 91 LT 225. There is a further difficulty that in the case of any highway that existed prior to 1836, or to a highway within the meaning of s 47 of the National Parks and Access to the Countryside Act 1949, such a highway will be maintainable at public expense and a freehold in the surface will be vested in the local highway authority; that gives rise to the question as to whether the freehold owner of the subjacent soil or the local highway authority is the proper party to effect a higher dedication.

under the Commons Registration Act 1965,[1] or the Commons Act 2006.[2] These are Class A greens that were originally allotted as such, Class B greens based on customary rights of the local inhabitants, and Class C greens based on 20 years user as of right. As the object of a Class A green was to allot land solely for the purpose of recreation, it is very unlikely that the owner would retain any residual rights out of which it could make grants of easements. Indeed it is unlawful to authorise the use of or to use any recreational allotment for any purposes other than those specified in the award or the Inclosure Acts.[3] Further such greens were frequently to be held in trust for recreational purposes.[4] In the case of a Class B green based on customary rights, such rights do not necessarily fully exploit the user of the green and may be limited having regard to the rights enjoyed, such as by time.[5] In such cases an owner may well be able to grant an easement as would not interfere with the customary rights. But otherwise, the limited power point in the decision in *Sheringham* could apply, and the owner could not make grants affecting statutory and customary rights to use the green. Further, and importantly, an obstruction of or interference with a right that lies either in statute or in custom would be a public nuisance; that would apply to each class of green. Accordingly an owner does not have the competence to make an express grant of an easement that would create a public nuisance.

The lack of competence in the second sense, of lack of power as a grantor, is illustrated by the following. In *Mills v Commission of the New Forest* certain statutes protective of the New Forest made the grant or taking of any interest in the common 'null and void'.[6] It followed that as the owner of the common had no power to make a grant of rights affecting the common, rights over the common could not be acquired by prescription. The significance of this decision is that the grant in issue would have been void and of no effect, rather than merely voidable. In *Oakley v Boston*[7] an easement of way was claimed by lost modern grant over land that at the relevant time had

---

[1]   Section 22.

[2]   Section 15.

[3]   Commons Act 1876, s 19.

[4]   Inclosure Act 1845, s 15.

[5]   *Fitch v Rawling* (1795) 2 H Bl 393.

[6]   (1856) 18 CB 60.

[7]   [1976] QB 270.

been glebe land. The Court of Appeal decided that as the servient owner at the time required the consent of the Ecclesiastical Commissioners to grant an easement,[1] and that as that body had not known of the acts of user, it could not be presumed that the Commissioners had given the necessary consent to a grant; therefore a valid lost modern grant could not be presumed.[2] The significance of this case is that the owner at the relevant time had the power to grant an easement, subject only to obtaining a consent, and that consent was required to be given by the consenting party being a party to the deed of grant. As Megaw LJ said, without that consent the grant would have been invalid.[3] However there was no discussion in *Oakley* as to whether a grant made without the necessary consent might have been only voidable. Finally, and possibly relevant to some owners of unenclosed areas, Goulding J, in considering whether a fiduciary owner could acquiesce where a party was purporting to exercise a right over land, pointed out that there were considerable difficulties in applying the doctrine of acquiescence to persons in a fiduciary position who had a duty only to alienate if satisfied of the permanent benefit of the transaction.[4]

5.5.3 Competent grantors: express or implied grants by local authorities

Commons and greens (unenclosed areas) are frequently owned by local authorities. Local authorities have power to grant rights in land they hold provided that such grants are not inconsistent with the purpose for which they hold the land.[5] Further, except with the Secretary of State's consent, a local authority shall not dispose of land for a consideration less than the best that can reasonably be obtained.[6] 'Land' includes the grant of an easement.[7] A local authority is therefore not empowered to grant an easement for less than the best

---

[1] Ecclesiastical Leasing Acts 1842–1858.

[2] The position would be the same for a claim based on 20 years under s 2 of the Prescription Act 1832.

[3] [1975] 3 All ER 405 at p 411.

[4] [1976] QB 270 at p 285.

[5] *Stourcliffe Estates Co Ltd v Bournemouth Corporation* [1910] 2 Ch 12; *British Transport Commission v Westmoreland County Council* [1958] AC 126, where dedication of a way as a public footpath was not incompatible with the owner's statutory objects to run a railway.

[6] Local Government Act 1972, s123(1) (principal councils as defined in s 270(1)), and s 127(2) (parish councils).

[7] Ibid, s 270(1).

consideration, and would be acting in breach of the law in purporting to do so. If such a transaction was void, this would preclude the prescriptive acquisition of an easement.[1] However it seems clear that such transactions are voidable, not void, where consent has not been obtained, and are not necessarily invalid as against the grantee.[2] But it is unclear whether transactions would be void if some other requirement was not satisfied, such as a failure to obtain the best consideration. As such a failure may be related to the giving or withholding of the Secretary of State's consent, it seems likely that any transaction that did not comply with statutory requirements would only be voidable and not void. Accordingly *Oakley* would not apply and a prescriptive easement could be acquired over unenclosed land owned by local authorities.

There are additional restrictions on local authorities when disposing of open space land, including the grant of easements over such land. These will apply particularly, but not exclusively, in the case of greens that were often allotted to the parish, and would now be held by the parish council. 'Open space' means any land '... used for the purposes of public recreation ...' as defined by s 270 of the Local Government Act 1972 and s 336 of the Town and Country Planning Act 1990. Before disposing of open space land, a local authority such as a parish council must give notice of their intention to do so, specifying the land in question, and advertise the same, and must consider any objections to the proposed disposal which may be made to them.[3] A green would normally be open space, as so defined. Again it seems likely that a failure to follow the required procedure would result only in a voidable, rather than a void grant. A local authority would therefore have power to dispose of land by the grant of an easement, and a prescriptive easement could be acquired.

Sometimes a local authority, such as a parish council, may acquire a green and be required to hold it upon a trust. Such land is sometimes acquired under s 9 of the Open Spaces Act 1906. If that is correct then by s 10 such an authority shall 'hold and administer the open space ... in trust to allow, and with a view to, the enjoyment thereof by the public as an open space within the meaning of [the] Act and under

---

[1]   *Mill v Commission of the New Forest* (1856) 18 CB 60.

[2]   Local Government Act 1972, s 128(2) and *R v Hackney London Borough Council, ex parte Structadene* [2001] 1 EGLR 15.

[3]   Ibid, s 123(2A).

proper control and regulation and for no other purpose'. These duties are subject to any conditions under which a green was originally acquired. These provisions place the owner of a green in the sort of fiduciary position that was considered in *Oakley*.[1] Lord Walker in *Brandwood* said that one consideration in relaxing the illegality principle was that the landowner did not hold his dispensing power in any sort of fiduciary capacity.[2] On that basis it is then arguable that an easement could not be prescriptively acquired over land held by a local authority or other body under the 1906 Act, or where allotted and held in trust, in the absence of some acquiescence. And even if there was some knowledge of the user of the way by that body, the claimant would still have to show that such acquiescence was wide enough to discharge the duty only to alienate if there was permanent benefit. If one considers the matter in terms of express grant, the grant of an easement of access over an area of a green where no recreational rights would actually be interfered with, might be justified if it gave rise to the payment of a substantial sum of money which could itself then be used for the general recreational interest over the green. But granting an easement of access over land which would demonstrably adversely affect the public recreational enjoyment would hardly ever be consistent with the duties of a body under the 1906 Act. The same point must apply to Class A greens that were allotted for recreational purposes and are held in trust by parish councils, quite apart from the bar on such use in s 19 of the Commons Act 1876.

5.5.4 Illegality principle: effect of criminal conduct on unenclosed areas and acquisition of easements of way

In one respect the decisions of the Court of Appeal in *Hanning* and the House of Lords in *Brandwood* were limited.[3] Section 193(1) of the 1925 Act, which confers public rights of air and exercise, applied to commons in urban and borough council areas from the date when the Act came into force on 1 January 1926.[4] In the case of rural commons, the section only applied where an owner effected the necessary dedication of the common.[5] Section 34(1) of the Road Traffic Act 1930

---

[1]   *Oakley v Boston* [1976] QB 270.

[2]   [2004] UKHL 14 para 56.

[3]   See **5.5.1** supra.

[4]   Councils that would not have been rural district councils prior to 1 April 1974.

[5]   Section 193(2).

came into force in that year. Where a prescriptive period expires before the coming into force of the public statute that makes a certain conduct illegal, the illegality principle had no application. Thus, in *Brandwood*, where Park J, at first instance, found that tracks accessing three of the houses had been used for more than 20 years before the date in 1928 when the lord of the manor had made a dedication applying s 193, the illegality principle did not have to be considered and easements by prescription by lost modern grant were acquired.[1] In *Hayling v Harper*[2] the issue concerned s 34(1) of the Road Traffic Act 1988 and the earlier enactment of the same criminal provision in s 14 of the Road Traffic Act 1930. It was accepted that an easement could be prescribed for under the doctrine of a lost modern grant based on a user that commenced prior to 1910, and this was not precluded by the illegality principle.[3]

The decision of the House of Lords in *Brandwood*, excluding the illegality principle in relation to the criminal conduct in s 193(4), was in part based on questions of public policy rather than pure legal reasoning. That makes the ratio decidendi the more difficult to analyse in terms of identifying principles capable of application to conduct made criminal under other public statutes. One particular matter did seem relevant to Lord Scott. The criminal conduct under s 193(4) was qualified by being without lawful authority, and that the servient owner could grant that authority. This point is capable of fairly straightforward reasoned application to other criminal acts that might be committed in prescribing for an easement over unenclosed areas.

Section 193(4) of the 1925 Act has now been addressed in *Brandwood*; the CROW Act 2000 prospectively repeals s 193(2).[4] But the decision in *Brandwood* provokes an examination of other public statutes that make conduct on unenclosed areas criminal, and a discussion as to whether the relaxation of the illegality principle might apply. There are a number of public statutes that criminalise defined conduct on

---

[1] Unlike prescription under the Prescription Act 1832, where the relevant prescriptive period is that before the proceedings, a lost modern grant can be established by any period of user of usually not less than 20 years.

[2] [2003] 3 EGLR 5.

[3] Ibid, paras [20]–[30].

[4] CROW Act 2000, s 102 and Sch 16.

unenclosed areas.[1] Section 34(1) of the Road Traffic Act 1988 is the first and obvious example, and was the illegality provision in issue in *Massey*.[2] However s 34(1) has two limbs; it is an offence to drive a vehicle without lawful authority '*(a) on to or upon any common land, moorland, or land of any other description, not being land forming a road, or (b) on any road being a footpath, bridleway or restricted byway ...'*. The conduct at (a) is similar to the conduct in issue in *Brandwood*, and, subject to any issue as to whether a green is '*land of any other description*', the illegality principle will not preclude a prescriptive acquisition in limb (a) cases. The only other question under this limb is whether or not the land in question is land '*... not being land forming part of a road'*.[3]

But the conduct at s 34(1)(b) might have some relevance if an easement of way is being claimed over a track across an unenclosed area, and the track runs either along or across a public highway such as a footpath. Whilst lack of lawful authority also qualifies limb (b), can it be assumed that the owner of an unenclosed area can in all circumstances give that authority in relation to a public highway on his land? In principle an owner of such land may grant an easement over land subject to public rights of way. The grant would be restricted, in the sense of itself being subject to, and not inconsistent with, the prior public rights of way. But what the owner could not give is authority for such user of the public highway as he has not retained for himself or which would amount to a public nuisance. A public nuisance is a criminal offence.[4] The notion of public nuisance in relation to public highways has relevance in two respects. First, whether an owner of an unenclosed area of land (or indeed of any land) can give consent in terms of s 34(1) of the 1988 Act. Second, and whether or not s 34(1) has application, whether user that amounts to public nuisance will always preclude the prescriptive acquisition of easement of way.

It is a public nuisance to obstruct a highway or hinder the public's free passage.[5] An act which '*prevents the convenient use of the way by*

---

[1]   This chapter principally addresses the problems of acquiring easements over unenclosed areas. However, as *Hayling v Harper* [2003] 3 EGLR 5 shows, some of these provisions may also have application to enclosed areas.

[2]   CROW Act 2000, s 67 of and Sch 7, para 5 will substitute an amended s 34.

[3]   The meaning of a road is not addressed in this chapter.

[4]   *Clerk & Lindsell on Torts*, 18th edn, para 19-03.

[5]   Ibid, para 19-106.

passengers' is a public nuisance.[1] Whether conduct is a public nuisance involves the notion of unreasonable use of the public highway.[2] But in *Sheringham Urban District Council v Holsey* a claim to a prescriptive right to use a public footpath by vehicles based on 40 years user failed as the user had from the beginning been a public nuisance.[3] Lord Scott in *Brandwood*, after considering *Hereford and Worcester County Council*,[4] accepted the general principle that it would not be open to an owner to dedicate a footpath as public vehicular highway if use by vehicles would have constituted a public nuisance to pedestrians using the footpath.[5] Whilst a public nuisance is more likely to be committed by use by vehicles proceeding along, rather than across a public footpath, one can envisage circumstances by which a user exercised across a public highway could be so unreasonable as to amount to a public nuisance; the illegality principle would be invoked and an easement could not be acquired by prescription (or indeed express grant).

In relation to public highways, s 131A of the Highways Act 1980 makes it an offence, without lawful authority or excuse, to disturb the surface of a footpath, a bridleway or other highway being a carriageway that is not made-up as to render it inconvenient for the exercise of the public right of way. As this offence is qualified by lawful authority, the illegality is capable of being waived. Where the whole of the surface of the way is vested in the owner, that owner could waive subject to any objection based on public nuisance; where the surface vests in the local highway authority, presumably only that authority could give consent.[6]

Some conduct on greens is subject to criminal penalties either because it would be a public nuisance, as discussed above, or because there are specific statutory offences. Section 12 of the Inclosure Act 1857 makes it an offence if '*any person … wilfully lay any …matter or thing …*

---

[1]　*R v Mathias* (1861) 2 F&F 570 per Byles J at p 573.

[2]　*Harper v Haden & Haden & Sons* [1932] 1 Ch 298.

[3]　(1904) 91 LT 225.

[4]　(1995) 71 P&CR 231.

[5]　[2004] UKHL 14 at paras 41–42. [2004] 2 AC 519, [2004] 2 All ER 305, [2004] 2 EGLR 15. There is a further difficulty, discussed above, about highways maintainable at public expense. Where a freehold in the surface is vested in the local highway authority; that gives rise to the question as to whether the freehold owner of the subjacent soil or the local highway authority is the proper party to effect a higher dedication.

[6]　See further at preceding footnote.

*or do any other act whatsoever to the injury of such town or village green
…, or to the interruption of the use or enjoyment thereof as a place for
exercise and recreation … '*; this part, unlike other parts of s 12, is not
qualified by *'without lawful authority'*. The Commons Act 1876
contains two provisions of relevance. Section 19 provides that it is
unlawful to use or authorise the use of an allotted green for purposes
other than those specified in the award or the Inclosure Acts. Section
29 makes any of the following a public nuisance: *'an encroachment on
or inclosure of a town or village green, also any erection thereon or
disturbance or interference with or occupation of the soil thereof which is
made otherwise than with a view to the better enjoyment of such town or
village green …'*.[1] Under s 12 of the 1857 Act and s 29 of the 1876 Act
the construction of a way, such as by providing a surface not in the
interests of the local inhabitants would amount to a public nuisance.
But, save in the case of allotted greens, the actual use of a way would
only be a public nuisance if it interfered with the rights of the local
inhabitants or in some way spoilt their use of the area for recreation.
That would certainly arise in the case of Class A allotted greens, but
may arise in the case of Class B customary greens depending on the
scope of the custom. The s 19 provision is in such uncompromising
terms that any transaction or grant in breach would probably be
treated as void rather than merely voidable, and would then invoke
lack of competency.

Schemes made under the Commons Act 1899 authorised the local
authorities to make local byelaws, and the byelaws may prohibit the
driving of vehicles on commons *'without lawful authority'*.[2] Finally,
under s 15 of the Open Spaces Act 1906, by-laws may be made
regulating greens. Such by-laws may or may not prohibit conduct in
the same way and subject to the same qualifications.

The Commons Act 2006 prohibits works which have the effect of
preventing or impeding access to or over the certain defined land, or
works for the resurfacing of land, without the consent of the
appropriate national authority.[3] The defined land includes any land
registered as common land and certain other land, such as land
regulated under the Commons Act 1876 or subject to a scheme under

---

[1] The 1876 Act applies to Greens which have been allotted for that purpose. What is doubtful is whether
 the legislation applies to a village green which arises through the exercise of customary rights.

[2] Commons (Schemes) Regulations 1982, SI 1982/209, Sch, Form 1, para 8(e).

[3] Section 38.

the Metropolitan Commons Act 1866 or the Commons Act 1899. The appropriate national authority in England is the Secretary of State, and in Wales, the National Assembly. Although the carrying out of works prohibited by the 2006 Act may not be criminal, there is an enforcement procedure in the county court.[1] It would therefore seem that the illegality principle is capable of having application, and this would prevent the acquisition of easements of way over the affected land by prescription (or express grant) if the exercise of the right involves any of the prohibited works.

In conclusion, lack of competency will defeat a claim to an easement by prescription if there could not have been a competent grantor. In the case of unenclosed areas, such as greens subject to allotted or customary rights, and/or owned in trust or under the 1906 Act, owners may lack competency to make grants. In any event, an owner can never permit what would be conduct that amounts to a public nuisance. The relaxation of the illegality principle is therefore limited. For the purposes of the prescriptive acquisition of easements, and the need to show that there would have been a competent grantor, it seems highly probable that those enactments that prohibit conduct on unenclosed areas 'without lawful authority' are likely to be accorded the same illegality principle relaxation as in *Brandwood*. Those enactments that are not so qualified would not give rise to any such relaxation.

5.5.5 Section 68 of the CROW Act 2000

This provision provided a statutory procedure for the acquisition of a right of way; it was enacted to address the problem created by *Hanning v Top Deck Travel Group Ltd*.[2] Section 68, which was repealed by the Commons Act 2006,[3] raised two issues: First, the scope of its application, especially following the decision of the House of Lords in *Bakewell Management Ltd v Brandwood*;[4] and second, the consequences of the provision in the Commons Act 2006 for its repeal.

---

[1]   See s 41.

[2]   (1993) 68 P&CR 14, as explained earlier in this chapter.

[3]   Came into force on 1 October 2006, see Commons Act 2006 (Commencement No 1, Transitional Provisions and Savings) (England) Order 2006, SI 2006/2504.

[4]   [2004] UKHL 14.

(a)   The scope of s 68

This provision applied where the owner or occupier from time to time of any premises had used as a means of access for vehicles to the premises and the use of the way '(a) *was an offence under an enactment applying to the land crossed by the way, but (b) would otherwise have been sufficient to create on or after the prescribed date, and to keep in existence, an easement giving a right of way for vehicles'.*[1] An 'enactment' includes any local or private Act, and a by-law, regulation or other provision having effect under an enactment.[2] The prescribed date was 5 May 1993.[3] The creation of an easement under this provision was in accordance with regulations.[4] An application for an easement was required to be made by the applicant serving a notice on the land owner within 12 months of the date when the regulations came into force (4 July 2002) or, if later, the date on which the relevant use of the way ceased.[5]

The time limits were unclear and confusing. The non-statutory guidance note on the regulations explained that it was only where the relevant user of the way had ceased and ended on or after 5 May 1993, that the first time limit of 4 July 2003 applied; the relevant user being user as of right such as can found a prescriptive easement.[6] The relevant user would cease, as such by a step being taken by the landowner to end the user as of right. That makes sense but it is not what the regulations state. The guidance note then stated that where the relevant user continues after 4 July 2003 applications may be made at any time provided they are made no later than 12 months of when the relevant user ceases or ends after that date, such as by action of the landowner.[7] Again that makes sense, but the regulations are not exactly clear on this point.

---

[1]   Section 68(1).

[2]   Section 68(5).

[3]   Vehicular Access across Common and other Land (England) Regulations 2002, SI 2002/1711, reg 4.

[4]   Section 68(2) and the Vehicular Access across Common and other Land (England) Regulations 2002, SI 2002/1711.

[5]   Vehicular Access across Common and other Land (England) Regulations 2002, SI 2002/1711, reg 6(2).

[6]   Defra, Common Land Branch, November 2002, para 12.

[7]   Ibid, para 13.

The first requirement under s 68 was that the use of the way must have been an offence under any enactment. The effect of the limitation of the illegality principle in *Brandwood* is to exclude those cases from s 68 where the acquisition of a prescriptive easement was not precluded by that principle. But where the illegality principle does apply, because the use of the way would be an offence, as discussed above, the section had application. Following the relaxation of the illegality principle in *Brandwood*, section 68 would only apply where an easement could have been acquired, but for the user being an offence. User might be an offence because it is a public nuisance or contrary to one or other of the statutory enactments considered above, such as s 12 of the Inclosure Act 1857 or s 29 of the Commons Act 1876. But s 68 will not apply where a prescriptive easement could not have been acquired because no express grant could have been made on grounds of lack of competency of the owner. That might arise where a green is held by a body as a fiduciary subject to the Open Space Act 1906, or is an allotted green held in trust. In *Burns v Kirby* the President of the Lands Tribunal considered that s 68 would apply to conduct unlawful under s 34(1)(a) of the Road Traffic Act 1988.[1]

Where, for example, an easement could be acquired prescriptively by reliance on a 20-year period during which no offence would have been committed, such as prior to the enactment of s 193 of the Law of Property Act or s 14(1) of the Road Traffic Act 1930, s 68 will not apply.

The second requirement was that the offence must apply to '*the land crossed by the way*'. In *Burns v Kirby* the Lands Tribunal decided that an easement could not be acquired under s 68 where the way was *along* a footpath or bridleway; a footpath or bridleway on a definitive map being treated as a road for the purposes of the offence under s 34(1)(b).[2] That was because, the President said, '*where a way was along a road, the normal use of the language would not permit it to be said that the road was crossed by the way*', in the terms used in s 68(1)(a).[3] But that construction assumes that the introductory words of s 34(1)(b), '*on any road being a footpath, bridleway of restricted byway*' will always apply to such public rights of way. A footpath or bridleway may be on land '*not being land forming part of a road*', in which case s 34(1)(a)

---

[1]   REF/4/2003 31 October 2003, para 15.

[2]   REF/4/2003 31 October 2003, para 20 and Road Traffic Act 1988 s 34(2).

[3]   Ibid.

would apply and the first issue would be whether the use of the public right of way was unlawful in a manner that would invoke the illegality principle apart from the *Brandwood* relaxation, such as by being a public nuisance. The linguistic argument accepted by the Lands Tribunal is a narrow one and gives insufficient consideration to the purpose of the provision.

The third requirement was that the use would otherwise have been sufficient to create an easement by prescription. Accordingly a landowner remains entitled to resist an application on the grounds that would have been available to him under the common law or the Prescription Act 1832.[1] In this regard the competency questions become relevant.[2] As already discussed above, the use of certain greens, such as those allotted and held in trust, would in most cases not found a prescriptive right of way.

Section 68 of the CROW Act 2000 was enacted to address the difficulties where a right of way could have been acquired by prescription, but for the fact that the necessary user would have been an offence that invoked the illegality principle. Under s 68, the Vehicular Access across Common and Other Land (England) Regulations 2002[3] were made. The regulations applied to any land crossed by a way used as a means of access for vehicles to particular premises. The owner of the premises was entitled to apply to the owner of the common land for the creation of an easement. In the case of any dispute, the matter was referred to the Lands Tribunal. Compensation was payable: 0.25% of the value of the claimant's premises where the premises existed on 31 November 1905, or 0.5% where they existed on 30 November 1930.

As discussed above the time limits for making claims were far from clear. By reg 6(2), an application for an easement had to be made before 3 July 2003 in respect of a way that was then still being used and in respect of which a prescriptive right could have been acquired but for the unlawful user (generally, 20-year user). Many owners of premises with access over common land will have been unaware of

---

[1]   Application is made to the Lands Tribunal: see *Burns and another v Kirby and another* REF/4/2003 31 October 2003.

[2]   In the case of a vehicular way being claimed over or along a public footpath or bridleway, there is a further difficulty, discussed above, about highways maintainable at public expense. Where a freehold in the surface is vested in the local highway authority; that gives rise to the question as to whether the freehold owner of the subjacent soil or the local highway authority is the proper party to effect a higher dedication.

[3]   SI 2002/1711.

this time-limit. Where the use of the relevant way ceases at a date after 3 July 2003, the application must be made within 12 months of such cessation.

The right to apply for an easement only arose where the user 'would otherwise have been sufficient to create on or after the prescribed date, and to keep in existence, an easement giving a right of way for vehicles'.[1] The prescribed date was 5 May 1993. The literal meaning of this limitation is that if the 20-year prescriptive period expired prior to this prescribed date, no claim can be made. The possible answer to this conundrum is to contend for a 20-year prescription period under the Prescription Act 1832; the prescriptive period is that immediately before the action or suit.[2] An alternative claim based on the doctrine of a lost modern grant does assume a grant on the date when user of the way first commenced and, if s 68(1) had the effect its literal interpretation suggested, would fall foul of the prescribed date bar if the 20-years' user expired before that date.

There was a strict timetable for the service by the landowner of notices under regs 7 and 8 of the 2002 Regulations. Where no notices are served, the claimant becomes entitled to an easement as of right upon payment into court of the compensation sum.[3]

(b)   Effect of repeal of s 68

The Commons Act 2006 makes provision for the repeal of s 68.[4] Presumably the policy justification for its repeal is that as the House of Lords allowed the relaxation of the illegality principle, and therefore allowed the acquisition of a right of way by prescription where a servient owner could have consented to an express grant, there was no good reason why an easement could be acquired under s 68 that could never be acquired by prescription because of the application of the illegality principle to those cases where no relaxation of the principle would have been granted by the courts. But, the repeal of s 68 will preclude the acquisition of certain easements where the illegality principle applies and would not have been relaxed. Section 68 was repealed on 1 October 2006.[5]

---

[1]   CROW Act 2000, s 68(1).

[2]   Prescription Act 1832, s 4.

[3]   Regulations 14 and 15.

[4]   Schedule 6, Part 5; repeal is expected in late 2006.

[5]   See Commons Act 2006 (Commencement No 1, Transitional Provisions and Savings) (England) Order 2006, SI 2006/2504.

Chapter 6

CREATION AND TRANSFER OF RIGHTS OF COMMON

6.1   INTRODUCTION

There are a number of ways in which rights of common were created in the past. In the case of rights enjoyed by copyholders (including customary freeholds – a type of copyhold), until the abolition of copyhold in 1922, rights akin to rights of common were acquired by copyholders by custom. Otherwise, rights of common were attached to freehold interests. These rights were of four kinds: rights appendant; rights appurtenant; rights in gross; or rights *pur cause de vicinage*.[1] Rights of common appendant must have existed prior to 1290,[2] and cannot therefore any longer be created. The other rights were capable of being created by grant or reservation, prescription or statute. Subject to the effect of the Commons Act 2006, these are the only methods by which rights of common can still be created today.

Save for the case of rights of common in gross, rights of common pass on the transfer of the land to which they are attached (the dominant land). Rights of common in gross are not attached to any land, and can therefore be transferred as such. Certain formalities are necessary for the transfer of any rights of common.

All rights of common subsisting at the time of the Commons Registration Act 1965 were required to be registered under that Act.[3] At the end of the registration period (31 July 1970) 'no rights of common were exercisable over any such land unless they were registered either under the 1965 Act or under the Land Registration Acts 1925 and 1936'.[4] The Commons Act 2006 maintains the requirement of registration.

---

[1]   See Chapter 4.

[2]   Possibly prior to 1189, see *Tyrringham's Case* (1584) 4 Co Rep 36b.

[3]   Section 1.

[4]   Section 1(2)(b).

The 1965 Act defined common land as including land subject to rights of common.[1] Provision was made for the registration of new commons.[2] The Commons Act 2006 restricts the scope for the creation of new rights of common.[3] In particular, a right of common cannot be created by virtue of prescription. In very limited circumstances rights of common can be created by statute.

This chapter also deals with the protection of rights of common (rather than common land), together with the legal and extra-legal remedies available to commoners where rights are being interfered with.

6.2   CREATION

6.2.1   Custom

Custom arises in two separate circumstances: custom in connection with the rights of the copyholders of a manor and originally enforceable in the manorial courts, although ultimately by the common law courts; and custom enforceable at common law.

(a)   *Custom and copyholders*

The copyholders in a manor did not own freehold legal estates. As rights of common proper were part of freehold interests, the rights of the copyholders to exercise similar rights on the uninclosed lands within the manor arose and were protected by the customs of the manor. Although copyholds started as grants of tenancies at the will of the lord of the manor, over time the copyhold interest acquired recognition as an estate of its own and was at the will of the lord only in name. Customs determined the characteristics of these estates, how long they lasted, how they could be inherited, and what additional rights ran with them. Customs varied from manor to manor, although manors in a particular locality or area of the country may have shared common customs. Customs were enforceable against the lord of the manor and others, eventually, in the common law courts.[4]

---

[1]   Section 22(1).

[2]   Section 13 and Commons Registration (New Land) Regulations 1969, SI 1969/1843.

[3]   Section 6.

[4]   In the sixteenth century the action of ejectment in the common law courts was extended to protect the interests of copyholders: see Simpson, *An Introduction to the History of Land Law* (1961), at p 145.

Customs concerned a number of matters within the manor, such as inheritance, services, as well as the use of the unenclosed lands. Customs were enforceable in and regulated by the customary court of the manor. This court would have regulated the use of the waste land of the manor by controlling the number of animals, and the times of the year when they could be let out.[1] The manorial courts were held until the abolition of copyhold in 1922.[2] Their use and effectiveness in relation to the control of customary rights exercisable over the unenclosed waste lands of the manor began to peter out following the alterations in agricultural practices and the inclosure of the commons. However, it seemed unlikely that the precise rights to use the waste land of the manor by the copyholders remained unchanged throughout the history of the manor. Accordingly, although these rights lay in custom, and would normally be of long usage, it seems possible that alterations in the local custom would have arisen from time to time and, accordingly, new rights created notwithstanding the strict rule in the common law courts that a custom must have existed prior to 1189.

Customary rights of common can therefore no longer be created. Where the common law rule that a customary right cannot exist if it can be shown not to have existed prior to 1189 applies, it may be possible to show by reference to decisions of the respective manorial courts that a particular customary right to use waste land of the manor was confirmed by a manorial court, and then became converted, with the conversion of the copyhold title, to a freehold interest. In practice this is no longer relevant in respect of registered commons because any unregistered rights of common that existed when the Commons Registration Act 1965 came into force can no longer be exercised.[3]

(b)   *Custom and the common law*

Outside the manorial courts, custom was enforceable at common law. However, a custom was only enforceable if local, ancient, reasonable and certain. Of these requirements, ancient meant that the custom had come into existence before 1189.[4] The effect of the abolition of

---

[1]   See Jessel, *The Law of the Manor*, at chapter 13.

[2]   Law of Property Act 1922.

[3]   Section 1(2)(b).

[4]   The commencement of legal memory; the accession of Richard I; see *Hammerton v Honey* (1876) 24 WR 603.

copyhold was to convert the copyhold into a freehold, and the customary rights of the copyholders to use the waste lands of the manor into rights of common.[1]

Custom is important in relation to town and village greens. The use of the green for the recreational purposes of the local inhabitants may be a custom that the common law will enforce.[2]

6.2.2   Express grant

(a)   Formal requirements

By 'grant' is meant a grant by deed of a legal interest. A right of common is a *profit à prendre* and capable of being a legal interest in land.[3] A *profit à prendre* can only exist as a legal interest if it is granted by deed.[4] To create a legal interest, the grant must be for an interest equivalent to an estate in fee simple absolute in possession or a term of years absolute.[5] A profit granted for any other term, such as for a life, will only be an equitable interest notwithstanding that the grant lies in a deed.[6] Further, an enforceable contract to grant a profit will only give the grantee an equitable right.[7] In the case of any contract or agreement made on or after 27 September 1989, the contract or agreement must comply with the Law of Property (Miscellaneous Provisions) Act 1989, s 2. In the case of an agreement to grant a *profit à prendre* made before 27 September 1989, there must either be a sufficient memorandum in writing that satisfies the Law of Property Act 1925, s 40 or the agreement must be supported by part performance.[8]

When fully in force, the Commons Act 2006 will replace and improve the registration system under the 1965 Act.[9] It will also make additional changes to the registration and status of rights of common. The 2006 Act adopts the same definition of a right of common as the

---

[1]   Law of Property Act 1922, Sch 12.

[2]   See Chapter 9.

[3]   Law of Property Act 1925, s 1(2)(a).

[4]   Ibid, s 52(1).

[5]   Ibid, s 1(2)(a).

[6]   Ibid, s 1(3).

[7]   *White v Taylor (No 2)* [1968] 1 Ch 160.

[8]   *Mason v Clarke* [1955] AC 778.

[9]   The relevant provisions will be progressively introduced during 2007 to 2008.

1965 Act,[1] and such a right therefore includes a cattlegate or beastgate and a right of sole or several vesture or herbage or of sole or several pasture. After the commencement of the relevant provisions, the following restrictions will apply to the creation of rights of common.

A right of common will only be able to be created by express grant if the land is not registered as a town or village green and the right is attached to, and therefore capable of benefiting identifiable, land.[2] The creation of a right of common will only have effect if it complies with such requirements as to form and content as regulations may provide,[3] and the creation of a right of common will not operate until on an application to have the right registered in a register of common land, or if the right is over land not registered as common land, the land is registered as common land.[4] An application to register the creation of a right of common consisting of a right to graze any animal will be refused if in the opinion of the commons registration authority the land over which it is created would be unable to sustain the exercise of that right, and if the land is already registered as a common land, any other rights of common registered as exercisable over the land.[5] Although the creation of new or additional rights of common may be rare, the registration authorities will no doubt have to take expert advice about any land in issue, whether already a common or not, can support further livestock. These new rules fit in with the policy behind the provisions of the 2006 Act to better manage common land.[6]

If the owner of land grants a *profit à prendre* to be enjoyed by one party to the exclusion of all other persons, the profit is a 'sole' or 'several' profit; whereas if the profit is granted to a person to be enjoyed with a number of other persons, including the owner of the land, it is called a profit 'in common'. It follows that every right of common is a *profit à prendre*, but not every *profit à prendre* is a right of common in the ordinary common law sense.[7] However, a sole right of vesture, herbage or pasture falls within the definition of

---

[1] See section 61(1).

[2] Section 6(3).

[3] Section 6(4).

[4] Section 6(5).

[5] Section 6(6).

[6] See Chapter 11 below.

[7] See *Gale on Easements* (17th edn), at para 1–129.

a right of common where that term is used in the Commons Registration Act 1965 and the Commons Act 2006.[1]

(b) Competence of the grantor

The grantor of a *profit à prendre* must have the necessary competence to grant the intended interest or interests. Thus persons entitled only to rights of common over common land would have no power to grant an easement of way over the common.[2] A person who owns a lease of land could grant a *profit à prendre* out of that lease for a term that was less than the term of the lease, but that person could not grant a *profit à prendre* in perpetuity. When the Commons Act 2006 is fully in force, the grant of a right of common outside the limits that may be permitted under that Act will be beyond the competence of an owner of common land.

(c) Exclusive right of grazing

In *Anderson v Bostock*[3] it was held that the grant of an exclusive right of grazing over a moor could not exist as an appurtenant right to land. Grazing rights have to be related to the needs or use of the dominant tenement and could not be of an exclusive and unlimited nature for such appurtenant rights are unknown to the law. An exclusive right to grazing without limit did not therefore pass to successors in title as an appurtenant right.

6.2.3 Reservation

A *profit à prendre* may be created by the express reservation of such a right in a deed of conveyance of the affected land. The purchaser acquires the land subject to the reserved rights. A reservation operates without a re-grant.[4] However, any ambiguity will be construed against the purchaser of the land as if there had been a re-grant by that person.[5] In practice the circumstance where rights of common might be created by reservation is probably limited to that where existing common land is sold and the owner reserves for

---

[1]   Section 22(1) of the 1965 Act defines 'rights of common', and s 61(1) of the 2006 Act defines 'right of common' in the same terms to include a right of sole or several vesture or herbage or of sole or several pasture.

[2]   *Paine & Co v St Neots Gas & Coke Co* [1939] 3 All ER 812.

[3]   [1976] Ch 312.

[4]   Law of Property Act 1925, s 65.

[5]   *St Edmundsbury & Ipswich Diocesan Board of Finance v Clark (No 2)* [1975] 1 WLR 468.

himself rights of common. The requirements of the Commons Act 2006 must be satisfied.[1]

6.2.4 Prescription

Any *profit à prendre* that lies in grant is capable of being acquired by prescription. Prescription is the legal idea by which the law concludes that there has been a grant of a *profit à prendre* by implication: an implied grant. Whatever may have been the position prior to the coming into force of the appropriate provisions of the Commons Act 2006, that Act provides that a right of common cannot at anytime be created over land by virtue of prescription.[2] Prescription is the acquisition of a right, such as a right of common, by actual user as of right for the minimum prescriptive period of not less than 20 years.[3] Accordingly what follows is a discussion of the methods of acquiring rights of common that applied prior to 31 July 1970, when all rights had to be registered, and may have applied to the period thereafter, and before the 2006 Act had application.

There are three methods of claiming a *profit à prendre* by prescription:

– at common law;
– under the doctrine of a lost modern grant; or
– under the Prescription Act 1832.

Each method is based on the idea that there has been a grant by deed. Rights of common appendant arise by operation of law and do not lie in grant. Accordingly, such rights cannot be acquired by prescription. An acquisition of a *profit à prendre* by way of prescription is not the same as the acquisition of customary rights.[4]

Under any of the three methods of prescription, there must be user of the claimed right, as of right, without permission, without secrecy, and without force. There is a further general requirement that the right claimed must be continuously used during the prescriptive period. However, continuity has regard to the nature of the right.

---

[1]   Section 6 as discussed above under express grant.

[2]   Section 6(1).

[3]   See Chapter 5 supra.

[4]   See *Halsbury's Laws of England* (4th edn) vol 6, at para 555 and *Hammerton v Honey* (1876) 24 WR 603; *Tyson v Smith* (1838) 9 Ad & El 406; *Mercer v Denne* [1905] 2 Ch 538; see also Chapter 3.

Thus a claim to a right of pasturage during certain times of the year does not require user outside those periods.[1]

(a)   Prescription at common law

Prescription at common law requires user since time immemorial (1189). In practice, proof of user for a sufficiently long period of time, exceeding 20 years, will normally suffice.[2] A claim based on prescription at common law can be defeated by showing that there could not have been such user so far back as 1189. Unity of ownership of the land over which the right is asserted and the land in respect of which the right is exercised will defeat a claim under this method of prescription because a person cannot have a profit over his own land. Further, such a claim will be defeated if there is evidence that the claimed right was not, as a matter of fact, exercised at some point since 1189.[3]

(b)   Lost modern grant

The doctrine of lost modern grant evolved to address some of the problems that arose in relation to proving user back to 1189 in the case of prescription at common law. Under this doctrine, there is a presumption that a grant was made of the right, but the grant has been lost.[4] The normal prescriptive period is a minimum of 20 years.[5] The claim can only be defeated by showing that there could not have been a capable grantor or grantee at the time of the supposed 'lost' grant. The fact that the person asserting the right believed, when so doing, that he had and was entitled to, a right, does not negate a claim to a right of common under the doctrine of lost modern grant.[6]

Where a person, purportedly entitled to rights of common that existed when the Commons Registration Act 1965 came into force, failed to appeal a decision of the Commons Commissioner not to confirm an application for the registration of those rights, those rights would cease to be exercisable under s 1(2)(b) when the Commissioner

---

[1]   *White v Taylor (No 2)* [1969] 1 Ch 160 at 192, [1969] 1 All ER 1015.

[2]   *R v Joliff* (1823) 2 B&C 54.

[3]   *Addington v Clode* (1775) 2 WmBl 989; *R v Ashby Folville Inhabitants* (1866) LR 1 QB 213; *Bryant v Foot* (1868) LR 3 QB 497.

[4]   *Cowlam v Slack* (1812) 15 East 108; *Tehidy Minerals Ltd v Norman* [1971] 2 QB 528, [1971] 2 All ER 475.

[5]   *Tehidy Minerals Ltd v Norman* [1971] 2 QB 528, [1971] 2 All ER 475.

[6]   *Earl de la Warr v Miles* (1881) 17 ChD 535.

decided the application was void and not at the earlier date of 31 July 1970. Lost modern grant cannot operate until the date of the Commissioner's decision.[1]

A right could not have been acquired by prescription where the acts justifying the right, for example grazing or the taking of estovers, would themselves be unlawful and where the illegality principle is not relaxed,[2] or there could never have been any lawful grant.[3]

(c)   The Prescription Act 1832

This Act provides for a minimum prescriptive period of 30 years without interruption. The right becomes absolute and indefeasible where a full period of 60 years is established unless the right was enjoyed by consent or agreement made by deed in writing.[4] The two periods of 30 years and 60 years are those immediately before any legal proceedings in which the issue is brought into question.[5] However, no act amounts to an interruption of user unless it has been submitted to or acquiesced in for one year. Consequently, a period of 29 years and one day, or 59 years and one day, is sufficient to found a right provided legal proceedings are commenced immediately on the expiration of the relevant 30- or 60-year period, so that a full year's interruption is not achieved. All the other requirements for the establishment of the profit by prescription apply under this Act. However, an oral consent given at the commencement of the 60-year period will not defeat a claim.[6]

---

[1]   *Dynevor (Lord) v Richardson* [1995] Ch 173. As the registration of the land as common land was earlier deemed void, this case is no authority for the proposition that a right of common can be acquired by prescription over registered common land; it leaves the question open.

[2]   *Hanning v Top Deck Travel Group Ltd* (1993) 68 P&CR 14; *Bakewell Management Ltd v Brandwood* [2004] UKHL 14 overruling 1 WLR 1429; see also Chapter 5.

[3]   *Neaverson v Peterborough RDC* [1902] 1 Ch 557; *Mill v New Forest Commissioners* (1856) 18 CB 60.

[4]   Section 1.

[5]   Section 4.

[6]   *Tickle v Brown* (1836) 4 Ad & El 369; *Earl de la Warr v Miles* (1881) 17 ChD 535.

(d) Conclusions on prescription

It must be remembered that after the coming into force of the appropriate provisions of the Commons Act 2006, rights of common cannot be created by prescription.[1]

6. 3 THE 1965 AND 2006 ACTS AND THE CREATION OF RIGHTS

The creation of rights of common (as distinct from a *profit à prendre* that does not amount to a right of common, such as a 'sole' or 'several' profit) has been profoundly affected by both the Commons Registration Act 1965 and the Commons 2006 Act. In order to understand the consequences for the creation of rights of common by prescription, one needs first to understand the position in relation to the creation of rights by *express* grant.

6.3.1 Express grant of rights of common over registered commons

By s 1(2) of the 1965 Act, no rights of common were exercisable over any common land that was registered under the Act unless those rights were registered under the 1965 Act or under the Land Registration Acts 1925 and 1936. All rights of common that existed at the commencement of the 1965 Act therefore had to be registered, or could not after the end of the registration period thereafter be exercised.

However, s 1(2) appeared to allow for the registration of new rights of common coming into existence after the end of the registration period of 31 July 1970. In theory the owner of the soil to a registered common could have created new or additional rights of common by express grant. Such expressly granted rights of common would not be exercisable over any registered common land until those rights were, themselves, registered under the Act. However, there seemed to have been no provision for the amendment of registers of rights of common created under the 1965 Act to allow for such new rights of common to be entered on existing registers.

Section 13 made provision for regulations to provide for the amendment where:

---

[1] Section 6(1).

'any rights registered under this Act are apportioned, extinguished or released, or are varied or transferred in such circumstances as may be prescribed.'

But there was no reference to rights that might be created over registered commons, although it might have been possible to contend that upon the creation of new rights existing registered rights were varied. Further, the consequential Commons Registration (New Land) Regulations 1969 specifically provided that no application could be entertained for the registration of rights of common over existing registered common land.[1]

The matter has now been addressed by the Commons Act 2006. Where rights are created by express grant that satisfy the requirements of s 6 and the regulations, as discussed above, provision is made for the registration of these new rights.[2]

6.3.2 Grant of new rights over land not registered as common land

In the period between the last date for the registration of rights of common under the 1965 Act (31 July 1970) and the date when the relevant provisions of the 2006 Act comes into force, the position will be different in relation to the creation by express grant of rights of common over any land that was not, at the time, registered common land. Such land would, upon the express grant of rights of common over it, have become common land in respect of which a new registration should have been effected under the 1965 Act, together with the newly created rights of common.[3]

However, after the relevant provisions of the Commons Act 2006 come into force, the restrictions on the grant of new rights of common apply to all land, whether or not it is registered common land.[4] Accordingly, a right of common will then only be created by express grant if the land is not registered as a town or village green and the right is attached to, and therefore capable of benefiting identifiable,

---

[1]   Regulation 3(2).

[2]   Section 6(5)–(6).

[3]   Commons Registration Act 1965, s 1 and Commons Registration (New Land) Regulations 1969, SI 1969/1843, reg 3.

[4]   Section 5 provides that Part 1 of the Act applies to all land in England and Wales except the New Forest, Epping Forest and the Forest of Dean.

land.[1] The grant must comply with such requirements as to form and content as regulations may provide,[2] and the creation of a right of common will not operate until the land is registered as common land.[3] An application to register the creation of a right of common consisting of a right to graze any animal will be refused if in the opinion of the commons registration authority the land over which it is created would be unable to sustain the exercise of that right. [4]

6.3.3   Acquisition of rights by prescription and the Commons Registration Act 1965

What follows is a brief discussion of the position during the period between the end of the registration of rights of common under the Commons Registration Act 1965 (31 July 1970) and the coming into force of the Commons Act 2006. The 2006 Act provides that a right of common cannot any longer be created by prescription, whether over registered common land or other land.

(a)   Registered commons

The acquisition of rights of common by prescription is founded upon the assumption of a grant (an implied grant). Accordingly, there is no reason why the observations in relation to express grants above should not also have applied in principle to prescription. During the prescriptive period, the person without any common rights but who was asserting a right of common by user as of right over a pre-2006 Act registered common, was arguably not exercising *rights of common* within the meaning of s 1(2)(b). That subsection must have been referring to rights that ought to have been registered prior to 31 July 1970, and were not, in other words, rights that were legal interests and capable of registration.

Section 1(2)(b) did not make it unlawful to use a common for a purpose that, upon the completion of a prescriptive period would, in the absence of the Act, then be a right of common acquired by prescription. There was therefore no reason why rights of common could not have been purportedly prescribed against a registered common. But on completion of the 20-year (or under the Prescription

---

[1]   Section 6(3).

[2]   Section 6(4).

[3]   Section 6(5).

[4]   Section 6(6).

Act 1832, 30-year) prescriptive period, the law would have assumed an implied grant at the commencement of the prescriptive period. However, it is arguable that s 1(2)(b) might then have had effect. The right acquired by prescription could not have been exercised. The contrary argument is that if the right did not exist when the 1965 Act came into force, the right did not require registration. The real difficulty, which is common to the creation of new express grants of rights of common, and to the acquisition of rights by prescription, is that the Act contained no clear provisions to add newly acquired rights over existing registered commons. One was left with the possible argument that the registered rights of common had been varied.[1]

(b)   Rights acquired by prescription over land not registered as common land

The position was quite different where rights have been acquired by prescription over land that is not registered as common land. Such land would have become new common land in respect of which a new registration can be effected under the 1965 Act, together with the newly created rights of common.[2] As from the date when the relevant provisions of the Commons Act 2006 comes into force, a right of common cannot be acquired by prescription.[3]

6.3.4   Registration of rights

The requirements for the registration of any newly created rights, and rights created between 1970 and the commencement of the provisions of the Commons Act 2006, are fully explained in Chapter 8.

6.4   TRANSFER

Rights of common appendant or appurtenant will pass with the conveyance of the land to which they are attached.[4] However, a right of common appendant passes with the land and can never be severed from it; it was acquired by operation of law, and not by grant.[5] Rights

---

[1]   Section 13. But Knox J in *Dynevor v Richardson* [1995] 1 All ER 109 would not seem to have precluded the acquisition of prescriptive rights in all cases.

[2]   Commons Registration Act 1965, s 1 and Commons Registration (New Land) Regulations 1969, SI 1969/1843, reg 3.

[3]   Commons Act 2006, s 6(1).

[4]   Law of Property Act 1925, s 62.

[5]   *Bennett v Reeve* (1740) Willes 227.

of common appurtenant can be severed from the land to which they are attached and then become rights of common in gross.[1] The Commons Act 2006 imposes restrictions on severance; see below at **6.6.4**.

Rights of common are interests in land, they are incorporeal hereditaments, and can only be conveyed or transferred by deed.[2] In the absence of express mention, in any deed or transfer of the dominant land to which rights of common are attached, such rights will pass pursuant to the word-saving provision in s 62(1) of the Law of Property Act 1925.[3]

The Commons Registration Act 1965 required rights of common to be registered. These rights were widely defined and included cattlegates or beastgates, rights of sole or several vesture or herbage or of sole or several pasture.[4] All such rights existing prior to 31 July 1970 were required to be registered.[5] Upon the transfer of any registered rights, application had to be made to register the transfer and the new owner as owner on the pre-2006 Act register of rights of common.[6] That position remains the same under the Commons Act 2006.[7]

6.5   STATUTE

Rights of common may be created by statute.[8] The effect of many inclosure awards made under private, and later, the public inclosure Acts of the nineteenth century, was the creation or variation of rights of common.

However, today, the most common circumstance for the creation of rights of common over land not subject to the same is in connection with compulsory acquisition of common land. The compulsory

---

[1]   *Bunn v Channen* (1813) 5 Taunt 244, *Bettinson v Langton* [2001] 3 All ER 417. Under Dartmoor Commons Act 1985, s 8 there is a prohibition against severance.

[2]   Law of Property Act 1925, s 51.

[3]   *White v Williams* [1922] 1 KB 727; *White v Taylor (No 2)* [1969] 1 Ch 160, [1968] 1 All ER 1015.

[4]   Section 22(1).

[5]   Section 4.

[6]   Section 13 and Commons Registration (General) Regulations 1966, SI 1966/1471, reg 29(1), as amended by Commons Registration (General) (Amendment) Regulations 1968, SI 1968/658.

[7]   Sections 12 and 14; registration is explained further in Chapter 8.

[8]   Acknowledged in s 6(2) of the Commons Act 2006.

purchase order may include suitable 'exchange' land to replace common land that is proposed to be acquired. The order may provide for the vesting of the exchange land in persons, and subject to the same rights, as the land being compulsorily acquired. The confirming Secretary of State must certify his satisfaction.[1] The Commons Act 2006 also contains provisions for exchange land.[2]

6.6   MISCELLANEOUS DISPOSITIONS

The topics of surrender and extinguishment, and deregistration and exchange, are more fully considered in Chapter 7 below.

6.6.1   Variation

The owner of the soil and a commoner may agree to vary a right of common by altering the land over which the right is exercised, or the extent of the right. When the relevant provisions of the Commons Act 2006 come into force, there will be restrictions on the ability to vary a right of common. A right will not be capable of variation where the right is exercisable over new land that is registered as a town or village greens,[3] or the right is to be varied to extend a right over a town or village green[4] any other variation will not have effect unless it complies as to form and content to be prescribed by regulations, and then only upon an application to register.[5] Where an application is made to register the variation of a right consisting of a right to graze any animal, the registration authority will be entitled to refuse registration where it is of the opinion that the land cannot sustain the exercise of the right.[6]

6.6.2   Surrender

At common law a right of common could always be surrendered by the commoner to the owner of the soil by a deed of release.[7] Where that was done, the right of common came to an end.[8] When the

---

[1]   Acquisition of Land Act 1981, s 19(1); see also Chapter 12.

[2]   See Chapter 8.

[3]   Section 7(2).

[4]   Section 7(3).

[5]   Section 7(4).

[6]   Section 7(5).

[7]   See further Chapter 7.

[8]   See Chapter 7.

relevant provisions of the Commons Act 2006 come into force, the surrender of a right of common will only have effect if it complies with such requirements as to form and content as will be prescribed by regulations, and will not operate until on an application to remove the right from the register of rights.[1] At common law a right of common is extinguished where ownership of both the soil and the land to which the right is attached merges in the same person (unity of possession); when the relevant provisions of the Commons Act 2006 are in force, a registered right of common cannot be extinguished by operation of common law.[2]

6.6.3   Apportionment

A right of common may be apportioned where the land to which it is attached is divided between two or more owners. When the relevant provisions of the Commons Act 2006 come into force, regulations will provide for the amendments, if any, which must be made to the registers of common land and of town and village greens.[3] Section 9 of the Act provides that to the extent that any instrument purports to apportion rights of common otherwise than *pro rata*, it will be void. Until the registration requirements of the 2006 Act come into force, an application can, but is not required to, be made under s 13 of the Commons Registration Act 1965 to register a variation of rights of common arising by apportionment.

6.6.4   Severance

In certain circumstances a right of common of pasture, which is attached to land, was capable of being severed from that land and then held in gross.[4] Other rights, such as estover rights, were not capable of being severed. Severance of rights of common on Dartmoor has been prohibited for some time.[5] Where a right is attached to land, and would otherwise be capable of severance, the Commons Act 2006 provides that the severance of such a right of common will no longer have effect unless it is authorised under Schedule 1 to the Act.[6] This restriction had retrospective effect to 28

---

[1]   Section 13(1).

[2]   Section 13(2).

[3]   Section 8.

[4]   See *Bettison v Langton* [2001] 3 All ER 417.

[5]   Dartmoor Commons Act 1985.

[6]   Section 9, which was deemed to have come into force on 28 June 2005.

June 2005.[1] Schedule 1 sets out three cases where the bar on severance may be relaxed. First, there will be a limited exception for rights of common that are acquired by a commons council or Natural England.[2] Second, temporary severance of rights may be permitted by an order made by the Secretary of State or under rules made by a commons council. An order came into force on 9 September 2006 permitting temporary severance by the leasing or licensing of rights of common for a period not exceeding 2 years, or the leasing or licensing of the land to which the right of common is attached, without that right.[3] Third, permanent severance of rights may be permitted in accordance with an order by the Secretary of State for a specified common or commons; this is an exception of last resort, and no such orders are presently planned.[4]

The effect of any severance, such as by the grant or licence, or otherwise, of any right of common, which is in breach of the 2006 Act, and is not authorised as discussed above, is as follows. The severance is void, the person claiming rights will not be entitled to them, any stock placed on a common in reliance to a void severance will be therefore unlawfully, and the common owner or any commoner can take any of the actions discussed later in this Chapter. Additionally the Secretary of State could take action under the Commons Act 2006.[5] It has also been suggested that a person who has unlawfully acquired rights will not be entitled to payments under the Single Payment Scheme or other grant schemes, and may not have immunity from the duty to take care conferred by section 7 of the Animals Act 1971 in respect of animals straying from unfenced land to a highway.[6]

6.6.5 Attachment and re-allocation of attached rights

This arises where a right of common is not appurtenant or attached to land. When the relevant provisions of the Commons Act 2006 are in force, regulations will provide for the manner, form and content by

---

[1] Section 9(7).

[2] For the powers of commons councils, see Chapter 11.

[3] Commons (Severance of Rights) (England) Order 2006 SI 2006/2145. A further order may be made that would permit temporary leasing or licensing of rights of common in relation to a particular common or area.

[4] See Defra, *Guidance Note on Severance*, revised August 2006.

[5] When s 46 is on force.

[6] Defra, *Guidance Note on Severance*, revised August 2006.

which an application may be made to attach a right held in gross to land.[1] The 2006 Act also contains provisions for the regulation of the re-allocation of attached rights where the land to which the rights are attached is no longer used for agricultural purposes, has planning permission for a non-agricultural use, or is subject to compulsory purchase.[2]

6.6.6   Letting

In August 2006 Defra made an order permitting the temporary letting or licensing of rights of common for no more than two years; or the leasing or licensing of land, to which a right of common is attached without the whole or part of the right of common, provided the owner of the land retains, for his own benefit, the right or part of the right of common not so leased or licensed.[3]

6.6.7   Registration under the Commons Act 2006

The registration requirements relating to any of the above miscellaneous dispositions are explained in Chapter 8.

6.7   PROTECTION OF RIGHTS OF COMMON

Rights of common are legal interests in land. Commoners are entitled to exercise their rights without interference or obstruction.

6.7.1   Extent of rights of common

The rights of the commoners are limited:[4]

> 'The interest which a commoner has in the common is, in the legal phrase, to eat the grass with the mouths of his cattle, or to take such other produce of the soil as he may be entitled to. Apart from this, he must not meddle at all with the soil, nor with the fruits or produce, even though by doing so he may eventually improve and meliorate the common.'

---

[1]   Section 10.

[2]   Section 11.

[3]   Commons Act 2006, Sch 1, para 2; the Commons (Severance of Rights) (England) Order 2006, SI 2006/2145.

[4]   *Halsbury's Laws of England* (4th edn) vol 6, at para 652 adapted from 1 Roll Abr 406, quoted in 1 Saund 353a.

In the case of rights of pasturage, the rights were quantified and registered under the Commons Registration Act 1965.[1] In respect of other rights, such as of estovers or of turbary, the extent of the rights must be determined in accordance with the principles considered in Chapter 4.

6.7.2 Liability for damage to the soil

Where the commoner is properly exercising his rights of common, he is not liable to the owner of the soil of the common for any damage that is directly and unavoidably caused by that exercise, for example by his cattle eating a stack put on the common by the owner.[2]

6.7.3 Legal remedies for interference with rights of common

(a)   *The scope of likely interference*

The commoner might suffer damage in a number of different ways. One or more of his fellow commoners might put more animals upon the common than they are entitled to which could diminish the available grazing. The commoner's animals might be physically prevented from grazing on the whole, or more likely part, of the common by the actions of either the owner of the soil or some third party. Each case needs to be separately considered.

(b)   *Overstocking by other commoners*

Where there is unlawful overstocking by another commoner, there is a right of *surcharging* to recover damages for the wrong.[3] Where there are two adjoining commons, the commoners of each common may enjoy rights *pur cause de vicinage* over the common that adjoins the one over which they have substantive rights. Whilst that gives a commoner a defence if his animals are found on the common adjoining his home common, it would not do so if he is over-stocking by reference to the rights he has on his own home common.

One solution to overstocking is for the commoners to persuade the owner of the soil to exercise his right to drive the common and remove the animals that are not entitled to be present.[4]

---

[1]   Section 15.

[2]   *Farmor v Hunt* (1611) Yelv 201; Cro Jac 271; *sub nom Farmer v Hunt* 80 ER 132.

[3]   See precedent in *Atkin's Court Forms*, vol 8(2).

[4]   See Chapter 5.

However, these problems are now likely to be addressed by the commons councils that are being set up under the Commons Act 2006. The councils will have a range of functions to manage commons. These are discussed more fully in Chapter 11 below.

(c)   Physical obstruction

Physical obstruction might occur by a person erecting a building or other works on the common, such as fences, or otherwise destroying or unlawfully removing the subject matter of the right of common. Where a person interferes with, or obstructs, the lawful exercise of a right of common, the appropriate remedy is nuisance for what is called *disturbance* to the right. Rights of common fall within that category of legal interests in land known as *profits à prendre*. Such rights, together with easements, are protected by, primarily, the law of nuisance. Damages and/or an injunction are the appropriate remedies.[1]

A commoner may bring legal proceedings for the wrongful taking of the subject-matter of his rights of common, such as the consumption of the pasture, and also for any wrong that, if not stopped, could grow into a legal right such as an easement.[2]

There is also the new power in the Commons Act 2006 to apply to the county court for an order to remove unauthorised works from a common.[3]

6.7.4   Self-help abatement

Abatement is the removal of the cause of the interference by the injured commoner without any recourse to the courts. A person suffering a nuisance is, in principle, entitled to abate it.[4] The law does not favour abatement and it should be restricted to simple cases that would not justify the expense of legal proceedings and urgent cases that required an immediate remedy.[5] A prior request is required, especially where the person liable in law did not actually cause the

---

[1]   *King v Brown, Durant & Co* [1913] 2 Ch 416; *Fitzgerald v Firbank* [1897] 2 Ch 96.

[2]   *King v Brown, Durant & Co* [1913] 2 Ch 416.

[3]   Section 41(2).

[4]   *Baten's Case* (1610) 9 Co Rep 54b; *Perry v Fitzhowe* (1845) 8 QB 775.

[5]   *Gale on Easements* (17th edn), at para 14–06, relying on *Burton v Winters* [1993] 1 WLR 1077.

injury or entry is required on the wrong-doer's property,[1] and abatement must be exercised without delay.[2]

The scope of abatement is probably quite limited. In *Hope v Osborne* it was held that a commoner cannot abate a nuisance caused by another party that merely interferes with his rights of common. His right of abatement is limited to a nuisance that wholly prevents him from exercising his rights.[3] Further, no more must be done than is strictly necessary to abate the nuisance.[4] For example, a commoner would be entitled to remove a fence that had been wrongly erected on the common preventing access by his animals.[5] However, the decision of the Court of Appeal in *Burton v Winters*[6] shows that there are limitations on the right to use the self-help remedy of abatement. It is a summary remedy justified only in clear and simple cases or in an emergency. The right ceases on the refusal of a court to grant an injunction.

6.7.5   Statutory remedies

A number of statutory provisions create statutory offences for interferences with commons.[7] In appropriate cases, such as unlawful fencing, commoners might find a more effective remedy by having recourse to these provisions by making a complaint and request for action to the body responsible for enforcement. When in force, there will be a right to apply to the county court under the Commons Act 2006 for an order to remove unauthorised works.[8]

---

[1]   *Lemmon v Webb* [1894] 3 Ch 1.

[2]   *Moffett v Brewer* (1848) Iowa 1 Greene 348; see also *Burton v Winter* [1993] 1 WLR 1077 and *Co-operative Wholesale Society v British Railway Board* [1995] NPC 200.

[3]   [1913] 2 Ch 349.

[4]   *Roberts v Rose* (1865) LR 1 Exch 82.

[5]   *Cooper v Marshall* (1757) 1 Burr 259 and *Kirby v Sadgrove* (1797) 1 Bos & P 13 (fence erected by lord of the manor inconsistent with the grant of rights of common); see also *Arlett v Ellis* (1827) 7 B&C 346.

[6]   [1993] 1 WLR 1077.

[7]   See Chapter 11.

[8]   Section 41(2).

Chapter 7

INCLOSURE AND EXTINGUISHMENT OF RIGHTS OF COMMON

7.1   INTRODUCTION

There are various ways in which rights of common can be brought to an end. Some of these depend upon the actions of parties or the characteristics of the subject matter of the right of common. The inclosure of commons – once an important cause of the extinguishment of rights of common – has been virtually obsolete for a number of years. Compulsory purchase has now become much more important in this context and this is considered separately at Chapter 12.

Where any rights of common have been terminated or extinguished, or any land ceased to be common land, then appropriate amendments and deletions can be made to the registers of common land and rights.[1] However, the Commons Act 2006 contains a number of important limitations on inclosure and the extinguishment of rights of common.

7.2   EXTINGUISHMENT WITHIN THE CONTROL OF THE PARTIES

7.2.1   Unity of ownership

The essential characteristic of a right of common is that it is a *profit à prendre* exercisable for the benefit of one parcel of land (the benefited land) over another parcel of land (the common land). If both the benefited land and the common land come to be within the ownership of the same person, the rights of common are extinguished by operation of law. As Coke said:[2]

---

[1]   Commons Registration Act 1965, s 13.

[2]   Co Litt 313a, quoted in *Gale on Easements* (17th edn), at para 12–02.

'[Profits à prendre] are said to be extinguished when they are gone forever, et tunc moriuntur, and can never be revived; that is, when one man hath as high and perdurable an estate in the one as in the other.'

There will not be extinguishment where, say, the freehold owner of the common acquires a lease of the dominant or benefited land to which rights of common are attached. Although the rights of common may be suspended for the duration of his ownership of the lease of the benefited land, once the lease has terminated, the rights are revived.[1]

7.2.2   Abandonment and non-use

Mere non-use of rights of common will generally be insufficient to establish an intention to abandon. As Alderson B said in *Ward v Ward*:[2]

'The presumption of abandonment cannot be made from the mere fact of non-user. There must be other circumstances in the case to raise that presumption. The right is acquired by adverse enjoyment. The non-user, therefore, must be the consequence of something which is adverse to the user.'

The period of non-user is therefore not particularly relevant. Non-use of a right of way for 175 years did not raise any presumption of abandonment in one case.[3] Much more relevant is whether the owner of the rights of common has made changes to the benefited land such as to show that he no longer has use for or intends to assert his rights of common. Demolishing a house with a right of common or turbary, with no intention of erecting a replacement, shows intentional abandonment.[4] In the case of rights of common of pasture, whether appendant or appurtenant, altering the character and use of the benefited land such that it could no longer be used for supporting the animals entitled to the pasturage, such as by building houses, does raise the presumption of abandonment.[5]

---

[1]   Co Litt 313a.

[2]   (1852) 7 Ex Ch 838 at 839 quoted in *Gale on Easements* (17th edn), at para 12–56.

[3]   *Benn v Hardinge* (1992) 66 P&CR 246

[4]   *Moore v Rawson* (1824) 3 B&C 332.

[5]   *Carr v Lambert* (1866) LR 1 Ex Ch 168; *Re Yateley Common, Hampshire* [1977] 1 All ER 505, [1977] 1 WLR 840.

7.2.3   Express release

Rights of common will be extinguished if the owner of the rights enters into an express deed of release. There has been doubt as to whether releasing rights of common over part of the affected land releases the whole of the right.[1]

7.2.4   Effect of the Commons Act 2006

The 2006 Act will provide that a registered right of common cannot be extinguished by operation of common law;[2] that will apply to extinguishment by unity of possession and non-use or abandonment. When the relevant provisions of the 2006 Act come into force, the surrender of a right of common will only have effect if it complies with such requirements as to form and content as will be prescribed by regulations, and will not operate until on an application to remove the right from the register of rights.[3]

7.3   BY STATUTE

7.3.1   Generally

Rights of common may be extinguished by statute in a number of ways. The most obvious today arises upon the exercise of powers of compulsory acquisition. Schedule 4 to the Compulsory Purchase Act 1965 contains a procedure for the determination of compensation to commoners and the extinction of their rights.[4] There are powers under the Town and Country Planning Act 1990 under which easements and other rights can be overridden.[5] Local planning authorities have wide powers to acquire land, compulsorily or by agreement, for planning purposes.[6] They may also appropriate land from one purpose to another.[7] Where any land has been acquired or appropriated by a local planning authority for planning purposes, the authority may appropriate the land for any other purpose for which

---

[1]   *Rotherham v Green* (1597) Cro Eliz 593; *Miles v Etteridge* (1692) 1 Show 349. But compare with *Benson v Chester* (1799) 8 Term Rep 396.

[2]   Section 13(2).

[3]   Section 13(1).

[4]   *Lewis v Mid Glamorgan County Council* [1995] 1 All ER 760; see also Chapter 12.

[5]   See s 237.

[6]   See ss 226–227.

[7]   Local Government Act 1972, s 122.

they are authorised to acquire land.[1] However, the right to appropriate land which is common land is subject to ministerial consent.[2] But where land has been acquired or appropriated for planning purposes, any building or other works carried out in accordance with planning permission authorises the interference with any easement or rights affecting that land. Two comments are called for here. First, the mere grant of planning permission will not, of itself, authorise works or building on common land; the additional controls considered in Chapter 11 have to be complied with. Secondly, a change of use is not authorised.[3]

For many years inclosure was only possible under the authority of a statute. This is considered further below.

7.3.2   Commons Registration Act 1965

Rights of common existing prior to the expiration of the registration period on 31 July 1970, but not registered by that date, are not thereafter exercisable.[4] That status of non-exercisability amounts to a type of statutory extinguishment of the rights. Although non-exercisability, as a concept, appears to leave the possibility of the rights becoming exercisable at some point, the Commons Act 2006 merely carries forward the registration of rights of common. However, where common land was not finally registered under the 1965 Act and is recognised as common land under certain specified enactments, such land can be registered under the 2006 Act.

7.3.3   Commons Act 2006

This Act contains several provisions for the extinguishment of rights of common over common land. The Act 2006 provides for the release and exchange of common land and town or village greens. The owner of such land may apply to the appropriate national authority (the Secretary of State in England, or the National Assembly for Wales) for land to cease to be registered (the release land).[5] If the release land is more than 200 square metres in area, the application must include a proposal that further land (the replacement land) is to be registered

---

[1]   See s 232(1) of the 1990 Act.

[2]   Section 232(2) of the 1990 Act and s 122 of the 1972 Act.

[3]   *Thames Water Utilities Ltd v Oxford City Council* [1999] 1 EGLR 167.

[4]   Section 1(2)(b).

[5]   Commons Act 2006, s 16(1).

as common land or as a town or village green in place of the release land.[1] The criteria for release are as follows. The replacement land must not already be registered as common land or a town or village green, and if the owner of the release land does not own the replacement land, the owner of the latter must join in the application.[2] In determining an application, the appropriate national authority must have regard to the interest of persons with rights in the release land, the interests of the neighbourhood, the public interest, and any other matter considered relevant.[3] Where the release land is less than 200 square metres, particular regard must be had to the persons with interests in it. The public interest includes nature conservation, conservation of the landscape, protection of public rights of access to any area of land, and the protection of archaeological remains and features of historic interest.[4]

Where an appropriate national authority grants an application for de-registration, it must make an order requiring the commons registration authority to remove the release land from the appropriate register of common land or of town or village greens, and to register any exchange land.[5] The effect of any order is that any rights of common over the release land are extinguished, and where replacement land is provided, those rights become exercisable over such land. Where the release land was subject to s 193 of the Law of Property Act 1925 (public rights of access), or to schemes under the Metropolitan Commons Act 1866, an Act under the Commons Act 1876 confirming a provisional order of the inclosure commissioners, a scheme under the Commons Act 1899, or s 1 of the Commons Act 1908, the effect of the order will be to cease the application of those provisions to the release land and to transfer them to the replacement land.[6]

---

[1]   Commons Act 2006, s 16(2)–(3).

[2]   Commons Act 2006, s 16(5).

[3]   Commons Act 2006, s 16(6).

[4]   Commons Act 2006, s 16(7)–(8).

[5]   Commons Act 2006, s 17(1)–(2).

[6]   Commons Act 2006, s 17.

7.4   INCLOSURE

7.4.1   Inclosure before 1845

The right of approvement was the first process by which surplus waste came to be inclosed. The right to do so was confirmed by the Commons Act 1236, as extended by the Commons Act 1285.[1] Generally the lord of the manor was required to leave sufficient pasture on the uninclosed waste or common for the commoners.[2] Although any approvement under the Commons Acts 1236–1285 required the consent of the Secretary of State,[3] the Commons Act 2006 will repeal the Commons Act 1285 and abolishes any right of approvement.[4] This provision came into force on 1 October 2006.[5]

Prior to 1845 a number of private Acts were passed authorising inclosure on a local basis.[6]

7.4.2   Inclosure post-1845

The Inclosure Act 1845 provided a comprehensive procedure for the inclosure of commons. A number of subsequent Acts made amendments to that Act. However, the Commons Act 1876 introduced a requirement that inclosure should not proceed without the approval of the Inclosure Commissioners and of Parliament. Such approval to be given only where the inclosure would be of benefit to the neighbourhood.

(a)   Inclosure Act 1845

By s 11 of the 1845 Act, the following descriptions of land could be inclosed:

–   all land subject to any rights of common whatsoever, and whether such rights may be exercised or enjoyed at all times, or may be exercised or enjoyed only during limited times, seasons

---

[1]   The Commons Act 2006 will repeal the Commons Act 1285.

[2]   *Arlett v Ellis* (1827) 7 B&C 346; *Robertson v Hartopp* (1889) 43 ChD 484.

[3]   Law of Commons Amendment Act 1893.

[4]   Section 47.

[5]   See Commons Act 2006 (Commencement No 1, Transitional Provisions and Savings) (England) Order 2006, SI 2006/2504.

[6]   Apparently 4,000 such Acts were passed between 1745 and 1845: see *Halsbury's Laws of England* (4th edn) vol 6, at para 704.

or periods, or be subject to any suspension or restriction whatsoever in respect of the time of the enjoyment thereof;

– all gated and stinted pastures in which the property of the soil or of some part thereof is in the owners of the cattlegates or other gates or stints, or any of them;

– all gated and stinted pastures in which no part of the property of the soil is in the owners of the cattlegates or other gates or stints, or any of them;

– all land held, occupied, or used in common, either at all times or during any time or season, or periodically, and either for all purposes or for any limited purpose, and whether the separate parcels of the several owners of the soil shall or shall not be known by metes or bounds or otherwise distinguishable;

– all land in which the property or right of or to the vesture or herbage, or any part thereof, during the whole or any part of the year, or the property or right of or to the wood or under-wood growing and to grow thereon, is separated from the property of the soil;

– and all lot meadows and other lands the occupation or enjoyment of the separate lots or parcels of which is subject to interchange among the respective owners in any known course of rotation or otherwise.

The New Forest and the Forest of Dean were excluded.[1]

Land within 15 miles of London or within certain distances of large towns was not to be inclosed without the previous direction of Parliament in each case.[2] In fact there is further legislation considered below in relation to the protection of metropolitan commons. Town and village greens were not to be inclosed, although there was provision for directing that greens should be allotted to the church wardens and overseers of the poor.[3]

The Act made provision for the making of applications for inclosure or regulation of a common by persons representing at least one-third in value of the interests in the affected land. An assistant Commissioner of the Inclosure Commissioners would hold a local inquiry, and would then report to the Inclosure Commissioners. If the

---

[1]   Section 13.

[2]   Section 14.

[3]   Section 15 and see Chapter 9.

Inclosure Commissioners were satisfied that inclosure or regulation should proceed, they would prepare a draft provisional order. Following further deposit of the draft provisional order, it would then be reported to Parliament and Parliament would confirm the order as a confirmatory Act. Following confirmation by Act of Parliament, a valuer was appointed to put the details of the Act into effect. One important matter was to deal with claims for compensation by commoners whose rights were affected or terminated. The valuer would also direct the allotment of the inclosed common between the persons entitled. This appeared in an award. A number of details such as ownership of roads and ways, fencing and straightening out boundaries, were also done in the award. Some land was allotted for public purposes, such as setting out new roads, and the residue was then divided and allotted between the various persons interested, including the lord of the manor and the other persons who had rights of common.

(b)   Commons Act 1876

This Act considerably restricted inclosure under the 1845 Act. The Inclosure Commissioners had to be persuaded that the application for inclosure would be for the benefit of the neighbourhood, and with a view to that benefit they were required to consider inserting the following provisions:[1]

–   free access to be secured to any particular points of view;
–   particular trees or objects of historical interest were to be preserved;
–   there was to be reserved, where a recreation ground was not set out, a privilege of playing games or of enjoying other species of recreation at such times and in such manner and on such parts of the common as might have been thought suitable;
–   carriage roads, bridle paths, and footpaths over the common were to be set out as appeared most commodious;
–   any other specified thing was to be done which it might be thought equitable and expedient, regard being had to the benefit of the neighbourhood.

---

[1]   Section 7.

That Act considerably altered the policy direction behind the inclosure and reflected a growing concern about the loss of common land in terms of its recreational and wider public benefit value.

(c) *Inclosure today*

These Acts, and others, made provision for the regulation of commons, including metropolitan commons.[1] Although the provisions relating to inclosure in the Inclosure Act 1845 and the Commons Act 1876 are still on the statute book, these powers have not been used for some considerable time, and must be regarded in the present political climate as being virtually obsolete. The Commons Act 2006 will repeal s 147 of the Inclosure Act 1845 (power to exchange land) and s 31 of the Commons Act 1876 (three months' notice of a claim to inclose to be given in local newspapers).[2] This provision came into force on 1 October 2006.[3] Section 147 of the 1845 Act was a provision that could have been used where a person wanted an access over common land that would interfere with rights of common, but was prepared to offer exchange land as recompence. This provision came into force on 1 October 2006.[4] But, most importantly, the 2006 Act has abolished any approvement.[5] Inclosure is no longer possible.

---

[1] See Chapter 11.

[2] Sections 48–49 and Sch 6, Part 3.

[3] See Commons Act 2006 (Commencement No 1, Transitional Provisions and Savings) (England) Order 2006, SI 2006/2504.

[4] See Commons Act 2006 (Commencement No 1, Transitional Provisions and Savings) (England) Order 2006, SI 2006/2504.

[5] Section 47.

Chapter 8

REGISTRATION OF COMMON LAND AND RIGHTS OF COMMON

8.1   INTRODUCTION

The Commons Registration Act 1965 gave effect to one of the recommendations of the *Royal Commission Report on Common Land*.[1] The 1965 Act made provision for the registration of commons, the ownership of common land and of rights of common. It also made provision for the registration of town and village greens.

In some respects the law of commons became frozen by the 1965 Act. Thereafter, the status of common land, and whether any rights of common could be exercised, depended entirely upon the entries in the registers. Further, rights of common of pasture, that had previously been held without stint, or limitation of numbers, but which depended on the carrying capacity of the land to which the rights were attached (*levancy* and *couchancy*), had to be registered with specified animal numbers. It is likely that excessive numbers were registered in many cases, but in any event the register determined the extent of the right.

The 1965 Act, however, threw up certain questions such as: could new rights of common be granted over an existing common and, if so, should these be registered? Could rights of common be acquired by prescription? Does the registered entry of rights of common determine for ever the extent of those rights? These questions, and many others, are now addressed by Part 1 of the Commons Act 2006. Part 1 of the 2006 Act contains provisions for the repeal of the Commons Registration Act 1965 and its replacement with a new improved registration system. Part 1 will be introduced in stages starting with a pilot scheme among a few registration authorities in late 2007. Defra will consult on the proposed regulations early in 2007

---

[1]   Cmnd 462 1958.

with a view to their introduction in late 2007 and the new registration requirements being brought fully into force from 2008 onwards.[1]

8.2   REGISTRATION: COMMONS

8.2.1   Registration under the Commons Registration Act 1965

Section 1 of the Commons Registration Act 1965 required the registration of:

(a) land in England or Wales which is common land or a town or village green;
(b) rights of common over such land; and
(c) persons claiming to be or found to be owners of such land or becoming the owners thereof by virtue of the 1965 Act.

It also directed that no rights of common over land which was capable of being registered under the 1965 Act could be registered under the Land Registration Acts of 1925 and 1936 (and their statutory successor, the Land Registration Act 2002).

The registration requirement was a continuing obligation. Although the initial registration period expired on 31 July 1970, and any rights of common not registered could not thereafter be exercised,[2] provision was made for registration of new commons coming into existence after that period.[3]

Every register of common land or of town or village green consisted of a register map and a register containing three parts for each register unit; a land section describing the land in each register unit by reference to the register map, the rights section containing registrations of the rights of common, and the ownership section containing the registration of the owner of any part of a register unit.[4]

---

[1]   The Defra website contains details of the developments and progress of implementation.

[2]   Commons Registration Act 1965, s 1(2)(b). This would probably include rights acquired by prescription where the prescriptive period had already been satisfied.

[3]   Ibid, s 13.

[4]   Reg 4 of the Commons Registration (General) Regulations 1966.

8.2.2 Registration under the Commons Act 2006

When Part 1 of the Commons Act 2006 is in force, a registration authority will be required to maintain a register of common land and a register of town and village greens.[1] The purpose of these registers will be to register the land as common land, or a town or village green, and, in either case, to register rights of common over either type of land.[2] These new registers will contain all land registered under the Commons Registration Act 1965 as common land and town or village greens, and all rights of common registered under that Act over either type of land.[3] As the 2006 Act contains its own provisions for the registration of further land as common land, the registration of new rights, and of new town or village greens, the new registers will also contain these new and additional registrations.[4] New and additional registrations are likely to come about because the 2006 Act makes provision for, among other matters, the limited creation of new rights of common,[5] the correction of registration mistakes under the 1965 Act,[6] and for registering new town or village greens not on the registers.[7] Registrations will therefore be possible for the matters set out below.

(a) New rights of common

As explained in Chapter 6, new rights of common can be created in limited circumstances.[8] The new right, which must be created by express grant, cannot be created over a town or village green and must be attached to land.[9] The new right will not take effect until registration, and if it is created over land not already registered as common land, that land must be registered as common land.[10] The other limitations on the grant of new rights are considered in Chapter 6.

---

[1] Section 1.

[2] Section 2.

[3] Section 3.

[4] Section 3.

[5] Section 6(2).

[6] Section 22 and Sch 2.

[7] Section 15.

[8] Commons Act 2006, s 6.

[9] Commons Act 2006, s 6(3).

[10] Commons Act 2006, s 6(5)(b).

(b)   Variation of a right of common

A right of common can be varied by being exercisable over new land in the various ways, or by an alteration in what can be done, as explained in Chapter 6.[1] A variation will not operate until it is registered.[2] The other limitations on the grant of new rights, and the prohibition of severance, and the exemptions to that prohibition, are also considered in Chapter 6.

(c)   Apportionment of a right of common

Where the land to which a right of common is attached is divided in some way, the disposition may apportion the right of common as between, or to one or more, of the divided parts. Regulations may be made under the 2006 Act requiring that an application may be made to amend the register to reflect the apportionment.[3]

(d)   Attachment of a right of common to land

Where a right of common is registered in a register of common land or town or village green, but is not registered as attached to land (a right in gross), the owner may apply for the right to be registered as attached to any land provided he is entitled to occupy that land or the person entitled to occupy the land consents.[4]

(e)   Re-allocation of attached rights

Where a right of common is registered in a register as attached to any land, the owner may apply to have the register amended so as to secure that the right does not attach to a relevant part of that land.[5] In effect to re-allocate the right to land other than the relevant part. This will apply in two circumstances. First, where the relevant part is not used for agricultural purposes. Second, it is the subject of a compulsory purchase order that has been confirmed (where confirmation is required), the relevant part is not vested in the acquiring authority, and is required for a use other than for agricultural purposes.

---

[1]   Commons Act 2006, s 7.

[2]   Commons Act 2006, s 7(4).

[3]   Commons Act 2006, s 8.

[4]   Commons Act 2006, s 10.

[5]   Commons Act 2006, s 11.

(f)   Transfer of rights in gross

A right held in gross is a right of common that is not attached to any land; the owner of the right may himself own no land or if he does, the right is not attached to, and does not pass with, that land. Such a right is more fully explained in Chapter 4. Such a right may have been created as a right in gross or it may have arisen as a result of being severed from land (severance).[1] Subject to limited exemptions, the severance of a right of common will be prohibited by the Commons Act 2006.[2] However, any transfer of a right of common that is a right in gross will not have effect until registered.[3]

(g)   Surrender and extinguishment

The surrender to any extent of a registered right of common will have to be in a form to be prescribed by regulations. It will also not have effect until the right is removed from the register on an application.[4]

(h)   Statutory dispositions

Certain statutory dispositions, particularly the compulsory acquisition of land, may involve the acquisition of common land or town or village greens, and the extinguishment of rights of common. This is more fully explained in Chapter 12. Acquisition can also involve acquiring exchange land to replace the lost common land. Regulations will be made to provide for the circumstances of when and how applications are to be made to amend the registers of common land and greens to give effect to such statutory dispositions.[5]

(i)   New Class C town or village greens

This category is explained in more detail in Chapter 9, and also below. Where a new Class C green is established, it may be registered.[6]

---

[1]   *Bettison v Langton* [2002] 1 AC 27, [2001] 3 All ER 417.

[2]   Commons Act 2006, s 9.

[3]   Commons Act 2006, s 12.

[4]   Commons Act 2006, s 13.

[5]   Commons Act 2006, s 14.

[6]   Commons Act 2006, s 15.

(j)   Deregistration and exchange

The Commons Act 2006 contains provisions for the release and exchange of common land and town or village greens. The owner of such land may apply to the appropriate national authority (the Secretary of State in England, or the National Assembly for Wales) for land to cease to be registered (the release land).[1] If the release land is more than 200 square metres in area, the application must include a proposal that further land (the replacement land) is to be registered as common land or as a town or village green in place of the release land.[2] The criteria for release, and for the orders that may be made permitting release are explained in more detail in Chapter 7. Where an appropriate national authority grants an application for deregistration, it must make an order requiring the commons registration authority to remove the release land from the appropriate register of common land or of town or village greens, and to register any exchange land.[3]

(k)   Corrections

A commons registration authority may amend the registers for the purpose of correcting a mistake made by the authority providing the correction will not affect the extent of any land registered as common land or as a town or village green, or what can be done by virtue of a right of common. This is considered further below.[4]

(l)   Non-registration or mistaken registration under the Commons Registration Act 1965

Schedule 2 to the Commons Act 2006 sets out a number of limited circumstances where mistakes in the registers made under the Commons Registration Act 1965 can be corrected. This is discussed more fully below.

(m)   Transitional registrations

Schedule 3 to the 2006 Act sets out certain transitional provisions for updating the registers. Regulations will be made that will deal with the details, who may make the application, and the time limits, but if

---

[1]   Commons Act 2006, s 16(1).

[2]   Commons Act 2006, s 16(2)–(3).

[3]   Commons Act 2006, s 17(1)–(2).

[4]   Commons Act 2006, s 19.

any of the following events have occurred then the registers can be updated:

- the creation of a right of common after 2 January 1970 and before the commencement these transitional provisions;
- any of the following dispositions after their registration under the 1965 Act and before the commencement of the transitional provisions: the surrender or variation of a right of common, the apportionment or severance of a right of common attached to land, the transfer of a right in gross;
- a disposition of registered common land or town or village green under certain statutory powers (principally compulsory acquisition);
- the giving of land in exchange.[1]

8.2.3   Information on 2006 Act registers

The registers under the Commons Act 2006 will not register ownership or contain an ownership section. Where ownership is registered in a register kept under the Commons Registration Act 1965, then such ownership must continue to be registered on that register.[2] However, if the Land Registry inform a registration authority that the land has a title registered under the Land Registration Act 2002, then the authority must remove the registration of ownership from the register.[3] The 2006 Act envisages that regulations will be made in due course that will require the maintenance of registration of ownership to cease.[4]

In relation to the registration of rights of common, the Commons Act 2006 will require the following information to be registered: the nature of the right, if the right is attached to land, the land to which it is attached, and if the right is not so attached, the owner of the right.[5]

The Commons Act 2006 provides that, save with statutory authority, no land or rights registered under the Act is to be removed from the registers;[6] it also provides that no right of common is to be registered

---

[1]   Commons Act 2006, Sch 3, para 2.
[2]   Commons Act 2006, Sch 3, para 8(1).
[3]   Commons Act 2006, Sch 3, para 8(2).
[4]   Commons Act 2006, Sch 3, para 8(3).
[5]   Section 3(4).
[6]   Section 3(6).

in the register of title kept under the Land Registration Act 2002 by the Land Registry.[1]

8.2.4   Meaning of common land and rights of common

(a)   Common land

Because most of the entries in the new registers to be kept under the Commons Act 2006 will be those first registered under the Commons Registration Act 1965, one needs to start with the definition of 'common land' in the 1965 Act:[2]

> '(a) land subject to rights of common (as defined in this Act) whether those rights are exercisable at all times or only during limited periods;
>
> (b) waste land of a manor not subject to rights of common;
>
> but does not include a town or village green or any land which forms part of a highway.'

Common land therefore had a specific meaning for the purposes of the 1965 Act. It was either land subject to rights of common, or it was waste land of a manor, not subject to rights of common. Although each needs to be considered in turn, the meaning of rights of common is crucial to both. As both expressions – common land and rights of common – were more widely defined under the Act than such expressions would have been understood prior to the Act, certain land and rights that would not have been understood as either common land or rights in common became registrable. The Commons Act 2006 does not contain any definition of common land. The reasons for this are probably as follows. First, as the registers to be kept under the 2006 Act must include all land and rights registered under the 1965 Act, a further definition of common land is not required for this purpose. Second, although the 2006 Act contains limited provisions for the creation of new rights of a common, it does contain its own definition of a right of common,[3] and provides only

---

[1]   Section 3(7).

[2]   Section 22(1).

[3]   Section 61(1).

that any land subject to a right of common must be registered as common land.[1]

(b)   Rights of common

The 1965 Act defined 'rights of common' as including:

> 'Cattlegates or beastgates (by whatever name known) and rights of sole or several vesture or herbage or of sole or several pasture, but does not include rights held for a term of years or from year to year.'

The definition of a right of common under the Commons Act 2006 is in the same terms save that it is expressed throughout in the singular.[2] The first thing to note is that under either the 1965 Act or the 2006 Act this is not an exclusive definition. Accordingly, rights of common, exercised by the commoners together with the owner of the relevant land, fall within this definition.[3]

Cattlegates and beastgates are stints or rights to pasture a specified number of beasts on land. Rights of sole or several vesture, herbage or pasture were rights exercisable by the sole owners to the exclusion of the owner of the land, and were not, strictly, rights of common because the owner was excluded.[4] It follows that land, which was not regarded as common land prior to the 1965 Act, was treated as common land for the purposes of that Act.

Rights attached to leases and tenancies or held for periods of time equivalent to leases or tenancies were excluded under the 1965 Act, and are also excluded under the 2006 Act. Thus, the freehold owner of land with attached rights of common was required to register his rights under the 1965 Act but, if the land was let to a farming tenant, together with the rights, the tenant's interest in the rights are not registered; the position will be the same under the 2006 Act. Rights of sole of pasture are frequently let for defined or periodic terms less than a fee simple, either together with a tenancy of land or quite separate from any tenancy; such rights were and are not registrable.

---

[1]   Section 6(5)(b).

[2]   Section 61(1).

[3]   See Chapter 4.

[4]   Ibid.

8.2.5   Land subject to rights of common

Returning to the definition of common land, if land was subject to rights of common, defined as widely as they were under the 1965 Act, then the common should have been registered, and its ownership and the rights of common over it.

Such land specifically included land where the rights of common were exercisable at all times or only during limited periods. Rights exercisable at all times should have caused no problems. However, rights exercisable only during limited periods would have been more problematical. In Chapter 3, reference was made to commonable lands, such as Lammas lands, or other lands that were derived from the open-field system of agriculture. Individuals owned strips of the open fields but the land was subject to rights of pasture in favour of all the owners during specified periods of the year (usually between reaping and sowing). The land would not normally have been regarded as the open 'common or waste' of a manor as commonly understood, but regarded by its owners as 'their' land subject only to the mutual rights at certain times of the year. Whilst the registration requirements alone may not be of much consequence to the owners, such owners might now be startled to discover that, as such commons are registered commons, there are now public rights of access on foot over all such commons.[1]

8.2.6   Waste land of the manor not subject to rights of common

Waste land of the manor not subject to rights of common would have been owned by the lord of the manor. It would have been his land which, because it was not subject to rights of common, he could have inclosed. Most of it would have been roadside waste, and few people would have regarded it as common land as generally understood. However, it was registrable under the 1965 Act, and its meaning was important. Further, the Commons Act 2006 provides that where waste land of a manor was not registered as common land under the Commons Registration Act 1965, because a Commons Commissioner considering a provisional registration determined that it was no longer waste land as it had ceased to be connected with a manor,[2]

---

[1]   CROW Act 2000.

[2]   For the reasons given by the Court of Appeal in *Box Parish Council v Lacey* [1980] Ch 109 and which were disapproved by the House of Lords in *Hampshire County Council v Milburn* [1990] 2 All ER 257 at 262.

then the registration authority shall, when the provisions are in force, register it as common land.[1]

In *A-G v Hanmer*[2] Watson B said:

> 'The true meaning of "wastes", or "waste lands", or "waste grounds of the manor", is the open, uncultivated and unoccupied lands parcel of the manor, or open lands parcel of the manor other than the demesne lands of the manor.'

As Lord Templeman said in *Hampshire County Council v Milburn*:[3]

> 'The manorial system which the Normans partly inherited and partly established displayed a variety of local laws and customs but in general there were three categories of land comprised in a manor. The demesne land belonged to the lord of the manor. Copyhold land was divided between the tenants of the lord of the manor. The remainder of the land consisted of uncultivated land, referred to as the waste of the manor. The waste land was the natural source of grazing, fodder and fuel for all the inhabitants of the manner. The waste land belonged to the lord of the manor subject to the rights of the tenants to enjoy in common the fruits or some of the fruits of the soil.'

The only difficulty with that description of the lands within the manor is that Lord Templeman did not add as a fourth category 'waste land not subject to any rights of common'.

Under the 1965 Act, any waste land that was subject to rights of common fell within the definition of 'common land', and was as such registrable. However, there was a separate requirement to ensure that waste land of the manor not subject to rights of common should also be registered. What if such waste land became separated, or severed from the ownership of the manor as such? Did such land cease to be waste land *of* the manor if it was no longer held *with* the manor? In *Re Chewton Common, Christchurch, Borough of Christchurch v Milligan*[4] Slade J said:

---

[1]   Sch 2, para 4(1).

[2]   (1858) 27 LJ Ch 837 at 840.

[3]   [1990] 2 All ER 257 at 258.

[4]   [1977] 3 All ER 509 at 514–515, [1977] 1 WLR 1242 at 1249–1250.

'The phrase "waste land of a manor" [in the 1965 Act], used in relation to a particular piece of land in the context of a statute passed some forty years after copyhold tenure had been abolished [in 1925], does not as a matter of legal language by any means necessarily import that the ownership of the land still rests with the Lord of the relevant manor. ... It is permissible to construe the phrase in this particular context of a post-1925 statute as meaning waste land which was once waste land of a manor in the days when copyhold tenure still existed.'

That approach was approved by the House of Lords in *Hampshire County Council v Milburn.*[1] Lord Templeman said:[2]

'... but the [1965] Act provided that waste land "not subject to rights of common" should be registered, whether there was an identifiable owner of that land or not and the Act did not provide for registration of such land to be vacated once the owner had been identified. The Royal Commission [on common land] clearly thought that common land should be preserved for the benefit of the public and registration was the first step to that end. Parliament cannot have intended that every identifiable piece of waste land which was required to be registered under the Act should cease to be affected by the Act by the voluntary act of the owner for the time being. ... "Waste land of a manor" means "waste land now or formerly of a manor" or "waste land of manorial origin".'

The House of Lords disapproved of the decision of the Court of Appeal in *Box Parish Council v Lacey*[3] where it had refused the registration of Box Hill Common, formerly waste land of the manor of Box, because it had become severed from the lordship of the manor in 1878. The effect of this decision, and any other decision of a Commons Commissioner refusing to confirm a provisional registration under the Commons Registration 1965 Act on the same ground, can be corrected when the relevant provisions of the Commons Act 2006 are in force.[4] Land will then be registrable as common land where: it was severed from the manor, prior to severance it was waste land of the manor, and it was the subject of a provisional registration under the 1965 Act.

---

[1]   [1990] 2 All ER 257.

[2]   Ibid, at 262.

[3]   [1980] Ch 109, [1979] 1 All ER 113.

[4]   Commons Act 2006, Sch 2, para 4.

The meaning of 'waste land of the manor' was also considered in *Re: Britford Common*[1] where Slade J said that:[2]

'It is implicit in [the definition in section 22 of the 1965 Act] that waste land of the manor must be (a) parcel of a manor; (b) open and uncultivated; (c) unoccupied; and (d) not comprised in the demesne lands of the manor. If it complies with all these four conditions, it constitutes "waste land of a manor".'

In the light of his later decision in *Re Chewton Common*, Slade J would probably have qualified condition (a) to read 'is or was parcel of a manor'.

The status of land as 'waste land of the manor' is not necessarily altered if such land should be the subject of compulsory acquisition. In *Lewis v Mid Glamorgan County Council*[3] the House of Lords was concerned with the compulsory acquisition of common land for the purposes of constructing a reservoir pursuant to the powers granted by a local Act. Although no notice to treat was served on the commoners as required by s 5 of the Compulsory Purchase Act 1965, the compensation procedure in Sch 4 to that Act was invoked and compensation was agreed and paid to the commoners' committee. The Water Authority later abandoned the reservoir project and sold the land to the local authority for use as a golf course. The House of Lords decided that although the local Act sanctioned the construction of the reservoir on the common, there was no Parliamentary sanction for the golf course development. Neither the local Act nor the Compulsory Purchase Act 1965, although providing for the compulsory acquisition of rights vested in the lords of the manor and the commoners, altered the classification of land as waste land of the manor. The land therefore remained part of the common. Although the rights of common may have been extinguished, the land was still waste land of the manor, not subject to rights of common, and was common land within the meaning of s 22(1)(b) of the 1965 Act.

---

[1]   [1977] 1 All ER 532.

[2]   Ibid, at 539.

[3]   [1995] 1 All ER 760.

8.3   REGISTRATION: TOWN OR VILLAGE GREENS

8.3.1   Registration under the Commons Registration Act 1965

Under the Commons Registration Act 1965, the definition of 'common land' excluded a town or village green or any land that formed part of a highway.[1] However, a town or village green was capable of being registered as such.[2] Accordingly, common land and greens were mutually exclusive. However, a green falling within the definition of a town or village green could be subject to rights of common. The 1965 Act appeared to allow the registration of rights of common over a green even though the green is not common land.[3] The Commons Act 2006 clarifies the position of rights over a town or village green. When Part 1 of the 2006 is in force, the register of a town or village green will register any rights of common exercisable over the green.[4]

Section 22(1) of the 1965 Act defined a town or village green as meaning:

'(1) … land which has been allotted by or under any Act for the exercise or recreation of the inhabitants of any locality or on which the inhabitants of any locality have a customary right to indulge in lawful sports and pastimes or which falls within subsection (1A) of this section.

(1A) Land falls within this subsection if it is land on which for not less than twenty years a significant number of the habitants of any locality, or of any neighbourhood within a locality, have indulged in lawful sports and pastimes as of right, and either

(a)   continue to do so, or

(b)   have ceased to do so for not more than such period as may be prescribed, or determined in accordance with prescribed provisions.'[5]

---

[1]   Commons Registration Act 1965, s 22(1).

[2]   Ibid, s 1(1)(a).

[3]   Ibid, ss 1(1) and 4(1).

[4]   Section 2(2)(b).

[5]   Commons Registration Act 1965, s 22(1) and (1A), as amended.

The three classes of green within this definition are discussed in Chapter 9. Class A is allotted land; Class B is land where the inhabitants have customary rights; and Class C, as originally enacted, is land where the inhabitants of any locality indulged in sports and pastimes as of right for not less than 20 years. With effect from 30 January 2001, the amended definition of a Class C green required that the user must be by a *significant* number of inhabitants of a locality or neighbourhood within a locality, and (in the absence of any regulations under s 22(1A)(b)) that user must *continue* to the date of any application for registration.[1]

Although a highway could not be registered as part of a common, there is no similar prohibition in the case of the registration of a green.[2]

8.3.2   Registration under the Commons Act 2006

When the relevant provisions of the Commons Act 2006 are in force, new Class C town or village greens will registrable. The definition of a Class C green is the same as under the 1965 Act save that it expressly states that the requisite 20 years user must continue to the date of an application for registration.[3] This accords with the decision of the House of Lords in *Oxfordshire County Council v Oxford City Council*.[4] The 2006 Act allows registration in certain defined circumstances where the user has ceased prior to the date of the application for registration. This, and the relevant time limits are fully considered in Chapter 9 below.

The registers of town or village greens may be amended in many of the circumstances listed at **8.2.2 *(a)–(m)*** above. The registers may also be updated under the transitional provisions to reflect certain dispositions also referred to at **8.2.2** above.

---

[1]   *Oxfordshire County Council v Oxford City Council* [2006] 2 WLR 1235.

[2]   Commons Registration Act 1965, s 22(1).

[3]   Section 15.

[4]   [2006] 2 WLR 1235.

8.4   REGISTRATION PROCESS

8.4.1   The registration authorities

The registration authorities for the purposes of the Commons Registration Act 1965 were:

–   where land is situated in a county or unitary authority, the county council or the unitary authority, respectively; and
–   where land is situated in Greater London, a London borough council in which the land is situated.[1]

Under the Commons Act 2006 the commons registration authorities will be:

–   a county council in England;
–   a district council in England for an area without a county council;
–   a London borough council;
–   a county council or county borough council in Wales.[2]

Where part of any land is in the area of one registration authority and part in that of another, the authorities may, by agreement, provide for one of them to be the registration authority in relation to the whole of the land.[3]

8.4.2   The registers under the Commons Registration Act 1965

For the purposes of registering common land, town and village greens, rights of common and the ownership of such land, the registration authorities under the Commons Registration Act 1965 were required to maintain:

–   a register of common land; and
–   a register of town or village greens.[4]

In the case of East Sussex County Council, many of its records, including registers required to be maintained under section 3, were destroyed by fire. Accordingly, the Commons Registration (East

---

[1]   Commons Registration Act 1965, s 2.

[2]   Commons Act 2006, s 4.

[3]   Commons Registration Act 1965, s 2(2); Commons Act 2006, s 4(3).

[4]   Commons Registration Act 1965, s 3.

Sussex) Act 1994 was enacted to enable the county council to reconstitute its registers.

Any register maintained under the Act is required to be open to inspection by the public at all reasonable times.[1]

8.4.3 The registers under the Commons Act 2006

When Part 1 of the Commons Act 2006 is in force, a commons registration authority will again be required to maintain a register of common land and a register of town or village greens.[2] The purpose of these registers will be to register the land as common land, or a town or village green, and, in either case, to register rights of common over either type of land.[3] These new registers will contain all land registered under the Commons Registration Act 1965 as common land and town or village greens, and all rights of common registered under that Act over either type of land.[4] As the 2006 Act contains its own provisions for the registration of additional land as common land, the registration of new rights, and of new Class C town or village greens, the new registers will also contain these new and additional registrations.[5] New and additional registrations are likely to come about because the 2006 Act makes provision for, among other matters, the limited creation of new rights of common,[6] for the correction of registration mistakes under the 1965 Act,[7] and for registering new town or village greens not on the registers.[8] These are considered in more detail below.

Registers kept under the 2006 Act are open to public inspection,[9] and regulations will be made for the form and effect of official copies.[10]

---

[1]   Ibid, s 3(2).

[2]   Commons Act 2006, s 1.

[3]   Section 2.

[4]   Section 3.

[5]   Section 3.

[6]   Section 6(2).

[7]   Section 22 and Sch 2.

[8]   Section 15.

[9]   Commons Act 2006, s 20.

[10] Commons Act 2006, s 21.

Provision has been made for the registers to be kept in an electronic form.[1]

8.4.4   Original application and provisional registration under the Commons Registration Act 1965

When the 2006 Act comes into force, the procedure for dealing with applications under the 1965 Act will remain relevant for a short period for the following reason. The 2006 Act makes provision for certain cases where there was non-registration of common land, or the mistaken registration of land as common land, under the 1965 Act. In order to understand the circumstances where those mistakes can be corrected, some knowledge of the 1965 procedure will be required.

In respect of any application made before 31 July 1970, this was required to be entered by the registration authority on the registers as a provisional registration, and so described.[2] In the case of an application for the registration of any land as common land or as a town or village green, such an application could have been made by any person. In any event, a registration authority was entitled to register any land as common land or a town or village green notwithstanding that no application had been made for that registration by any other person.[3] The registration authority was required, in any event, to register any land in any case where it registered any rights over it.[4]

A registration remained provisional until it became final in accordance with the provisions of the 1965 Act. An application would become final following the expiration of the various procedures for the making and hearing of objections. In the case of an undisputed application, that is where either no objection was made to the registration under s 4 or if objections were made and all of them were withdrawn, the registration became final at the end of the period

---

[1]   Commons Act 2006, s 25.

[2]   Commons Registration Act 1965, s 4(1).

[3]   Ibid, s 4(2)(a).

[4]   Ibid, s 4(2)(b).

during which such objections could have been made, or at the date of the withdrawal.[1]

8.4.5 Notification and objections to registration under the Commons Registration Act 1965

Section 5 of the 1965 Act made provision for the giving of notices by the registration authority of applications for registration, and for the making of objections. The time-limits for the making of an application for registration under s 4, and for advancing objections under s 5, have now long expired.

8.4.6 Exemptions

Certain land was exempted from registration.[2] The registration requirements of the 1965 Act did not apply to the New Forest, Epping Forest or the Forest of Dean; the same exemptions apply under the Commons Act 2006.[3] Also, the registration requirements of the 1965 Act did not apply to any land exempted under an order made by the Minister. The Commons Registration (Exempted Land) Regulations 1965[4] made provision for such exemption, although the criteria for the selection of commons exempted from registration are not entirely clear. The exempted commons are distributed throughout England, although there are a number located in the South East, including Mitcham Common and Kenley Commons in London, and Oxshott Heath, Esher in Surrey.

8.4.7 Quantification of grazing rights

Where a right of common consisted of or included a right, not limited by number, to graze animals or animals of any class, such a right was treated, for the purposes of registration, as exercisable in relation to no more animals, or animals of that class, than a definite number.[5] Any application for the registration of such a right was required to state the numbers of animals to be entered on the registers, or as the case may be, the numbers of animals of different classes to be so

---

[1]   Ibid, s 7.

[2]   Ibid, s 11.

[3]   Commons Act 2006, s 5(2).

[4]   SI 1965/2001.

[5]   Commons Registration Act 1965, s 15(1).

entered.[1] When any such registration became final, the right was accordingly exercisable in relation to animals not exceeding the number of animals registered or such other number as Parliament might later determine.[2]

The Commons Act 2006 provides for the creation of commons councils.[3] The councils will have powers to make rules relating to the exercise of grazing rights, including the imposition of conditions limiting the exercise of rights.[4]

8.4.8   Subsequent registration under the Land Registration Acts

If the ownership of any land has been registered under the Commons Registration Act 1965 and, subsequently, that ownership is registered under the Land Registration Acts,[5] then when the Land Registry inform the registration authority of that subsequent registration, the authority must delete the entry in the ownership register under the 1965 Act.[6] The position will be the same when the Commons Act 2006 is in force.[7]

8.4.9   Registrations under the Commons Act 2006

The registers that will be required to be kept under the Commons Act 2006 will contain the registrations of common land, of town or village greens, and of rights of common registered under the Commons Registration Act 1965; they will also include additional registrations permitted under the 2006 Act. As explained above, the 2006 Act makes provision for the limited creation of new rights of common, for the registration of new Class C town or village greens, and for the correction of various mistakes under the Commons Registration Act 1965. The relevant regulations governing these new and additional registrations are likely to be made from 2007 onwards. The circumstances where new rights of common can be created are explained in Chapter 6. The registration of Class C greens is dealt

---

1   Ibid, s 15(2).

2   Ibid, s 15(3).

3   Commons Act 2006, s 26.

4   Commons Act 2006, s 31(3)–(4).

5   Land Registration Acts 1925 and 1936, now the Land Registration Act 2002.

6   Commons Registration Act 1965, s 12.

7   Commons Act 2006, Sch 3, para 8(2).

with in Chapter 9. The correction of various mistakes is dealt with later in this chapter, and see also **8.2.2** above.

Regulations are yet to be made as to the making and determination of any application for the amendment of a register of common land or town or village green.[1] It is apparent that any application under Part 1 of the 2006 Act, whether for adding new rights of common, varying existing rights, adding a new green, or for correcting mistakes, will be treated as an application to vary the appropriate register. The regulations will make provision for:

(a) the steps to be taken by a person before making an application;
(b) the form of the application;
(c) the information or evidence to be supplied with the application;
(d) the fee payable on an application;
(e) the persons to be notified of an application;
(f) the publication of the application;
(g) the making of objections to the application;
(h) the persons to be consulted, or whose advice must be sought, in relation to the application;
(i) the holding of an inquiry before determination of an application;
(j) the evidence to be taken into account in making a determination and the weight to be given to the evidence;
(k) the persons to be notified of any determination;
(l) the publication of a determination;
(m) the amendments to be made by the commons registration authority to a register of common land or town or village greens pursuant to the determination;
(n) the time at which any such amendments are to be regarded as having been made.[2]

Regulations will also be made to make provision as to the persons entitled to make the application in any of the above cases.[3]

---

[1] Commons Act 2006, s 24(1).

[2] Commons Act 2006, s 24(2).

[3] Commons Act 2006, s 24(3).

8.5   EFFECT OF REGISTRATION

8.5.1   Effect of provisional registration under the Commons Registration Act 1965

Until a registration became final under the 1965 Act, a provisional registration was not conclusive as to the matters registered. Accordingly, any rights of common that had provisional registration depended upon proof of title, through express grant or evidence supporting prescription, for their validity. A provisional registration remained subject to objection and the determination of any objections by a Commons Commissioner.[1]

8.5.2   Effect of final registration under the Commons Registration Act 1965

If no objection was made to a provisional registration, or if all objections were withdrawn, the registration became final at the end of the objection period or the withdrawal of the objection.[2] If an objection was made to the provisional registration of land as common land, or as a green, or to the provisional registration of any ownership or rights of common over such land, the registration became final upon the decision of the Commons Commissioner dismissing all such objections.[3]

The effect of registration of any land as common land or as a town or village green, or of any rights of common over any such land, was conclusive evidence of the matters registered.[4] This could mean that land achieving final registration under the 1965 Act as common land retained that legal status even where the land never fell within the definition of common land under the Act. In *Corpus Christi College, Oxford v Gloucestershire County Council*,[5] land that had never been waste land of the manor was provisionally registered as common land, and rights of common over it were also provisionally registered. The owners successfully objected to the provisional registration of the rights of common, and these were deleted from the register. There was no objection to the provisional registration of the land as

---

[1]   Commons Registration Act 1965.

[2]   Commons Registration Act 1965, s 7(1).

[3]   Commons Registration Act 1965, s 6.

[4]   Commons Registration Act 1965, s 10.

[5]   [1982] 3 WLR 849, [1982] 3 All ER 995.

common land. The Court of Appeal held that even though the land was not subject to rights of common, and had never been waste land of the manor, s 10 of the Act deemed the land common land: the final registration of the land as common land was conclusive as to that status.

A court will not normally go behind a registration that has become final by virtue of s 10. Thus *R v Norfolk County Council, ex parte Perry*,[1] where a bungalow had been built on land in the ownership of the applicant, the land had acquired final registration status following a provisional registration to which no objections were made. It was held that the registration was conclusive.

One effect of the conclusive nature of a final registration of land as common land is that such land is regarded as a registered common for the purpose of the public rights of access under the CROW Act 2000.[2]

Another effect of the conclusive registration of land as a town or village green may depend on the basis of the rights over the land claimed by the applicants. If the green was registered on the basis of the proof of customary rights, those rights may be exercised. However, if the green was registered on the basis of 20 years' use by inhabitants indulging in sports and pastimes (Class C green),[3] it has been doubted whether the Act confers rights on the public.[4] However, in *Oxfordshire County Council v Oxford City Council* the House of Lords decided that the act of registration confers on the land the status of a green; registration gives rise to rights for the relevant inhabitants to use the land generally for lawful sports and pastimes even where these activities may be more extensive than the activities relied on in support of an application for registration.[5]

It follows that there is some land registered under the Commons Registration Act 1965 that should never have been registered. The

---

[1]   (1996) 74 P&CR 1.

[2]   See Chapter 10.

[3]   Under s 22(1A) of the 1965 Act.

[4]   *New Windsor Corporation v Mellor* [1975] Ch 380 per Lord Denning MR at pp 391H–392G; and *R (Laing Homes Ltd) v Buckinghamshire County Council* [2003] EWHC 1578 (Admin); [2003] 3 PLR 60.

[5]   [2006] 2 WLR 1235.

Commons Act 2006 contains a number of provisions to correct certain mistakes. These are explained below.

8.5.3   Effect of registration under the Commons Act 2006

Save in the case of certain rights of common, and certain transitional purposes, the 2006 Act does not contain the equivalent of s 10 of the Commons Registration Act 1965 by which registration was conclusive evidence of the matters registered. One probably arrives at the same position under the 2006 Act in the following way. Land registered under the 2006 Act is that registered under the 1965 Act and that registered under Part 1 of the 2006 Act. The land that was registered under the 1965 Act would have been subject to the conclusive provision in s 10 of that Act. The land that may come to be additionally registered under the 2006 Act will, in the case of common land, be subject to the rights of common that may be added or varied by virtue of registration (see **8.2.2** above), and in the case of town or village greens, by virtue of the registration of land that satisfies the definition of a Class C green.

The 2006 Act makes express provision for the conclusiveness of certain entries where land is registered as common land or as a town or village green. Where such land is registered as being subject to a right of common, then –

–   if the land would not otherwise have been subject to that right, it is deemed to be subject to the right of common;[1]
–   if the right is registered as attached to any land, the right shall, if it would not otherwise have attached to that land, be deemed to have become so attached upon registration of its attachment;[2]
–   if the right is not registered as attached to any land, the person registered as the owner of the right shall, if he would not otherwise have been its owner, be deemed to have become its owner on registration.[3]

---

[1]   Commons Act 2006, s 18(2).
[2]   Commons Act 2006, s 18(3).
[3]   Commons Act 2006, s 18(4).

8.6 EFFECT OF FAILURE TO REGISTER

8.6.1 Commons Registration Act 1965

(a) *Rights of common*

The registration period ceased on 31 July 1970. After the end of that period, no land capable of being registered under the 1965 Act shall be deemed to be common land or a town or village green unless it was so registered, and no rights of common shall be exercisable over any such land unless they were registered under either the 1965 Act or under the Land Registration Acts 1925 to 2002: see s 1(2) of the 1965 Act.

The words in section 1(2) that 'no rights of common shall be exercisable over any such land unless they are registered ...,' mean that where rights of common existed prior to the expiration of the registration period, and were therefore lawfully exercisable, the effect of non-registration meant that such rights were lost completely. It also meant that if no rights of common were registered in respect of land that had been common land, such land ceased to be common land. Thus in *Central Electricity Generating Board v Clwyd County Council*[1] the County Council provisionally registered an area of land as common land notwithstanding that an application to register the rights of common had not been made within the prescribed period of time. It was held that since 'common land' means land subject to rights of common, and no rights of common were registered within the prescribed period, any rights which might have existed were no longer exercisable by virtue of s 1(2) of the 1965 Act. Further, the fact that such rights of common were no longer exercisable meant that they had been extinguished and the area was no longer common land. However, the decision in that case was brought into question in *Corpus Christi College, Oxford v Gloucestershire County Council*.[2]

The same point arose in *Re Turnworth Down*[3] where, again, rights of common had not been registered within the prescribed period. However, the complication in this case was that the relevant rights – rights to cut furze – had been awarded under an inclosure award made pursuant to a private Act of Parliament of 1801. In relation to

---

[1]   [1976] 1 WLR 151.

[2]   [1982] 3 WLR 849, [1982] 3 All ER 995.

[3]   [1977] 2 All ER 105.

an application to register the land as common land, it was argued on behalf of the applicant that, as the rights to cut furze had been created by statute, they could only be extinguished if that statute was repealed by a subsequent statute, and s 1(2)(b) of the 1965 Act did not have that effect. That argument was rejected. It was held that all rights of common including those created by an earlier Act were subject to the provisions of the 1965 Act and that, therefore, the failure to register the rights to cut furze within the prescribed period meant that such rights had been extinguished. It followed that the land was not subject to rights of common and could not be registered as common land.

Where an application was made to register rights of common, and the Commons Commissioner upholds an objection, there was a period by which an appeal could be brought. If such an appeal was not brought, s 1(2)(b) operates to extinguish a provisional registration of rights when that provisional registration becomes void as a result of the Commons Commissioner's determination.[1]

(b)   Correcting non-registration under the Commons Act 2006

The provisions of the 2006 Act for addressing some of the problems of the non-registration of rights of common and of common land are explained below.

(c)   Town and village greens

In respect of town or village greens, in *Oxfordshire County Council v Oxford City Council*,[2] Lightman J decided that the provision in s 1(2) of the 1965 Act that non-registration had the effect that the land shall not be deemed to be a green, meant that the rights of local inhabitants in respect of greens registrable but unregistered by 31 July 1970 were extinguished, and a fresh period of qualifying user was required to revive the green. That period would be 20 years in respect of a Class C green. In the Court of Appeal Carnwath LJ accepted that even if a green did enjoy historic rights, they would have been extinguished by s 1(2). The issue, which was not directly addressed in the House of Lords, is probably rather academic in the sense that if the state of affairs that can constitute a Class C green continues, an application for registration can be made.

---

[1]   *Lord Dynevor v Richardson* [1995] 1 All ER 109.

[2]   [2004] EWHC 12, [2004] PLSCS 16.

(d)   Unclaimed land: town or village green

Section 8 of the Commons Registration Act 1965 made provision for the vesting of unclaimed land. Where the registration of any land as common land or as a town or village green became final, then unless the land was registered under the Land Registration Acts,[1] the registration authority was required to refer the question of ownership to a Commons Commissioner.[2]

After the giving of notices by the registration authority, the Commons Commissioner was required to inquire into the matter and, if satisfied that any person was the owner, direct the registration authority to register that person as owner.[3] If the Commons Commissioner was not so satisfied, and the land was a town or village green, he was required to direct that the registration authority register as owner a specified local authority.[4] The local authorities were, in the case of land where there was a parish or community council, such a council, ie in London, the London borough council, elsewhere, the district council.[5]

On registration of the ownership of a town or village green in the name of the appropriate local authority, then, unless the land was regulated under the Commons Act 1899, ss 10 and 15 of the Open Spaces Act 1906 (power to manage and make by-laws) would apply as if the authority had acquired ownership under the 1906 Act.[6]

(e)   Unclaimed land: common land

Where the registration of any land as common land became final, but no person was registered under the Land Registration Acts as the owner of the land,[7] then, until the land is vested under any provisions that Parliament might later make, any local authority for the area became entitled to take such steps for the protection of the land against unlawful interference as could be taken by an owner in

---

[1]   Land Registration Acts 1925 and 1936, now Land Registration Act 2002.

[2]   Commons Registration Act 1965, s 8(1).

[3]   Commons Registration Act 1965, s 8(2).

[4]   Commons Registration Act 1965, s 8(3).

[5]   Commons Registration Act 1965, s 8(5).

[6]   Commons Registration Act 1965, s 8(4); see also Chapters 9 and 11 for powers of management.

[7]   Land Registration Acts 1925 and 1936, now Land Registration Act 2002.

possession of the land, and the authority may institute proceedings for any offence committed in respect of the land.[1]

8.6.2   Non-registration: the Commons Act 2006

(a)   *Non-registration of rights*

The various new rights, and the dispositions that are capable of being registered under the 2006 Act, are set out at **8.2.2** above. In all cases the relevant disposition will not have effect unless on an application for registration. In the case of the transitional provisions for the registration of various rights and dispositions occurring between the registrations and registration periods under the 1965 Act and the commencement of the relevant provisions of the 2006 Act, as explained below at **8.8**, then at the end of the transitional period for registration, any right of common capable of but which is not registered will be extinguished.[2]

(b)   *Unclaimed land*

The 2006 Act contains provisions enabling local authorities to take steps to protect common land or town or village greens where the owner cannot be identified.[3] This is further considered in Chapter 11. When commons councils are established, they will have such wide powers to manage common land or town or village greens that the question of actual ownership may no longer really matter. The functions of commons councils are explained in Chapter 11. Section 8 of the 1965 Act, which allowed the vesting of unclaimed town or village greens in a local authority, has been repealed.[4] Any vesting under the 1965 Act remains unaffected. But, unless the land that did vest under s 8 is regulated by a scheme under the Commons Act 1899, ss 10 and 15 of the Open Spaces Act 1906 will continue to apply as if the local authority had acquired ownership under the 1906 Act.[5]

---

[1]   Commons Registration Act 1965, s 9.

[2]   Commons Act 2006, Sch 3, para 3.

[3]   Commons Act 2006, s 45.

[4]   See Commons Act 2006 (Commencement No 1, Transitional Provisions and Savings) (England) Order 2006, SI 2006/2504.

[5]   Commons Act 2006, Sch 3, para 9.

8.7   AMENDMENTS, RECTIFICATIONS AND NEW COMMONS UNDER THE COMMONS REGISTRATION ACT 1965

When the Commons Act 2006 is fully in force, the provisions in this section of the present chapter will be repealed. Accordingly they remain relevant only for a short period of time; but they are also relevant to understanding some of the changes that the 2006 Act will bring about to deal with amendments and rectifications of the registers.

8.7.1   The amendment of registers under the Commons Registration Act 1965

Regulations under s 13 of the 1965 Act provide for the amendment of the registers where:

–   any land registered under the Act ceases to be common land or a town or village green (now repealed);[1] or
–   any land becomes common land or a town or village green; or
–   any rights registered under the Act are apportioned, extinguished or released, or are varied or transferred in such circumstances as may be prescribed.

8.7.2   Creation of rights of common after 2 January 1970

There are two principal ways in which rights of common can be created:

–   by express grant or reservation;
–   by prescription, namely actual use as of right for the minimum 20-year prescriptive period.

The way in which rights of common can be created or acquired is explained in more detail in Chapter 6. The Commons Registration (New Land) Regulations 1969 made provision for the registration of land becoming common land for the first time after 2 January 1970 and of rights in respect of such land. However, neither the 1965 Act, nor the 1969 Regulations permitted registration of rights of common

---

[1]   See Commons Act 2006 (Commencement No 1, Transitional Provisions and Savings) (England) Order 2006, SI 2006/2504.

created after 2 January 1970 over land that was registered under s 4 of the 1965 Act.[1]

The Commons Registration (New Land) Regulations 1969 provided for those cases where, after 2 January 1970:

− any land became common land;
− any land becomes a town or village green.

Such land could be included in the appropriate register and there could be registration of the rights of common over such land.[2] Where rights of common are created by express grant by deed after 2 January 1970, and they are created over land that is not at the time of creation registered common land, then such land would have become common land at the date of such creation. Accordingly, both the new common land and the new rights of common are capable of being registered under reg 3 of the 1969 Regulations.

The position concerning the acquisition of rights of common over land that is not common land by prescription was less clear, and is explained in Chapter 6. Prescription depends upon establishing user as of right for the minimum 20-year prescription period. Whilst the right might have been exercisable as of right during the 20-year period, the right does not become a *profit à prendre* and a legal interest in land until the first day after the expiration of the 20-year period. That is the day upon which rights of common acquired by prescription can be said to have been 'created'. For the purposes of reg 3 of the 1969 Regulations, that would be the date when the land over which such rights have been acquired, where it is not already registered common land, 'becomes common land'. Such rights thereafter become registrable. Accordingly, it would not seem to matter that some part of the 20-year prescriptive period preceded 3 January 1970. Until the expiration of the 20-year period, it cannot be said that rights of common were exercisable, within the meaning of s 1(2)(b) of the 1965 Act, because although the person exercising those rights may have thought he was entitled to do so and was exercising them 'as of right' he was not actually exercising rights of common as such. Accordingly, the purported exercise of rights prior to 3 January 1970 was not at that time capable of registration and therefore are not

---

1   Commons Registration (New Land) Regulations 1969, SI 1969/1843, reg 3(2). See further Chapter 6.

2   Ibid, reg 3(1).

rights that cease to be exercisable by virtue of s 1(2)(b). Accordingly, provided the prescriptive period had not expired prior to 31 July 1970, it was arguable that such rights could have been registered over land that was not common land.

It would seem that the same argument could have been applied to the acquisition of rights of common by prescription where the whole of the prescriptive 20-year period fell after 2 January 1970. Indeed, this approach appears to be confirmed by the notes to the forms prescribed by the 1969 Regulations. Note 5 to form 31, which is concerned with the registration of rights of common over new common land after 2 January 1970, sets out how land can become subject to rights of common:

– by or under an Act of Parliament;
– by a grant by the owner of land of rights of common over it;
– by rights of common being acquired over it by prescription;
– by substitution or exchange for other land which has ceased to be common land under:
  (a) ss 147 and 148 of the Inclosure Act 1845; or
  (b) para 11 of Sch 1 to the Acquisition of Land (Authorisation Procedure) Act 1946;[1] or
  (c) any other enactment providing, on the exchange of land, for the transfer of rights trusts or incidents attaching to the land given in exchange from that land to the land taken in exchange and vice versa.

The arguments set out above in support of the registration of rights of common acquired by prescription will shortly be negated when the relevant provisions of the Commons Act 2006 are in force. Section 6(1) provides that a right of common cannot be created by virtue of prescription.

8.7.3   New town or village greens under the Commons Registration Act 1965

The position of new town or village greens is slightly different. In *Oxfordshire County Council v Oxford City Council*,[2] the House of Lords decided that land only becomes a Class C green on registration. There

---

[1]   See now Acquisition of Land Act 1981.

[2]   [2006] 2 WLR 1235.

is no legal basis for treating land as having the status of a green by virtue of any earlier period of user. On registration the land becomes a green. Where an application was made to register a Class C green after the date when the amended definition of s 22(1) came into force (30 January 2001), the applicant must show continuity of user to the date of the application for registration.[1] It was also made clear in the *Oxford* case that a registration authority may allow for amendments to an application, including an alteration in the extent of the land, unless fairness requires the republication of a new application.[2]

8.7.4   New common land under the Commons Registration Act 1965 and land registration

Regulation 3(3) of the Commons Registration (New Land) Regulations 1969 provided that no person may be registered under the 1969 Regulations as the owner of any land which is already registered under the Land Registration Acts 1925 to 1966. However, the position concerning rights of common has become more complicated following the commencement of the Land Registration Act 2002. Prior to the coming into force of that Act, the general principle under the Land Registration Act 1925, and the Land Registration Rules 1925,[3] was that rights of common were neither required nor capable of substantive registration, although were capable of being entered as appurtenant rights to a substantively registered interest. In other words, on the registration of the transfer of land having the benefit of rights of common, such benefit might be described in the Property Register of the registered title. It followed that rights of common that were not registered in any way under the Land Registration Act 1925 were binding on purchasers of a registered title.[4]

The Land Registration Act 2002 provides that where easements or profits (and the latter include rights of common) are granted or reserved after the Act comes into force, they will not override a subsequent registrable disposition unless they are first registered.[5]

---

[1]   *Oxfordshire County Council v Oxford City Council* [2006] 2 WLR 1235.

[2]   Ibid.

[3]   SR&O 1925/1093.

[4]   They were overriding interests within the meaning of Land Registration Act 1925, s 70(1).

[5]   See s 27(2)(d).

However, the grant of a right of common that is registrable under the Commons Registration Act 1965 is not registrable under the 2002 Act.

8.7.5 Applications to register new commons and greens under the Commons Registration Act 1965

Where an application is made under the Commons Registration (New Land) Regulations 1969, the registration authority must send notice to every person believed to be an owner, lessee, tenant or occupier of any part of the land affected by the application, or to be likely to wish to object to the application. It must also publish a notice and affix a notice on any part of the land where possible. The notices must give not less than 6 weeks within which objections can be made.[1] The registration authority must then consider any objections that are in writing and shall send the applicant a copy of every statement in objection. It shall not reject the application without giving the applicant a reasonable opportunity of dealing with the matters contained in the statements of objection and with any other matter in relation to the application which appears to the authority to afford prima facie grounds for rejecting the application.[2] If the registration authority accepts an application, it makes the necessary registration as a registration under s 13 of the 1965 Act.[3] However, it should not normally make a decision without first holding a non-statutory inquiry or hearing.[4] A procedure approved by the Court of Appeal in *R (Whitmey) v Commons Commissioners*; the procedure does not breach the Convention on Human Rights and Freedoms because the decision of the registration authority can still be challenged by judicial review or under s 14(b) of the 1965 Act.[5] If the registration authority rejects the application, it must give to the applicant the reasons for the rejection.

In the case of an application to register a green that has come into existence after 2 January 1970, the application can be amended where it would be reasonable to allow an amendment, but the registration authority is not required to accept each and every of the grounds or

---

[1]   Commons Registration (New Land) Regulations 1969, SI 1969/1843, reg 5.

[2]   Ibid, reg 6.

[3]   Ibid, reg 7.

[4]   *R (Cheltenham Builders Ltd) v South Gloucestershire District Council* [2003] EWHC 2803 (Admin).

[5]   [2005] QB 282, [2004] 3 WLR 1342.

dates used in an application for registration of land as a green. Thus the statement of the date on which the land became a green is a guide to the case intended to be made by the applicant, but it is not and cannot be taken to be writ in stone. A registration authority may register as a green a lesser area than that advanced in an application provided it is not substantially different and where it considers that the part omitted does not have the status of a green.[1] Guidance was also given by Lightman J in *Oxfordshire County Council v Oxford City Council* as to how an application for registration of a green should be considered where either some of the land is inaccessible or is crossed with tracks that are, or may become, public rights of way, although such guidance was declined in both the Court of Appeal and the House of Lords.[2]

The 1969 Regulations do not contain any further rights of appeal, whether by way of a public local enquiry or a hearing before the Commons Commissioners. If an application for registration of new common land or of a new town or village green or of rights of common over new common land is rejected, the only remedy available to the disappointed applicant is to make an application for judicial review into the High Court. On the other hand, if an application succeeds or partly succeeds, and the registration authority then effects an amendment or addition to the registers pursuant to s 13 of the 1965 Act, s 14 of the 1965 Act empowers the High Court to order that a register be amended if it appears to the court that no amendment or a different amendment ought to have been made and that the error cannot be corrected in pursuance of regulations made under the Act, and that the court deems it just to rectify the register.[3] Alternatively, an application can be made for judicial review.[4]

---

[1]   *Oxfordshire County Council v Oxford City Council* [2006] 2 WLR 1235, app from [2006] Ch 43, [2005] 3 WLR 1043, [2005] 3 All ER 961, and app from [2004] Ch 253, [2004] 2 WLR 1291, [2004] 1 EGLR 105.

[2]   Ibid.

[3]   Section 14(b); the public have an interest: see also *Re Anstey Common* [1985] 1 Ch 329, 341A.

[4]   *R (Cheltenham Builders Ltd) v South Gloucestershire District Council* [2003] EWHC 2803 (Admin).

8.7.6 Land ceasing to be common land and alterations to rights of common: Commons Registration Act 1965

Provision was made by the Commons Registration (General) Regulations 1966[1] for the amendment of the registers where land has ceased to be common land, or rights of common have been altered or varied in some way.[2]

Land would cease to be common land within the meaning of s 22(1) of the 1965 Act where it was no longer subject to rights of common.[3] That might happen where, for example, there has been a release of the rights of common to the owner of the soil, or where the ownership of the soil and of the lands to which rights of common are attached are merged together in a single owner. Regulation 27 of the 1966 Regulations permit the owner of the soil to apply for the removal of the land from the registers.

Following the compulsory purchase of common land, land may be provided by way of exchange and as substituted land.[4] There were also provisions for exchange of land in ss 147 and 148 of the Inclosure Act 1845; these provisions will be repealed by the Commons Act 2006. Regulation 28 of the 1966 Regulations provided for the amendment of the registers to accommodate such substituted land.

Where any right of common has been apportioned, varied, extinguished or released, or, having become a right in gross, has been transferred, application can be made under reg 29 of the 1966 Regulations for the amendment of the register.[5]

---

[1] SI 1966/1471.

[2] Section 13 of the 1965 Act.

[3] In *Corpus Christi College, Oxford v Gloucestershire County Council* [1982] 3 All ER 995, the Court of Appeal decided that land had not ceased to be common land, within the meaning of s 13 of the 1965 Act, where the provisional registration of rights of common had not been confirmed, and no objection had been made against the registration of the land as common land.

[4] See Chapter 12 and the Acquisitions of Land Act 1981, s 19(2).

[5] See also Chapter 6.

8.7.7 Rectification under the Commons Registration Act 1965

The High Court has power to order the amendment of a register under the 1965 Act, where it deems it just, in the following circumstances:[1]

- if the registration of any land or rights of common has become final and the court is satisfied that any person was induced by fraud to withdraw an objection to the registration or to refrain from making an objection; or
- the register has been amended in pursuance of s 13 and it appears to the court that no amendment or a different amendment ought to have been made and that the error cannot be corrected in pursuance of regulations under the Act. The court is not restricted to errors of law and can consider the overall merits of the amendment.[2] The court has a wide discretion.[3]

8.7.8 Dwelling-houses and rectification

The Commons Registration Act 1965 contained a defect. No adequate requirement was made so that when land was provisionally registered, the owner should be notified of that provisional registration. Accordingly, there were occasions when land consisting of a dwelling-house, or ancillary to a dwelling-house, was given final registration without the relevant owners making an objection.

That defect was addressed by the Common Land (Rectification of Registers) Act 1989. This provided that where land consisting of a dwelling-house or land ancillary to a dwelling-house has had that characteristic since 5 August 1945, a notice could be given by any person within 3 years of the Act objecting to the inclusion of such land on either the register of common land or of town or village greens.[4] On receipt of such a notice, the registration authority was required to refer the matter to a Commons Commissioner to inquire

---

[1]   Section 14.

[2]   *R v Suffolk County Council, ex parte Steed* (1995) 70 P&CR 487. Alternatively, a registration can be quashed by judicial review: see *R (Cheltenham Builders Ltd) v South Gloucestershire District Council* [2003] EWHC 2803 (Admin).

[3]   *Secretary of State for Health v Birmingham City Council* (per Vinelott J) (unreported) 20 July 1995; see also *Oxfordshire County Council v Oxford City Council* [2004] EWHC 12, [2004] PLSCS 16.

[4]   Section 1(1)–(2).

into it and make a decision as to whether the register required modification.[1]

In *Re Land at Freshfields*[2] the applicant owned an area of land, adjoining his house and garden, that had been used as pasture for grazing cattle and growing hay. This area had been registered as common land under the 1965 Act. The Commons Commissioner had been entitled to dismiss the applicant's application under the 1989 Act to have the land removed from the register; the land could not be described as 'garden' within the meaning of the 1989 Act. However, in *Storey v Commons Commissioner*[3] the Commissioner was wrong to conclude that an orchard some distance from a dwelling-house could not be part of the 'garden'; it was a question of fact whether land was 'garden'. Land did not have to be used and enjoyed as ancillary to a single dwelling-house for the whole period after 5 August 1945.

For the position under the Commons Act 2006, see below.

8.7.9 Commons Commissioners and appeals

As explained above, in relation to the hearing of objections to provisional registrations under the Commons Registration Act 1965, Commons Commissioners dealt with these and made decisions binding on the registration authorities. The Lord Chancellor appointed Commons Commissioners from lawyers and a panel of assessors with special knowledge to assist the Commissioners.[4] Provision was made for the award of costs.[5]

Any person aggrieved by the decision of a Commons Commissioner as being erroneous in law is entitled to require a case to be stated for the decision of the High Court.[6]

Where a registration authority is required to make a decision about altering or adding an entry to the registers under s 13, it should

---

[1] Section 1(4).

[2] (1993) 66 P&CR 9.

[3] (1993) 66 P&CR 206, applying *Cresstock Investments Ltd v Commons Commissioner* [1992] 1 WLR 1088.

[4] Commons Registration Act 1965, s 17(1).

[5] Ibid, s 17(4).

[6] Commons Registration Act 1965, s 18(1).

normally consider holding a non-statutory inquiry or hearing.[1] The person holding the inquiry would be appointed by the authority and would not hold the position of a Commons Commissioner.

The Court of Appeal has now decided that a Commons Commissioner does not have jurisdiction under s 13 of the 1965 Act to determine whether land has become a town or village green.[2] The registration authority makes the decision, although it may do so on the recommendations of a person appointed to hold a non-statutory inquiry.[3]

8.8   RECTIFICATION OF REGISTERS UNDER THE COMMONS ACT 2006

A number of matters have been identified in this and other chapters where there has either been non-registration or mistaken registration of rights of common, of common land, or of town or village greens under the Commons Registration Act 1965. Schedule 2 to the Commons Act 2006 sets out a number of matters were such non-registration or mistaken registration can be rectified.

8.8.1   Non-registration of common land

Where any land not registered as common land or as a town or village green satisfies the following conditions, a commons registration authority shall register the land as common land upon the application of any person before such date as regulations may specify, or on a proposal by the authority before a specified date –

– the land was not finally registered as common land or as a town or village green under the 1965 Act;
– the land is regulated by an Act made under the Commons Act 1876 confirming a provisional order of the Inclosure Commissioners, is subject to a scheme under the Metropolitan Commons Act 1866 or the Commons Act 1899, regulated as common land under a local or personal Act, or is otherwise

---

[1]   *R (Cheltenham Builders Ltd) v South Gloucestershire District Council* [2003] EWHC 2803 (Admin), following *R v Suffolk County Council, ex parte Steed* (1995) 70 P&CR 487 at 500.

[2]   *R (Witmey) v Commons Commissioners* [2005] QB 282, [2004] 3 WLR 1342.

[3]   Ibid.

recognised or designated as common land by or under an enactment;

- the land is in England or Wales and is not the New Forest, Epping Forest or the Forest of Dean;
- the land satisfies any other conditions that may be specified by regulations yet to be made.[1]

8.8.2 Non-registration of town or village greens

Where any land not registered as a town or village green or as common land satisfies the following conditions, a commons registration authority shall register the land as a town or village green upon the application of any person before such date as regulations may specify, or on a proposal by the authority before a specified date –

- on 31 July 1970 the land was allotted by or under any Act for the exercise or recreation of the inhabitants of any locality;
- was not at the time finally registered as a town or village green or as common land under the 1965 Act;
- continues to be land allotted, as above;
- the land is in England or Wales and is not the New Forest, Epping Forest or the Forest of Dean;
- the land satisfies any other conditions that may be specified by regulations yet to be made.[2]

8.8.3 Unregistered waste land of manor

Where any land not registered as common land or as a town or village green satisfies the following conditions, a commons registration authority shall register the land as common land upon the application of any person before such date as regulations may specify, or on a proposal by the authority before a specified date –

- the land was provisionally registered as common land under s 4 of the 1965 Act;
- an objection was made in relation to the provisional registration; and
- the provisional registration was cancelled for one of three reasons: first, where the provisional registration was referred to a

---

[1]   Commons Act 2006, Sch 2, para 2.

[2]   Commons Act 2006, Sch 2, para 3.

commons commissioner who determined that although the land had been waste land of a manor, it had ceased to be connected with the manor, and refused to confirm the provisional registration; second, the provisional registration was referred to a commons commissioner who determined that the land was not subject to rights of common and was not waste land of a manor; or third, the person making the application for provisional registration agreed to its cancellation.[1]

8.8.4   Town or village green wrongly registered as common land

Where any land registered as common land is land that satisfies the following conditions, a commons registration authority shall register the land as a town or village green upon the application of any person before such date as regulations may specify, or on a proposal by the authority before a specified date –

–   the land was provisionally registered as common land under s 4 of the 1965 Act;
–   the provisional registration became final;
–   immediately before its provisional registration, the land was a town or village green within the 1965 Act as originally enacted.[2]

8.8.5   Buildings registered as common land

Where any land registered as common land is land that satisfies the following conditions, a commons registration authority shall remove the land from its register of common land upon the application of any person before such date as regulations may specify, or on a proposal by the authority before a specified date –

–   the land was provisionally registered as common land under s 4 of the 1965 Act;
–   on the date of the provisional registration the land was covered by a building or was within the curtilage of a building;
–   the provisional registration became final; and
–   since the date of the provisional registration the land has at all times been, and still is, covered by a building or within the curtilage of a building.[3]

---

[1]   Commons Act 2006, Sch 2, para 4; this addresses the problem identified in *Hampshire County Council v Milburn* [1990] 2 All ER 257.

[2]   Commons Act 2006, Sch 2, para 5.

[3]   Commons Act 2006, Sch 2, para 6.

8.8.6 Other land wrongly registered as common land

Where any land registered as common land is land that satisfies the following conditions, a commons registration authority shall remove the land from its register of common land upon the application of any person before such date as regulations may specify, or on a proposal by the authority before a specified date –

- the land was provisionally registered as common land under s 4 of the 1965 Act;
- the provisional registration was not referred to a commons commissioner under s 5 of the 1965 Act;
- the provisional registration became final; and
- immediately before its provisional registration the land was not land subject to rights of common, waste land of a manor, a town or village green within the meaning of the 1965 Act as originally enacted, or land of a description specified in s 11 of the Inclosure Act 1845.[1]

8.8.7 Buildings registered as town or village green

Where any land registered as a town or village green is land that satisfies the following conditions, a commons registration authority shall remove the land from its register of town and village greens upon the application of any person before such date as regulations may specify, or on a proposal by the authority before a specified date –

- the land was provisionally registered as town or village green under s 4 of the 1965 Act;
- on the date of the provisional registration the land was covered by a building or was within the curtilage of a building;
- the provisional registration became final; and
- since the date of the provisional registration the land has at all times been, and still is, covered by a building or within the curtilage of a building.[2]

8.8.8 Other land wrongly registered as town or village green

Where any land registered as a town or village green satisfies the following conditions, a commons registration authority shall remove

---

[1] Commons Act 2006, Sch 2, para 7.

[2] Commons Act 2006, Sch 2, para 8.

the land from its register of town or village greens upon the application of any person before such date as regulations may specify, or on a proposal by the authority before a specified date –

- the land was provisionally registered as a town or village under s 4 of the 1965 Act;
- the provisional registration was not referred to a commons commissioner under s 5 of the 1965 Act;
- the provisional registration became final; and
- immediately before its provisional registration the land was not common land within the meaning of the 1965 Act;
- immediately before its provisional registration the land was not a town or village green for the following reasons: throughout the 20 years preceding the date of its provisional registration the land was, by reason of its physical nature, unusable by members of the public for the purposes of lawful sports and pastimes, and was not, and still is not, allotted by or under Act for the exercise or recreation of the inhabitants of any locality.[1]

---

[1]   Commons Act 2006, Sch 2, para 9.

Chapter 9

TOWN AND VILLAGE GREENS

9.1   INTRODUCTION

What is a town or village green? In *New Windsor Corporation v Mellor*,[1] Lord Denning MR explained the background to customary rights to a village green:[2]

> 'Today we look back far in time. To a town or village green. The turf is old. Animals have grazed there for hundreds of years. Nowadays they are pleasant stretches of grass where people sit and talk. Sometimes they play cricket or kick a ball about. But in mediaeval times it was the place where young men mustered with their bows and arrows. They shot at the butts. There might be stocks there where offenders were put for their petty misdemeanours. In the month of May they set up a maypole and danced around it. We have no record of when it all began.'

He then introduced an excerpt from the poem 'Forefathers' by Edmund Blunden:

> 'On the green they watched their sons
>
> Playing til too dark to see,
>
> As their fathers watched them once,
>
> As my father once watched me.'

Town and village greens are the quintessential features of the village in England and Wales and, to a lesser extent, the smaller county towns. Although today associated with leisure activities, their pre-1066 origins no doubt lay in the obvious need for some form of open space in any village where communal activities of one sort or another,

---

[1]   [1975] 1 Ch 380.

[2]   Ibid, at 386c.

whether for leisure or non-leisure purposes, could be carried out. By the Norman period the following description would have been true of many village greens:[1]

> 'Through the village ran the highway. This was not a metalled road as we know it but a broad area, muddy in winter and dusty in summer, along which travellers made their way as best they could, detouring round potholes and rough patches over the adjoining land. Wandering pedlars sold their goods on the green and visiting showmen set up their booths there. The young folk met and the older ones gossiped in good weather and cottagers put out their geese to graze.'

Many town or village greens would have been, and may remain, subject to rights of common, particularly rights of pasture. But the town or village greens that have never been subject to rights of common were almost certainly always part of the waste lands of the manor.[2] In the nineteenth century, it was the practice for Inclosure Commissioners to allot areas in a town or village for recreational purposes, in connection with the inclosing of commons. Town or village greens are also frequently subject to customary rights for leisure and other purposes, whether or not they are either part of the waste lands of the manor or subject to rights of common.

An area may look like a town or village green, because it is an open, probably green, space within or near the centre of a town or a village. However, town or village greens do not all have the same origins, and the public will not necessarily enjoy public rights of access for the same purposes over each of them.

This chapter considers the legal basis of town and village greens, and their regulation and protection. Although the original registration process of town or village greens under the Commons Registration Act 1965 was considered more fully in Chapter 8, the 1965 Act is briefly considered, together with the changes to the registration of new greens made by the Commons Act 2006.

---

[1]   See Jessel *The Law of the Manor* (1998), at p 8.

[2]   See Chapter 2.

9.2   REGISTRATION OF GREENS UNDER THE COMMONS REGISTRATION ACT 1965

9.2.1   Registration

Section 1(1) of the 1965 Act provided that:

'There shall be registered, in accordance with the provisions of this Act and subject to the exceptions mentioned thereon –

(a) land in England or Wales which is common land or a town or village green;

(b) rights of common over such land; and

(c) persons claiming to be or found to be owners of such land or becoming the owners thereof by virtue of this Act.'

Section 3 of the 1965 Act required the registration authorities to maintain a separate register of town or village greens. As originally enacted, the 1965 Act defined a town or village green as meaning:[1]

'… land which has been allotted by or under any Act for the exercise or recreation of the inhabitants of any locality or on which the inhabitants of any locality have a customary right to indulge in lawful sports and pastimes *or on which the inhabitants of any locality have indulged in such sports and pastimes as of right for not less than 20 years.*'

This definition identifies three classes of greens. The definition of the third of these three classes was amended with effect from 30 January 2001; the italicised words set out above were deleted and replaced with 'or which falls within subsection (1A) of this section', together with the following:[2]

'(1A) Land falls within this subsection if it is land on which for not less than twenty years a significant number of the inhabitants of any locality, or of any neighbourhood within a locality, have indulged in lawful sports and pastimes as of right, and [either] –

(a) continue to do so, …'

---

[1]   Section 22(1).

[2]   Subsections 22(1A) and (1B) were introduced by CROW Act 2000, s 98 with effect from 30 January 2001.

This definition included a provision for regulations that would specify a period of time within which an application had to be made where user was no longer continuing; no regulations were ever made. The classification into three classes was referred to by Carnwath J in *R v Suffolk County Council, ex parte Steed*:[1] Class A, allotted land; Class B, land subject to customary right to indulge in lawful sports and pastimes; and Class C, land on which for more than 20 years a significant number of inhabitants indulged in lawful sports and pastimes (as amended). The original unamended definition of a Class C green applied whenever the 20-year qualifying period of user (which can be any period of 20 years) expired prior to 30 January 2001; that user did not have to continue up to the date of any application to register the green. The definition of a Class C green, as amended in 2000, required the additional requirement of a significant number of local inhabitants, although they can be of any locality within a neighbourhood, and that the user continues. The question as to whether an applicant had to prove user to the date of the application or the date of the registration was answered in the first sense by the House of Lords in *Oxfordshire County Council v Oxford City Council*.[2]

Registrations of greens under the Commons Registration Act 1965 will therefore include greens of all three classes, and these registrations will be continued when the Commons Act 2006 is in force.

9.2.2   Class A: allotted land

This category of land is described as 'land which has been allotted by or under any Act for the exercise or recreation of the inhabitants of any locality'.[3] Prior to the enactment of the Inclosure Act 1845, inclosure awards frequently allotted areas of land, particularly town and village greens, for the purposes of exercise and of recreation. The Inclosure Act 1845 contained several provisions for the allotment of land for exercise and recreation in the awards of the Inclosure Commissioners.

---

[1]   [1995] QB 487 at 491; also by Lord Hoffmann in *R v Oxfordshire County Council, ex parte Sunningwell Parish Council* [1999] 2 EGLR 94 at 95E and by Sullivan J in *R (Cheltenham Builders Ltd) v South Gloucestershire District Council* [2003] EWHC 2803.

[2]   [2006] 2 WLR 1235.

[3]   Commons Registration Act 1965, s 22(1).

Under the 1845 Act any existing town or village green could not be subject to inclosure.[1] Further, it was lawful for the Commissioners to allot any existing green to the church wardens and overseers of the poor of the parish to hold that land in trust to allow the same to be used for the purposes of exercise and recreation, provided that such allotted green should be of equal or greater extent to any previously existing. The boundary of such an allotted green was to be marked where it adjoined inclosed land.[2]

When first enacted, the 1845 Act required the Inclosure Commissioners to consider allotting part of the waste lands of the manor for the purposes of exercise and recreation. An allotment of between four and 10 acres was to be provided according to the size of the population of the parish.[3] Allotments for exercise and recreation would normally be made to the church wardens and overseers of the relevant parishes.[4] It has been said that the effect of allotments for exercise and recreation was to extinguish any rights of common over the affected land.[5] This seems doubtful as the provision dealing with the extinguishment of rights of common appears to be directed to the allotments that were made for the purposes of inclosure. The management obligations in relation to allotted greens or areas for exercise and recreation are considered below. It became the invariable practice of the Inclosure Commissioners after 1845 to allot land for the purposes of exercise and recreation.

Although the nature and origin of customary rights is considered below, it was quite usual for greens allotted under s 15 of the 1845 Act to have been subject to customary rights.

Under the Commons Act 2006, it will be possible to register Class A greens that were mistakenly omitted from registration prior to the 31 July 1970 under the Commons Registration Act 1965: for the limitations on this, see below.

---

[1] Section 15. See also Chapter 7 for an explanation of this Act.

[2] Section 15.

[3] Section 31.

[4] Section 73.

[5] See Gadsden *The Law of Commons*, at p 380 relying on s 106 of the 1845 Act.

9.2.3   Class B: Customary rights to indulge in lawful sports and pastimes

Customary rights are recognised by the common law where certain requirements are satisfied. Such rights must have been exercisable only by members of some identifiable local community, in relation to a particular locality.[1] They must be certain, reasonable and continuous, and have existed from time immemorial (1189). In *Mercer v Denne* it was said that:[2]

> 'Most cases with regard to validity of custom are difficult of decision. The fact is that reason recoils from the proposition that legal memory goes back to an arbitrary date at the beginning of the reign of Richard I., A.D. 1189, and, if one finds proof of uninterrupted modern usage, there is a natural inclination to presume the previous existence of the custom right back to 1189, even though the facts may be such as to force upon reason the conclusion that the modern usage could not in fact have been adopted for more than a few generations.'

It seems certain that, apart from allotted greens (considered above), town or village greens had their origins as either waste lands of the manor or as land subject to rights of common. Either way the owner of the soil would have been the owner of the manor. Customary rights can therefore be acquired over both waste lands of the manor and land subject to rights of common. It is also clear that the customary rights can be acquired over land that would not ordinarily be described as a town or village green, they might be acquired over an area of private enclosed land, if the necessary requirements are satisfied.[3]

The requirements for establishing a customary right are as follows.

(a)   Local inhabitants

A customary right may only be exercised by the members of some identifiable local community. The definition of 'any locality', in

---

[1]   *R v Oxfordshire County Council, ex parte Sunningwell Parish Council* [2000] AC 335 and *R v Suffolk County Council, ex parte Steed* (1995) 70 P&CR 487.

[2]   *Mercer v Denne* [1905] 2 Ch 538, *per* Vaughan Williams LJ at 577.

[3]   *Hall v Nottingham* (1875) 1 Ex D 1.

s 22(1) of the 1965 Act, therefore probably means '*the* locality'. As Sir George Jessel MR said in *Hammerton v Honey:*[1]

> 'What must be the usage proved? It must not only be consistent with the custom alleged, but, if I may use the expression, not too wide. For instance, if you allege a custom for certain persons to dance on a green, and you prove in support of that allegation, not only that some people danced, but that everybody else in the world who chose danced and played cricket, you have got beyond your custom.'

In *Bourke v Davis*[2] it was said that a custom is good if confined to inhabitants of a particular district. In *Edward v Jenkins*, Kekewich J, after considering the decision in *Fitch v Rawling*[3] said:[4]

> 'I do not, therefore, find in any of the cases anything that would justify me in saying that the use of the word "district" means more than the particular division known to the law in which the particular property is situate. It may be situate in a parish, or in a manor, or there might be some other division. But I cannot see how a number of parishes can, without specific evidence, be said to be situated in a particular district so that land in one of the parishes is land in a particular district.'

Although *Fitch v Rawling* was not referred to in *Ministry of Defence v Wiltshire County Council*,[5] Harman J decided that the residents of three streets in the vicinity of the open land in question did not constitute a defined body of persons recognised in law as an entity, such as a parish or manor, and were therefore not capable of exercising a customary right.

In *Edwards v Jenkins*,[6] Kekewich J decided that a custom could not be claimed on behalf of the inhabitants of three parishes, because three parishes did not constitute a district, such as a parish or a manor. In *New Windsor Corporation v Mellor*[7] Lord Denning MR said that he did not think that that was correct. He added:

---

[1]   (1876) 24 WR 603.

[2]   (1889) 44 ChD 110.

[3]   (1795) 2 H Bl 393.

[4]   [1896] 1 Ch 308, at 313.

[5]   [1995] 4 All ER 931.

[6]   [1896] 1 Ch 308.

[7]   [1975] 1 Ch 380.

'So long as the locality is certain, that is enough.'

Gadsden suggests this observation is highly persuasive and that it ought to be a question of fact in each case as to the extent of the locality which is relevant for establishing a customary right, and that there is no reason why a housing estate, whatever its extent, should not be regarded as a locality.[1] There must, however, be some doubt about that approach. Customary rights must be ancient, certain, reasonable and continuous. They are 'ancient' if they are shown to have commenced prior to 1189, the beginning of legal memory. Apart from the fact that a housing estate today can probably be shown not to have existed in 1189, this approach, and Lord Denning's disapproval, fails to take into account that a customary right must, at least in theory, lie in grant. As Heath J said in *Fitch v Rawling:*[2]

> 'The lord might have granted such a privilege, as is claimed by the ... custom, before the time of memory.'

That recognises the unlikelihood of any grant being made by the lord of the manor in favour of inhabitants outside the manor, or possibly the parish. In *R (Cheltenham Builders Ltd) v South Gloucestershire District Council*, Sullivan J concluded that 'locality' was an administrative unit.[3]

(b)   Ancient, certain, reasonable and continuous

The other essential characteristics of a custom are: immemorial existence, reasonableness, certainty, and continuity.[4] Although every custom must have been in existence since 1189, there is a presumption of such immemorial existence if proof of user in living memory is shown. However, that presumption is rebuttable by proof that the user could not have taken place since 1189.[5]

Reasonableness has no single test, but embraces notions of reasonableness considered in relation to all the circumstances, the nature of the custom, the land over which it is claimed and

---

[1]   See Gadsden *The Law of Commons*, at p 379.

[2]   (1795) 2 H Bl 393 at 399.

[3]   [2003] EWHC 2803 (Admin).

[4]   *Halsbury's Laws of England* (4th edn) vol 21(1), at para 606.

[5]   *Hammerton v Honey* (1876) 24 WR 603.

consistency with other rights and laws.[1] Certainty requires definite limits to the rights claimed, the locality it is claimed over and the persons claiming it.[2] Continuity requires the absence of interruption since 1189. That does not mean use everyday, or even every year, but no interruption to the exercise of the right as a right. It certainly does not mean that the right must be capable of being exercised every day as many rights are only claimed in respect of defined periods each year.[3]

(c)   Nature of the activities

Both non-leisure and leisure activities have been recognised as customary rights. Thus in *Mercer v Denne*[4] a custom was established for fishermen drying nets on land. The relevance of the nature of the activity that founds a customary right arises because of the registration requirements of the Commons Registration Act 1965 and the various provisions that protect and regulate town and village greens. For the purposes of the 1965 Act, where a customary right was claimed, this was limited to where the inhabitants of any locality had a customary right to indulge in lawful sports and pastimes. As we shall see below, in relation to the regulation and management of town and village greens, the various provisions are restricted to town and village greens used for recreational purposes. Accordingly, the only customary rights that are generally relevant to town and village greens are those involving recreational pastimes.

Customary rights which have been upheld include archery,[5] dancing[6] and playing cricket.[7]

(d)   Conclusions

The requirements set out above will prevent the establishment of a customary right at common law in many circumstances. The additional Class C category of greens, based on 20 years' use for

---

[1]   *Wolstanton Ltd v Newcastle-under-Lyme Borough Council* [1940] AC 860, [1940] 3 All ER 101, HL.

[2]   *Hammerton v Honey* (1876) 24 WR 603.

[3]   *New Windsor Corporation v Mellor* [1974] 2 All ER 510.

[4]   [1905] 2 Ch 538.

[5]   *New Windsor Corporation v Mellor* [1975] 1 Ch 380.

[6]   *Hall v Nottingham* (1875) 1 Ex D 1.

[7]   *Fitch v Rawling* (1795) 2 H Bl 393.

lawful sports and pastimes addressed some of the defects in establishing such user as a customary right.

9.2.4   Class C: lawful sports and pastimes as of right for 20 years

Because in future any new greens will only be registerable as Class C greens, these are more fully described below under the Commons Act 2006.

9.2.5   Effect of non-registration under the Commons Registration Act 1965

In respect of town or village greens existing at the date when the 1965 Act came into force, the period of registration expired on 31 July 1970. The 1965 Act then provided that at the end of that period 'no land capable of being registered under the Act shall be deemed to be ... a town or village green unless it is so registered'.[1] It has been said that whilst land subject to a customary right to indulge in lawful sports and pastimes (Class B) might cease to have that status by reason of non-registration, land falling within the other two classes of town or village greens would probably retain their status.[2] In *Oxfordshire County Council v Oxford City Council*, the House of Lords approved the conclusion of Carnwath LJ in the Court of Appeal that by reason of the conclusive provisions in s 10 of the 1965 Act, there was no legal basis for treating land as having the status of a green if it was not registered, notwithstanding that the land might at some earlier time have satisfied the statutory definition of a green.[3]

However, the Commons Act 2006 contains provisions for the registration, within strict time limits, of Class A greens (allotted land) that were mistakenly omitted from registration prior to 31 July 1970 under the Commons Registration Act 1965: see below.

9.2.6   Registration of new greens under the Commons Registration Act 1965

Because the new provisions relating to the registration of town or village greens in the Commons Act 2006 will not be in force until 2007 or 2008, registration of new greens will continue for a while under the

---

[1]   Section 1(2)(a).

[2]   See Gadsden *The Law of Commons*, at p 385.

[3]   *Oxfordshire County Council v Oxford City Council* [2006] 2 WLR 1235, 1251, approving [2006] Ch 43, 72 on this point.

1965 Act. Where any land becomes a town or village green after 31 July 1970, the 1965 Act made provision for the amendment of the registers so that a new town or village green can be included.[1] The procedure usually required the registration authority to hold a non-statutory inquiry or hearing; a decision to register may be challenged by judicial review or by an application under s 14 of the 1965 Act.[2] Only Class C greens can now come into existence. Class C greens within the meaning of the unamended definition may be registered where the 20-year qualifying period was satisfied prior to 30 January 2001 (any period of 20 years will suffice). Where the 20-year qualifying period expires after that date, the amended definition of a Class C green applies, and the user must be by a significant number of inhabitants, and continue until the date of the application for registration.[3] Guidance on the form and treatment of applications was considered in Chapter 8. As the relevant provisions of the Commons Act 2006 are likely to come into force from 2007 onwards, the entitlement to register a new green under the Commons Registration Act 1965 will be short lived.

9.3 REGISTRATION OF NEW GREENS UNDER THE COMMONS ACT 2006

9.3.1 What land can be registered as a green

When s 15 of the 2006 Act is in force, the only new greens that will be registrable will be those within Class C.[4] Any person can apply for registration.[5] As explained below, it must be shown that certain defined inhabitants have indulged in lawful sports and pastimes for not less than 20 years user as of right. In determining the period of 20 years, there is to be disregarded any period during which access to the land was prohibited to the public by reason of any enactment.[6] The more formal details of the application for registration are dealt with in Chapter 8 above. A full discussion of all the requirements of a Class C green is set out later in this chapter.

---

[1]   Section 13 and Commons Registration (General) Regulations 1966, SI 1966/1471 as amended by Commons Registration (New Land) Regulations 1969, SI 1969/1843.

[2]   *R (Cheltenham Builders Ltd) v South Gloucestershire District Council* [2003] EWHC 2803.

[3]   *Oxfordshire County Council v Oxford City Council* [2006] 2 WLR 1235.

[4]   Section 15.

[5]   Section 15(1).

[6]   Section 15(6).

The 2006 Act amends the definition of Class C greens and requires the registration authority to register land as a green where:[1]

> '(a) a significant number of the inhabitants of any locality, or of any neighbourhood within a locality, have indulged as of right in lawful sports and pastimes on the land for a period of at least 20 years; and
>
> (b) they continue to do so at the time of the application'

Where the requirement in (a) above is satisfied by the minimum 20 years user, it is possible that some enactment might prohibit the user, or the landowner might try to stop the user being as of right by granting permission, so that the user does not continue to the date of an application for registration in terms of (b) above. Section 15(7) addresses that possibility. It provides that a user that was lawful is regarded as continuing notwithstanding some prohibition by an enactment. It also provides that if permission is granted for the user, the user will continue 'as of right'.

The requirement in (b) above, that the user must continue to the time of the application for registration, is modified in two circumstances. The first modification applies when the relevant user ceases before an application is made, but after the date when s 15 of the 2006 Act comes into force:[2]

> '(a) a significant number of the inhabitants of any locality, or of any neighbourhood within a locality, indulged as of right in lawful sports and pastimes on the land for a period of at least 20 years; and
>
> (b) they ceased to do so before the time of the application but after the commencement of this section; and
>
> (c) the application is made within the period of two years beginning with the cessation referred to in paragraph (b).'

A relevant user of land for sports and pastimes may cease, or cease to be as of right, because the owner of the affected land takes steps to prevent the user, such as by fencing or other obstructions, or attempts to negate user as of right by granting permission. Indeed the owner may have obtained planning permission for development, and even

---

[1]   Section 15(2).

[2]   Section 15(3).

commenced work on the land in accordance with that permission. Even if works are carried out under a planning permission, the modification above allows a 2-year period within which an application must be made. It follows that there could be a 2-year period of uncertainty to persons developing land where the development land may have been used for sports and pastimes. The second modification addresses the same problem where the relevant user ceases before s 15 of the 2006 Act is in force; it uses a 5-year period, but is subject to s 15(5) of the Act:[1]

> '(a) a significant number of the inhabitants of any locality, or of any neighbourhood within a locality, indulged as of right in lawful sports and pastimes on the land for a period of at least 20 years; and
>
> (b) they ceased to do so before the commencement of this section; and
>
> (c) the application is made within the period of five years beginning with the cessation referred to in paragraph (b).'

But the entitlement to make an application to register land as a green under this second modification will not apply where:[2]

> '(a) planning permission was granted before 23 June 2006 in respect of the land;
>
> (b) construction works were commenced before that date in accordance with that planning permission on the land or any other land in respect of which the permission was granted; and
>
> (c) the land –
>
> > (i) has by reason of any works carried out in accordance with that planning permission become permanently unusable by members of the public for the purposes of lawful sports and pastimes; or
> >
> > (ii) will by reason of any works proposed to be carried out in accordance with that planning permission become permanently unusable by members of the public for those purposes.'

---

[1]   Section 15(4).

[2]   Section 15(5).

Section 15(5) therefore prevents land being registered as a green by reason of works carried out, or to be carried out, under a planning permission that has or will prevent lawful sports and pastimes. There are important limitations to this exclusion from registration. First, the planning permission must have been granted before 23 June 2006, and some construction works must have commenced before that date. Further, the exclusion only applies where the cessation of the lawful sports and pastimes was before the date when s 15 comes into force (probably in 2007).

9.3.2   How applications are determined

As the processing of applications for the registration of town or village greens is the same as those for applications to register rights of common, the registration process is more fully explained in Chapter 8.

9.3.3   Application by owner for registration

Under s 15(8) of the Commons Act 2006 the owner of any land may apply to a registration authority to register that land as a town or village green. The consent of any tenant with a lease of more than seven years, and any chargee, will be required.[1] Although it may be quite difficult to envisage a landowner wishing to have his own land registered as a village green, there may be such public-spirited individuals. It is more likely that a local authority may wish to take advantage of this provision in order to confer additional protection on appropriate land.

9.3.4   Deregistration and exchange

The Commons Act 2006 contains provisions for the deregistration of town or village greens in certain limited circumstances. As the scope and procedure of these provisions also applies to common land, these matters are fully explained in Chapter 8.

9.4   COMMONS ACT 2006: CORRECTIONS AND NON- OR MISTAKEN REGISTRATION

The Commons Act 2006 contains a number of provisions to correct mistakes in the registers, or to add land that should have been

---

[1]   Section 15(9).

registered as a town or village green or remove land that should not have been registered.

9.4.1   Corrections

A registration authority may amend any part of its register of town or village greens to correct a mistake in making or amending an entry, to remove a duplicate entry, to update any name or address, or to take account of any accretion or diluvion (addition or loss due to action of water).[1] Where a mistake is being corrected, the amendment cannot affect the extent of the land or what can be done by virtue of any right of common.[2]

9.4.2   Non-registration of town or village greens

Schedule 2 to the Commons Act 2006 contains provisions for the registration of Class A greens.[3] The registration authority must be satisfied that on 31 July 1970 (last date for registration under the 1965 Act) the green was land allotted under any Act for the exercise or recreation of the inhabitants of the locality, it was not finally registered under the 1965 Act, and the land continues to be allotted land. Regulations may be made that may specify other conditions.

9.4.3   Green wrongly registered as common land

A number of town or village greens were wrongly registered under the Commons Registration Act 1965 as common land, and not as greens. The Commons Act 2006 contains powers for a registration authority to remove the land from the register of common land and register it as in the register of town or village greens.[4]

9.4.4   Buildings registered as town or village green

Where, on the date when land was provisionally registered under the Commons Registration Act 1965 as a green, it was covered by a building or was within the curtilage of a building, the registration authority can remove the land from registration provided the provisional registration became final and the land remains covered

---

[1]   Commons Act 2006, s 19.

[2]   Commons Act 2006, s 19(2)(b).

[3]   Commons Act 2006, Sch 2, para 3.

[4]   Commons Act 2006, Sch 2, para 5.

by a building or is within the curtilage of a building.[1] Regulations will be made setting down a time limit for applications for deregistration.

9.4.5   Other land wrongly registered as a town or village green

Land can also be removed from the register where it was not a town or village green immediately before its provisional registration under the Commons Registration Act 1965.[2] The land will be regarded as not having been a green only if, throughout the 20 years preceding the date of provisional registration, it was unusable for lawful sports and pastimes and was not allotted under any Act for exercise and recreation. The land to be removed must have been the subject of a provisional registration that was not referred to a Commons Commissioner under s 5 of the Commons Registration Act 1965, and therefore became final. Regulations will be made setting down a time limit for applications for deregistration.

9.5   CLASS C: USE OF LAND FOR LAWFUL SPORTS AND PASTIMES AS OF RIGHT FOR 20 YEARS

9.5.1   Deficiencies in requirements for customary rights

This category, introduced in 1965, was first amended by the Countryside and Rights of Way (CROW) Act 2000, with effect from 30 January 2001. The amendment introduced the need for a *significant* number of inhabitants to have indulged in lawful sports and pastimes, and that such inhabitants could be the inhabitants not merely of a locality, but also of any neighbourhood within a locality – this latter change addressing the difficulty in *Ministry of Defence v Wiltshire County Council*.[3] When s 15 of the Commons Act 2006 is in force, this provision retains the same definition of Class C greens as that as amended in 2001 with one important exception. As explained above, in relation to the registration of new greens under the 2006 Act, s 15 makes clear that the 20 years user must continue until the date when an application for registration is made; there is also provision for where the user is interrupted.

The purpose of a Class C green is clear. Under the common law an easement or a profit may be acquired by implication which arises

---

[1]   Commons Act 2006, Sch 2, para 8.

[2]   Commons Act 2006, Sch 2, para 9.

[3]   [1995] 4 All ER 931.

where a minimum of 20 years' use without permission, without secrecy, and without force, can be established (30 years for profits under the Prescription Act 1832). A claim to customary rights can be defeated by showing that the rights could not have been exercised before 1189. Accordingly, a claim to public rights of exercise and recreation would fail at common law.[1] The identification of the locality has also caused problems.

When s 15 of the Commons Act 2006 is in force, Class C greens will be the only type of new town or village green capable of registration in the future. The amended definition of Class C greens that are registrable is as discussed above. The further requirements of Class C are as follows.

9.5.2 Significant number of inhabitants

A significant number of inhabitants must have indulged in lawful sports and pastimes. There is little guidance on the meaning of a 'significant number of the inhabitants' of either any locality or of a neighbourhood within a locality in the Act. This should be given its ordinary meaning such that a claim by only a few inhabitants could constitute a 'significant number' in appropriate cases. In *R (Alfred McAlpine Homes Ltd) v Staffordshire County Council*, it was held that a 'significant number' need not be considerable or substantial; it was a matter of impression for the decision-maker on the evidence put before him and what mattered was that the number of people using the land in question had to be sufficient to indicate that their use of the land signifies that it is a general use by the local community for informal recreation, rather than occasional use by individuals as trespassers.[2] It is not necessary that a significant number of inhabitants must be the applicants for registration as a town or village green. In one case only four local residents made the application.[3]

9.5.3 Any locality or neighbourhood within a locality

A claim can be made by the inhabitants of any locality, or of any neighbourhood within a locality. The meaning of 'the inhabitants of any locality' was considered above in relation to customary rights. A

---

1   *New Windsor Corporation v Mellor* [1975] 1 Ch 380 at 391.

2   [2002] 2 PLR 1, at para 71.

3   *R (Beresford) v Sunderland City Council* [2002] QB 874.

'locality' suggested a manor or a parish or some other recognised unit. It is sufficient if the land is used predominantly by inhabitants of the village.[1] What is now clear is that an area less than a locality is sufficient to support a claim. This circumvents the problem that the applicants faced in *Ministry of Defence v Wiltshire County Council* where the residents of three streets were held not to constitute a locality.[2] But a 'locality' is not an arbitrary line on a map; it means an administrative unit and a 'neighbourhood' within a locality means an area with a sufficient degree of cohesiveness.[3]

9.5.4   As of right

The applicants must show that the inhabitants have indulged in lawful sports and pastimes *as of right*. The meaning of *as of right* was considered in *R v Oxfordshire County Council, ex parte Sunningwell Parish Council.*[4] In that case the church authorities were the owners of 10 acres of glebe land on which they had obtained planning permission to build some houses. The parish council contended that the glebe was land on which the inhabitants of the locality had indulged in sports and pastimes as of right for not less than 20 years. The House of Lords decided that where a use had to be established *as of right*, user that was apparently *as of right* could not be discounted merely because many of the users over a long period were subjectively indifferent as to whether a right existed, or even had private knowledge that it did not. It was sufficient that the glebe was used predominantly by inhabitants even if there was occasional use by non-inhabitants. A balance had to be struck between neighbourly tolerance of trespass and the acquisition of rights by user; there had been sufficient quality of user as of right. Toleration was not inconsistent with user as of right.[5]

In *R (Beresford) v Sunderland City Council*, the commons registration authority had refused an application for an area to be registered as a town green, pursuant to s 13 of the 1965 Act, on the ground that the inhabitants had indulged in sports and pastimes with the permission

---

[1]   *R v Oxfordshire County Council, ex parte Sunningwell Parish Council* [1999] 2 EGLR 94, at 99D.

[2]   [1995] 4 All ER 931.

[3]   *R (Cheltenham Builders Ltd) v South Gloucestershire District Council* [2003] EWHC 2803 (Admin).

[4]   [1999] 2 EGLR 94 in which *R v Suffolk County Council, ex parte Steed* [1997] 1 EGLR 131 was said to be wrongly decided.

[5]   [1999] 2 EGLR 94, at 99F.

or implied licence of the landowner; the inhabitants had not indulged in sports or pastimes *as of right*.[1] The House of Lords held that the claim to a use of the land *as of right* was not defeated by implied permission. The land had been owned by public or local authorities and their provision of the land was not, on the evidence, indicative of a precatory permission; the application for registration of the area as a town green could proceed.

In *R (Laing Homes Ltd) v Buckinghamshire County Council*, Sullivan J had to consider whether rights could be exercisable, *as of right*, over some fields used for taking an annual hay crop. In concluding that the matter had to be remitted to the registration authority for reconsideration, he said that the proper approach was to consider how the exercise of the activities appeared to the owner of the land:[2]

> 'Thus, the proper approach is not to examine the extent to which those using the land for recreational purposes were interrupted by the landowner's agricultural activities, but to ask whether those using the fields for recreational purposes were interrupting [the landowners' licensee's] agricultural use of the land in such a manner, or to such an extent, that [the landowners] should have been aware that the recreational users believed that they were exercising a public right. If the starting point is, "how would the matter have appeared to [the landowners]?" it would not be reasonable to expect [the landowners] to resist the recreational use of their field so long as such use did not interfere with their licensee's ... use of them, for taking an annual hay crop.'

In *Oxfordshire County Council v Oxford City Council*, Lord Hoffmann doubted whether Sullivan J was entitled to conclude that low-level agricultural activities must be regarded as having been inconsistent with use for sports and pastimes.[3] In *Laing* Sullivan J also considered that public statements made by members of the public against the development of the fields, in relation to planning applications, were inconsistent with a claim *as of right*.[4] The problem with showing 'user as of right' was considered in *R (Cheltenham Builders Ltd) v South*

---

1   [2004] 1 All ER 160, [2003] 3 WLR 1306, on appeal from [2001] 3 PLR 120.

2   *R (Laing Homes Ltd) v Buckinghamshire County Council* [2003] EWHC 1578 (Admin) at para 82, [2003] 3 PLR 60.

3   [2006] 2 WLR 1235, 1255.

4   *R (Laing Homes Ltd) v Buckinghamshire County Council* [2003] EWHC 1578 (Admin) at para 82, [2003] 3 PLR 60.

Gloucestershire District Council,[1] where Sullivan J considered that it was sufficient to show user up to the date of the application for registration; a point now confirmed by the House of Lords in *Oxfordshire County Council v Oxford City Council,*[2] and further confirmed in the Commons Act 2006.[3]

9.5.5   20-year period and lack of continuity

In *Ministry of Defence v Wiltshire County Council* Harman J thought, but without deciding the question, that under the definition of a Class C green in s 22(1) of the 1965 Act, an applicant for registration had to show a minimum of 20 years use continuing to the date of the application.[4] The amendments made by the CROW Act 2000 (s 22(1A)(a)) required the use to continue, without stating to what date. It did make alternative provision where a use had ceased for no more than a prescribed period of time. The prescribed period allowed for the possibility that the landowner may have prevented use for a period of time sufficient to negate 20 years user continuing up to the date of application. But no regulations were ever made prescribing any period. In *R (Cheltenham Builders Ltd) v South Gloucestershire District Council,* Sullivan J concluded that user must continue to the date of the application, but that where an application was withdrawn after the landowner objected, there had not been continuity of user as of right thereafter.[5] In *Oxfordshire County Council v Oxford City Council* the House of Lords confirmed that user as of right had to continue to the date of application.[6]

An application for registration of a Class C green under the Commons Registration Act 1965, made after 30 January 2001, must satisfy the definition of a green as amended in 2001 by the CROW Act 2000: see above.[7] An application may be made at any time thereafter so long as user is continuing.[8]

---

[1]   [2003] EWHC 2803 (Admin).

[2]   [2006] 2 WLR 1235.

[3]   Section 15(2).

[4]   [1995] 4 All ER 931.

[5]   [2003] EWHC 2803 (Admin), [2004] 1 EGLR 85, [2003] 4 PLR 95.

[6]   [2006] 2 WLR 1235.

[7]   *Oxfordshire County Council v Oxford City Council* [2006] 2 WLR 1235.

[8]   Ibid.

When s 15 of the Commons Act 2006 is in force, and 20 years user can be established, the user must continue until the time of the application for registration.[1] This is in accordance with the decision of the House of Lords in *Oxfordshire County Council v Oxford City Council*.[2] In determining the 20 years user, any period during which the user was prohibited by an enactment is to be disregarded.[3] Even if the 20 years user is satisfied, it is possible that the landowner might try to stop the user being as of right by granting permission, so that the user does not continue to the date of an application for registration 'as of right'. Section 15(7) addresses that possibility. It provides that if permission is granted for the user, the user will continue 'as of right'.

The requirement in s 15(2)(b) of the 2006 Act, that the user must continue to the time of the application for registration, is modified in two circumstances. First, where the user ceases before the time of the application, and after s 15 of the 2006 Act comes into force, an application must be made within a 2-year period.[4] Second, where the user ceases before s 15 comes into force, an application must be made within a 5-year period.[5] However, the right to apply within this 5-year period does not arise where, before 23 June 2006, construction works have been carried out with planning permission, and the land has become permanently unusable.[6] This is further explained above under registration.

9.5.6 Lawful sports and pastimes

Finally, the expression 'lawful sports and pastimes' was considered in *R v Oxfordshire County Council, ex parte Sunningwell Parish Council*.[7] The rights claimed were for:[8]

> '... such outdoor pursuits as walking their dogs, playing family and children's games, flying kites, picking blackberries, fishing in the stream and tobogganing down the slope when snow falls.'

---

[1] Commons Act 2006, s 15(2).

[2] *Oxfordshire County Council v Oxford City Council* [2006] 2 WLR 1235.

[3] Commons Act 2006, s 15(6).

[4] Section 15(3).

[5] Section 15(4).

[6] Section 15(5).

[7] [1999] 2 EGLR 94.

[8] Ibid, at 95C.

Lord Hoffmann said that 'sports and pastimes' was a composite class, so that an activity that was a sport or a pastime would be within it.[1] In *R (Laing Homes Ltd) v Buckinghamshire County Council* Sullivan J considered that the use of footpaths for walking dogs through fields might not constitute the necessary sports or pastimes.[2] The situation where the public use defined tracks over land can cause difficulties as to whether the use of those tracks will give rise to public rights of way only, or rights of user as a Class C green. Also, where tracks across land are already public rights of way can a Class C green user be established? In *Oxfordshire County Council v Oxford City Council*,[3] Lightman J stated that in the first situation the user of the tracks will generally only establish public rights of way unless the user is wider in scope or the tracks are of such character that user of them cannot give rise to a presumption of dedication at common law as a public highway, but user of such tracks for pedestrian recreational purposes may readily qualify as user as a Class C green. The answer must depend how the matter would have appeared to the owner of the land.[4] In the second situation the user will generally be referable to the public rights of way unless the user is only explicable to a Class C green; the matter being viewed from the position of the landowner. When the *Oxford* case went on appeal to the House of Lords, the House agreed with the Court of Appeal that it would not be appropriate to give any guidance on the evidentiary matters relating to the use of the tracks and the other land.[5]

9.5.7   Effect of registration of green based on 20 years of public use

Registration of a Class C green gives the green the status of a green upon which the inhabitants are then entitled to indulge in any lawful sports or pastimes; it is irrelevant that their 20 years user was based on only a restricted number of activities.[6] In *Oxfordshire County*

---

[1]   Ibid, at 98L.

[2]   *R (Laing Homes Ltd) v Buckinghamshire County Council* [2003] EWHC 1578 (Admin), [2003] 3 PLR 60. Dog-walking and playing with children was accepted by Carnwath J in *R v Suffolk County Council, ex parte Steed* (1995) 70 P&CR 487 at 503.

[3]   *Oxfordshire County Council v Oxford City Council* [2004] EWHC 12, [2004] PLSCS 16.

[4]   [2004] EWHC 12. [2004] PLSCS 16 and *R v Oxfordshire County Council, ex parte Sunningwell Parish Council* [2001] 1 AC 335, pp 352H–353A.

[5]   *Oxfordshire County Council v Oxford City Council* [2006] 2 WLR 1235, 1256.

[6]   *Oxfordshire County Council v Oxford City Council* [2006] 2 WLR 1235 overruling *New Windsor Corporation v Mellor* [1975] Ch 380 per Lord Denning MR at 391H–392G; and *R (Laing Homes Ltd) v Buckinghamshire County Council* [2003] EWHC 1578 (Admin), [2003] 3 PLR 60.

Council v Oxford City Council Lord Hoffmann concluded that the only rational construction of s 10 of the Commons Registration Act 1965 was that land registered as a Class C green can be used generally for sports and pastimes.[1] He also concluded that the effect of registration on the landowner was not a breach of Article 1 of the First Protocol to the European Convention on Human Rights and Freedoms.[2]

9.6   REGULATION AND PROTECTION

9.6.1   Ownership

Town or village greens that were allotted for exercise or recreation for the inhabitants of any locality, under the Inclosure Act 1845, or earlier Inclosure Acts, will usually now be owned by the parish or town council, or, in urban areas, the district or borough council. In the case of town or village greens subject to customary rights, or which have been registered as such under the Commons Registration Act 1965, on the ground that they have been used for sports and pastimes for at least 20 years, their ownership is far less certain. The land may be privately owned and may never have been a green properly so described. A town or village green is more usually part of the uninclosed land in what was, or remains, a village. That land would originally have been owned by the lord of the manor.

Under s 1(1)(a) of the Commons Registration Act 1965, land in England or Wales which is a town or village green was required to have been registered. There should also have been registered persons claiming to be or found to be owners of such land.[3] Where any land was registered as a town or village green, but no person was registered as its owner, either under the Commons Registration Act 1965 or the Land Registration Acts 1925 and 1936, there was provision under the 1965 Act for the ownership of a town or village green to be vested in a local authority.[4] In the case of land in a parish or community where there is a parish or community council, that council is the appropriate local authority. If the land is regulated by a scheme under the Commons Act 1899, the appropriate local authority is the parish or community council only if the powers of management

---

[1]   *Oxfordshire County Council v Oxford City Council* [2006] 2 WLR 1235, 1253.

[2]   *Oxfordshire County Council v Oxford City Council* [2006] 2 WLR 1235, 1255.

[3]   Section 1(1)(c).

[4]   Commons Registration Act 1965, s 8(3).

under Part I of the 1899 Act are being exercised by that council.[1] In the case of land in a London borough, the local authority is the borough council.[2] In all other cases, the appropriate local authority is the council or the district in which the land is situated.[3]

Under the Commons Act 2006, where land is registered as a town or village green, but no person is registered as the owner of the land, the local authority may take steps to protect the land. They may take all steps that the true owner could take and institute proceedings for any offence.[4] In England the local authority means a county, district or parish council, in London, a borough council, and in Wales, a county, county borough or community council.

9.6.2   Effect of rights of common

No doubt many town or village greens were subject to rights of common[5] and such land would have been subject to the rights of the commoners. Whether the rights of recreation prevail over, or are subject to, the rights of the commoners or the rights of the owner to any produce, probably depends upon the manner by which the recreational rights were acquired. In *Fitch v Fitch*[6] it was held that the rights of an owner to cut hay prevailed over the recreational rights of the local inhabitants. However, one can see that there may be circumstances where the recreational rights were acquired by such use as did prevail over the rights of the commoners or the owner. The possible conflict between the recreational rights of the local inhabitants and the rights of commoners remains because rights of common were registrable under the Commons Registration Act 1965 in respect of a town or village green.[7] Although the definition of *common* land under the Commons Registration Act 1965 excluded a town or village green,[8] rights of common may nonetheless be registered and exercised over a town or village green.[9] That is

---

1   Ibid, s 8(5)(a).

2   Ibid, s 8(5)(b).

3   Ibid, s 8(5)(c).

4   Commons Act 2006, s 45.

5   *Ratcliffe v Jowers* (1891) 8 TLR 6 (Barnes Green, London).

6   (1797) 2 Esp 543.

7   Section 4(1).

8   Section 22(1).

9   Section 4(1).

continued under the Commons Act 2006,[1] save that new rights of common cannot be created over land registered as a green.[2]

9.6.3 Management powers and duties

There are several statutory provisions that contain management powers and duties. These statutory provisions are not restricted to town or village greens.

(a) Metropolitan Commons Acts 1866–1878

These Acts applied to land which was subject to rights of common in 1866, the whole or any part of which was situated within the Metropolitan Police District as defined at the date of the passing of the Act.[3] Under the 1866 Act, schemes of regulation were made for many metropolitan commons, including by-laws and regulations for the prevention of nuisances and the preservation of order.[4] It would appear that the purpose of a scheme under the 1866 Act is:

> 'for the establishment of local management with a view to the expenditure of money on the drainage, levelling, and improvement of a metropolitan common, and to the making of bylaws and regulations for the prevention of nuisances and the preservation of order thereon.'

(b) Commons Act 1899

Under this Act the council of an urban district may make a scheme for the regulation and management of any common within their district with a view to the expenditure of money on the drainage, levelling and improvement of the common, and to the making of bylaws and regulations for the prevention of nuisances and the preservation of order on the commons.[5] Although this Act was principally concerned with the making of schemes of regulation affecting commons, the expression 'common' was deemed to include any town or village green.[6]

---

[1] Section 2(2)(b).

[2] Section 6(3).

[3] Sections 3 and 4.

[4] Section 6.

[5] Section 1. See further at Chapter 11.

[6] Section 15.

(c)   Open Spaces Act 1906

This Act contains a number of powers for trustees and local authorities in relation to the management of open spaces. An 'open space' is defined as meaning any land, whether inclosed or not, on which there are no buildings or of which not more than one-twentieth part is covered with buildings, and the whole or the remainder of which is laid out as a garden or is used for purposes of recreation, or lies waste and unoccupied.[1] That definition would plainly include a town or village green. Under the Act, a local authority includes a parish council.[2] Land may be acquired by, or transferred to, a local authority pursuant to powers under the Act.[3] Where an open space has been acquired by a local authority under the Act, that authority is required to hold and administer the open space in trust for the public and may carry out works of improvement.[4] There is a power to make by-laws.[5]

(d)   Criminal offences: nuisance and inclosure

Section 12 of the Inclosure Act 1857 makes it an offence to create nuisances of various forms on an allotted town or village green without lawful authority.[6] Section 29 of the Commons Act 1876 deems encroachment, enclosure or any erection on a green a public nuisance. These two provisions apply to greens, however, and whenever created and whether registered under the 1965 Act or not, including, by virtue of s 10 of the Commons Registration Act 1965, Class C greens.[7] If land has the status of a green prior to its registration, the owner might fear prosecution for acts contrary to these two provisions. These offences require *mens rea* and cannot give rise to any exposure to prosecution where the existence of the green is not established and known. The language of the legislation makes plain that the prohibited acts continue 'once and for all' and are not 'continuing' offences. Accordingly, putting up a building in ignorance of the fact that the land is a green is no offence, and it is not

---

[1]   Section 20.

[2]   Section 1.

[3]   See ss 2–7 and 9.

[4]   Section 10.

[5]   Section 15.

[6]   Such as the erection of an electric fence: *Rabett v Poole* (unreported county court decision).

[7]   *Oxfordshire County Council v Oxford City Council* [2006] 2 WLR 1235.

a criminal offence to refrain from removing it when the true facts are known.[1]

(e) Commons councils and schemes

The Commons Act 2006 contains provisions for the creation of commons councils. These bodies will have responsibility for the management of agricultural activities, vegetation and rights of common.[2] Whether they will be established in respect of greens that are not subject to rights of common remains to be seen. The functions of commons councils are more fully explained in Chapter 11.

9.6.4 Buildings and other works on town or village greens

Parish councils and others owning town or village greens may wish to carry out works, such as the provision of car parks and the erection of buildings, such as sports pavilions or public lavatories. A number of provisions prevent the erection of works, or make it a criminal offence to carry out certain activities on town or village greens, although much may depend on the precise legal status of the green in issue.[3] Where the green is subject to customary rights of sports and pastimes, and such activities have been acquired by 20 years' use, no works can be carried out that would interfere or obstruct the lawful exercise of those rights. The test is probably whether the rights can be exercised as conveniently as before.[4] The erection of a cricket pavilion on a small part of a very large village green is hardly likely to give rise to an actionable interference with the lawful rights of the inhabitants. Indeed, the very same inhabitants may have been pressing for just such a facility. But the construction of a car park on a relatively small green might well constitute an actionable interference.

In the case of greens that have been allotted under an inclosure award, a number of provisions make the carrying out of works on those greens a criminal offence.[5] The Commons Act 1876 prohibits any encroachment or inclosure on a green, although it does allow

---

[1] Ibid.

[2] Commons Act 2006, ss 26–31.

[3] Section 94 of the Law of Property Act 1925 requires ministerial consent to any fence or inclosure on a green that is common land.

[4] See *Gale on Easements* (17th edn), at chapter 13.

[5] The Inclosure Act 1848, s 10, the Inclosure Act 1857, s 12, and the Commons Act 1876, s 29.

works carried out with a view to its better enjoyment.[1] This would include the erection of a cricket pavilion.

Section 38 of the Commons Act 2006 will prohibit certain works on land to which the section applies. The works include fencing, the construction of buildings and the digging of trenches. Section 38 applies to registered common land, and certain other land that is not registered common land. This other land is land regulated under the Commons Act 1876 or subject to a scheme under the Metropolitan Commons Act 1866 or the Commons Act 1899. Such land may well be a town or village green as defined in that legislation, as discussed above in relation to this nineteenth century legislation, but not all town or village greens will therefore be protected by s 38.

9.6.5   Driving on greens

Driving vehicles over town and village greens can be a criminal offence. Under the Road Traffic Act 1988, s 34 it is an offence to drive a motor vehicle without lawful authority onto any common land or any other land of whatever description not being land forming part of a road. There is an exception where a person drives no more than 15 yards for the purposes of parking.

Some town or village greens may be subject to dedication for the purposes of the Law of Property Act 1925, s 193. Under that provision any person who, without lawful authority, drives on such land commits a criminal offence.[2]

Because it is unlawful to drive on a village green, a right of way cannot be acquired by prescription, as the user would have been in breach of the law.[3]

---

[1]   Section 29. See *Rabett v Poole* (unreported county court decision).

[2]   Section 193(4).

[3]   See Chapter 6.

Chapter 10

PUBLIC ACCESS TO COMMONS

10.1   INTRODUCTION

Prior to the widespread inclosure of common land, up to the nineteenth century, the common land to a village was proportionately larger in extent than today (if indeed any remains) and socially and economically more important. For the reasons explained in Chapter 2, common land played an important role in the rural economy. To local people, almost entirely employed in agriculture, or activities related to agriculture, there simply was no notion of public rights of access onto the common separate from the rights and incidents of rights of common. With the massive urbanisation of the nineteenth century, and the disengagement of many people from agricultural activities, many commons came to be seen to have separate or additional recreational purposes. Separate from the exercise of rights of common, the use of common land for general recreational purposes must be authorised by the law in some manner. Common land is, after all, land owned by the owner of the soil and, so far as that person is concerned, is subject only to the rights of common.

Outside the exercise of rights of common, the law authorises recreational use, which would otherwise be a trespass on common land, by the recognition of customary or other common law rights or by statute. The most significant statutory rights of access are now found in the Countryside and Rights of Way (CROW) Act 2000.

In practice, the public may have rights of access over common land (or, for that matter, town and village greens) along public highways. Public highways include public footpaths and bridleways.

10.2   COMMON LAW RIGHTS OF ACCESS TO COMMONS

The common law has come to recognise two principal recreational rights over land. Neither category is unique to common land. Common law rights of access for recreational use may arise over private land that is not common land, and customary rights are frequently found in relation to town and village greens, which may not necessarily have been subject to rights of common.

10.2.1 Easement of recreation

In *Re Ellenborough Park*,[1] it was held that the owner of land could have, for the benefit of that land, an easement over land adjoining or nearby that permitted the owner full enjoyment of a pleasure ground. A similar right was held to be an easement in the earlier case of *Duncan v Louch*,[2] and a right of common use of a garden was an easement in *Mulvaney v Gough*.[3]

The rights in *Re Ellenborough Park* were expressly granted in conveyances of a number of properties surrounding the pleasure ground in question. However, any right that lies in grant is also capable of being acquired by implied grant, such as where there has been a use of land, without force, without secrecy, and without permission.[4] Whilst it may be theoretically possible for an individual landowner to seek to claim an implied easement in this way, it is far more likely that where common land has been used for recreational purposes by one person in the locality, it will have been enjoyed by many others. In such circumstances the particular owner may not necessarily be asserting an implied easement for the direct benefit of his property, but he may be asserting as a member of a class, the public, rights of a customary nature, considered below.

10.2.2 Customary rights

From time to time the courts have upheld customary rights. In *New Windsor Corporation v Mellor*[5] Lord Denning MR explained the background to customary rights:

> 'Today we look back far in time. To a town or village green. The turf is old. Animals have grazed there for hundreds of years. Nowadays they are pleasant stretches of grass where people sit and talk. Sometimes they play cricket or kick a ball about. But in mediaeval times it was a

---

[1]   [1956] 1 Ch 131.

[2]   (1845) 6 QB 904.

[3]   [2002] 3 EGLR 72.

[4]   *Gale on Easements* (17th edn, 2002), at paras 4–73 to 4–86.

[5]   [1975] 1 Ch 380.

place where young men mustered with their bows and arrows. They shot at the butts. There might be stocks there where offenders were put for their petty misdemeanours. In the month of May they set up a maypole and danced around it. We have no record of when it all began.'

He then continued:[1]

'The villagers have an undoubted right to play games on their green. But whence comes their right? Not in deeds or in statutes. Only in custom from time immemorial. Rarely has it ever been challenged, ... To be good, of course, a custom must be reasonable. ... The result is that, in many village greens, no one knows who is the owner of the land. But everyone knows that the villagers have a right to play games on it. If anyone should disturb or hinder the exercise of that right, any one of the inhabitants can sue to enforce the right of all, stating that he does so on behalf of himself and all others. ... He can stop any fences being erected, or any holes being dug, or pipes laid, if they would interfere unreasonably with the exercise by the villagers of their right. And such a right, once acquired by custom, cannot be lost by disuse or abandonment. It can only be abolished or extinguished by Act of Parliament. ... in my opinion, [the land in question] is subject to a customary right in the inhabitants to indulge in lawful sports and pastimes on that land.'

Customary rights must be exercisable only by members of some identifiable local community.[2] The rights must be exercisable as of right in relation to a particular locality.[3]

Customary rights must be ancient, certain, reasonable and continuous.[4] A custom is said to be 'ancient' if it commenced prior to 1189 – the beginning of legal memory. However, in practice proof of long user will be sufficient, unless there is evidence that the custom commenced after 1189.[5] A customary right can still be established

---

[1]   Ibid, at p 386F.

[2]   *R v Oxfordshire County Council, ex parte Sunningwell Parish Council* [2000] AC 335.

[3]   *R v Suffolk County Council, ex parte Steed* (1995) 70 P&CR 487. However, in *Ministry of Defence v Wiltshire County Council* [1995] 4 All ER 931, the residents of three streets were held not to constitute a locality. See also *R (Laing Homes Ltd) v Buckinghamshire County Council* [2003] EWHC 1978 (Admin), [2003] 3 PLR 60.

[4]   *Lockwood v Wood* (1844) 6 QB 64.

[5]   *Simpson v Wells* (1872) LR 7 QB 214.

even where the nature of the custom changes. The playing of cricket, for example, may replace the playing of some earlier types of games.

Although customary rights may well arise in relation to a common properly so called, they are more likely to be found in respect of town and village greens, where this topic is more fully explored.[1]

10.3   COUNTRYSIDE AND RIGHTS OF WAY ACT 2000

The CROW Act 2000 provides the public with a new right of access on foot only to registered common land, as well as other open uncultivated land such as mountain, moor, heath and down. All such land is known as 'Access Land'.[2] Save in the case of registered common land, other areas of Access Land had first to be identified by a mapping exercise that was carried out by the Countryside Agency. The CROW Act 2000 contains provisions for the exclusion or restriction of public access onto Access Land.

The Countryside Agency amalgamated with English Nature, the body concerned with nature conservation, to form Natural England as from October 2006.

The new right of access came into force on 31 October 2005 in relation to all land shown as Access Land on maps in conclusive form before that date.

10.3.1 Rights of access

Section 2(1) of the CROW Act 2000 contains the general right of the public to enter and remain on any 'Access Land' for the purposes of open air recreation on foot only. Such rights of access may only be exercised where 'Access Land' has been included on a conclusive map prepared by the Countryside Agency (now Natural England) (or the Countryside Council for Wales). Section 1 of the Act defines Access Land as meaning any land which:

(a)   is shown as open country on a map in conclusive form issued by the appropriate countryside body;
(b)   is shown on such a map as registered common land;

---

[1]   See Chapter 9.

[2]   Occupiers Liability Act 1957 will not apply to persons exercising a right of access. In any event, any duty of care excludes certain risks: see s 13(1)–(2).

(c) is registered common land in any area outside Inner London for which no such map relating to registered common land has been issued;

(d) is situated more than 600 metres above sea level in any area for which no such map relating to open country has been issued; or

(e) is dedicated to the purposes of access under s 16 of the Act.

However, Access Land does not include 'excepted land' or land which is treated by s 15(1) of the Act as being accessible to the public apart from the CROW Act 2000.[1] 'Excepted land' is explained below. Land that is treated as being accessible under s 15(1) includes land that at any time:

(a) is subject to access rights under s 193 of the Law of Property Act 1925: see below;

(b) is subject to a local or private Act or a scheme made under Part I of the Commons Act 1899 giving rights of access for open-air recreation. By reason of s 15(2) of the CROW Act 2000 such rights are exercisable by the public at large;

(c) is subject to an access agreement or order under the National Parks and Access to the Countryside Act 1949;

(d) that the public have access to it under s 17 of the Ancient Monuments and Archaeological Areas Act 1979.

'The appropriate countryside body' means, in relation to England, the Countryside Agency, or since October 2006, Natural England, and, in relation to Wales, the Countryside Council for Wales.

The following definitions are important. 'Open country' is land which appears to the appropriate countryside body as consisting wholly or predominantly of mountain, moor, heath or down, and is not registered common land.[2] 'Registered common land' means:

(a) land which is registered as common land under the Commons Registration Act 1965, and whose registration under that Act has become final, and when Part 1 of the Commons Act 2006 is fully in force, land in a register of common land kept under the 2006 Act.

---

[1] Section 1(1).

[2] Section 1(2).

Until Part 1 of the Commons Act 2006 is in force, the following is also within the meaning of registered common land:

(b) subject to an exception considered below, land which was registered as common land under the 1965 Act on 30 November 2000 – the date when the CROW Act 2000 was enacted – or on any date after that day, but has subsequently ceased to be registered as common land under the 1965 Act.

Accordingly, the general rule is that where common land was on 30 November 2000, or some subsequent date, registered under the 1965 Act, but is then removed, it remains 'registered common land' for the purposes of the public rights of access under the CROW Act 2000. The exceptions to the general rule are as follows. Land that is omitted from the register of common land under the 1965 Act following an application to amend the register of common land made before 30 November 2000, and land that ceases to be common land by reason of powers of compulsory purchase or the provision of substitute common land under the 1965 Act.[1]

When Part 1 of the 2006 Act is fully in force, the additional category of land deemed to be registered at (b) will no longer apply. Thus, if land ceases to be registered common land, the access rights will also cease.

10.3.2 Exceptions

Schedule 1 to the CROW Act 2000 sets out a list of 'excepted land'; such land cannot be Access Land to which the public will have rights of access. The excepted land includes the following:

(1) land on which the soil is being, or has at any time within the previous 12 months been, disturbed by any ploughing or drilling undertaken for the purposes of planting or sowing crops or trees;
(2) land covered by buildings or the curtilage of such land;
(3) land within 20 metres of a dwelling;
(4) land used as a park or garden;
(5) land used for the getting of minerals by surface working (including quarrying);
(6) land used for the purposes of a railway or tramway;

---

[1]   Section 1(3) and (4).

(7) land used for the purposes of a golf course, racecourse or aerodrome;

(8) land which does not fall within any of the categories above, but which is covered by works used for the purposes of a statutory undertaking or for telecommunications apparatus, or the curtilage of any such land;

(9) land where development is being carried out such that it will fall within any of the categories set out above;

(10) land within 20 metres of a building which is used for housing livestock, not being a temporary or moveable structure;

(11) land covered by pens in use for the temporary reception or detention of livestock;

(12) land habitually used for the training of racehorses; and

(13) land the use of which is regulated under the Military Lands Acts.

Whilst the exceptions set out above may make some sense in relation to Access Land other than registered common land, it is not easy to see how the exceptions will work in practice in relation to registered common land itself. There must be many cases of dwellings or buildings used for housing livestock that are located within 20 metres of the boundaries of existing common land. As explained above, Access Land is required to be mapped[1] and, strictly, any area of registered common land to which one or more of the exceptions set out above apply, must not be excluded from the draft, provisional and conclusive maps. Although no marked or physical boundary will appear on the ground, the public will be trespassing if they pass into the 20-metre boundary around dwellings and livestock buildings and it is unclear how that could ever be adequately 'policed'.[2]

10.3.3 Restrictions

The Act contains certain provisions for the exclusion or restriction of the public right of access.[3] The owner (or any tenant) of Access Land may give notice to the appropriate countryside body in accordance with regulations excluding or restricting access to any land on one or

---

[1] Strictly, it is all registered common land and all open country that must be mapped. The maps may therefore include areas that will not be Access Land because one or more of the exceptions will apply.

[2] But see s 20 for duty of Countryside Agency to inform the public of the extent of Access Land.

[3] See Chapter 11.

more days specified in the notice.[1] The number of days on which access is excluded or restricted is limited to 28 in each calendar year.[2] Access may not be excluded or restricted on Christmas Day, Good Friday or any Bank Holiday or on more than 4 days in any calendar year which are either Saturday or Sunday, on any Saturday between 1 June and 11 August, in any year, or on any Sunday between 1 June and 30 September in any year.[3]

It is likely that the purpose of this provision allowing exclusion or restriction of access on a certain number of days in each calendar year is to enable shooting to take place. As that is unlikely over registered common land, this particular exclusion may have little importance in relation to such land.

Section 23 contains provisions allowing the restriction on dogs onto Access Land.[4] During specified periods, the right of access onto land consisting of moor managed for the breeding and shooting of grouse may not be exercised with dogs. Similarly, the owner of land used in connection with lambing may take steps such that the right of access may only be exercised by persons who do not take dogs into any field or inclosure on land in which there are sheep. As any field or inclosure is unlikely to include registered common land, this exclusion will not be relevant where common land is used for the pasturing of sheep.

Public rights of access may also be excluded or restricted where the appropriate countryside body allows an application by the owner for the purposes of land management.[5] The public rights of access may also be excluded or restricted for the purpose of avoiding risk of fire or danger to the public.[6] Public rights of access may also be excluded or restricted on certain grounds of nature conservation and heritage

---

[1]   Access to the Countryside (Exclusions and Restrictions) (England) Regulations 2003, SI 2003/2713 and Access to the Countryside (Exclusions and Restrictions) (Wales) Regulations 2003, SI 2003/142.

[2]   Ibid. For the manner and form of notice, see reg 4.

[3]   Section 22.

[4]   Access to the Countryside (Exclusions and Restrictions) (England) Regulations 2003, SI 2003/2713, reg 5 and Access to the Countryside (Exclusions and Restrictions) (Wales) Regulations 2003, SI 2003/142.

[5]   Section 24.

[6]   Section 25.

preservation.[1] Regulations provide for the giving of notices, the making of directions and for appeals.[2]

10.3.4 Additional land open to access

Certain other land, which cannot be Access Land, is treated as being accessible to the public apart from the CROW Act 2000. Such land includes land:

(a) that is common land to which the Law of Property Act 1925, s 193 applies (see below);
(b) that is subject to public rights of access to land within the meaning of Part I of the Commons Act 1899;
(c) that is subject to an access agreement or access order under Part V of the National Parks and Access to the Countryside Act 1949; or
(d) that is subject to public rights of access under the Ancient Monuments and Archaeological Areas Act 1979, s 19.

10.3.5 By-laws

The CROW Act 2000 contains provisions for the making of by-laws regulating public rights of access,[3] for the appointment of wardens,[4] and for the erection and maintenance of notices indicating the boundaries of Access Land and any exclusions or restrictions.[5]

10.3.6 Mapping of open country

By s 4 of the CROW Act 2000, it was the duty of the Countryside Agency (now Natural England) to prepare maps showing all open country, and all registered common land. In respect of Wales, the same duty fell on the Countryside Council for Wales. A map prepared under this section must distinguish between open country and registered common land, but need not distinguish between different categories of open country.[6] The appropriate countryside body could have decided not to show areas of open country which

---

[1] Section 26.

[2] Access to the Countryside (Exclusions and Restrictions) (England) Regulations 2003, SI 2003/2713, Access to the Countryside (Exclusions and Restrictions) (Wales) Regulations 2003, SI 2003/142.

[3] Section 17.

[4] Section 18.

[5] Section 19.

[6] Section 4(4).

were so small that their inclusion would serve no useful purpose and could determine that any boundary of an area of open country was to be treated as coinciding with a particular physical feature. In other words, where commonsense suggests that natural features would provide a natural boundary, that decision was made.[1]

By s 5 of the Act, the appropriate countryside body was required to:

(a) issue in draft form any map prepared by them under s 4;
(b) consider representations received by them within a prescribed period with respect to the showing of, or the failure to show, any area of land on the map as registered common land or as open country;
(c) confirm the map with or without modifications;
(d) if the map was confirmed without modifications, issue it in provisional form; and
(e) if the map was confirmed with modifications, prepare a map incorporating the modifications, and issue that map in provisional form.[2]

10.3.7 Representations against maps

Regulation 5 of the Access to the Countryside (Maps in Draft Form) (England) Regulations 2001[3] provided that where the appropriate countryside body issued a map in draft form, it then had to publish a notice that (amongst other things):

(a) invited representations with respect of the showing of, or the failure to show, any area of land on the map in draft form as registered common land or open country;
(b) stated that representations on the map in draft form must be made so as to be received by the Agency within a period of 3 months beginning with the date of issue;
(c) stated the manner in which representations must be made to the appropriate countryside body including the effect of reg 12(2) and (3); and
(d) stated the general effect of the right conferred on the public by s 2(1).

---

[1] Section 4(5).

[2] Access to the Countryside (Correction of Provisional and Conclusive Maps) (England) Regulations 2003, SI 2003/1591 provide for the correction of provisional and conclusive maps.

[3] SI 2001/3301.

Regulation 12(1) provided that where the appropriate countryside body issued a map in draft form, it should consider:

'... any representations, with respect to the showing of, or the failure to show, any area of land on the map as registered common land or as open country, received by them within a period of three months beginning with the date of issue.'

That duty was limited to, in effect, a consideration of discrepancies between the map of registered common land under the Commons Registration Act 1965, and the draft map prepared by the appropriate countryside body under the CROW Act 2000. Regulation 12(2) made provision for the information that must be contained in any representation, so as to identify the representor, the location and extent of the land to which the representation relates, and the interest in the land that the representor had.

The scope of the representations that could have been made by or on behalf of, for example, land-owners, in relation to the maps in draft form, was extremely limited. In the case of common land, the representation right was limited to making representations that the map in draft form included land that was *not* registered common land. That required a very careful comparison of the relevant maps. If there was a discrepancy, then a landowner could have advanced a representation. There was no general right to object to the inclusion of registered common land on the maps that were prepared. The mapping process brought to the attention of many landowners that their land was registered common land for probably the first time; although there was nothing that they could have done at the time, there are provisions in the Commons Act 2006 to have land removed from the register of common land that should not have been registered in the first place.[1]

10.3.8 Consultations

Regulation 4 of the Regulations made provision for consultation of the maps in draft form. The persons who were to be consulted include only those listed in the Schedule to the Regulations. These included the Countryside Council for Wales and the Historic Buildings and Monuments Commission for England. In any event, the consultation requirement was limited to an invitation to make

---

[1] Commons Act 2006, Sch 2.

representations in respect to the showing of, or the failure to show, any area of land on the map in draft form as registered common land (or as open country).

10.3.9 Confirmation of maps

After the appropriate countryside body considered any representations received by it with respect of the showing of, or the failure to show, any area of land on the map as registered common land, its duty under s 5 of the CROW Act 2000 was to confirm the map with or without modifications. If the map was confirmed without modifications, the appropriate countryside body issued it in provisional form, and where the map was confirmed with modifications, it prepared a map incorporating the modifications, and issued that map in provisional form.[1]

10.3.10 Appeals

By s 6 of the Act, any person having an interest in any land was entitled to appeal against the showing of that land on a map in provisional form as registered common land or as open country. In the case of land in England, the appeal was to the Secretary of State and in Wales, it was to the National Assembly for Wales.[2] An appeal relating to the showing of any land as registered common land could be brought only on the ground that the land was not registered common land.[3] Accordingly, the right of appeal in relation to common land was limited to the case where land is shown on a map in provisional form as registered common land, where it should not be so included, as it is not common land registered under the Commons Registration Act 1965. In relation to any land that was shown as open country, an appeal may only be brought on the ground that the land did not consist wholly or predominantly of mountain, moor, heath or down, or the discretion to use as the boundary of the area of open country some particular physical feature has not been exercised properly.[4]

---

[1] Section 5. There are powers of correction in Access to the Countryside (Correction of Provisional and Conclusive Maps) (England) Regulations 2003, SI 2003/1591.

[2] Section 6(1).

[3] Section 6(2).

[4] Section 6(3).

Under s 7 of the Act, the Secretary of State (or the National Assembly for Wales) was entitled to hold either a hearing or a public local inquiry.[1] The Secretary of State appointed an inspector to hold the hearing or public local inquiry and to prepare a report containing conclusions and recommendations. Following the hearing of the appeal, and the consideration of the inspector's report, the Secretary of State (or the National Assembly for Wales) was entitled to approve the whole or part of the map which was the subject of the appeal, with or without modifications, or require the appropriate countryside body to prepare a new map relating to all or part of the area covered by the map which was the subject of the appeal.[2] Under s 8 of the CROW Act 2000, the Secretary of State (or the National Assembly for Wales) may appoint any person to exercise on his or its behalf the function of determining any appeals or any matters involved in such appeals.

10.3.11   Maps in conclusive form

The appropriate countryside body was required to issue a map in conclusive form where no appeal has been brought under s 6 within the time-limit or, where an appeal was been brought, the appeal was determined by the map or part of it being approved without modifications, or the appeal was withdrawn. Where an appeal was determined by the map or part of it being approved with modifications, the appropriate countryside body then prepared a map in conclusive form incorporating the modifications.[3]

Under s 10, maps in conclusive form must be reviewed from time to time. The first review should be undertaken not more than 10 years after the issue of the map in conclusive form, and subsequent reviews at not more than 10-year intervals.

10.4   SECTION 193 OF LAW OF PROPERTY ACT 1925

Section 193(1) of the Law of Property Act 1925 provides for public access over common lands in the following circumstances:

---

[1]   Section 7.

[2]   Section 6(4).

[3]   Section 9.

'Members of the public shall, subject as hereinafter provided, have rights of access for air and exercise to any land which is a metropolitan common within the meaning of the Metropolitan Commons Acts 1866 to 1898, or manorial waste, or a common, which is wholly or partly situated within an area which immediately before 1 April 1974 was a borough or urban district, and to any land which at the commencement of this Act is subject to rights of common and to which this section may from time to time be applied in manner hereinafter provided.'

That subsection makes provision for access to specified categories of commons and other land in the circumstances explained below.

10.4.1 Definition of a common under s 193

The terms 'manorial waste, or a common' are not expressly defined for the purposes of s 193. 'Manorial waste' probably has the same meaning as the waste land of a manor. In *Attorney-General v Hanmer*[1] it was said that:

'The true meaning of "wastes", or "waste lands", or "waste grounds of the manor", is the open, uncultivated and unoccupied lands parcel of the manor, or open lands parcel of the manor other than the demesne lands of the manor.'

In *Hampshire County Council v Millburn*[2] Lord Templeman accepted that, for the purposes of the Commons Registration Act 1965, s 22(1) meant:

'...."waste land of a manor" means "waste land now or formerly of a manor" or "waste land of manorial origin".'

It therefore may not matter that a particular area of manorial waste is no longer actually held with, and is part of, a manor.

The word 'common' was probably meant to have a wide general meaning. Section 193(1) itself separately distinguishes land 'subject to rights of common' in connection with the dedication of rural commons. That supposes that land might be a common without necessarily being land subject to rights of common. Somewhat confusingly, s 193(1)(d) provides that rights of access under the

---

[1]   (1858) 27 LJ Ch 837 at 840.

[2]   [1990] 2 All ER 257 at 262j.

section shall cease to apply to any land over which the commonable rights are extinguished under any statutory provision. That poses the question as to whether the two expressions, within the same subsection, of 'rights of common' and 'commonable rights' were intended to have the same or different meanings. It is unlikely that those expressions were intended to have different meanings. The expression 'commonable rights' was probably used merely as a more convenient linguistic description of the land to which rights of access would cease where commonable rights were extinguished.

10.4.2 Metropolitan commons

The Metropolitan Commons Act 1866 defined the term 'common' as meaning land subject at the time of the passing of the Act to any right of common, and any land subject to be included under the provisions of the Inclosure Act 1845.[1] Land subject to be included under the provisions of the Inclosure Act 1845 is widely defined as all lands subject to any rights of common whatsoever, and whether such rights may be exercised or enjoyed at all times, or may be exercised or enjoyed only during times, seasons or periods.[2] The 1866 Act applies to any commons, as so defined, the whole or any part of which is situated within the Metropolitan Police District as defined at the date of the passing of the Act.[3] However, under the deregistration provisions of the Commons Act 2006, where land is released and deregistered it will cease to be subject to a scheme under the 1866 Act, although any replacement land may be made subjected to the scheme.[4]

10.4.3 Borough or urban commons

Prior to 1 April 1974, local government in England and Wales consisted of the first tier county councils and the second tier of urban and rural district councils. Additionally, there were separate unitary authorities known as county borough councils. Accordingly, the public have had rights of access for air and exercise since 1 January 1926 over any common or manorial waste that fell within the boundaries of a pre-April 1974 borough or urban district council. This

---

[1] Section 3 as amended by Metropolitan Commons Act 1869, s 2.

[2] Section 11 continues with a very full description of such lands.

[3] Section 4. The extent of the Metropolitan Police District was defined by Metropolitan Police Act 1829, ss 4 and 34 and Metropolitan Police Act 1839, s 2.

[4] Commons Act 2006, s 17(6)–(8).

was never very logical as some commons in rural areas actually fell within urban district council boundaries, and conversely some commons or manorial wastes in urban and built up areas fell outside those boundaries and were within the areas of rural district councils.

10.4.4 Rural common subject to dedication

Section 193(1) of the Law of Property Act 1925 did not automatically create rights of air and exercise in favour of the public over rural commons, that is those commons lying outside the boundaries of pre-April 1974 borough and urban district council areas. By s 193(2):

> 'The lord of the manor or other person entitled to the soil of any land subject to rights of common may by deed, revocable or irrevocable, declare that this section shall apply to the land, and upon such deed being deposited with the Minister the land shall, so long as the deed remains operative, be land to which this section applies.'

Since 1926, the owners of a large number of commons have executed deeds of dedication under s 193. However, a large number of commons remain without the benefit of such dedication and, accordingly, in the absence of any other statutory provisions, are not subject to general public rights of access. The CROW Act 2000 contains provisions for the repeal of s 193(2); presumably the justification for this is that a s 193(2) dedication will no longer be necessary with public rights of access over all registered common land, and because the CROW Act 2000 allows a landowner to make a voluntary dedication of land as open to public access.[1]

The provision for the dedication applies only to land 'subject to rights of common'. Accordingly, even if land can fall within the definition of a 'common', if it is not subject to rights of common, s 193 cannot be applied to it by dedication.

10.4.5 Extent of rights of public access

Where s 193 applies to a manorial waste or a common, the public has access for 'air and exercise'. The right does include the right to ride

---

[1] Section 16.

horses over such common land, as riding would have been a normal way of taking air and exercise in 1925.[1]

Section 193(4) contains limitations on what may be done on a common to which the section applies:

> 'Any person who, without lawful authority, draws or drives upon any land to which this section applies any carriage, cart, caravan, truck, or other vehicle, or camps or lights any fire thereon, or who fails to observe any limitation or condition imposed by the Minister under this section in respect of any such land, shall be liable [of a criminal offence].'

The Minister can make an order, known as an order of limitation, on the application of any person entitled to the soil of the land, or entitled to any commonable rights affecting the land. An order of limitation may impose such limitations and conditions as to the exercise of the rights of access or as to the extent of the land to be affected as, in the opinion of the Minister, are necessary or desirable for preventing injury to the land or any interest in the land, for conserving flora, fauna, or geological or physiographical features of the land, or for protecting objects of historical interest.[2] An order of limitation will be published in the form of permanent notices on or near the affected land.

10.4.6   Effect of subsequent legislation

Under the Commons Registration Act 1965,[3] land over which rights of common were exercised was required to be registered. The 1965 Act also provided that s 1(2) shall not affect the application to any land registered under the 1965 Act of s 193 of the Law of Property Act 1925.[4] Section 1(2) provided that where there was a failure to register rights of common, they shall cease to be exercisable. The purpose of that saving provision was probably included to ensure that if rights of common were not exercised, and that non-exercisability was deemed to be equivalent to extinguishment, the rights of access under

---

1   *R v Secretary of State for the Environment, Transport and the Regions, ex parte Billson* [1998] 2 All ER 587, contrary to Gadsden *The Law of Commons* (1988), at chapter 11.

2   Section 193(1)(b).

3   Section 1(2)(b).

4   Section 21(1).

s 193 would continue.[1] However, under the deregistration provisions of the Commons Act 2006, where land is released and deregistered it will cease to be subject to s 193, although any replacement land may be made subjected to s 193.[2]

10.5   ADDITIONAL STATUTORY RIGHTS OF ACCESS

10.5.1   Commons Act 1876

This Act contains provisions for the regulation and inclosure of commons other than metropolitan commons within the meaning of the Metropolitan Commons Acts 1866 and 1869.[3] A provisional order, which requires confirmation as an Act of Parliament, may make provision for the benefit of the neighbourhood and, in particular, may provide for free access to be secured to any particular points of view, and that there be reserved, where a recreation ground is not set out, a privilege of playing games or of enjoying other forms of recreation at such times and in such manner and on such parts of the common as may be thought suitable.[4] Bylaws may be made for regulating public access. However, under the deregistration provisions of the Commons Act 2006, where land is released and deregistered it will cease to be subject to a scheme under the 1876 Act, although any replacement land may be made subjected to the scheme.[5]

10.5.2   Commons Act 1899

This Act contains provisions for the regulation of any common within the area of a district council. The scheme of regulation may contain any of the provisions for the benefit of the neighbourhood which are mentioned in the Commons Act 1876, s 7.[6] The Commons (Schemes) Regulations 1982[7] and the Commons (Schemes) (Welsh Forms)

---

[1]   See *Central Electricity Generating Board v Clwyd County Council* [1976] 1 WLR 151.

[2]   Commons Act 2006, s 17(6)–(8).

[3]   A 'metropolitan common' is defined by Metropolitan Commons Act 1866, s 4 as any common the whole or any part of which is situated within the Metropolitan Police District as defined at the passing of that Act.

[4]   Section 7.

[5]   Commons Act 2006, s 17(6)–(8).

[6]   Section 1.

[7]   SI 1982/209.

Regulations 1982[1] make provision for a model form of scheme. Paragraph 4 of the model scheme provides that:

> 'The inhabitants of the neighbourhood shall have a right of free access to every part of the common and a privilege of playing games and of enjoying other kinds of recreation thereon, subject to any bylaws made by the Council under this Scheme.'

The scheme also includes provisions for the making of by-laws regulating the use of, and activities on, a regulated common. However, under the deregistration provisions of the Commons Act 2006, where land is released and deregistered it will cease to be subject to a scheme under the 1899 Act, although any replacement land may be made subjected to the scheme.[2]

10.5.3 National Parks and Access to the Countryside Act 1949

This Act makes provision for the making of access orders or access agreements under which the public has access for open air recreation to 'open country', being any area that consists wholly or predominantly of mountain, moor, heath, down, cliff or foreshore.[3] Schedule 2 to the Act sets out a number of general restrictions that must be observed by persons exercising the right of access. The effect of the interrelationship between the statutory right of access and the general restrictions is that any person who fails to comply with the restrictions when on land the subject of an access order or agreement is treated as a trespasser. Unlike a deed of dedication under the Law of Property Act 1925, s 193, where criminal sanctions are imposed on those breaching the prohibited acts, there are no criminal sanctions affecting visitors to land within access orders or access areas. In the past, the attraction to a landowner in entering into an access agreement, rather than a deed of dedication, is that compensation and/or grants have been available.

---

[1]   SI 1982/667.

[2]   Commons Act 2006, s 17(6)–(8).

[3]   Sections 59–65.

10.6   LOCAL ACTS

Many commons are regulated by individual local Acts of Parliament. Although each Act must be carefully considered as to its terms, many make provision for public rights of access. Such Acts include the Epping Forest Act 1878, the Wimbledon and Putney Common Act 1871, the Dartmoor Commons Act 1985 and the Ashdown Forest Act 1974.

Chapter 11

REGULATION AND MANAGEMENT OF COMMON LANDS

11.1   INTRODUCTION

Common land was largely regulated and managed according to the customs of the manor. This took place through the manorial courts acting through the steward to the lord of the manor. However, the nineteenth century legislation on commons introduced powers of regulation and management concerning the exercise of rights of common and of public recreation and access where so provided. During the twentieth century legislation was concerned with the protection of the scientific and ecological aspects of common land. The Commons Registration Act 1965 made provision only for the registration of commons. The Commons Act 2006 contains powers to create commons councils that will have very broad functions to manage commons in the widest sense. A useful guide to the issues relating to the management of commons was published in 2005.[1]

11.2   MANAGEMENT BY THE OWNER OF THE SOIL

All common land is owned by someone. Where commons are owned by local authorities, these authorities may have active management policies. These are usually directed to the management of the common for public recreation in respect of those commons to which the public have rights of access. Local authorities will generally be able to use most of the powers referred to below.

In the case of commons owned by non-local authorities, where the owner also possesses the manorship, such persons will have all the powers of management incidental to the ownership of any legal estate in land, subject only to the rights of the commoners and the various statutory prohibitions against inclosure, fencing or the making of erections.

---

[1]   *A Common Purpose: Guide to agreeing Management on Common Land*: see Defra website.

In the case of commons in the upland areas where the use is primarily for grazing purposes by those holding rights of common, the owner of the common may himself utilise his own right to pasture his animals. He may, therefore, take a fairly active interest in the careful management of the common in the wider general interests of the commoners.[1]

In those cases where commons are owned by non-local authority owners and where commoners' rights are no longer actively exercised, the principal value of the common may lie in public access and recreation where that is authorised. Such owners may have little incentive in most cases to pursue active management policies for public recreation and access purposes. However, access agreements have been made under s 64 of the National Parks and Access to the Countryside Act 1949. The effect of such agreements is to permit access to the public to open land. The access agreement may make provision for payments by the local planning authority to the owner in consideration of the making of the agreement and by way of contributions towards expenditure.

11.3   REGULATION OF NON-METROPOLITAN COMMONS

A series of Acts between the Inclosure Act 1845 and the Commons Act 1899 make provision for the regulation of commons.[2] Although now repealed, s 113 of the Inclosure Act 1845 made provision for a regulated pasture. The procedure, and the powers of the Inclosure Commissioners, the Assistance Commissioner, and the valuer were the same in relation to the making of a provisional order, and an award as in the case of inclosure.[3] The basic steps – the making of a draft provisional order, its advertisement and submission to the Secretary of State for approval, and subsequent confirmation of the provisional order by Parliament – were therefore the same as in the case of inclosure orders.[4] Where an order provided for the regulation of a common, the order could include provision for the adjustment of rights. This included the determination of the persons entitled to rights of common, what those rights should be, and the rights and

---

[1]   See Chapter 5 on the incidence of the ownership of common land.

[2]   Inclosure Act 1845, Commons Act 1876, Commons (Expenses) Act 1878, Commons Act 1879, Commonable Rights Compensation Act 1882, and Commons Act 1899.

[3]   See Chapter 7.

[4]   Ibid.

liabilities of the owner.[1] However, the order could make provision for the improvement of the common. This might include the draining, manuring or levelling of the common, the planting of trees, the making of by-laws and regulations, the general management of the common, and the appointment from time to time of conservators.[2] Following the confirmation of the Act, an award would then be made of a regulated pasture. The effect of this was that:[3]

> 'All rights of common, and all rights whatever by the [regulation] intended to be extinguished, belonging to or claimed by any person whomsoever, in or upon such lands, shall cease, determine, and be forever extinguished.'

The ownership of a regulated pasture would be with the stint holders in proportion to the value of their respective stints.[4] The award normally gave powers of management and control to the stint holders.

The provisions related to regulated pastures are no longer in force. Strictly, a regulated pasture is not land subject to rights of common.[5] However, under the Commons Registration Act 1965, s 11 and the Commons Registration (Exempted Land) Regulations 1965, there was exempted from registration regulated pasture where no rights of common had been exercised over the land for at least 30 years. Nevertheless, some regulated pastures have been registered.

11.4   REGULATION OF METROPOLITAN COMMONS

Provision was made for the regulation of metropolitan commons under a number of Acts.[6] Under the Metropolitan Commons Acts, a 'common' was defined as meaning land that was on 10 August 1866 subject to any rights of common and land that could be the subject of inclosure under the Inclosure Act 1845.[7] A metropolitan common was

---

[1]   Commons Act 1876, s 4.

[2]   Commons Act 1876, s 5.

[3]   Inclosure Act 1845, ss 106 and 114.

[4]   Ibid, s 116.

[5]   Ibid.

[6]   Metropolitan Commons Act 1866, Metropolitan Commons Amendment Act 1869, Metropolitan Commons Act 1887, and Metropolitan Commons Act 1898.

[7]   Metropolitan Commons Act 1866, s 3.

any common, the whole or any part of which was situated within the Metropolitan Police District on 10 August 1866. Section 5 of the Metropolitan Commons Act 1866 prohibited inclosure of metropolitan commons, except for the purposes of widening a highway. The purposes of the Metropolitan Commons Acts were to create schemes for the establishment of local management, the carrying out of improvements, and the making of by-laws.[1] However under the deregistration provisions of the Commons Act 2006, where land is released and deregistered it will cease to be subject to a scheme under the 1866 Act, although any replacement land may be made subjected to the scheme.[2]

11.5 REGULATION OF COMMONS UNDER THE COMMONS ACT 1899

The Commons Act 1899 contained powers for urban district councils to make schemes for the regulation and management of any common within their district with a view to the expenditure of money on the drainage, levelling, and improvement of the common, and to the making of by-laws and regulations for the prevention of nuisances and the preservation of order on the common.[3] When a scheme is made, it must be advertised, and objections can then be made to it.[4] The council can approve the scheme unless objections of dissent are received from the owner or persons representing at least one-third in value of the ownership in the common.[5] A draft scheme is prescribed by regulations.[6] The scheme provides for the works that may be carried out to improve and manage the common, and also the rights of free access. Compensation is payable to any person with an interest in a common made the subject of a scheme.[7] There are powers to make by-laws.[8] However under the deregistration provisions of the Commons Act 2006, where land is released and deregistered it will

---

[1] Metropolitan Commons Act 1866, s 6. None of the provisions of Commons Act 1876 were applicable to any metropolitan common: s 35.

[2] Commons Act 2006, s 17(6)–(8).

[3] Section 1.

[4] Section 2.

[5] Ibid.

[6] Commons (Schemes) Regulations 1982, SI 1982/209.

[7] Section 6.

[8] Section 10.

cease to be subject to a scheme under the 1899 Act, although any replacement land may be made subjected to the scheme.[1]

11.5.1 Commons Act 1908

This Act regulates the turning out onto commons of entire animals (uncastrated males). The Act contains powers by which the persons entitled to turn animals onto a common may resolve at a meeting by a majority in value of their interest to make regulations. These may determine the times and the conditions under which entire animals of any class or description or age specified in the regulation may be put on the common.[2] The Act provides that regulations require the confirmation of the Secretary of State.[3]

11.6 LOCAL REGULATION OF COMMONS

A number of commons are subject to specific Acts for their regulation. These include the New Forest,[4] Epping Forest,[5] Ashdown Forest[6] and Dartmoor.[7] The local Acts generally provide for the regulation and management of the respective commons, and for public access subject to by-laws.

11.7 MANAGEMENT OF COMMONS UNDER THE COMMONS ACT 2006

When Part 2 of the Commons Act 2006 is in force, the appropriate national authority (either the Secretary of State, in relation to England, or the National Assembly for Wales) will have wide powers to establish commons councils. An order establishing a commons council for a common will confer a wide range of functions relating to the management of common land.

---

[1] Commons Act 2006, s 17(6)–(8).

[2] Section 1.

[3] Ibid.

[4] New Forest Acts 1877 to 1970.

[5] Epping Forest Acts 1878 and 1880.

[6] Ashdown Forest Act 1974.

[7] Dartmoor Commons Act 1985.

11.7.1 Establishment of commons councils

Where land is registered as common land, or is registered as a town or village green and is subject to rights of common, the appropriate national authority may, for any area or areas of such land establish by an order a commons council.[1] The procedure for establishing a commons council requires the appropriate national authority to publish a draft of the proposed order and to invite representations about it. The order will name the commons council and specify the area or areas of land for which the council is to be established. On receipt of representations, the appropriate national authority may cause a local inquiry to be held. They may not make an order unless satisfied that there is substantial support for the making of the order. The appropriate national authority must have particular regard to any representations received from persons having rights in relation to or occupying the land, persons who are entitled to exercise rights of common over such land, and persons with functions under an enactment which relates to the maintenance or management of any such land.[2] Regulations will be made prescribing the constitution and administration of commons councils; it is intended that in most cases a standard constitution will apply to all councils.[3] The constitution will include terms relating to the membership of the council, the participation in the council by other persons, the proceedings of the council, and the keeping and publication of accounts, reports and other information. Further terms will deal with the membership of councils and the frequency and procedure for meetings.[4]

11.7.2 Functions of commons councils

An order establishing a commons council will confer on the council functions relating to any one or more of the following –

(a) the management of agricultural activities on the land for which the council is established;

(b) the management of vegetation on the land;

(c) the management of rights of common on the land.[5]

---

[1]   Commons Act 2006, s 26.

[2]   Commons Act 2006, s 27.

[3]   Commons Act 2006, s 29.

[4]   Commons Act 2006, s 30.

[5]   Commons Act 2006, s 31.

The functions which may be conferred on a commons council will include, in particular, functions of –

(a) making rules relating to agricultural activities, the management of vegetation and the exercise of rights of common on the land for which the council is established;
(b) making rules relating to the leasing or licensing of rights of common;
(c) preparing and maintaining a register of grazing;
(d) establishing and maintaining boundaries;
(e) removing unlawful boundaries and other encroachments;
(f) removing animals unlawfully permitted to graze.[1]

In relation to the rule-making functions of a commons council, these rules may have the effect of limiting or imposing conditions on the exercise of rights of common over, or in the exercise of rights to use the surplus of, the land for which the council is established, and requiring the provision of information to the commons council in relation to the exercise of those rights.[2]

Where a council exercises the function of removing animals unlawfully permitted to graze, it may dispose of any animal it removes, and recover from the owner of the animal the costs that it may reasonably incur in removing and disposing of it.[3] A commons council must discharge its functions having regard to any guidance given by the appropriate national authority and the public interest in relation to the land for which it is established. The public interest includes interest in nature conservation, the conservation of the landscape, the protection of public rights of access to any area of land, and the protection of archaeological remains and features of historic interest.[4]

In connection with the exercise of its functions, a commons council will have ancillary powers to do anything which it considers will facilitate, or will be conducive or incidental to, the carrying out of its functions. This will include powers to enter into agreements, prepare and adopt management plans, raise money, acquire or dispose of

---

[1] Commons Act 2006, s 31(3).
[2] Commons Act 2006, s 31(4).
[3] Commons Act 2006, s 31(5).
[4] Commons Act 2006, s 31(6)–(7).

land, and employ staff.[1] There is a specific power of a commons
council to raise money that includes the power to require the
payment of fees in connection with the exercise of rights of common
over, or the exercise of rights to use the surface of, the land for which
the council is established, and participation in the council.[2]

11.7.3   The requirement for consents

Although the powers conferred on a commons council by the
Commons Act 2006 may not be exercised without the consent of a
person with an interest in the affected land, where that person's
consent would otherwise be required, lack of such consent will not
always matter. A commons council does not need the consent of a
person who has a right of common over the land for which it is
established in order to do anything on the land.[3] A commons council
does not need the consent of any other person with an interest in the
land for which it is established in order to do anything on the land
where what is proposed to be done could be done without that
person's consent by any person who has a right of common over the
land.[4] In other words a commons council does not need the consent of
the owner of the common if what it proposes to do could be done by
a commoner without the owner's consent. There are two possible
examples of this where a commoner can do things on the common
without the consent of the owner. First, he has a right of self-help
abatement where, for example, a fence or other obstruction has been
wrongly erected on the common preventing access for his animals.[5]
Second, the grazing of animals in the exercise of the right of common
of pasture. Within the scope of his right, a commoner does not need
the consent of an owner to exercise such a right. It would follow that
a commons council could exercise a commoner's rights to take
pasture without either the commoner's consent or that of the owner.

Where a commons council wishes to obtain the consent of any person
with an interest in the land, for which the council is established, in
respect of anything it proposes to do on the land, it may serve a
notice on that person. That notice must specify what the council
proposes to do, the time within which the person on whom it is

---

[1]   Commons Act 2006, s 32(1)–(2).

[2]   Commons Act 2006, s 32(3).

[3]   Commons Act 2006, s 33(2).

[4]   Commons Act 2006, s 33(3).

[5]   See Chapter 6 above, and *Cooper v Marshall* (1757) 1 BURR 259.

served may object (not less than 28 days), and the manner in which he may object.[1] If no objection is received from a person receiving such a notice within the specified time limit, he is to be regarded as having given his consent to the matters proposed in the notice.[2] A person with an interest in land is regarded as a person who owns the land or is entitled to exercise any right over the land.[3]

11.7.4 Enforcement of rules

It will be a criminal offence to breach any rule which is made with the consent of the appropriate national authority pursuant to the rule-making function conferred on a commons council. A commons council may take proceedings in relation to an offence; it may apply to a county court for an order to secure compliance with any rule if it is of the opinion that proceedings for an offence would provide an ineffectual remedy against the person who has failed to comply with the rule.[4] It is certainly possible that rules may be made regulating the number of animals that may be placed on a common, and the periods of the year during which they may graze. A county court order compelling a commoner to remove animals may be a more effectual remedy than merely fining the commoner.

11.7.5 Supplementary matters

The Commons Act 2006 makes provision for a number of supplemental matters in relation to the powers and functions of commons councils. The appropriate national authority may, when it makes an order establishing a commons council, make provision to –

(a) vary or abolish the jurisdiction of certain ancient courts referred to in Part 1 of Sch 4 to the Administration of Justice Act 1977;[5]
(b) vary or revoke any regulations or arrangements made under the Commons Act 1908;
(c) vary or revoke any scheme made under the Commons Act 1899, or any arrangement arising under such a scheme;

---

[1]   Commons Act 2006, s 33(4)–(5).

[2]   Commons Act 2006, s 33(6).

[3]   Commons Act 2006, s 33(9).

[4]   Commons Act 2006, s 34.

[5]   Although the jurisdiction to try legal disputes was withdrawn in 1977, Courts Leet, Courts Baron and the Customary Courts of Manors were entitled to sit to transact any other customary business.

(d) vary or revoke any Act made under the Commons Act 1876 confirming a provisional order of the Inclosure Commissioners or any other arrangement arising under such an Act; and

(e) vary or revoke any local or personal Act, or any scheme or arrangement under such an Act, which relates to the management or maintenance of, or the exercise of rights of common over, the land.[1]

However, in making provision in an order for any of the matters specified in (c) to (e) above, the appropriate national authority cannot include anything that would have the effect of abolishing or restricting a right of access of whatever nature exercisable by members of the public generally or by any section of the public.[2]

The appropriate national authority may make an order revoking any previous order establishing a commons council only if it is satisfied that the council has ceased to operate, it is failing to discharge its functions in an effective manner, or is, in discharging its functions, failing to have sufficient regard to the public interest.[3]

11.7.6 Intervention powers

Where the owner of a registered common cannot be identified, a local authority has power to take steps to protect the land from unlawful interference, and to institute proceedings.[4] There are additional provisions to deal with unauthorised agricultural activities on registered commons, or town or village greens that are detrimental to the persons having rights in the land or the public interest.[5] The appropriate national authority may serve a notice requiring activities to cease. There is an opportunity to make representations, and an entitlement for the authority to enforce a notice by seeking a court order.[6]

---

[1]   Commons Act 2006, s 36(1)–(2).

[2]   Commons Act 2006, s 36(3).

[3]   Commons Act 2006, s 37.

[4]   Commons Act 2006, s 45. This provision came into force on 1 October 2006 – see Commons Act 2006 (Commencement No 1, Transitional Provisions and Savings) (England) Order 2006, SI 2006/2504.

[5]   Commons Act 2006, s 46(1).

[6]   Commons Act 2006, s 46.

11.8   NATURE RESERVES AND SITES OF SPECIAL SCIENTIFIC INTEREST

Nearly 50% of the common land in England is wholly or partially designated as a site of special scientific interest (SSSI). The Wildlife and Countryside Act 1981, as amended by the Countryside and Rights of Way (CROW) Act 2000, makes provision for sites of special scientific interest.[1] The responsible authority in England is Natural England, and in Wales, the Countryside Council for Wales.

11.8.1 Notification

Where Natural England (or the Countryside Council for Wales) is of the opinion that any area of land is of special interest, it must notify that fact to the local planning authority, to every owner and occupier of the land, and to the Secretary of State.[2] The notification must specify the time (not less than three months) within which, and the manner in which, representations or objections can be made.[3] A notification must:

- specify the flora, fauna, or geological or physiographical features that makes the land of special interest;
- specify any operations likely to damage that flora, fauna or other features; and
- shall contain a statement of the authorities' views about the management of the land, including any views about conservation and enhancement.

Natural England (or the Countryside Council for Wales) may give notice within nine months that either they have confirmed the notification or are withdrawing it.

11.8.2 Protection of SSSIs

So long as a notification remains in force, the owner or occupier of any land included in a SSSI shall not carry out, cause or permit to be carried out on the land any operation that is prohibited by the notification unless he has given notice to Natural England (or the Countryside Council for Wales) of the proposed operation and:

---

[1]   Sections 28–28R.

[2]   Section 28(1).

[3]   Section 28(3).

- Natural England (or the Countryside Council for Wales) give written consent;
- the operation is carried out in accordance with an agreement made under the National Parks and Access to the Countryside Act 1949 or the Countryside Act 1968; or
- the operation is carried out in accordance with a management scheme or management notice under the 1981 Act itself.[1]

It is a criminal offence to carry out operations without the necessary consents or agreements.[2]

The 1981 Act makes provision for appeals in connection with the refusal of consent to carry out operations, or the grant of consent subject to conditions. The appeal is to the Secretary of State.[3] There is also provision for the making of a restoration order where a person is convicted of an offence of destroying or damaging any of the flora, fauna or geological or physiographical features that make the land of special interest.[4]

Natural England (or the Countryside Council for Wales) may formulate management schemes for all or part of a SSSI. These schemes may provide for the conservation or restoration of the flora, fauna, or geological or physiographical features that make the land of special interest.[5] There is a scheme for the service of notices of the making of management schemes and for a consideration of any representations or objections. Where a management scheme has been made, and it appears to Natural England (or the Countryside Council for Wales) that an owner or occupier is not giving effect to a provision of the management scheme, and there is inadequate conservation or restoration, then they may serve a management notice requiring works or other matters to be done.[6] Again, there is a scheme of appeals against management notices.[7]

---

[1]   Section 28E.

[2]   Section 28P.

[3]   Section 28F.

[4]   Section 31.

[5]   Section 28J.

[6]   Section 28K.

[7]   Section 28L.

The 1981 Act also contains a power by which Natural England (or the Countryside Council for Wales) may compulsorily purchase of all or any part of a SSSI where the relevant body is satisfied that they are unable to conclude on reasonable terms an agreement with the owner or occupier as to the management of the land, or an agreement that has been made has been breached in such a way that the land is not being managed satisfactory.[1]

11.8.3 Effect of sites of special scientific interest

The possible consequences to commoners of the designation of a common as a site of special scientific interest are illustrated by the decision in *Owen v Blathwayt*.[2] In that case, a number of tenanted farms enjoyed sheep-grazing rights over land that had once been a common. The land was designated as a site of special scientific interest but Natural England (in fact its statutory predecessor) consented to one of the tenants grazing animals on the land, provided there was no more than a specified number during winter months and a higher specified number during the rest of the year. As these numbers were substantially lower than the number of animals that could be maintained on the tenant's holding, this led to a dispute with the other tenants with similar sheep-grazing rights as to whether a rule of priority applied so that the first grantee of rights could displace the others on the land. The court held that all tenants claiming grazing rights had to regard themselves as having equal status. The same principles would probably apply to common land.

The House of Lords in *Bettison v Langton* confirmed that where rights of common of pasture are appurtenant to land, they may be severed from the land and be held by a purchaser (and his successors) in gross.[3] The requirement under the Commons Registration Act 1965 to register specific numbers of animals resulted in excessive numbers being entered, which has given rise to severe overgrazing and conservation management problems. Where rights of common of grazing are severed from land, this could produce enormous problems in enforcing conservation policies under, for example, the Wildlife and Countryside Act 1981.[4] When the Commons Act 2006 is

---

[1] Section 28N.

[2] [2002] EWHC 2231, [2003] 1 P&CR 28.

[3] [2001] 3 All ER 417.

[4] Sydenham, 'Managing Common Land for Environmental Benefit: The Difficulties After Bettison v Langton', *Environmental Law Review*, 4.1(1), March 2002.

fully in force, and commons councils are set up with management powers, many of these problems will be addressed.

In *Southern Water Authority v The Nature Conservancy Council*, the term 'occupier' was given a wide interpretation as including anyone with a stable relationship with the land and which was not transient. Accordingly, the persons holding common rights would fall within that status and be entitled to notification, and subject to the obligations in relation to sites of special scientific interest.[1]

11.8.4   The Commons Act 2006

The difficulties of reconciling conservation regulation under the Wildlife and Countryside Act 1981 and the rights of commoners, with registered rights under the Commons Registration Act 1965 has long been a subject for discussion.[2] Although the Commons Registration Act 1965, s 13 permits the amendment of the registers following the transfer of common rights, there is no duty to notify changes in ownership. The commons registers are often out of date, inaccurate, and unrepresentative of the current land use on the common. This has made for difficulties in identifying all commoners with registered rights, especially having regard to the powers and duties of the statutory predecessors to Natural England under the Wildlife and Countryside Act 1981, s 28.[3] In the past proposals were advanced for the introduction of legislative regulating the numbers of stock that could be grazed on commons in order to address the acute problems in some areas of overgrazing, often arising out of inflated numbers of animals registered under the Commons Registration Act 1965.[4] The Department of the Environment Transport and the Regions, produced guidance on the management of commons, together with a model constitution for what was then called a commons association.[5]

---

[1]   [1992] 3 All ER 481.

[2]   Rodgers, 'Environmental Management of Common Land: Towards a Legal Framework?', *Environmental Law Review*, March 2002.

[3]   Ibid.

[4]   Ibid.

[5]   *The Good Practice Guide on Managing the Use of Common Land* (DETR, 1998); and *MAFF Guidelines for Joint ESA Agreements with Commoners*.

Parliament has now legislated in the form of the Commons Act 2006. This Act addresses the problem of the severance of rights of common: see Chapter 6 above. Part 2 of the Act contains powers to create commons councils with wide powers to manage common land: see above.

11.9   THE COUNTRYSIDE AND RIGHTS OF WAY ACT 2000

Public rights of access on foot are now available under this Act; these are more fully explained in Chapter 10. Subject to a number of exceptions, 'Access Land', under the CROW Act 2000, includes all registered common land. There are limited rights for owners of Access Land to exclude or restrict public access, for example:

–   along specified routes or ways;
–   by entering the land only at a specified place or places;
–   by persons who do not take dogs on the land; or
–   by persons who satisfy any other specified conditions.[1]

The Act also makes provision for the exclusion or restriction of access where the appropriate authority makes a direction for the purposes of the management of the land by its owner.[2] There is also a right to seek the exclusion or restriction of access for no more than 28 days each calendar year.[3] It will be some time before it is clear how these management arrangements will operate under this Act, especially in relation to common land. But one can see the likelihood of restrictions on access during, for example, the lambing season.[4]

11.10   FENCES ON COMMONS

There are two matters here, namely whether there are any obligations to fence or provide some other form of stockproof inclosure around the boundary of a common, to prevent the escape of animals, and whether, and in what circumstances, fencing can be erected on a common.

---

[1]   Sections 2(1) and 21(3).

[2]   Section 24(1).

[3]   Section 22.

[4]   See now Access to the Countryside (Exclusions and Restrictions) (England) Regulations 2003, SI 2003/2713 and Access to the Countryside (Exclusions and Restrictions) (Wales) Regulations 2003, SI 2003/142.

11.10.1 Duty to fence

A duty on owners of properties adjoining a common may arise as a matter of custom to fence to prevent the animals on the common straying out.[1] In an earlier case the same result was achieved by the implication of an easement to fence; the obligation falling on the owners of properties adjoining the common.[2] The standard of fencing must be suited to the animals likely to be upon the common.[3]

11.10.2 Right to erect fences

In the case of commonable lands, stinted and regulated pastures, which have been the subject of allotment or regulation schemes, the terms of the award will determine liability as to fencing.

With regard to fencing on common land, the Law of Property Act 1925, s 194(1) provided that:

> 'The erection of any building or fence, or the construction of any other work, whereby access to land to which this section applies is prevented or impeded, shall not be lawful unless the consent of the [Secretary of State] thereto is obtained, ...'

Section 194 applied to any land which at the commencement of the 1925 Act was then subject to rights of common (1 January 1926).[4] The restrictions on buildings or fences ceased to apply to any land over which the rights of common were extinguished under any statutory provision, or to any land over which the rights of common were otherwise extinguished if the county council in which the land was situated passes a resolution and that is approved by the Secretary of State.[5] When the Secretary of State is considering an application for consent, he is not obliged to hold a public local inquiry.[6]

---

[1]   *Egerton v Harding* [1975] QB 62.

[2]   *Crow v Wood* [1971] 1 QB 77.

[3]   *Coaker v Willcocks* [1911] 1 KB 649, *affirmed* [1911] 2 KB 124.

[4]   Section 194(4). A temporary electric fence is unauthorised: see *Rabett v Poole* (unreported county court decision).

[5]   Section 194(3).

[6]   *R (Ashbrook) v Secretary of State for the Environment, Food and Rural Affairs* [2005] 1 All ER 166.

The Secretary of State gave consent to the erection of fences on Ashdown Forest; the purpose of the fences was to manage sheep with a view to maintain the 'openness' of parts of the forest.

However, when Part 3 of the Commons Act 2006 is in force, s 194 of the Law of Property Act 1925 will be repealed and replaced by new provisions prohibiting works on commons and greens: see below. The special position of the National Trust is considered at the end of this chapter.

11.11   PROHIBITION OF WORKS ON COMMONS

The two principal provisions that prohibit the construction of works on commons are s 147 of the Inclosure Act 1845 and s 194 of the Law of Property Act 1925. The former restricted the enclosure of commons and town or village greens unless certain criteria were satisfied, and thereby prevented the erection of fences or works.[1] The latter applies also to fencing on common land, and is discussed above. The Commons Act 2006 contains a number of provisions for the prohibition of works on commons without consent. These provisions are likely to be in force by late 2007. As explained above in relation to fences on commons, s 194 of the Law of Property Act 1925 prohibits works on commons without the consent of the Secretary of State. This provision will be repealed when the appropriate provisions of the 2006 Act come into force.

11.11.1 Works prohibited without consent

Save with the consent of the appropriate national authority, no person may carry out any 'restricted works' on –

(a)   any registered common land;
(b)   any land not so registered but which is –
       regulated by an Act made under the Commons Act 1876 confirming a provisional order of the Inclosure Commissioners; or
       subject to a scheme under the Metropolitan Commons Act 1866;
(c)   land not falling within any of the above which is in the New Forest and is subject to rights of common.[2]

---

[1]   See Chapter 7.

[2]   Commons Act 2006, s 38(1) and (5).

The 'restricted works' are works which have the effect of preventing or impeding access to the relevant common, or works for the resurfacing of land. The 'restricted works' also include the erection of fencing, the construction of buildings and other structures, and the digging of ditches and trenches and the building of embankments. The resurfacing of land is that which consists of the laying of concrete, tarmacadam, coated roadstone or similar material, provided it is not the repair of an existing surface made of such materials.[1] It follows that the construction of a new access over common land involving resurfacing would be a restricted work that cannot be carried out without the consent of the appropriate national authority. The appropriate national authority in England is Natural England, and in Wales, the Countryside Council for Wales. The following works are not prohibited –

(a) works on any land where the works are, or include, works carried out under a power conferred in relation to that land under any enactment;

(b) works on any land where the works are carried out under a power conferred by any enactment applying to common land;

(c) works authorised under a scheme under the Metropolitan Commons Act 1866 or the Commons Act 1899 without any requirement for any person to consent to the works;

(d) works for the installation of electronic communications apparatus for the purposes of an electronic communications code network.

That last item of non-prohibited work is somewhat surprising. It would appear that, subject to any other consents or permissions required under the Town and Country Planning Act 1990, the erection of a mobile phone mast on common land is not a prohibited work.

11.11.2 The procedure for consents

Where an application for consent for restricted works is made to the appropriate national authority, that body must have regard to the interests of persons having rights in relation to, or occupying, the land (including the commoners), the interests of the neighbourhood, the public interest, and any other matter considered to be relevant. The public interest includes interest in nature conservation, the

---

[1]   Commons Act 2006, s 38(2)–(4).

conservation of the landscape, the protection of public rights of access to any area of land, and the protection of archaeological remains and features of historic interest.[1] On an application for consent to carry out restricted works, consent may be given in relation to all or part of the proposed works, and subject to such modifications and conditions as the appropriate national authority thinks fit. Regulations may be made to specify a time limit for the making of applications. Consent may be given in relation to works which have been commenced or completed.[2]

The Commons Act 2006 makes provision for the making of regulations that will govern the procedure for the making and determination of applications for consent to carry out restricted works.

11.11.3 Enforcement

The new protection controls apply to all registered common land. When any 'restricted works' are carried out on land that is subject to s 38 of the 2006 Act without consent, then *any* person may apply to the county court for an order requiring the removal of the works and the restoration of the land to the condition it was in before the works were carried out. Where consent was given, but the works have not been carried out in accordance with any term of the consent, for an order that the works be carried out in such manner and subject to such conditions as the order may specify.

11.11.4 Existing schemes

At any time there may be schemes that are currently in force made under either the Metropolitan Commons Act 1866 or the Commons Act 1899. Such schemes may contain a provision prohibiting the carrying out of works but providing no procedure for consenting. In such circumstances, the consent of an appropriate national authority to 'restricted works' is sufficient to ensure that such works do not contravene any provision or the schemes made under either the 1866 or the 1899 Acts subject to the additional consent of the owner of the land affected.[3]

---

[1]   Commons Act 2006, s 39(1)–(2).

[2]   Commons Act 2006, s 39(3)–(7).

[3]   Commons Act 2006, s 42.

11.11.5 Exemption

Section 43 of the Commons Act 2006 contains provisions by which the appropriate national authority may make an order providing that the prohibition on the carrying out of works on common land in s 38 is not to apply in certain cases. The order will specify the persons, the works, the land, or the descriptions of persons, works and land, that are exempted from the restriction on the carrying out of works on certain common land. An exemption can only be made where the works are likely to be necessary or expedient on any land for the following purposes:

(a)   use of land by members of the public for the purposes of open-air recreation pursuant to any right of access;

(b)   the exercise of rights of common;

(c)   nature conservation;

(d)   the protection of archaeological remains or features of historic interest;

(e)   the use of land for sporting or recreational purposes.[1]

Schedule 4 to the Commons Act 2006 makes amendments to a number of statutory provisions to enable those provisions to be consistent with the prohibition of works in ss 38–40 of the 2006 Act.

11.12   DRIVING VEHICLES OVER COMMON LAND

It is an offence under the Road Traffic Act 1988 to drive a motor vehicle without lawful authority upon any common land not forming part of a road. The Law of Property Act 1925, s 193 applies to urban commons and commons to which the section was specifically applied to by declaration from time to time.[2] In respect of common land to which s 193 applies:

> 'Any person who, without lawful authority, draws or drives upon any land to which this section applies any carriage, cart, caravan, truck, or other vehicle, or camps or lights any fire thereon, or who fails to observe any limitation or condition imposed by the Minister under this section in respect of any such land, shall be liable on summary conviction to a fine ...'

---

[1]   Commons Act 2006, s 43(3)–(4).

[2]   See Chapter 10.

11.13   NATIONAL TRUST COMMON LAND

Under s 29 of the National Trust Act 1971, the Trust is required to keep all commons open and unbuilt on as open spaces for recreation and the enjoyment of the public. Under s 23 of the National Trust Act 1971, ministerial consent is required for any buildings or other works on Trust-owned commons if public access would be affected. Section 23 permits the erection of fencing where the National Trust thinks that it is bona fide to do so.[1]

---

[1]   *National Trust v Ashbrook* [1997] 4 All ER 76.

CHAPTER 12

COMPULSORY ACQUISITION AND COMMON LANDS

12.1 INTRODUCTION

Many public authorities and other bodies have powers of compulsory purchase. These powers may authorise the compulsory acquisition of land or of rights over land. Common land is not immune from compulsory acquisition, although there are a number of procedural safeguards. There are special provisions for the assessment of compensation payable to the owners of common land, and to the commoners.

A full explanation of the legislation and powers of compulsory acquisition is beyond the scope of this book. However, the basic principles are as follows. The power to acquire land or rights in land is found in an Act of Parliament. Powers in public Acts of Parliament are available to central government and local authorities for such purposes as the acquisition of land and rights for the purposes of creating and improving public highways (see the Highways Act 1980). Other legislation contains powers to acquire land for specific projects, such as the Channel Tunnel Railway (see the Channel Tunnel Railway Act 1996). Increasing use is made of the powers in the Transport and Works Act 1992 to make works orders for such projects as railways and light tramways. A power to acquire land or rights compulsorily is exercisable only after the making and confirmation of a compulsory purchase order or, in the case of the Transport and Works Act 1992, a works order. Such orders are made by the authority possessing powers of compulsory acquisition and then confirmed by the relevant Secretary of State. It is in relation to the procedures for the making and confirmation of compulsory purchase orders that the legislation contains special provisions concerning common land.

12.2   COMPULSORY ACQUISITION OF LAND

Where a compulsory purchase order authorises the purchase of any land forming part of a common, open space or fuel or field garden allotment, the order is subject to what is called special Parliamentary procedure unless excluded by a certificate issued by the Secretary of State (see the Acquisition of Land Act 1981, s 19(1)).

12.2.1 Certificate excluding special Parliamentary procedure

The Secretary of State may only issue a certificate where he is satisfied:

'(a) that there has been or will be given in exchange for land as described above, other land, not being less in area and being equally advantageous to the persons, if any, entitled to rights of common or other rights, and to the public, and that the land given in exchange has been or will be vested in the persons in whom the land purchased was vested and subject to the like rights, trusts and incidents as attached to the land purchased, or[1]

(b) that the land is being purchased in order to secure its preservation or improve its management,[2] or

(c) that the land does not exceed 250 square yards in extent or is required for the widening or drainage of an existing highway or partly for the widening and partly for the drainage of such a highway and that the giving in exchange of other land is unnecessary, whether in the interests of the persons, if any, entitled to rights of common or other rights or in the interests of the public.'[3]

In relation to the above exclusions, the word 'common' is defined as including any land subject to be inclosed under the Inclosure Acts 1845 to 1882, and any town or village green.[4] The word 'open space' is defined as meaning any land laid out as a public garden, or used

---

[1]   Section 19(1)(a).

[2]   Section 19(1)(aa).

[3]   Section 19(1)(b).

[4]   Section 19(4).

for the purposes of public recreation, or land being a disused burial ground.[1]

In *Greenwich London Borough Council v the Secretary of State for the Environment*,[2] the court had to consider the meaning of the words 'equally advantageous' in paragraph (a) above. In connection with a compulsory purchase order that included some ancient woodland, a certificate had been issued in respect of exchange land that was to be planted with trees. However, during a period of about 15 years, to enable the trees to become established, the public would only have restricted access. Hutchison J said:

> 'It seemed likely that Parliament would have intended to permit a degree of flexibility, leaving it to the Secretary of State to judge whether advantages of one sort could be off set against advantages of a different sort.'

He added that the Secretary of State acted lawfully if he was:

> 'satisfied of equal advantage at the date of exchange on the basis that advantages that the exchange land would have in the future meant that it was equally advantageous to users of the order land and the public at large at the date of exchange.'

Where the Secretary of State is proposing to give a certificate, he must direct the acquiring authority to give public notice of his intention so to do.[3] The Secretary of State then affords an opportunity to all persons interested to make representations and objections in relation to his proposal to give a certificate. After causing a public local inquiry to be held in any case where it appears to him to be expedient so to do, and having regard to any representations or objections made, the Secretary of State may give his certificate. Before doing so he is required to consider any representations and objections made and, if an inquiry has been held, the report of the person who held the inquiry.[4]

---

[1]   Section 19(4).

[2]   [1993] Env LR 344.

[3]   Section 19(2).

[4]   Section 19(2).

12.2.2 Exchange land

A compulsory purchase order may provide for the vesting of exchange land in the persons and is subject to the same rights as the land being compulsorily acquired. It may also provide for the discharging of the land being compulsorily acquired of all rights to which it was previously subject.[1] There is one exception to this; that arises where the Secretary of State gives a certificate where land is already common or open space land and is being purchased in order to secure its preservation or improve its management.

Although the Secretary of State is not bound to hold a public local inquiry, he should only decline to do so where the issues relating to the provision of, for example, exchange land are relatively straightforward and can be fully covered in written submissions, and where it would be difficult to see how the Secretary of State could obtain further assistance. Exchange land does not have to replicate the land being compulsorily acquired.[2]

Under the Commons Act 2006, any exchange land will require registration under the appropriate register of common land or town or village greens in accordance with regulations that are yet to be made.[3] The 2006 Act will also require that certain variations in a right of common must be registered; presumably that will apply where either a right is acquired without any exchange land, or is transferred to, or will additionally be over, the exchange land.[4]

12.2.3 Special Parliamentary procedure

Where a certificate is not issued, as described above, a compulsory purchase order is of no effect until it has been laid before Parliament by the Secretary of State and comes into force in accordance with the provisions of the Statutory Orders (Special Procedure) Act 1945. A notice of an intention to lay an order before Parliament must be published in the *London Gazette*.[5] A period of time is allowed for the presentation of petitions by way of general objection or for the amendment to the order. A petition may be presented by any person

---

[1]   Section 19(2A).

[2]   *Waltham Forest District Council v Secretary of State for the Environment* [1993] EGCS 34.

[3]   Commons Act 2006, s 14(2).

[4]   Commons Act 2006, s 7.

[5]   Statutory Orders (Special Procedures) Act 1945, s 2(1).

in accordance with the standing orders of Parliament. Petitions may be of general objection, or for some amendment. An order may be annulled by resolution of either House of Parliament, or referred to a joint committee of both Houses for consideration of any petition.[1] If the joint committee report that the order should not be approved, or if amendments are made which are unacceptable to the Secretary of State, the order can only be authorised by the introduction of a Bill and its confirmation by Acts of Parliament.[2] In those cases where the committee report the order without amendment, it will come into operation without further formal confirmation procedures.[3]

Special Parliamentary procedure provides Parliament with a measure of control over controversial proposals for the compulsory acquisition of common land. The procedure also allows the making of petitions for consideration by an appropriate committee.

12.3 ACQUISITION OF RIGHTS OVER COMMONS

Where a compulsory purchase order authorises the acquisition of a right over land forming part of a common, open space or fuel or field garden allotment, it shall be subject to special Parliamentary procedure except where excluded by a certificate of the Secretary of State.[4] The Secretary of State may only issue a certificate excluding special Parliamentary procedure where he is satisfied that:

(a) the land, when burdened with the right sought to be compulsorily acquired, will be no less advantageous to those persons in whom it is vested and other persons, if any, entitled to rights of common or other rights, and to the public, than it was before;[5] or

(b) the right, which is being acquired compulsorily, is being acquired in order to secure the preservation or improvement of the management of the land;[6] or

---

[1] Sections 3–5.

[2] Section 6(2).

[3] Section 6(1).

[4] Acquisition of Land Act 1981, Sch 3, para 6(1).

[5] Ibid, para 6(1)(a).

[6] Ibid, para 6(1)(aa).

(c) there has been or will be given in exchange for the right being compulsorily acquired additional land that will be adequate to compensate the owner of the common and those entitled to rights of common or other rights over it for the disadvantages which will result from the acquisition of the right. The additional land must either have been, or will be vested in the owner of the land over which the right is to be acquired, and be made subject to the like rights as attached to that land apart from the compulsory purchase order;[1] or

(d) the land affected by the right to be acquired does not exceed 250 square yards in extent, and the giving of other land in exchange for the right is unnecessary, whether in the interests of the persons, if any, entitled to rights of common of other rights or in the interests of the public.[2]

Where land is being acquired by a compulsory purchase order under the Highways Act 1980, a certificate can be issued under paragraph (d) above where, in the alternative to the land being acquired not exceeding 250 square yards, only rights are required in connection with the widening or drainage of an existing highway or in connection partly with the widening and partly with the drainage of such a highway.[3]

Where the Secretary of State is proposing to issue a certificate under any of the grounds set out above, the procedures for publicity, the making of objections and representations and the holding of a local public inquiry or otherwise, more fully explained at para **12.2.1** above, will apply.

Where a compulsory purchase order is concerned with the acquisition of rights, and no certificate can be issued excluding special Parliamentary procedure, or the Secretary of State decides not to do so, the special Parliamentary procedure described at para **12.2.3** above will apply.

---

[1]   Ibid, para 6(1)(b).

[2]   Ibid, para 6(1)(c).

[3]   Ibid, para 6(2).

12.4   COMPENSATION FOR THE FREEHOLD

12.4.1 Value of land taken

In the case of the acquisition of common land, the freehold will have to be compulsorily acquired. There are no special rules for the assessment of compensation for the acquisition of such a freehold. The owner of the freehold will be entitled to the value of his interest assessed in accordance with the compensation rules. These rules are set out in the Land Compensation Act 1961. Certain rules concern the basis of finding the open market value of the freehold interest; in broad terms, one assumes a sale by a willing seller in the open market.[1] Further rules deal with any planning assumptions that can be made; these may be relevant to the determination of the open market value.[2]

Where a piece of common land is being compulsorily acquired, the freehold is unlikely to have a very high value. However, the following factors should be considered:

(a) The value of the residue of rights left to the owner of the soil, such as his entitlement to timber, minerals or any rights he has in common with the commoners, such as rights of grazing.
(b) Whether the rights of the commoners might be extinguished in the manner allowed under the Commons Act 2006.[3] Extinguishment by merger of the ownership of the common with land to which the rights were attached is believed to have occurred in respect of Copthorne Common where the owner of the soil was able to acquire the property of the only remaining commoner with registered common rights, although extinguishment by operation of law will no longer be possible.[4]
(c) All commons within the Metropolitan Police District, or within the areas once boroughs or urban districts (as they existed before local government reorganisation in 1974), are subject to a public right of access for air and exercise. A similar right applies to commons outside those areas if the owner of the soil has made a declaration allowing for this under s 193 of the Law of Property Act 1925. Most common land is registered common land under

---

[1]   Land Compensation Act 1961, s 5(2).

[2]   Ibid, ss 14–18.

[3]   Commons Act 2006, s 13(1).

[4]   Commons Act 2006, s 13(3).

the Commons Registration Act 1965, and will be under the Commons Act 2006. All registered common land is land over which the public will have rights of access under the Countryside and Rights of Way (CROW) Act 2000.

(d) Where the soil of a common carries with it ownership of the lord of the manor, a manorship may have considerable value. Whether this adds to the value of the land taken, or goes to any claim for injurious affection or severance, will depend on the circumstances.

12.4.2 Injurious affection and severance compensation

In addition to the value of any land taken, compensation is also payable for the effect of severance or injurious affection on any retained land of a claimant owner.[1] It follows that the owner of the soil may have a claim for compensation for the diminution in value of the retained part of the common. There may be a similar claim where the ownership of the soil is with the lord of the manor, and the retained interest in the manorship is similarly diminished in value.

12.4.3 Payment of compensation and conveyance

The compensation in respect of the right in the soil of any of the land subject to compulsory purchase and subject to any rights of common must be paid to the lord of the manor, if he is so entitled, or to any other such party who owns the soil, other than the commoners.[2] On payment or tender to the lord of the manor, or such other party as is entitled to the ownership of the soil, of the compensation agreed or awarded in respect of the right in the soil of any common land, the lord of the manor or such other party shall convey the land to the acquiring authority. The conveyance has the effect of vesting the land in the acquiring authority as if the lord of the manor or other party had owned the freehold at the time of executing the conveyance.[3] In default of such a conveyance, it shall be lawful for the acquiring authority, if it thinks fit, to execute a deed poll and, after paying the compensation monies into court, the land shall vest absolutely in the acquiring authority.[4]

---

[1]   Compulsory Purchase Act 1965, s 7.

[2]   Ibid, Sch 4, para 1(1).

[3]   Ibid, para 2(1)–(2).

[4]   Ibid, para 2(3).

The provisions discussed in this section apply only where the commoners are not also entitled to ownership of the soil. In the case of a common where the soil is owned by the commoners, not infrequent in Wales, the compensation provisions discussed under the next heading are appropriate.

12.5 COMPENSATION FOR THE COMMONERS

Schedule 4 to the Compulsory Purchase Act 1965 sets out the procedure for the assessment of compensation payable to the commoners on the compulsory acquisition of common land.

Two situations are covered by these provisions: the assessment of compensation where the commoners are also the owners of the soil, and the assessment of compensation payable to the commoners where the right in the soil does not belong to the commoners. In either situation, compensation must be determined by agreement between the acquiring authority and a committee of the persons entitled to commonable or other rights in the land appointed under the provisions of Sch 4.[1]

12.5.1 Meeting of commoners

The acquiring authority may convene a meeting of the commoners having rights over the land subject to compulsory purchase after giving notice in a local newspaper and fixing a notice on the door of the parish church in the locality.[2] The meeting may appoint a committee consisting of not more than five commoners, and the decision of the majority of persons present at the meeting shall bind the minority and all absent parties.[3]

The acquiring authority may negotiate with the committee. If a sum of compensation is agreed, that agreement is binding on all persons interested in the commonable rights.[4] Compensation may be paid to the committee or any three of them. The compensation may be apportioned by the committee among the commoners, according to

---

[1]   Ibid, para 3.

[2]   Ibid, para 4.

[3]   Ibid, para 4(5).

[4]   *Hipperson and others v Newbury District Council* (unreported 1998).

their respective interests, and the acquiring authority is not bound to see to the apportionment or to the application of the compensation, nor are they liable for any misapplication or non-application of the compensation.[1] If the committee fails to agree with the acquiring authority as to the amount of compensation, the dispute is referred to and determined by the Lands Tribunal.[2]

Where there has been a failure to hold an effective meeting, or the meeting fails to appoint a committee, the amount of the compensation is determined by a surveyor selected from the members of the Lands Tribunal.[3] On the payment of compensation to the committee, or any three of them or, where appropriate, into court, the acquiring authority may execute a deed poll; this will vest in the authority the common land freed and discharged from all the commonable rights.

Where the committee has difficulties in apportioning compensation, or there are difficulties about its investment, there are a number of powers that deal with this particular problem.[4]

12.5.2 Exchange land

Where the acquiring authority has provided exchange land to replace the common land being acquired, the granting of an exchange land certificate does not, by itself, preclude the payment of compensation to the commoners.[5] In one case the Lands Tribunal considered that the value of commoners' rights transferred to the exchange land represented in whole, or in part, the compensation which was payable for the acquisition of the rights in common which subsisted in the land acquired.[6]

12.5.3 Valuation of rights of common

Most common rights, such as grazing rights, are attached to land. In certain areas the existence of such rights is a significant factor in the

---

[1]   Para 5(1)–(3).

[2]   Compulsory Purchase Act 1965, Sch 4, para 5(4).

[3]   Ibid, para 6.

[4]   See Inclosure Act 1852, s 22 and Commonable Compensation Rights Act 1882, s 2.

[5]   *McKay v The City of London Corporation* (1966) 17 P&CR 264.

[6]   *Lay v Norfolk County Council* [1997] RVR 9 and *Freeman v Middlesex County Council* (1965) 16 P&CR 253.

value of farmland. If the land to which common rights are annexed is valued, first with those rights and, second, after those rights have been acquired as a result of the taking of the common, the difference can be said to be attributable to the value of the common rights. As the value of common rights over the same common may differ from holding to holding, the procedure of treating for compensation through a committee rather than directly is not always satisfactory.

12.5.4 Disputes

If there is disagreement among the commoners as to how the compensation should be apportioned or invested, the committee may make application in writing to the Secretary of State at the Department of the Environment, Food and Rural Affairs, who has powers to make an award binding on the parties.[1]

12.5.5 Effect of payment of compensation

The payment of compensation does not alter the status of the land as common land, as such. Therefore, unless inclosure is authorised, the land remains common land and cannot be inclosed. Further, the procedure under Sch 4 does not extinguish any public rights of access, only the commoners' rights.[2] Prior to the Commons Act 2006 the commoners' rights were extinguished upon the deed vesting the land or their rights in the acquiring authority.[3]

However, the Commons Act 2006 now makes provision for the consequences of a compulsory acquisition and, where applicable, the provision of exchange land. Certain statutory dispositions, including the compulsory acquisition of land, may involve the acquisition of common land or town or village greens, and the extinguishment of rights of common. Acquisition can also involve acquiring exchange land to replace the lost common land. Regulations will be made to provide for the circumstances of when and how applications are to be made to amend the registers of common land and greens to give effect to such statutory dispositions.[4]

---

[1]   Inclosure Acts 1852–54 and Commonable Compensation Rights Act 1882.

[2]   *Lewis v Mid-Glamorgan County Council* [1995] 1 All ER 760.

[3]   *Hipperson and others v Newbury District Council* (unreported 1998).

[4]   Commons Act 2006, s 14.

12.6   REGISTRATIONS UNDER THE COMMONS ACT 2006

12.6.1   Transitional registrations

Where land was compulsorily acquired, the Commons Registration Act 1965 made no provision for the amendment of the registers to reflect the extinguishment or variation of rights of common, and to reflect the provision of exchange land. Sch 3 to the Commons Act 2006 sets out certain transitional provisions for updating the registers. Regulations will be made that will deal with the details about who may make the application for the updating of the registers, and the time limits. But where any relevant instrument, such as one made under the Acquisition of Land Act 1981, has resulted in the surrender or variation of a right of common, the apportionment or the severance of a right, or the transfer of a right in gross, then the registers can be amended.

12.6.2   Re-allocation of attached rights

Where a right of common is registered in a register as attached to any land, the owner may apply to have the register amended so as to secure that the right does not attach to a relevant part of that land.[1] In effect to re-allocate the right to land other than the relevant part. This can apply where land is the subject of a compulsory purchase order that has been confirmed (where confirmation is required), the relevant part is not vested in the acquiring authority, and is required for a use other than for agricultural purposes.

---

[1]   Commons Act 2006, s 11.

APPENDIX

LEGISLATION

COMMONS ACT 2006

2006 CHAPTER 26

PART 1

REGISTRATION

An Act to make provision about common land and town or village greens; and for connected purposes. [19th July 2006]

BE IT ENACTED by the Queen's most Excellent Majesty, by and with the advice and consent of the Lords Spiritual and Temporal, and Commons, in this present Parliament assembled, and by the authority of the same, as follows: –

PART 1
REGISTRATION
Introductory

1   Registers of common land and greens

Each commons registration authority shall continue to keep –

(a)   a register known as a register of common land; and

(b)   a register known as a register of town or village greens.

2   Purpose of registers

(1)   The purpose of a register of common land is –

(a)   to register land as common land; and

(b)   to register rights of common exercisable over land registered as common land.

(2)   The purpose of a register of town or village greens is –

(a)   to register land as a town or village green; and

(b)   to register rights of common exercisable over land registered as a town or village green.

3   Content of registers

(1)   The land registered as common land in a register of common land is, subject to this Part, to be –

(a)   the land so registered in it at the commencement of this section; and

(b)   such other land as may be so registered in it under this Part.

(2)   The land registered as a town or village green in a register of town or village greens is, subject to this Part, to be –

(a)   the land so registered in it at the commencement of this section; and

(b)   such other land as may be so registered in it under this Part.

(3)   The rights of common registered in a register of common land or town or village greens are, subject to this Part, to be –

(a)   the rights registered in it at the commencement of this section; and

(b)   such other rights as may be so registered in it under this Part.

(4)   The following information is to be registered in a register of common land or town or village greens in respect of a right of common registered in it –

(a)   the nature of the right;

(b)   if the right is attached to any land, the land to which it is attached;

(c)   if the right is not so attached, the owner of the right.

(5)   Regulations may –

(a)   require or permit other information to be included in a register of common land or town or village greens;

(b)   make provision as to the form in which any information is to be presented in such a register.

(6)   Except as provided under this Part or any other enactment –

(a)   no land registered as common land or as a town or village green is to be removed from the register in which it is so registered;

(b)   no right of common registered in a register of common land or town or village greens is to be removed from that register.

(7)   No right of common over land to which this Part applies is to be registered in the register of title.

4   Commons registration authorities

(1)   The following are commons registration authorities –

(a)   a county council in England;

(b)   a district council in England for an area without a county council;

(c)   a London borough council; and

(d)   a county or county borough council in Wales.

(2)   For the purposes of this Part, the commons registration authority in relation to any land is the authority in whose area the land is situated.

(3)   Where any land falls within the area of two or more commons registration authorities, the authorities may by agreement provide for one of them to be the commons registration authority in relation to the whole of the land.

5   Land to which Part 1 applies

(1)   This Part applies to all land in England and Wales, subject as follows.

(2)   This Part does not apply to –

(a)   the New Forest; or

(b)   Epping Forest.

(3)   This Part shall not be taken to apply to the Forest of Dean.

(4)   If any question arises under this Part whether any land is part of the forests mentioned in this section it is to be referred to and decided by the appropriate national authority.

Registration of rights of common

6   Creation

(1)   A right of common cannot at any time after the commencement of this section be created over land to which this Part applies by virtue of prescription.

(2)   A right of common cannot at any time after the commencement of this section be created in any other way over land to which this Part applies except –

(a)   as specified in subsection (3); or

(b)   pursuant to any other enactment.

(3)   A right of common may be created over land to which this Part applies by way of express grant if –

(a)   the land is not registered as a town or village green; and

(b)   the right is attached to land.

(4)   The creation of a right of common in accordance with subsection (3) only has effect if it complies with such requirements as to form and content as regulations may provide.

(5)   The creation of a right of common in accordance with subsection (3) does not operate at law until on an application under this section –

(a)   the right is registered in a register of common land; and

(b)   if the right is created over land not registered as common land, the land is registered in a register of common land.

(6)   An application under this section to register the creation of a right of common consisting of a right to graze any animal is to be refused if in the opinion of the commons registration authority the land over which it is created would be unable to sustain the exercise of –

(a)   that right; and

(b)   if the land is already registered as common land, any other rights of common registered as exercisable over the land.

7   Variation

(1)   For the purposes of this section a right of common is varied if by virtue of any disposition –

(a)   the right becomes exercisable over new land to which this Part applies instead of all or part of the land over which it was exercisable;

(b)   the right becomes exercisable over new land to which this Part applies in addition to the land over which it is already exercisable;

(c)   there is any other alteration in what can be done by virtue of the right.

(2)   A right of common which is registered in a register of common land or town or village greens cannot at any time after the commencement of this section be varied so as to become exercisable over new land if that land is at the time registered as a town or village green.

(3)   A right of common which is registered in a register of town or village greens cannot at any time after the commencement of this section be varied so as to extend what can be done by virtue of the right.

(4)   The variation of a right of common which is registered in a register of common land or town or village greens –

(a)   only has effect if it complies with such requirements as to form and content as regulations may provide; and

(b)   does not operate at law until, on an application under this section, the register is amended so as to record the variation.

(5)   An application under this section to record a variation of a right of common consisting of a right to graze any animal is to be refused if in the opinion of the commons registration authority the land over which the right is or is to be exercisable would, in consequence of the variation, be unable to sustain the exercise of –

(a)   that right; and
(b)   if the land is already registered as common land, any other rights of common registered as exercisable over the land.

8   Apportionment

(1)   Regulations may make provision as to the amendments to be made to a register of common land or town or village greens where a right of common which is registered in a register of common land or town or village greens as attached to any land is apportioned by virtue of any disposition affecting the land.

(2)   Regulations under subsection (1) may provide that a register is only to be amended when –

(a)   a disposition relating to an apportioned right itself falls to be registered under this Part; or
(b)   the register falls to be amended under section 11.

(3)   Where at any time –

(a)   a right of common which is registered in a register of common land or town or village greens as attached to any land has been apportioned by virtue of any disposition affecting the land, and
(b)   no amendments have been made under subsection (1) in respect of the apportionment of that right, the rights of common subsisting as a result of the apportionment shall be regarded as rights which are registered in that register as attached to the land to which they attach as a result of the apportionment.

9   Severance

(1)   This section applies to a right of common which –

(a)   is registered in a register of common land or town or village greens as attached to any land; and
(b)   would, apart from this section, be capable of being severed from that land.

(2)   A right of common to which this section applies is not at any time on or after the day on which this section comes into force capable of being severed from the land to which it is attached, except –

(a)   where the severance is authorised by or under Schedule 1; or
(b)   where the severance is authorised by or under any other Act.

(3)   Where any instrument made on or after the day on which this section comes into force would effect a disposition in relation to a right of common to which this section applies in contravention of subsection (2), the instrument is void to the extent that it would effect such a disposition.

(4)   Where by virtue of any instrument made on or after the day on which this section comes into force –

(a)   a disposition takes effect in relation to land to which a right of common to which this section applies is attached, and

(b)   the disposition would have the effect of contravening subsection (2), the disposition also has effect in relation to the right notwithstanding anything in the instrument to the contrary.

(5)   Where by virtue of any instrument made on or after the day on which this section comes into force a right of common to which this section applies falls to be apportioned between different parts of the land to which it is attached, the instrument is void to the extent that it purports to apportion the right otherwise than rateably.

(6)   Nothing in this section affects any instrument made before, or made pursuant to a contract made in writing before, the day on which this section comes into force.

(7)   This section and Schedule 1 shall be deemed to have come into force on 28 June 2005 (and an order under paragraph 2 of that Schedule may have effect as from that date).

Commencement – 9 September 2006, SI 2006/2145.

10   Attachment

(1)   This section applies to any right of common which is registered in a register of common land or town or village greens but is not registered as attached to any land.

(2)   The owner of the right may apply to the commons registration authority for the right to be registered in that register as attached to any land, provided that –

(a)   he is entitled to occupy the land; or

(b)   the person entitled to occupy the land has consented to the application.

11   Re-allocation of attached rights

(1)   Where –

(a)   a right of common is registered in a register of common land or town or village greens as attached to any land, and

(b)   subsection (2), (3) or (4) applies in relation to part of the land ('the relevant part'),

the owner of the land may apply to the commons registration authority for the register to be amended so as to secure that the right does not attach to the relevant part.

(2) This subsection applies where the relevant part is not used for agricultural purposes.

(3) This subsection applies where planning permission has been granted for use of the relevant part for purposes which are not agricultural purposes.

(4) This subsection applies where –

    (a) an order authorising the compulsory purchase of the relevant part by any authority has been made in accordance with the Acquisition of Land Act 1981 (c 67) (and, if the order requires to be confirmed under Part 2 of that Act, has been so confirmed);

    (b) the relevant part has not vested in the authority; and

    (c) the relevant part is required for use other than use for agricultural purposes.

(5) Regulations may for the purposes of subsections (2) to (4) make provision as to what is or is not to be regarded as use of land for agricultural purposes.

(6) Regulations may provide that an application under this section is not to be granted without the consent of any person specified in the regulations.

12 Transfer of rights in gross

The transfer of a right of common which is registered in a register of common land or town or village greens but is not registered as attached to any land –

    (a) only has effect if it complies with such requirements as to form and content as regulations may provide; and

    (b) does not operate at law until, on an application under this section, the transferee is registered in the register as the owner of the right.

13 Surrender and extinguishment

(1) The surrender to any extent of a right of common which is registered in a register of common land or town or village greens –

    (a) only has effect if it complies with such requirements as to form and content as regulations may provide; and

    (b) does not operate at law until, on an application under this section, the right is removed from the register.

(2) The reference in subsection (1) to a surrender of a right of common does not include a disposition having the effect referred to in section 7(1)(a).

(3) A right of common which is registered in a register of common land or town or village greens cannot be extinguished by operation of common law.

Registration, deregistration and exchange of land

14   Statutory dispositions

(1)   Regulations may make provision as to the amendment of a register of common land or town or village greens where by virtue of any relevant instrument –

(a)   a disposition is made in relation to land registered in it as common land or as a town or village green; or

(b)   a disposition is made in relation to a right of common registered in it.

(2)   Regulations may provide that, where –

(a)   by virtue of any relevant instrument a disposition is made in relation to land registered as common land or as a town or village green,

(b)   by virtue of regulations under subsection (1) the land ceases to be so registered, and

(c)   in connection with the disposition other land is given in exchange,

the land given in exchange is to be registered as common land or as a town or village green.

(3)   In this section, 'relevant instrument' means –

(a)   any order, deed or other instrument made under or pursuant to the Acquisition of Land Act 1981 (c 67);

(b)   a conveyance made for the purposes of section 13 of the New Parishes Measure 1943 (No. 1);

(c)   any other instrument made under or pursuant to any enactment.

(4)   Regulations under this section may require the making of an application to a commons registration authority for amendment of a register of common land or town or village greens.

(5)   Regulations under this section may provide that a relevant instrument, so far as relating to land registered as common land or as a town or village green or to any right of common, is not to operate at law until any requirement for which they provide is complied with.

15   Registration of greens

(1)   Any person may apply to the commons registration authority to register land to which this Part applies as a town or village green in a case where subsection (2), (3) or (4) applies.

(2)   This subsection applies where –

(a)   a significant number of the inhabitants of any locality, or of any neighbourhood within a locality, have indulged as of right in lawful sports and pastimes on the land for a period of at least 20 years; and

(b)   they continue to do so at the time of the application.

(3)   This subsection applies where –

(a)   a significant number of the inhabitants of any locality, or of any neighbourhood within a locality, indulged as of right in lawful sports and pastimes on the land for a period of at least 20 years;

(b)   they ceased to do so before the time of the application but after the commencement of this section; and

(c)   the application is made within the period of two years beginning with the cessation referred to in paragraph (b).

(4)   This subsection applies (subject to subsection (5)) where –

(a)   a significant number of the inhabitants of any locality, or of any neighbourhood within a locality, indulged as of right in lawful sports and pastimes on the land for a period of at least 20 years;

(b)   they ceased to do so before the commencement of this section; and

(c)   the application is made within the period of five years beginning with the cessation referred to in paragraph (b).

(5)   Subsection (4) does not apply in relation to any land where –

(a)   planning permission was granted before 23 June 2006 in respect of the land;

(b)   construction works were commenced before that date in accordance with that planning permission on the land or any other land in respect of which the permission was granted; and

(c)   the land –

    (i)   has by reason of any works carried out in accordance with that planning permission become permanently unusable by members of the public for the purposes of lawful sports and pastimes; or

    (ii)   will by reason of any works proposed to be carried out in accordance with that planning permission become permanently unusable by members of the public for those purposes.

(6)   In determining the period of 20 years referred to in subsections (2)(a), (3)(a) and (4)(a), there is to be disregarded any period during which access to the land was prohibited to members of the public by reason of any enactment.

(7)   For the purposes of subsection (2)(b) in a case where the condition in subsection (2)(a) is satisfied –

(a)   where persons indulge as of right in lawful sports and pastimes immediately before access to the land is prohibited as specified in subsection (6), those persons are to be regarded as continuing so to indulge; and

(b)   where permission is granted in respect of use of the land for the purposes of lawful sports and pastimes, the permission is to be disregarded in determining whether persons continue to indulge in lawful sports and pastimes on the land 'as of right'.

(8)   The owner of any land may apply to the commons registration authority to register the land as a town or village green.

(9)   An application under subsection (8) may only be made with the consent of any relevant leaseholder of, and the proprietor of any relevant charge over, the land.

(10)   In subsection (9) –

'relevant charge' means –

    (a)   in relation to land which is registered in the register of title, a registered charge within the meaning of the Land Registration Act 2002 (c 9);

    (b)   in relation to land which is not so registered –

        (i)   a charge registered under the Land Charges Act 1972 (c 61); or

        (ii)   a legal mortgage, within the meaning of the Law of Property Act 1925 (c 20), which is not registered under the Land Charges Act 1972;

'relevant leaseholder' means a leaseholder under a lease for a term of more than seven years from the date on which the lease was granted.

16   Deregistration and exchange: applications

(1)   The owner of any land registered as common land or as a town or village green may apply to the appropriate national authority for the land ('the release land') to cease to be so registered.

(2)   If the release land is more than 200 square metres in area, the application must include a proposal under subsection (3).

(3)   A proposal under this subsection is a proposal that land specified in the application ('replacement land') be registered as common land or as a town or village green in place of the release land.

(4)   If the release land is not more than 200 square metres in area, the application may include a proposal under subsection (3).

(5)   Where the application includes a proposal under subsection (3) –

    (a)   the replacement land must be land to which this Part applies;

    (b)   the replacement land must not already be registered as common land or as a town or village green; and

    (c)   if the owner of the release land does not own the replacement land, the owner of the replacement land must join in the application.

(6)   In determining the application, the appropriate national authority shall have regard to –

    (a)   the interests of persons having rights in relation to, or occupying, the release land (and in particular persons exercising rights of common over it);

    (b)   the interests of the neighbourhood;

    (c)   the public interest;

    (d)   any other matter considered to be relevant.

(7)   The appropriate national authority shall in a case where –

    (a)   the release land is not more than 200 square metres in area, and

    (b)   the application does not include a proposal under subsection (3), have particular regard under subsection (6) to the extent to which the absence of such a proposal is prejudicial to the interests specified in paragraphs (a) to (c) of that subsection.

(8)   The reference in subsection (6)(c) to the public interest includes the public interest in –

(a)   nature conservation;

(b)   the conservation of the landscape;

(c)   the protection of public rights of access to any area of land; and

(d)   the protection of archaeological remains and features of historic interest.

(9)   An application under this section may only be made with the consent of any relevant leaseholder of, and the proprietor of any relevant charge over –

(a)   the release land;

(b)   any replacement land.

(10)   In subsection (9) 'relevant charge' and 'relevant leaseholder' have the meanings given by section 15(10).

17   Deregistration and exchange: orders

(1)   Where the appropriate national authority grants an application under section 16 it must make an order requiring the commons registration authority to remove the release land from its register of common land or town or village greens.

(2)   Where the application included a proposal to register replacement land, the order shall also require the commons registration authority –

(a)   to register the replacement land as common land or as a town or village green in place of the release land; and

(b)   to register as exercisable over the replacement land any rights of common which, immediately before the relevant date, are registered as exercisable over the release land.

(3)   A commons registration authority must take such other steps on receiving an order under this section as regulations may require.

(4)   Where immediately before the relevant date any rights of common are registered as exercisable over the release land, those rights are on that date extinguished in relation to that land.

(5)   Where immediately before the relevant date any rights are exercisable over the release land by virtue of its being, or being part of, a town or village green –

(a)   those rights are extinguished on that date in respect of the release land; and

(b)   where any replacement land is registered in its place, those rights shall become exercisable as from that date over the replacement land instead.

(6)   Where immediately before the relevant date the release land was registered as common land and any relevant provision applied in relation to it –

(a)   the provision shall on that date cease to apply to the release land; and

(b)   where any replacement land is registered in its place, the provision shall on that date apply to the replacement land instead.

(7)   An order under this section may contain –

(a)   provision disapplying the effect of subsection (5)(b) or (6)(b) in relation to any replacement land;

(b)   supplementary provision as to the effect in relation to any replacement land of –

  (i)   any rights exercisable over the release land by virtue of its being, or being part of, a town or village green;
  (ii)   any relevant provision;

(c)   supplementary provision as to the effect in relation to the release land or any replacement land of any local or personal Act.

(8)   In subsections (6) and (7) 'relevant provision' means a provision contained in, or made under –

(a)   section 193 of the Law of Property Act 1925 (c 20);
(b)   a scheme under the Metropolitan Commons Act 1866 (c 122);
(c)   an Act under the Commons Act 1876 (c 56) confirming a provisional order of the Inclosure Commissioners;
(d)   a scheme under the Commons Act 1899 (c 30);
(e)   section 1 of the Commons Act 1908 (c 44).

(9)   In this section, 'relevant date' means the date on which the commons registration authority amends its register as required under subsections (1) and (2).

(10)   Regulations may make provision for the publication of an order under this section.

Conclusiveness and correction of the registers

18   Conclusiveness

(1)   This section applies to land registered as common land, or as a town or village green, which is registered as being subject to a right of common.

(2)   If the land would not otherwise have been subject to that right, it shall be deemed to have become subject to that right, as specified in the register, upon its registration.

(3)   If the right is registered as attached to any land, the right shall, if it would not otherwise have attached to that land, be deemed to have become so attached upon registration of its attachment.

(4)   If the right is not registered as attached to any land, the person registered as the owner of the right shall, if he would not otherwise have been its owner, be deemed to have become its owner upon his registration.

(5)   Nothing in subsection (2) affects any constraint on the exercise of a right of common where the constraint does not appear in the register.

(6)   It is immaterial whether the registration referred to in subsection (2), (3) or (4) occurred before or after the commencement of this section.

19   Correction

(1)   A commons registration authority may amend its register of common land or town or village greens for any purpose referred to in subsection (2).

(2) Those purposes are –

(a) correcting a mistake made by the commons registration authority in making or amending an entry in the register;

(b) correcting any other mistake, where the amendment would not affect –

(i) the extent of any land registered as common land or as a town or village green; or

(ii) what can be done by virtue of a right of common;

(c) removing a duplicate entry from the register;

(d) updating the details of any name or address referred to in an entry;

(e) updating any entry in the register relating to land registered as common land or as a town or village green to take account of accretion or diluvion.

(3) References in this section to a mistake include –

(a) a mistaken omission, and

(b) an unclear or ambiguous description,

and it is immaterial for the purposes of this section whether a mistake was made before or after the commencement of this section.

(4) An amendment may be made by a commons registration authority –

(a) on its own initiative; or

(b) on the application of any person.

(5) A mistake in a register may not be corrected under this section if the authority considers that, by reason of reliance reasonably placed on the register by any person or for any other reason, it would in all the circumstances be unfair to do so.

(6) Regulations may make further provision as to the criteria to be applied in determining an application or proposal under this section.

(7) The High Court may order a commons registration authority to amend its register of common land or town or village greens if the High Court is satisfied that –

(a) any entry in the register, or any information in an entry, was at any time included in the register as a result of fraud; and

(b) it would be just to amend the register.

Information etc

20   Inspection

(1) Any person may inspect and make copies of, or of any part of –

(a) a register of common land or town or village greens;

(b) any document kept by a commons registration authority which is referred to in such a register;

(c) any other document kept by a commons registration authority which relates to an application made at any time in relation to such a register.

(2) The right in subsection (1) is subject to regulations which may, in particular –

    (a)   provide for exceptions to the right;

    (b)   impose conditions on its exercise.

(3)   Conditions under subsection (2)(b) may include conditions requiring the payment of a fee (which may be a fee determined by a commons registration authority).

21   Official copies

(1)   An official copy of, or of any part of –

    (a)   a register of common land or town or village greens,

    (b)   any document kept by a commons registration authority which is referred to in such a register, or

    (c)   any other document kept by a commons registration authority which relates to an application made at any time in relation to such a register,

is admissible in evidence to the same extent as the original.

(2)   Regulations may make provision for the issue of official copies and may in particular make provision about –

    (a)   the form of official copies;

    (b)   who may issue official copies;

    (c)   applications for official copies;

    (d)   the conditions to be met by applicants for official copies.

(3)   Conditions under subsection (2)(d) may include conditions requiring the payment of a fee (which may be a fee determined by a commons registration authority).

Transitory and transitional provision

22   Non-registration or mistaken registration under the 1965 Act

Schedule 2 (non-registration or mistaken registration under the Commons Registration Act 1965 (c 64)) has effect.

23   Transitional

(1)   Schedule 3 (transitional provision) has effect.

(2)   Nothing in Schedule 3 affects the power to make transitional provision and savings in an order under section 56; and an order under that section may modify any provision made by that Schedule.

Commencement – 1 October 2006, SI 2006/2504so far as it relates to Sch 3, para 9.

Supplementary

24   Applications etc

(1)   Regulations may make provision as to the making and determination of any application for the amendment of a register of common land or town or village greens under or for the purposes of this Part.

(2)   Regulations under subsection (1) may in particular make provision as to –

(a)   the steps to be taken by a person before making an application;

(b)   the form of an application;

(c)   the information or evidence to be supplied with an application;

(d)   the fee payable on an application (which may be a fee determined by the person to whom the application is made);

(e)   the persons to be notified of an application;

(f)   the publication of an application;

(g)   the making of objections to an application;

(h)   the persons who must be consulted, or whose advice must be sought, in relation to an application;

(i)   the holding of an inquiry before determination of an application;

(j)   the evidence to be taken into account in making a determination and the weight to be given to any evidence;

(k)   the persons to be notified of any determination;

(l)   the publication of a determination;

(m)   the amendments to be made by a commons registration authority to a register of common land or town or village greens pursuant to a determination;

(n)   the time at which any such amendments are to be regarded as having been made.

(3)   In the case of an application made for the purposes of any of –

(a)   sections 6 to 8, 12 and 13,

(b)   paragraph 1 or 3 of Schedule 1,

(c)   paragraph 2 or 3 of Schedule 2, and

(d)   paragraph 2(5)(a) of Schedule 3,

regulations under subsection (1) may make provision as to the persons entitled to make the application.

(4)   An application made for the purposes of any of –

(a)   sections 6, 7, 10, 11, 12, 13 and 15, and

(b)   paragraph 1 or 3 of Schedule 1,

shall, subject to any provision made by or under this Part, be granted.

(5)   Regulations under subsection (1) may include provision for the appropriate national authority to appoint a person to discharge any or all of its functions in relation to an application made to it under section 16.

(6)   Regulations may make provision as to the making and determination of any proposal by a commons registration authority to amend a register on its own initiative pursuant to section 19, Schedule 2 or paragraph 2(5)(b) of Schedule 3.

(7)   Regulations under subsection (6) may in particular make provision as to –

    (a)   the persons to be notified of a proposal;

    (b)   the publication of a proposal (and the information or evidence to be published with a proposal);

    (c)   the making of objections to a proposal;

    (d)   the persons who must be consulted, or whose advice must be sought, in relation to a proposal;

    (e)   the holding of an inquiry before determination of a proposal;

    (f)   the evidence to be taken into account in making a determination and the weight to be given to any evidence;

    (g)   the persons to be notified of any determination;

    (h)   the publication of a determination;

    (i)   the amendments to be made by a commons registration authority to a register of common land or town or village greens pursuant to a determination.

(8)   Regulations under this section may include provision for –

    (a)   the appropriate national authority to appoint persons as eligible to discharge functions of a commons registration authority in relation to applications made to, or proposals made by, the commons registration authority; and

    (b)   the appointment of one or more of those persons to discharge functions of the commons registration authority in the case of any description of application or proposal.

(9)   Regulations under this section may provide for the Church Commissioners to act with respect to any land or rights belonging to an ecclesiastical benefice of the Church of England which is vacant.

25   Electronic registers

(1)   Regulations may require or permit the whole or any part of a register kept under this Part to be kept in electronic form.

(2)   Regulations under subsection (1) may include provision as to –

    (a)   requirements to be complied with in relation to the recording of information in electronic form;

    (b)   the certification of information recorded in electronic form (including the status of print-outs of such information).

(3)   Regulations under subsection (1) may also include provision as to the process of converting a register, or part of a register, into electronic form.

(4)   The provision referred to in subsection (3) includes in particular provision –

    (a)   as to the publicity to be given to such a conversion;

    (b)   requiring a provisional electronic version to be made available for inspection and comment;

(c) as to the holding of an inquiry in relation to any question arising as a result of the conversion.

PART 2
MANAGEMENT

Commons councils

26 Establishment

(1) The appropriate national authority may, for any area or areas of land to which this section applies, establish a body corporate to carry out functions conferred under this Part.

(2) This section applies to any land that –

(a) is registered as common land; or
(b) is registered as a town or village green and is subject to rights of common.

(3) A body corporate established under this section is to be known as a 'commons council'.

(4) A commons council is to be established by order.

(5) An order establishing a commons council must specify –

(a) the name of the council;
(b) the area or areas of land for which the council is established.

27 Procedure for establishment

(1) This section applies where the appropriate national authority proposes to make an order under section 26 establishing a commons council.

(2) The appropriate national authority must –

(a) publish a draft of the proposed order in such manner as it thinks fit; and
(b) invite representations about it.

(3) The appropriate national authority may cause a local inquiry to be held.

(4) The appropriate national authority may not make the proposed order unless, having regard to –

(a) any representations received pursuant to subsection (2)(b), and
(b) the result of any local inquiry held under subsection (3),

it is satisfied that there is substantial support for the making of the order.

(5) For the purposes of subsection (4) the appropriate national authority must have particular regard to representations received pursuant to subsection (2)(b) from –

(a) persons having rights (other than rights of common) in relation to, or occupying, land specified in the draft order;
(b) persons who are entitled to exercise rights of common (and in particular

persons exercising rights of common) over any such land; and

(c)   persons with functions under an enactment which relate to the maintenance or management of any such land.

Status and constitution of commons councils

28   Status

(1)   A commons council is not to be regarded as the servant or agent of the Crown or as enjoying any status, immunity or privilege of the Crown.

(2)   The property of a commons council is not to be regarded as the property of, or as property held on behalf of, the Crown.

(3)   A commons council is not to be regarded as an authority to which section 28G of the Wildlife and Countryside Act 1981 (c 69) applies.

29   Constitution

(1)   The appropriate national authority must by regulations prescribe standard terms as to the constitution and administration of commons councils (in this Part, the 'standard constitution').

(2)   The terms of the standard constitution apply to every commons council, subject as follows.

(3)   An order under section 26 may also make provision as to the constitution and administration of a commons council.

(4)   Provision which may be made under subsection (3) includes in particular –

(a)   provision supplementary to any term of the standard constitution;
(b)   provision disapplying any such term;
(c)   provision replacing any such term.

(5)   Where in relation to a commons council –

(a)   provision is made under subsection (3) that is inconsistent with any term of the standard constitution, and
(b)   any such term has not been expressly disapplied under that subsection, the provision made under subsection (3) prevails, to the extent of the inconsistency, over the term of the standard constitution.

(6)   Terms of the standard constitution prescribed by regulations under subsection (1) may be amended by further regulations under that subsection; and this section applies in relation to such terms as amended as it applies in relation to the terms as first prescribed.

30   Constitution: supplementary

(1)   This section applies in relation to terms as to the constitution and administration of a commons council contained in –

(a)   the standard constitution; or
(b)   an order under section 26.

(2)   The terms may in particular include terms as to –

    (a)   the membership of the council;
    (b)   participation in the council by persons other than members;
    (c)   the proceedings of the council;
    (d)   the keeping and publication of accounts, annual reports and other information relating to the council.

(3)   The terms referred to in subsection (2)(a) include in particular terms as to –

    (a)   the appointment of members (by election or otherwise);
    (b)   the term for which members are appointed;
    (c)   co-option of members;
    (d)   the conduct of members;
    (e)   resignation and disqualification of members;
    (f)   termination and renewal of membership;
    (g)   payment of allowances to members.

(4)   The terms referred to in subsection (2)(b) include in particular terms as to –

    (a)   entitlement to elect members;
    (b)   entitlement to attend meetings.

(5)   The terms referred to in subsection (2)(c) include in particular terms as to –

    (a)   the frequency of meetings;
    (b)   voting procedures at meetings;
    (c)   committees and sub-committees.

(6)   The terms referred to in subsection (2)(d) include in particular terms as to –

    (a)   the appointment of auditors;
    (b)   the preparation and publication of accounts;
    (c)   the preparation and publication of annual reports.

(7)   Subject to any terms made of the kind referred to in subsection (2)(c), a commons council may regulate its own proceedings.

Functions of commons councils

31   Functions

(1)   An order under section 26 is to confer on a commons council functions relating to any one or more of the following –

    (a)   the management of agricultural activities on the land for which the council is established;
    (b)   the management of vegetation on the land;
    (c)   the management of rights of common on the land.

(2)   The functions conferred on a commons council under subsection (1) must be those the appropriate national authority considers appropriate in the case of that council.

(3)   The functions which may be conferred on a commons council under subsection (1) include in particular functions of –

   (a)   making rules relating to agricultural activities, the management of vegetation and the exercise of rights of common on the land for which the council is established;

   (b)   making rules relating to the leasing or licensing of rights of common;

   (c)   preparing and maintaining a register of grazing;

   (d)   establishing and maintaining boundaries;

   (e)   removing unlawful boundaries and other encroachments;

   (f)   removing animals unlawfully permitted to graze.

(4)   Rules made by virtue of subsection (3)(a) may have the effect of –

   (a)   limiting or imposing conditions on the exercise of rights of common over, or the exercise of rights to use the surplus of, the land for which the council is established;

   (b)   requiring the provision of information to the commons council in relation to the exercise of those rights.

(5)   In exercising a function conferred under subsection (3)(f), a commons council may –

   (a)   dispose of any animal it removes; and

   (b)   recover from the owner of the animal the costs that it may reasonably incur in removing and disposing of it.

(6)   A commons council must discharge its functions having regard to –

   (a)   any guidance given by the appropriate national authority; and

   (b)   the public interest in relation to the land for which it is established.

(7)   The reference in subsection (6)(b) to the public interest includes the public interest in –

   (a)   nature conservation;

   (b)   the conservation of the landscape;

   (c)   the protection of public rights of access to any area of land; and

   (d)   the protection of archaeological remains and features of historic interest.

32   Ancillary powers

(1)   A commons council has the power to do anything which it considers will facilitate, or is conducive or incidental to, the carrying out of its functions.

(2)   The power conferred by subsection (1) includes power to –

   (a)   enter into agreements;

   (b)   prepare and adopt management plans;

   (c)   raise money (including by applying for funds from any source);

   (d)   acquire or dispose of land;

   (e)   employ staff.

(3)   The power of a commons council to raise money as specified in subsection (2)(c) includes power to require the payment of fees in connection with –

(a)   the exercise of rights of common over, or the exercise of rights to use the surplus of, the land for which the council is established, and

(b)   participation in the council,

and any such fees owed to the council may be recovered as a debt due to it.

33   Consent

(1)   Subject to subsections (2) and (3), nothing in this Part authorises a commons council to do anything on the land for which it is established without the consent of a person with an interest in the land, where that person's consent would otherwise be required.

(2)   A commons council does not need the consent of a person who has a right of common over the land for which it is established in order to do anything on the land.

(3)   A commons council does not need the consent of any other person with an interest in the land for which it is established in order to do anything on the land where what is proposed to be done could be done without that person's consent by any person who has a right of common over the land.

(4)   Where a commons council wishes to obtain the consent of any person with an interest in the land for which the council is established in respect of anything it proposes to do on the land, it may serve a notice on him.

(5)   A notice under subsection (4) must specify –

(a)   what the commons council proposes to do;

(b)   the time within which the person on whom it is served may object (which may not be less than 28 days after service of the notice); and

(c)   the manner in which he may object.

(6)   If the person on whom a notice under subsection (4) is served does not object within the time and in the manner specified in the notice, he is to be regarded as having given his consent in relation to the proposal specified in the notice.

(7)   Where a commons council proposes to serve a notice on a person under subsection (4) but is unable after reasonable enquiry to ascertain his name or proper address –

(a)   the council may post the notice on the land; and

(b)   the notice is to be treated as having been served on the person at the time the notice is posted.

(8)   An order under section 26 may make further provision as to the form and service of notices under subsection (4).

(9)   For the purposes of this section, a person with an interest in any land is a person who –

(a)   owns the land; or

(b)   is entitled to exercise any right over the land.

34   Enforcement of rules

(1)   A person who breaches a rule to which subsection (2) applies is guilty of an offence.

(2)   This subsection applies to a rule which –

    (a)   is made with the consent of the appropriate national authority pursuant to a function of making rules conferred on a commons council under section 31; and

    (b)   specifies that a person who contravenes it is guilty of an offence under this section.

(3)   A person guilty of an offence under subsection (1) is liable on summary conviction to –

    (a)   a fine not exceeding level 4 on the standard scale; and

    (b)   in the case of a continuing offence, to a further fine not exceeding one half of level 1 on the standard scale for each day during which the offence continues after conviction.

(4)   A commons council may bring proceedings in relation to an offence under subsection (1) in respect of breach of any rule made by it to which subsection (2) applies.

(5)   A commons council may apply to a county court for an order to secure compliance with any rule that it has made pursuant to a function of making rules conferred on it under section 31.

(6)   But a commons council may only make an application under subsection (5) for the purpose of securing compliance with a rule to which subsection (2) applies if it is of the opinion that proceedings for an offence under subsection (1) would provide an ineffectual remedy against the person who has failed to comply with the rule.

(7)   On an application under subsection (5) the court may make such an order as it thinks fit.

35   Rules: supplementary

(1)   Any power to make rules conferred on a commons council under section 31 includes power to vary or revoke the rules made by the council.

(2)   An order under section 26 conferring a power to make rules may provide for the procedure to be followed in the exercise of the power (and may in particular require the consent of the appropriate national authority to be obtained before rules are made).

(3)   The appropriate national authority may by direction revoke any rule made by a commons council.

(4)   A direction under subsection (3) must set out the reason why the rule is being revoked.

(5)   Before revoking any rule under subsection (3) the appropriate national authority must consult –

(a)   the commons council; and

(b)   any other person it thinks appropriate.

Commons councils: supplementary

36   Consequential provision

(1)   The appropriate national authority may by order under section 26 make any provision specified in subsection (2) if it appears to the authority desirable to do so in consequence of functions conferred on a commons council in relation to any land.

(2)   The provision referred to in subsection (1) is provision to –

(a)   vary or abolish the jurisdiction so far as relating to the land of any court of a description referred to in Part 1 of Schedule 4 to the Administration of Justice Act 1977 (c 38) (certain ancient courts);

(b)   vary or revoke any regulations or arrangement made under the Commons Act 1908 (c 44);

(c)   vary or revoke any scheme made under the Commons Act 1899 (c 30), or any arrangement arising under such a scheme;

(d)   vary or revoke any Act made under the Commons Act 1876 (c 56) confirming a provisional order of the Inclosure Commissioners or any arrangement arising under such an Act;

(e)   vary or revoke any local or personal Act, or any scheme or arrangement under such an Act, which relates to the management or maintenance of, or the exercise of rights of common over, the land.

(3)   The appropriate national authority may not under subsection (1) make provision specified in subsection (2)(c) to (e) to the extent that to do so would have the effect of abolishing or restricting a right of access of whatever nature exercisable by members of the public generally or by any section of the public.

37   Variation and revocation of establishment orders

(1)   The appropriate national authority may by order under section 26 revoke a previous order under that section establishing a commons council only if it is satisfied that –

(a)   the council has ceased to operate;

(b)   the council is failing to discharge its functions in an effective manner; or

(c)   the council is, in discharging its functions, failing to have sufficient regard to the public interest as required by section 31.

(2)   An order under section 26 revoking a previous order under that section may include –

(a)   provision for the transfer of rights, property and liabilities of the commons council;

(b)   provision amending any enactment previously amended under section 36 in relation to the council.

(3)   Section 27 applies to an order under section 26 varying or revoking a previous order under that section as it applies to an order under that section establishing a commons council (but as if the references in section 27 to land specified in the order were to land affected by the variation or revocation).

PART 3

WORKS

38   Prohibition on works without consent

(1)   A person may not, except with the consent of the appropriate national authority, carry out any restricted works on land to which this section applies.

(2)   In subsection (1) 'restricted works' are –

(a)   works which have the effect of preventing or impeding access to or over any land to which this section applies;
(b)   works for the resurfacing of land.

(3)   The reference to works in subsection (2)(a) includes in particular –

(a)   the erection of fencing;
(b)   the construction of buildings and other structures;
(c)   the digging of ditches and trenches and the building of embankments.

(4)   For the purposes of subsection (2)(b) works are for the resurfacing of land if they consist of the laying of concrete, tarmacadam, coated roadstone or similar material on the land (but not if they consist only of the repair of an existing surface of the land made of such material).

(5)   This section applies to –

(a)   any land registered as common land;
(b)   land not so registered which is –

(i)   regulated by an Act made under the Commons Act 1876 (c 56) confirming a provisional order of the Inclosure Commissioners; or
(ii)   subject to a scheme under the Metropolitan Commons Act 1866 (c 122) or the Commons Act 1899 (c 30);

(c)   land not falling within paragraph (a) or (b) which is in the New Forest and is subject to rights of common.

(6)   The prohibition in subsection (1) does not apply to –

(a)   works on any land where those works, or works of a description which includes those works, are carried out under a power conferred in relation to that particular land by or under any enactment;
(b)   works on any land where the works are carried out under a power conferred by or under any enactment applying to common land;
(c)   works authorised under a scheme under the Metropolitan Commons Act 1866 or the Commons Act 1899 without any requirement for any person to consent to the works;

    (d)   works for the installation of electronic communications apparatus for the purposes of an electronic communications code network.

(7)   In subsection (6)(a) the reference to an enactment does not include Part 2 of this Act.

(8)   For the purposes of subsection (6)(b), an enactment applies to common land if it is expressed to apply (generally) to –

    (a)   registered common land;

    (b)   common land; or

    (c)   any common or commons, commonable land, land subject to inclosure under any enactment or other land of a similar description.

(9)   Subject to the following provisions of this Part, consent given to works under subsection (1) of this section constitutes consent for the purposes of that subsection only.

39   Consent: general

(1)   In determining an application for consent under subsection (1) of section 38 in relation to works on land to which that section applies, the appropriate national authority shall have regard to –

    (a)   the interests of persons having rights in relation to, or occupying, the land (and in particular persons exercising rights of common over it);

    (b)   the interests of the neighbourhood;

    (c)   the public interest;

    (d)   any other matter considered to be relevant.

(2)   The reference in subsection (1)(c) to the public interest includes the public interest in –

    (a)   nature conservation;

    (b)   the conservation of the landscape;

    (c)   the protection of public rights of access to any area of land; and

    (d)   the protection of archaeological remains and features of historic interest.

(3)   Consent may be given under section 38(1) –

    (a)   in relation to all or part of the proposed works;

    (b)   subject to such modifications and conditions relating to the proposed works as the appropriate national authority thinks fit.

(4)   In considering the effect in relation to any land of proposed works under this section, the appropriate national authority may consider that effect in conjunction with the effect in relation to that land of any other works for which consent has previously been given under section 38(1) above or section 194 of the Law of Property Act 1925 (c 20).

(5)   Where the appropriate national authority imposes any modification or condition in relation to any consent given under section 38(1), it may on the application of any person carrying out or proposing to carry out works in accordance with the consent vary or revoke that modification or condition.

(6)   Regulations may specify a time limit for the making of applications under subsection (5).

(7)   Consent may be given under section 38(1) in relation to works which have been commenced or completed; and any consent so given has effect from the time of commencement of the works.

40   Consent: procedure

(1)   Regulations may make provision as to the procedure to be followed in the making and determination of applications under sections 38(1) and 39(5).

(2)   Regulations under this section may in particular include provision –

(a)   as to the steps to be taken by an applicant before submitting an application;

(b)   as to the form and content of an application;

(c)   as to the procedure to be followed in making an application;

(d)   as to the evidence to be supplied in support of an application;

(e)   as to the fees payable in relation to an application;

(f)   as to the steps to be taken by the appropriate national authority upon receipt of an application;

(g)   for the appointment by the appropriate national authority of a person to discharge any (or all) of its functions in relation to the determination of an application;

(h)   for the making of representations or objections in relation to an application;

(i)   for the holding of a hearing or local inquiry in relation to an application;

(j)   for the publication of a determination of an application and the notification of interested persons.

41   Enforcement

(1)   Where any works are carried out on land to which section 38 applies in contravention of subsection (1) of that section, any person may apply to the county court in whose area the land is situated.

(2)   On an application under this section the court may make an order –

(a)   in any case, for removal of the works and restoration of the land to the condition it was in before the works were carried out;

(b)   in a case where consent has been given under section 38(1) but the works have not been carried out in accordance with any term of that consent, for the works to be carried out in such manner and subject to such conditions as the order may specify.

42   Schemes

(1)   This section applies in relation to works on relevant land where, by virtue of section 38(1), the works may not be carried out without the consent of the appropriate national authority.

(2)   In subsection (1) 'relevant land' means land which is subject to –

(a)   a scheme under the Metropolitan Commons Act 1866 (c 122) which is in force at the commencement of this section; or

(b)   a scheme under the Commons Act 1899 (c 30) which is in force at the commencement of this section.

(3)   Where –

(a)   any provision of the scheme referred to in subsection (2) would also prohibit the carrying out of the works, and

(b)   the scheme does not allow for any person to consent to the works to be carried out, the works do not contravene that provision if they are carried out with (and in accordance with the terms of) the consent of the appropriate national authority under section 38(1) and of any owner of the land (if not the person carrying out the works).

(4)   Regulations may make provision as to the procedure to be followed in obtaining the consent of an owner under subsection (3) (and may include provision for the consent of an owner to be regarded as having been given where he has not objected within a period of time specified in the regulations).

(5)   Where any provision of the scheme referred to in subsection (2) would also prohibit the carrying out of the works without the consent of the appropriate national authority –

(a)   consent given under section 38(1) is to be regarded as consent given under the scheme; and

(b)   consent may not be sought separately under the scheme.

43   Power to exempt

(1)   The appropriate national authority may by order provide that section 38 is not to apply to –

(a)   the carrying out by a specified person of specified works on specified land; or

(b)   the carrying out by a specified person, or a person of a specified description, of works of a specified description on –

(i)   any land; or
(ii)   land of a specified description.

(2)   The appropriate national authority may only make an order under subsection (1)(a) if it is satisfied that the works specified in the order are necessary or expedient for any of the purposes in subsection (4).

(3)   The appropriate national authority may only make an order under subsection (1)(b) if it is satisfied that works of the description specified in the order are likely to be necessary or expedient on any land, or on land of the description specified in the order, for any of the purposes in subsection (4).

(4)   The purposes referred to in subsections (2) and (3) are –

(a)   use of land by members of the public for the purposes of open-air recreation pursuant to any right of access;

(b)   the exercise of rights of common;

(c)   nature conservation;

(d)   the protection of archaeological remains or features of historic interest;

(e)   the use of the land for sporting or recreational purposes.

(5)   Where –

(a)   any land was at any time before the commencement of this section land to which section 194 of the Law of Property Act 1925 (c 20) applied, but

(b)   at any such time that section ceased to apply to the land by virtue of subsection (3)(a) of that section,

the appropriate national authority may by order provide that section 38 is not to apply to the carrying out of works, or works of a description specified in the order, on that land.

(6)   Where any land is the subject of a resolution under section 194(3)(b) of the Law of Property Act 1925 (c 20) immediately before the commencement of this section, the appropriate national authority may by order provide that section 38 is not to apply to the carrying out of works, or works of a description specified in the order, on that land.

(7)   An order under this section may provide that section 38 is not to apply only if the works to which the order relates are carried out in accordance with the terms of the order.

(8)   In subsection (1) 'specified' means specified in an order under that subsection.

44   Supplementary

(1)   Schedule 4 (which makes supplementary provision relating to works on common land) has effect. [1]

(2)   A national authority may for any purpose specified in subsection (3) by order amend –

(a)   any local or personal Act passed before this Act which contains provision for that authority to consent to works on land which is common land; and

(b)   any Act made under the Commons Act 1876 (c 56) confirming a provisional order of the Inclosure Commissioners which contains provision for that authority to consent to works on land to which the Act applies.

(3)   The purposes referred to in subsection (2) are –

(a)   that of securing that sections 39 and 40 apply to an application for the consent referred to in paragraph (a) or (b) of subsection (2) as they apply to an application for consent under section 38(1);

(b)   that of securing that section 41 applies in relation to the carrying out of works in contravention of the provision referred to in paragraph (a) or (b) of subsection (2) as it applies to works carried out in contravention of section 38(1).

(4)   In subsection (2) –

'national authority' means –

(a)   the Secretary of State; and
(b)   the National Assembly for Wales;

'common land' means –

(a)   any land registered as common land; and
(b)   any land not so registered which is subject to a scheme under the Metropolitan Commons Act 1866 (c 122) or the Commons Act 1899 (c 30).

Commencement – 1 October 2006, SI 2006/2504 so far as it relates to Sch 4, para 6.

PART 4
MISCELLANEOUS

Intervention powers

45   Powers of local authorities over unclaimed land

(1)   This section applies where –

(a)   land is registered as common land or a town or village green;
(b)   no person is registered in the register of title as the owner of the land; and
(c)   it appears to a local authority in whose area the land or any part of it is situated that the owner cannot be identified.

(2)   The local authority may –

(a)   take any steps to protect the land against unlawful interference that could be taken by an owner in possession of the land; and
(b)   institute proceedings against any person for any offence committed in respect of the land (but without prejudice to any power exercisable apart from this section).

(3)   In this section 'local authority' means –

(a)   a county, district or parish council in England;
(b)   a London borough council; and
(c)   a county, county borough or community council in Wales.

Commencement – 1 October 2006, SI 2006/2504.

46   Powers relating to unauthorised agricultural activities

(1)   This section applies where it appears to the appropriate national authority that –

(a)   a person is carrying out, or causing to be carried out by virtue of any arrangements, an agricultural activity on land which –

(i)   is registered as common land; or
(ii)   is registered as a town or village green and is subject to rights of common;

(b)   the activity is unauthorised; and
(c)   the activity is detrimental to –

    (i)   the interests of persons having rights in relation to, or occupying, the land; or

    (ii)   the public interest.

(2)   The appropriate national authority may, subject to the following provisions of this section, serve a notice on the person requiring him to do any one or more of the following –

    (a)   within such reasonable period as may be specified in the notice to stop carrying out the activity, or stop causing it to be carried out, to the extent that it is unauthorised;

    (b)   not to carry out, or cause to be carried out, any other unauthorised agricultural activity on the land which would be detrimental to the matters specified in subsection (1)(c)(i) and (ii);

    (c)   to supply the authority with such information relating to agricultural activities on the land carried out, or caused to be carried out, by him as it may reasonably require.

(3)   Before serving a notice under this section the appropriate national authority must, to the extent that it is appropriate and practicable in all the circumstances to do so –

    (a)   notify the persons specified in subsection (4) of its intention to serve the notice; and

    (b)   publicise its intention to do so (in such manner as it thinks fit).

(4)   The persons referred to in subsection (3)(a) are –

    (a)   any commons council for the land;

    (b)   any other person with functions under any enactment which relate to the maintenance or management of the land; and

    (c)   any person appearing to the authority to own or occupy the land.

(5)   Any notification or publication under subsection (3) may specify a period within which representations about the proposed notice may be made.

(6)   In deciding whether to serve a notice under this section the appropriate national authority must have regard to –

    (a)   any criminal or civil proceedings that have been or may be commenced in relation to the activity; and

    (b)   any steps taken by a commons council in relation to the activity.

(7)   If a person on whom a notice is served under this section fails to comply with it –

    (a)   the appropriate national authority may apply to a county court for an order requiring him to do so; and

    (b)   the court may make such an order for the purpose of securing compliance with the notice as it thinks fit.

(8)   For the purposes of this section, activity is unauthorised if the person carrying it out or causing it to be carried out –

    (a)   has no right or entitlement by virtue of his ownership or occupation of the land, or pursuant to any right of common, to do so; or

(b)   is not doing so with the authority of the person or persons entitled to give such authority.

(9)   The reference in subsection (1)(c)(ii) to the public interest includes the public interest in –

(a)   nature conservation;
(b)   the conservation of the landscape;
(c)   the protection of public rights of access to any area of land; and
(d)   the protection of archaeological remains and features of historic interest.

(10)   Section 123(1) to (5) of the Environment Act 1995 (c 25) applies in relation to the service of a notice under this section as it applies in relation to the service of a notice under that Act.

Abolition of powers of approvement and inclosure etc

47   Approvement

(1)   The Commons Act 1285 (13 Edw 1 c 46) (power of approvement) shall cease to have effect.

(2)   Any power of approvement of a common which subsists at common law is abolished.

Commencement – 1 October 2006, SI 2006/2504.

48   Inclosure

(1)   Section 147 of the Inclosure Act 1845 (c 118) (power to exchange common land for other land) shall cease to have effect.

(2)   The following shall cease to have effect –

(a)   section 2 of the Gifts for Churches Act 1811 (c 115);
(b)   in section 2 of the School Sites Act 1841 (c 38), the words from 'Provided also, that where any portion' to 'such conveyance;';
(c)   in section 1 of the Literary and Scientific Institutions Act 1854 (c 112),

the words from 'Provided also' to the end.

49   Notice of inclosure

(1)   Section 31 of the Commons Act 1876 (c 56) (three months' notice of claim to inclose to be given in local papers) shall cease to have effect.

(2)   In section 3 of the Metropolitan Commons Act 1878 (c 71), for 'Sections thirty and thirty-one' substitute 'Section 30'.

Commencement – 1 October 2006, SI 2006/2504.

Commons Act 1899

50   Schemes under the Commons Act 1899

(1)   The Commons Act 1899 (c 30) is amended as follows.

(2)   In section 1 (power of councils to make schemes for the regulation of commons) –

    (a)   in subsection (1), for the words from 'their district' to the end substitute 'in the public interest';

    (b)   after that subsection insert –

'(1A) In subsection (1), the reference to the public interest includes the public interest in –

    (a)   nature conservation;

    (b)   the conservation of the landscape;

    (c)   the protection of public rights of access to any area of land; and

    (d)   the protection of archaeological remains and features of historic interest.'

(3)   In that section, in subsection (3), omit the words from ', and for' to the end.

(4)   In that section, after subsection (3) insert –

'(4)   Regulations under subsection (3) may –

    (a)   prescribe alternative forms;

    (b)   permit exceptions or modifications to be made to any prescribed form.'

(5)   In section 2 (procedure for making scheme) –

    (a)   for subsections (1) to (3) and the first paragraph of subsection (4) substitute –

'(1)   A council is to make and approve a scheme under this Part of this Act in the prescribed manner.';

    (b)   renumber the second paragraph of subsection (4) as subsection (2).

(6)   For section 9 (power to amend scheme) substitute –

'9   Power to amend or revoke scheme

(1)   A scheme under this Part of this Act for any common may, in prescribed circumstances, be amended in the prescribed manner.

(2)   A scheme under this Part of this Act for any common may, where a new scheme is made under this Part of this Act for the whole of that common, be revoked in the prescribed manner.'

(7)   For section 10 (byelaws) substitute –

'10   **Byelaws**

(1)   A council which has made a scheme under this Part of this Act in relation to any common may make byelaws for the prevention of nuisances and the preservation of order on the common.

(2)   Sections 236 to 238 of the Local Government Act 1972 (which relate to the procedure for making byelaws, authorise byelaws to impose fines not exceeding level 2 on the standard scale, and provide for the proof of byelaws in legal proceedings) apply to all byelaws under this section.'

Vehicular access

51   Vehicular access

Section 68 of the Countryside and Rights of Way Act 2000 (c 37) shall cease to have effect.

Commencement – 1 October 2006, SI 2006/2504.

PART 5

SUPPLEMENTARY AND GENERAL

Amendments and repeals

52   Minor and consequential amendments

Schedule 5 (minor and consequential amendments) has effect.

Commencement – 1 October 2006, SI 2006/2504 so far as it relates to Sch 5, para 7(5) and para 7(1) so far as it relates to para 7(5).

53   Repeals

Schedule 6 (repeals, including consequential repeals and repeals of spent and obsolete enactments) has effect.

Commencement – 1 October 2006, SI 2006/2504 so far as it relates to Sch 6, Parts 1, 2 and 3 as specified.

54   Power to amend enactments relating to common land or greens

(1)   The appropriate national authority may by order amend any relevant Act so as to secure that –

(a)   a provision of that Act applying to common land does not apply to land to which Part 1 applies and which is not registered as common land;

(b)   such a provision applies to either or both of the following –

(i)   land registered as common land, or particular descriptions or areas of such land;

(ii)   land to which Part 1 does not apply, or particular descriptions or areas of such land.

(2)   The appropriate national authority may by order amend any relevant Act so as to secure that –

(a)   a provision of that Act which is expressed to apply to a town or village green does not apply to land to which Part 1 applies and which is not registered as a town or village green;

(b)   such a provision applies to either or both of the following –

(i)   land registered as a town or village green, or particular descriptions or areas of such land;

(ii)   land to which Part 1 does not apply, or particular descriptions or areas of such land.

(3)   In this section, 'relevant Act' means any public general Act passed before this Act.

(4)   For the purposes of subsection (1) a provision applies to common land if it is expressed to apply (generally) to common land, any common or commons, commonable land, land subject to inclosure under any enactment or other land of a similar description.

55   Power to amend enactments conferring functions on national authorities

(1)   A national authority may by order amend or repeal any provision of a local or personal Act passed before this Act which applies to common land for any of the following purposes –

(a)   to remove any function of the national authority which relates to the common land;

(b)   to transfer such a function from the national authority to another person;

(c)   to remove a requirement that the national authority be consulted, or that its consent be obtained, in respect of –

(i)   any act or omission relating to the common land; or

(ii)   any act or omission of a person concerned with the management of the common land;

(d)   to substitute for a requirement referred to in paragraph (c) a requirement that a person other than the national authority be consulted, or his consent obtained, in relation to the act or omission.

(2)   In subsection (1), 'common land' means –

(a)   any land registered as common land or as a town or village green;

(b)   any land referred to in section 5(2); and

(c)   any land not falling within paragraph (a) or (b) which is subject to a scheme under the Metropolitan Commons Act 1866 (c 122) or the Commons Act 1899 (c 30).

(3)   A national authority may by order amend or repeal any provision of an Act made under the Commons Act 1876 (c 56) confirming a provisional order of the Inclosure Commissioners for any of the following purposes –

(a)   to remove any function of the national authority which relates to land to which the Act applies;

(b)   to transfer such a function from the national authority to another person;

(c)   to remove a requirement that the national authority be consulted, or that its consent be obtained, in respect of –

(i)   any act or omission relating to land to which the Act applies; or

(ii)   any act or omission of a person concerned with the management of such land;

(d)   to substitute for a requirement referred to in paragraph (c) a requirement that a person other than the national authority be consulted, or his consent obtained, in relation to the act or omission.

(4)   In this section 'national authority' means –

(a)   the Secretary of State; and

(b)   the National Assembly for Wales.

Commencement and transitional provision

56   Commencement

(1)   The preceding provisions of this Act, except section 9 and Schedule 1 and sections 54 and 55, come into force in accordance with provision made by order by the appropriate national authority.

(2)   Sections 54 and 55 come into force at the end of the period of two months beginning with the day on which this Act is passed.

57   Severance: transitional

(1)   In relation to any area of England and Wales, the reference in subsection (1) of section 9 to a register of common land or town or village greens shall, during the relevant period in relation to that area, be read as a reference to such a register kept under the Commons Registration Act 1965 (c 64).

(2)   Sub-paragraph (6) of paragraph 1 of Schedule 1 shall not have effect in relation to a right of common severed (in accordance with that paragraph) from land in any area of England and Wales during the relevant period in relation to that area.

(3)   In this section, the 'relevant period', in relation to an area of England and Wales, is the period which –

(a)   begins with the coming into force of this section; and

(b)   ends with the coming into force of section 1 in relation to that area.

(4)   This section is deemed to have come into force on 28 June 2005.

58   Natural England

Any reference in a provision of this Act to Natural England shall, in relation to any time after the coming into force of that provision but before the coming into force of section 1(4) of the Natural Environment and Rural Communities Act 2006, be read as a reference to English Nature.

General

59   Orders and regulations

(1)   An order or regulations under this Act may make –

    (a)   transitional, consequential, incidental and supplemental provision or savings;

    (b)   different provision for different purposes or areas.

(2)   An order or regulations under this Act, other than an order under section 17, must be made by statutory instrument.

(3)   A statutory instrument containing regulations under section 29(1) or an order under section 54 or 55 may not be made by the Secretary of State (alone or jointly with the National Assembly for Wales) unless a draft has been laid before and approved by a resolution of each House of Parliament.

(4)   Subject to subsection (3), a statutory instrument containing any order or regulations made under this Act by the Secretary of State (alone or jointly with the National Assembly for Wales) other than an order under section 56 shall be subject to annulment in pursuance of a resolution of either House of Parliament.

60   Crown application

(1)   This Act (and any provision made under it) binds the Crown.

(2)   This section does not impose criminal liability on the Crown in relation to an offence under section 34(1).

(3)   Subsection (2) does not affect the criminal liability of persons in the service of the Crown.

61   Interpretation

(1)   In this Act –

'appropriate national authority' means –

    (a)   the Secretary of State, in relation to England; and

    (b)   the National Assembly for Wales, in relation to Wales;

'commons council' means a commons council established under Part 2;

'land' includes land covered by water;

'nature conservation' means the conservation of flora and fauna and geological and physiographical features;

'regulations' means regulations made by the appropriate national authority;

'register of title' means the register kept under section 1 of the Land Registration Act 2002 (c 9);

'right of common' includes a cattlegate or beastgate (by whatever name known) and a right of sole or several vesture or herbage or of sole or several pasture, but does not include a right held for a term of years or from year to year.

(2) In this Act –

    (a) any reference to land registered as common land or a town or village green is to land so registered in a register of common land or town or village greens;

    (b) any reference to a register of common land or town or village greens is to such a register kept under Part 1 of this Act.

(3) In this Act –

    (a) references to the ownership or the owner of any land are references to the ownership of a legal estate in fee simple in the land or to the person holding that estate;

    (b) references to land registered in the register of title are references to land the fee simple of which is so registered.

62   Short title

This Act may be cited as the Commons Act 2006.

63   Extent

This Act extends to England and Wales only.

SCHEDULES

SCHEDULE 1
Section 9
AUTHORISED SEVERANCE

Severance by transfer to public bodies

(1) A right of common to which section 9 applies may on or after the day on which this Schedule comes into force be severed permanently from the land to which it is attached by being transferred on its own to –

    (a) any commons council established for the land over which the right is exercisable;

    (b) Natural England (where the land or any part of it is in England); or

    (c) the Countryside Council for Wales (where the land or any part of it is in Wales).

(2) Where a person proposes to sever a right of common to which section 9 applies by a transfer under sub-paragraph (1)(b) or (c), Natural England or the Countryside Council for Wales as the case may be must –

(a) give notice of the proposal to the owner of the land over which the right is exercisable unless his name and address cannot reasonably be ascertained;

(b) in a case where there is no commons council established for the land, give notice of the proposal to such persons (if any) as they consider represent the interests of persons exercising rights of common over the land.

(3) A notice under sub-paragraph (2) must be given at least two months before the transfer and must –

(a) specify the name and address of the owner of the land to which the right is attached;

(b) describe the right proposed to be transferred, giving such details as regulations may specify;

(c) state the proposed consideration for the transfer; and

(d) give such other information as regulations may specify.

(4) Where a right of common to which section 9 applies is exercisable over land for which a commons council is established, the right may only be severed by a transfer under sub-paragraph (1)(b) or (c) if that council consents to the transfer.

(5) In a case where there is no commons council established for the land over which a right of common to which section 9 applies is exercisable, the appropriate national authority may by order provide that a person with functions of management conferred by any enactment in relation to that land is to be regarded, for any or all purposes of this paragraph, as a commons council established for the land.

(6) The severance of a right of common by its transfer under sub-paragraph (1) –

(a) only has effect if the transfer complies with such requirements as to form and content as regulations may provide; and

(b) does not operate at law until, on an application under this Schedule, the transferee is registered as the owner of the right in the register of common land or of town or village greens in which the right is registered.

Temporary severance by letting or leasing

2 (1) A right of common to which section 9 applies may, on or after the day on which this Schedule comes into force, to any extent be severed temporarily from the land to which it is attached by virtue of the right, or all or part of the land, being leased or licensed on its own in accordance with –

(a) provision made by order by the appropriate national authority; or

(b) rules made in relation to the land by a commons council under section 31.

(2) Provision under sub-paragraph (1)(a) and rules referred to in sub-paragraph (1)(b) may be framed by reference to –

(a) particular land or descriptions of land;

(b)   descriptions of persons to whom rights of common may be leased or licensed.

(3)   Where –

(a)   provision under sub-paragraph (1)(a) applies in relation to any land, and
(b)   rules referred to in sub-paragraph (1)(b) also apply in relation to that land and are inconsistent with that provision, the rules prevail over that provision, to the extent of the inconsistency, in relation to that land.

(4)   The appropriate national authority may by order provide that the leasing or licensing of a right of common (whether authorised by provision under sub-paragraph (1)(a) or by rules referred to in sub-paragraph (1)(b)) must comply with such requirements as to form and content as the order may provide.

Severance authorised by order

3 (1) The appropriate national authority may by order make provision authorising rights of common to which section 9 applies to be severed permanently from the land to which they are attached by transfer in accordance with that provision.

(2)   Provision under sub-paragraph (1) is to be framed by reference to –

(a)   particular land over which the rights of common are exercisable, or
(b)   particular descriptions of such land,

and may authorise transfers to particular persons, particular descriptions of persons or any person.

(3)   The appropriate national authority must, before making any provision under sub-paragraph (1) in relation to any land, consult such persons (if any) as it considers represent the interests of –

(a)   persons who own the land;
(b)   persons who exercise rights of common over the land.

(4)   Provision under sub-paragraph (1) may include provision securing that the owner of any land over which a right of common is exercisable is to be notified, and his consent obtained, before the right may be transferred.

(5)   Provision referred to in sub-paragraph (4) may include –

(a)   provision as to the circumstances in which notification may be regarded as having been given; or
(b)   provision as to the circumstances in which consent may be regarded as having been obtained.

(6)   Provision referred to in sub-paragraph (5)(b) may include –

(a)   provision for consent to be regarded as having been obtained if it is withheld unreasonably;
(b)   provision for the circumstances in which consent is to be regarded as withheld unreasonably;
(c)   provision for the resolution of disputes.

(7) The severance of a right of common by its transfer under provision under sub-paragraph (1) –

  (a) only has effect if the transfer complies with such requirements as to form and content as regulations may provide; and

  (b) does not operate at law until, on an application under this Schedule, the transferee is registered as the owner of the right in the register of common land or of town or village greens in which the right is registered.

(8) Provision under sub-paragraph (1) may include provision to secure the result that where –

  (a) the person to whom the right of common is transferred is the owner of land to which rights of common are attached, and

  (b) those rights are exercisable over the same land, or substantially the same land, as the right of common being transferred, the transferee must, when making an application as specified in subparagraph (7)(b), apply to the commons registration authority for the right to be registered as attached to the land referred to in paragraph (a).

SCHEDULE 2

Section 22

NON-REGISTRATION OR MISTAKEN REGISTRATION UNDER THE 1965 ACT

Introductory

1   In this Schedule 'the 1965 Act' means the Commons Registration Act 1965 (c 64).

Non-registration of common land

2 (1) If a commons registration authority is satisfied that any land not registered as common land or as a town or village green is land to which this paragraph applies, the authority shall, subject to this paragraph, register the land as common land in its register of common land.

(2) This paragraph applies to any land which –

  (a) was not at any time finally registered as common land or as a town or village green under the 1965 Act;

  (b) is land which is –

    (i)   regulated by an Act made under the Commons Act 1876 (c 56) confirming a provisional order of the Inclosure Commissioners;

    (ii)   subject to a scheme under Metropolitan Commons Act 1866 (c 122) or the Commons Act 1899 (c 30);

    (iii) regulated as common land under a local or personal Act; or

    (iv)   otherwise recognised or designated as common land by or under an enactment;

  (c) is land to which this Part applies; and

  (d) satisfies such other conditions as regulations may specify.

(3)   A commons registration authority may only register land under subparagraph (1) acting on –

(a)   the application of any person made before such date as regulations may specify; or

(b)   a proposal made and published by the authority before such date as regulations may specify.

Non-registration of town or village green

3 (1) If a commons registration authority is satisfied that any land not registered as a town or village green or as common land is land to which this paragraph applies, the authority shall, subject to this paragraph, register the land as a town or village green in its register of town or village greens.

(2)   This paragraph applies to any land which –

(a)   on 31 July 1970 was land allotted by or under any Act for the exercise or recreation of the inhabitants of any locality;

(b)   was not at any time finally registered as a town or village green or as common land under the 1965 Act;

(c)   continues to be land allotted as specified in paragraph (a);

(d)   is land to which this Part applies; and

(e)   satisfies such other conditions as regulations may specify.

(3)   A commons registration authority may only register land under subparagraph (1) acting on –

(a)   the application of any person made before such date as regulations may specify; or

(b)   a proposal made and published by the authority before such date as regulations may specify.

Waste land of a manor not registered as common land

4 (1) If a commons registration authority is satisfied that any land not registered as common land or as a town or village green is land to which this paragraph applies, the authority shall, subject to this paragraph, register the land as common land in its register of common land.

(2)   This paragraph applies to land which at the time of the application under sub-paragraph (1) is waste land of a manor and where, before the commencement of this paragraph –

(a)   the land was provisionally registered as common land under section 4 of the 1965 Act;

(b)   an objection was made in relation to the provisional registration; and

(c)   the provisional registration was cancelled in the circumstances specified in sub-paragraph (3), (4) or (5).

(3)   The circumstances in this sub-paragraph are that –

(a)   the provisional registration was referred to a Commons Commissioner under section 5 of the 1965 Act;

    (b)   the Commissioner determined that, although the land had been waste land of a manor at some earlier time, it was not such land at the time of the determination because it had ceased to be connected with the manor; and

    (c)   for that reason only the Commissioner refused to confirm the provisional registration.

(4)   The circumstances in this sub-paragraph are that –

    (a)   the provisional registration was referred to a Commons Commissioner under section 5 of the 1965 Act;

    (b)   the Commissioner determined that the land was not subject to rights of common and for that reason refused to confirm the provisional registration; and

    (c)   the Commissioner did not consider whether the land was waste land of a manor.

(5)   The circumstances in this sub-paragraph are that the person on whose application the provisional registration was made requested or agreed to its cancellation (whether before or after its referral to a Commons Commissioner).

(6)   A commons registration authority may only register land under subparagraph (1) acting on –

    (a)   the application of any person made before such date as regulations may specify; or

    (b)   a proposal made and published by the authority before such date as regulations may specify.

Town or village green wrongly registered as common land

5 (1) If a commons registration authority is satisfied that any land registered as common land is land to which this paragraph applies, the authority shall, subject to this paragraph, remove the land from its register of common land and register it in its register of town or village greens.

(2)   This paragraph applies to land where –

    (a)   the land was provisionally registered as common land under section 4 of the 1965 Act;

    (b)   the provisional registration became final; but

    (c)   immediately before its provisional registration, the land was a town or village green within the meaning of that Act as originally enacted.

(3)   A commons registration authority may only remove and register land under sub-paragraph (1) acting on –

    (a)   the application of any person made before such date as regulations may specify; or

    (b)   a proposal made and published by the authority before such date as regulations may specify.

Buildings registered as common land

6 (1) If a commons registration authority is satisfied that any land registered as common land is land to which this paragraph applies, the authority shall, subject to this paragraph, remove that land from its register of common land.

(2) This paragraph applies to land where –

(a) the land was provisionally registered as common land under section 4 of the 1965 Act;

(b) on the date of the provisional registration the land was covered by a building or was within the curtilage of a building;

(c) the provisional registration became final; and

(d) since the date of the provisional registration the land has at all times been, and still is, covered by a building or within the curtilage of a building.

(3) A commons registration authority may only remove land under subparagraph (1) acting on –

(a) the application of any person made before such date as regulations may specify; or

(b) a proposal made and published by the authority before such date as regulations may specify.

Other land wrongly registered as common land

7 (1) If a commons registration authority is satisfied that any land registered as common land is land to which this paragraph applies, the authority shall, subject to this paragraph, remove the land from its register of common land.

(2) This paragraph applies to land where –

(a) the land was provisionally registered as common land under section 4 of the 1965 Act;

(b) the provisional registration of the land as common land was not referred to a Commons Commissioner under section 5 of the 1965 Act;

(c) the provisional registration became final; and

(d) immediately before its provisional registration the land was not any of the following –

(i) land subject to rights of common;

(ii) waste land of a manor;

(iii) a town or village green within the meaning of the 1965 Act as originally enacted; or

(iv) land of a description specified in section 11 of the Inclosure Act 1845 (c 118).

(3) A commons registration authority may only remove land under subparagraph (1) acting on –

(a) the application of any person made before such date as regulations may specify; or

(b) a proposal made and published by the authority before such date as regulations may specify.

Buildings registered as town or village green

8 (1) If a commons registration authority is satisfied that any land registered as a town or village green is land to which this paragraph applies, the authority shall, subject to this paragraph, remove that land from its register of town or village greens.

(2)   This paragraph applies to land where –

(a)   the land was provisionally registered as a town or village green under section 4 of the 1965 Act;

(b)   on the date of the provisional registration the land was covered by a building or was within the curtilage of a building;

(c)   the provisional registration became final; and

(d)   since the date of the provisional registration the land has at all times been, and still is, covered by a building or within the curtilage of a building.

(3)   A commons registration authority may only remove land under subparagraph (1) acting on –

(a)   the application of any person made before such date as regulations may specify; or

(b)   a proposal made and published by the authority before such date as regulations may specify.

Other land wrongly registered as town or village green

9 (1) If a commons registration authority is satisfied that any land registered as a town or village green is land to which this paragraph applies, the authority shall, subject to this paragraph, remove the land from its register of town or village greens.

(2)   This paragraph applies to land where –

(a)   the land was provisionally registered as a town or village green under section 4 of the 1965 Act;

(b)   the provisional registration of the land as a town or village green was not referred to a Commons Commissioner under section 5 of the 1965 Act;

(c)   the provisional registration became final; and

(d)   immediately before its provisional registration the land was not –

(i)   common land within the meaning of that Act; or

(ii) a town or village green.

(3)   For the purposes of sub-paragraph (2)(d)(ii), land is to be taken not to have been a town or village green immediately before its provisional registration if (and only if) –

(a)   throughout the period of 20 years preceding the date of its provisional registration the land was, by reason of its physical nature, unusable by members of the public for the purposes of lawful sports and pastimes; and

(b)   immediately before its provisional registration the land was not, and at the time of the application under this paragraph still is not, allotted by or under any Act for the exercise or recreation of the inhabitants of any locality.

(4) A commons registration authority may only remove land under subparagraph (1) acting on –

  (a) the application of any person made before such date as regulations may specify; or

  (b) a proposal made and published by the authority before such date as regulations may specify.

Costs

10 (1) Regulations may make provision as to the payment of costs which pursuant to an application under this Schedule are incurred by the applicant, an objector or the person determining the application.

(2) That provision may in particular include provision –

  (a) for the payment of costs by the applicant, an objector or a commons registration authority;

  (b) for the person determining an application or the appropriate national authority to determine who is liable to pay costs and how much they are liable to pay.

SCHEDULE 3

Section 23

REGISTRATION: TRANSITIONAL PROVISION

Interpretation

1 In this Schedule 'the 1965 Act' means the Commons Registration Act 1965 (c 64).

Transitional period for updating registers

2 (1) Regulations may make provision for commons registration authorities, during a period specified in the regulations ('the transitional period'), to amend their registers of common land and town or village greens in consequence of qualifying events which were not registered under the 1965 Act.

(2) The following are qualifying events for the purposes of this Schedule –

  (a) the creation of a right of common (by any means, including prescription), where occurring in relation to land to which this Part applies at any time –

    (i) after 2 January 1970; and

    (ii) before the commencement of this paragraph;

  (b) any relevant disposition in relation to a right of common registered under the 1965 Act, or any extinguishment of such a right, where occurring at any time –

    (i) after the date of the registration of the right under that Act; and

    (ii) before the commencement of this paragraph;

(c)   a disposition occurring before the commencement of this paragraph by virtue of any relevant instrument in relation to land which at the time of the disposition was registered as common land or a town or village green under the 1965 Act;

(d)   the giving of land in exchange for any land subject to a disposition referred to in paragraph (c).

(3)   In sub-paragraph (2)(b) 'relevant disposition' means –

     (a)   the surrender of a right of common;

     (b)   the variation of a right of common;

     (c)   in the case of a right of common attached to land, the apportionment or severance of the right;

     (d)   in the case of a right not attached to land, the transfer of the right.

(4)   In sub-paragraph (2)(c) 'relevant instrument' means –

     (a)   any order, deed or other instrument made under or pursuant to the Acquisition of Land Act 1981 (c 67);

     (b)   a conveyance made for the purposes of section 13 of the New Parishes Measure 1943 (No. 1);

     (c)   any other instrument made under or pursuant to any enactment.

(5)   Regulations under this paragraph may include provision for commons registration authorities to amend their registers as specified in subparagraph (1) –

     (a)   on the application of a person specified in the regulations; or

     (b)   on their own initiative.

(6)   Regulations under sub-paragraph (5)(b) may include provision requiring a commons registration authority to take steps to discover information relating to qualifying events, including in particular requiring an authority to –

     (a)   carry out a review of information already contained in a register of common land or town or village greens;

     (b)   publicise the review;

     (c)   invite persons to supply information for, or to apply for amendment of, the register.

3   At the end of the transitional period, any right of common which –

     (a)   is not registered in a register of common land or town or village greens, but

     (b)   was capable of being so registered under paragraph 2, is by virtue of this paragraph at that time extinguished.

4 (1) Regulations may make provision for commons registration authorities to amend their registers of common land or town or village greens after the end of the transitional period, in circumstances specified in the regulations, in consequence of qualifying events.

(2)   Regulations under this paragraph may provide that paragraph 3 is to be treated as not having applied to any right of common which is registered pursuant to the regulations.

5   Regulations under paragraph 2 or 4 may in particular include provision as to what is or is not to be regarded as severance of a right of common for the purposes of those regulations.

Effect of repeals

6   The repeal by this Act of section 1(2)(b) of the 1965 Act does not affect the extinguishment of rights of common occurring by virtue of that provision.

7   The repeal by this Act of section 21(1) of the 1965 Act does not affect the application of section 193 of the Law of Property Act 1925 (c 20) in relation to any land.

Ownership of common land or town or village green

8 (1) Where the ownership of any land is registered in any register under the 1965 Act immediately before the commencement of this Schedule the ownership shall, subject to this Part, continue to be registered in that register.

(2)   Where the ownership of land continues to be registered in a register of common land or town or village greens pursuant to sub-paragraph (1), if the commons registration authority is notified by the Chief Land Registrar that the land has been registered in the register of title, the authority shall –

(a)   remove the registration of ownership; and
(b)   indicate in the register in such manner as may be specified in regulations that the land has been registered in the register of title.

(3)   Regulations may require commons registration authorities –

(a)   to remove registration of ownership of land from their registers of common land and town or village greens;
(b)   to keep or otherwise deal with documents received by them in connection with the registration of ownership of land in such manner as the regulations may specify.

Vesting of unclaimed land

9 (1) The repeal by this Act of section 8 of the 1965 Act does not affect the vesting of land in any local authority (within the meaning of that Act) occurring by virtue of that provision.

(2)   Unless land so vesting is regulated by a scheme under the Commons Act 1899 (c 30), sections 10 and 15 of the Open Spaces Act 1906 (c 25) (power to manage and make byelaws) shall continue to apply to it as if the local authority had acquired the ownership under that Act of 1906.

Commencement – 1 October 2006, SI 2006/2504.

SCHEDULE 4

Section 44

WORKS: SUPPLEMENTARY

Metropolitan commons

1   In section 5 of the Metropolitan Commons Act 1866 (c 122) (prohibition on inclosure), after 'inclosure of a metropolitan common' substitute 'which is under the control and management of a London borough council'.

2 (1) The Schedule to the Ministry of Housing and Local Government Provisional Order Confirmation (Greater London Parks and Open Spaces) Act 1967 (c xxix) is amended as follows.

(2)   In article 12 (restriction on powers in relation to commons), in paragraph (1) omit '(which consent the Minister may give in such cases as he thinks fit)'.

(3)   In that article, after paragraph (2) insert –

'(2A) Sections 39 and 40 of the Commons Act 2006 apply in relation to an application for consent under paragraph (1) as they apply in relation to an application for consent under section 38(1) of that Act.

(2B) Section 41 of that Act applies in relation to the carrying out of works in contravention of paragraph (1) as it applies to works carried out in contravention of section 38(1) of that Act (and as if references to consent under that provision were to consent under paragraph (1)).'

(4)   Omit paragraph (3) of that article.

(5)   In article 17 (street improvement), in paragraph (1), after 'enactment' insert 'or in any scheme made under, or confirmed by, any enactment'.

(6)   In that article –

       (a)   in paragraph (2), omit the words from 'and the Minister' to the end;
       (b)   after that paragraph insert –

'(2A) Where an application is made for consent under paragraph (2) in the case of any common, section 40 of the Commons Act 2006 applies in relation to the application as it applies in relation to an application for consent under section 38(1) of that Act.

(2B) Where an application is made for consent under paragraph (2) in any other case, the Minister before giving any consent shall have regard to any representations made to him in the manner specified in paragraph (3).';

       (c)   in paragraph (3), after 'paragraph (2)' insert 'in a case to which paragraph (2B) applies'.

National Trust property

3 (1) Section 29 of the National Trust Act 1907 (c cxxxvi) (powers exercisable over common or commonable land) is amended as follows.

(2)   Renumber the existing provision as subsection (1).

(3) In that subsection, for 'consists of common or commonable land' substitute 'is land to which this section applies'.

(4) After that subsection insert –

'(2) This section applies to –
- (a) any land registered as common land;
- (b) land not so registered which is –

    (i) regulated by an Act made under the Commons Act 1876 confirming a provisional order of the Inclosure Commissioners; or
    (ii) subject to a scheme under the Metropolitan Commons Act 1866 or the Commons Act 1899; and
- (c) land not falling within paragraph (a) or (b) which is in the New Forest and is subject to rights of common.'

4 (1) Section 23 of the National Trust Act 1971 (c vi) (powers over common land) is amended as follows.

(2) In subsection (2), omit the words from ', and in giving' to the end.

(3) After that subsection insert –

'(2A) Sections 39 and 40 of the Commons Act 2006 apply in relation to an application for consent under subsection (2) of this section as they apply in relation to an application for consent under section 38(1) of that Act.

(2B) Section 41 of that Act applies in relation to the carrying out of works in contravention of subsection (2) of this section as it applies to works carried out in contravention of section 38(1) of that Act (and as if references to consent under that provision were to consent under subsection (2) of this section).

(2C) Nothing in section 38 of the Commons Act 2006 applies in relation to land to which section 29 of the Act of 1907 applies.'

New parishes

5 In section 15 of the New Parishes Measure 1943 (No. 1) (land subject to rights of common), in subsection (1), for the words from 'without the consent' to the end substitute 'without the consent of the Secretary of State and sections 39 and 40 of the Commons Act 2006 apply in relation to an application for such consent as they apply in relation to an application for consent under section 38(1) of that Act.'

Transitional provision

6 In its application to any works carried out on or after 28 June 2005 but before the day on which section 38(1) above comes into force, section 194(2) of the Law of Property Act 1925 (c 20) shall have effect as if the words 'interested in the common' were omitted.

Commencement – 1 October 2006, SI 2006/2504.

7   The prohibition in section 38(1) does not apply to works carried out in connection with the taking or working of minerals if –

(a)   the works were granted planning permission under any enactment before the commencement of section 38;

(b)   the works are carried out in accordance with that planning permission in the period allowed for the works to be carried out (subject to any extension of time granted before or after the commencement of that section).

SCHEDULE 5

Section 52

MINOR AND CONSEQUENTIAL AMENDMENTS

Countryside Act 1968 (c 41)

1 (1) The Countryside Act 1968 is amended as follows.

(2)   In section 9(6), for the definition of 'common land' substitute –

'"common land" means –

(a)   land registered as common land in a register of common land kept under Part 1 of the Commons Act 2006;

(b)   land to which Part 1 of that Act does not apply and which is subject to rights of common within the meaning of that Act;'.

(3)   In Schedule 2, in paragraph 7, for the words from 'section 22(1)' to the end substitute 'the principal section'.

Animals Act 1971 (c 22)

2   In section 11 of the Animals Act 1971, for the definitions of 'common land' and 'town or village green' substitute –

'"common land" means –

(a)   land registered as common land in a register of common land kept under Part 1 of the Commons Act 2006;

(b)   land to which Part 1 of that Act does not apply and which is subject to rights of common within the meaning of that Act;

"town or village green" means land registered as a town or village green in a register of town or village greens kept under Part 1 of the Commons Act 2006;'.

Wildlife and Countryside Act 1981 (c 69)

3   In section 52(2C) of the Wildlife and Countryside Act 1981 –

(a)   for 'common land' (in the first place where it occurs) substitute 'subject to rights of common (within the meaning of the Commons Act 2006)';

(b)   for the words from 'the commoners' to the end of the subsection substitute 'the persons with such rights or any of them and any commons council established under Part 2 of the Commons Act 2006 for that land'.

Norfolk and Suffolk Broads Act 1988 (c 4)

4   In Schedule 3 to the Norfolk and Suffolk Broads Act 1988, in paragraph 38(1)(d), for 'section 9 of the Commons Registration Act 1965' substitute 'section 45 of the Commons Act 2006'.

Criminal Justice and Public Order Act 1994 (c 33)
5   In section 61(9) of the Criminal Justice and Public Order Act 1994 –

(a)   for the definition of 'common land' substitute –

'"common land" means –

(a)   land registered as common land in a register of common land kept under Part 1 of the Commons Act 2006; and
(b)   land to which Part 1 of that Act does not apply and which is subject to rights of common as defined in that Act;';
(b)   in the definition of 'commoner', for the words from 'as defined' to the end substitute 'as so defined;';
(c)   in the definition of 'the local authority', for 'section 9 of the Commons Registration Act 1965' substitute 'section 45 of the Commons Act 2006'.

Environment Act 1995 (c 25)

6   In Schedule 9 to the Environment Act 1995, in paragraph 1 –

(a)   in sub-paragraph (2)(d), for 'section 9 of the Commons Registration Act 1965' substitute 'section 45 of the Commons Act 2006';
(b)   in sub-paragraph (6), for 'the Commons Registration Act 1965' substitute 'Part 1 of the Commons Act 2006'.

Countryside and Rights of Way Act 2000 (c 37)

7 (1) The Countryside and Rights of Way Act 2000 is amended as follows.

(2)   In section 1, in subsection (3) –

(a)   for paragraph (a) substitute 'land which is registered as common land in a register of common land kept under Part 1 of the Commons Act 2006.';
(b)   omit paragraph (b).

(3)   In that section, omit subsection (4).

(4)   In section 45(1), in the definition of 'rights of common', for 'the Commons Registration Act 1965' substitute 'the Commons Act 2006'.

(5)   In section 46(2), for 'section' substitute 'subsection'.

Commencement – sub-para (5) in force 1 October 2006, SI 2006/2504.

Land Registration Act 2002 (c 9)

8 (1) The Land Registration Act 2002 is amended as follows.

(2)　In section 27(2)(d), for 'the Commons Registration Act 1965 (c 64)' substitute 'Part 1 of the Commons Act 2006'.

(3)　In section 33(d), for 'the Commons Registration Act 1965 (c 64)' substitute 'Part 1 of the Commons Act 2006'.

(4)　In Schedule 3, in paragraph 3(1), for 'the Commons Registration Act 1965 (c 64)' substitute 'Part 1 of the Commons Act 2006'.

SCHEDULE 6

Section 53

REPEALS

PART 1

REPEALS RELATING TO REGISTRATION

Short title and chapter	*Extent of repeal*
Commons Registration Act 1965 (c 64)	The whole Act.[1]
Parliamentary Commissioner Act 1967 (c 13)	In Schedule 4, the paragraph relating to Commons Commissioners.
Local Government Act 1972 (c 70)	Section 189(1) and (2). [2]
Local Government Act 1985 (c 51)	In Schedule 8, paragraph 10(6). [3]
Dartmoor Commons Act 1985 (c xxxvii)	Section 8. [4]
Common Land (Rectification of Registers) Act 1989 (c 18)	The whole Act.
Courts and Legal Services Act 1990 (c 41)	In Schedule 10, paragraph 26.
Tribunals and Inquiries Act 1992 (c 53)	In Schedule 1, in Part 1, the entry relating to Commons Commissioners and assessors.
Judicial Pensions and Retirement Act 1993 (c 8)	In Schedule 6, paragraph 26.

Short title and chapter	Extent of repeal
Countryside and Rights of Way Act 2000 (c 37)	Section 1(3)(b) and (4).
	Section 46(1).[5]
	Section 98.
Land Registration Act 2002 (c 9)	In Schedule 11, paragraph 7.
Greenham and Crookham Commons Act 2002 (c i)	Section 33(1).[6]
Constitutional Reform Act 2005 (c 4)	In Schedule 7, in paragraph 4, the entry relating to the Commons Registration Act 1965.
	In Schedule 14, in Part 3, the entries relating (c 4) –cont. to –
	(a) Commons Commissioner and Chief Commons Commissioner; and
	(b) Substitute Chief Commons Commissioner.

Commencement – 1 October 2006, SI 2006/2504: [1] ss 8, 9 ad 13(a); [2] all sections; [3] all sections; [4] all sections; [5] s 46(1); [6] all sections.

PART 2
REPEALS RELATING TO WORKS

Short title and chapter	Extent of repeal
Metropolitan Commons Act 1866 (c 122)	Section 21. [1]
Commons Act 1876 (c 56)	In section 30, the words from 'Any person aggrieved' to the end of the section.[2]
	Section 36.
Commons Act 1899 (c 30)	Section 21. [3]

Short title and chapter	*Extent of repeal*
Law of Property Act 1925 (c 20)	Section 194.
Administration of Justice (Appeals) Act 1934 (c 40)	In the Schedule, the reference to subsection (2) of section 194 of the Law of Property Act 1925.
Compulsory Purchase Act 1965 (c 56)	In Schedule 7, the entry relating to the Commons Act 1899. [4]
Ministry of Housing and Local Government Provisional Order Confirmation (Greater London Parks and Open Spaces) Act 1967 (c xxix)	In article 12 of the Schedule – (a) in paragraph (1), the words '(which consent the Minister may give in such cases as he thinks fit)'; and (b) paragraph (3). In article 17(2) of the Schedule, the words from 'and the Minister' to the end.
National Trust Act 1971 (c vi)	In section 23(2), the words from ', and in giving' to the end.
Norfolk and Suffolk Broads Act 1988 (c 4)	In Schedule 3, paragraph 38(1)(b).
Local Government (Wales) Act 1994 (c 19)	In Schedule 16, paragraph 7(2).
Environment Act 1995 (c 25)	In Schedule 9, paragraph 1(2)(b).
Communications Act 2003 (c 21)	In Schedule 17, paragraph 3.

Commencement – 1 October 2006, SI 2006/2504: [1] all sections; [2] all sections; [3] all sections; [4] all sections.

PART 3
REPEALS RELATING TO APPROVEMENT AND INCLOSURE

Short title and chapter	*Extent of repeal*
Commons Act 1285 (13 Edw 1 c 46)	The whole Act. [1]

Short title and chapter	Extent of repeal
Gifts for Churches Act 1811 (c 115)	Section 2.
School Sites Act 1841 (c 38)	In section 2, the words from 'Provided also, that where any portion' to 'such conveyance;'.
Inclosure Act 1845 (c 118)	Section 147.
Inclosure Act 1847 (c 111)	Section 4.
Literary and Scientific Institutions Act 1854 (c 112)	In section 1, the words from 'Provided also' to the end.
Inclosure Act 1857 (c 31)	Sections 4 and 5.
Commons Act 1876 (c 56)	Section 31.
Law of Commons Amendment Act 1893 (c 57)	The whole Act. [2]
Commons Act 1899 (c 30)	In Schedule 1, the references to –

In Schedule 1, the references to –

(a)   the Poor Relief Act 1601;

(b)   the Gifts for Churches Act 1811;

(c)   the Church Building Act 1818;

(d)   the Poor Relief Act 1831;

(e)   the Crown Lands Allotments Act 1831;

(f)   the Union and Parish Property Act 1835;

(g)   the School Sites Act 1841;

(h)   the Literary and Scientific Institutions Act 1854.

Commencement – 1 October 2006, SI 2006/2504 [1] all sections; [2] all sections.

PART 4
REPEAL RELATING TO SCHEMES UNDER THE
COMMONS ACT 1899

Short title and chapter	Extent of repeal
Commons Act 1899 (c 30)	In section 1(3), the words from ', and for' to the end.

PART 5
REPEAL RELATING TO VEHICULAR ACCESS

Short title and chapter	Extent of repeal
Countryside and Rights of Way Act 2000 (c 37)	Section 68.

COMMONS REGISTRATION ACT 1965

(1965 c 64)

An Act to provide for the registration of common land and of town or village greens; to amend the law as to prescriptive claims to rights of common; and for purposes connected therewith

[5 August 1965]

1 Registration of commons and towns or village greens and ownership of and rights over them

(1) There shall be registered, in accordance with the provisions of this Act and subject to the exceptions mentioned therein –

    (a) land in England or Wales which is common land or a town or village green;

    (b) rights of common over such land; and

    (c) persons claiming to be or found to be owners of such land or becoming the owners thereof by virtue of this Act;

and no rights of common over land which is capable of being registered under this Act shall be registered [in the register of title].

(2) After the end of such period, not being less than three years from the commencement of this Act, as the Minister may by order determine –

    (a) no land capable of being registered under this Act shall be deemed to be common land or a town or village green unless it is so registered; and

    (b) no rights of common shall be exercisable over any such land unless they are registered either under this Act or [in the register of title].

(3) Where any land is registered under this Act but no person is registered as the owner thereof under this Act or [in the register of title], it shall –

    (a) if it is a town or village green, be vested in accordance with the following provisions of this Act; and

    (b) if it is common land, be vested as Parliament may hereafter determine.

Amendment – Land Registration Act 2002, s 133, Sch 11.

2 Registration authorities

(1) The registration authority for the purposes of this Act shall be –

    (a) in relation to any land situated in any county ... , the council of that county [or, if the county is a metropolitan county, the council of the metropolitan district in which the land is situated] ... ; and

    (b) in relation to any land situated in Greater London, the [council of the London borough in which the land is situated];

except where an agreement under this section otherwise provides.

(2) Where part of any land is in the area of one registration authority and part in that of another the authorities may by agreement provide for one of them to be the registration authority in relation to the whole of the land.

Amendment – Local Government Act 1972, s 272(1), Sch 30; Local Government Act 1985, s 16, Sch 8.

3 The registers

(1) For the purposes of registering such land as is mentioned in section 1(1) of this Act and rights of common over and ownership of such land every registration authority shall maintain –

(a) a register of common land; and
(b) a register of town or village greens;

and regulations under this Act may require or authorise a registration authority to note on those registers such other information as may be prescribed.

(2) Any register maintained under this Act shall be open to inspection by the public at all reasonable times.

4 Provisional registration

(1) Subject to the provisions of this section, a registration authority shall register any land as common land or a town or village green or, as the case may be, any rights of common over or ownership of such land, on application duly made to it and accompanied by such declaration and such other documents (if any) as may be prescribed for the purpose of verification or of proving compliance with any prescribed conditions.

(2) An application for the registration of any land as common land or as a town or village green may be made by any person, and a registration authority –

(a) may so register any land notwithstanding that no application for that registration has been made, and
(b) shall so register any land in any case where it registers any rights over it under this section.

(3) No person shall be registered under this section as the owner of any land which is registered [in the register of title] and no person shall be registered under this section as the owner of any other land unless the land itself is registered under this section.

(4) Where, in pursuance of an application under this section, any land would fall to be registered as common land or as a town or village green, but the land is already so registered, the registration authority shall not register it again but shall note the application in the register.

(5) A registration under this section shall be provisional only until it has become final under the following provisions of this Act.

(6) An application for registration under this section shall not be entertained if made after such date, not less than three years from the commencement of this Act, as the Minister may by order specify; and different dates may be so specified for different classes of applications.

(7) Every local authority shall take such steps as may be prescribed for informing the public of the period within which and the manner in which applications for registration under this section may be made.

Amendment – Land Registration Act 2002, s 133, Sch 11.

5 Notification of, and objections to, registration

(1) A registration authority shall give such notices and take such other steps as may be prescribed for informing the public of any registration made by it under section 4 of this Act, of the times and places where copies of the relevant entries in the register may be inspected and of the period during which and the manner in which objections to the registration may be made to the authority.

(2) The period during which objections to any registration under section 4 of this Act may be made shall be such period, ending not less than two years after the date of the registration, as may be prescribed.

(3) Where any land or rights over land are registered under section 4 of this Act but no person is so registered as the owner of the land the registration authority may, if it thinks fit, make an objection to the registration notwithstanding that it has no interest in the land.

(4) Where an objection to a registration under section 4 of this Act is made, the registration authority shall note the objection on the register and shall give such notice as may be prescribed to the person (if any) on whose application the registration was made and to any person whose application is noted under section 4(4) of this Act.

(5) Where a person to whom notice has been given under subsection (4) of this section so requests or where the registration was made otherwise than on the application of any person, the registration authority may, if it thinks fit, cancel or modify a registration to which objection is made under this section.

(6) Where such an objection is made, then, unless the objection is withdrawn or the registration cancelled before the end of such period as may be prescribed, the registration authority shall refer the matter to a Commons Commissioner.

(7) An objection to the registration of any land as common land or as a town or village green shall be treated for the purposes of this Act as being also an objection to any registration (whenever made) under section 4 of this Act of any rights over the land.

(8) A registration authority shall take such steps as may be prescribed for informing the public of any objection which they have noted on the register under this section and of the times and places where copies of the relevant entries in the register may be inspected.

(9) Where regulations under this Act require copies of any entries in a register to be sent by the registration authority to another local authority they may require

that other authority to make the copies available for inspection in such manner as may be prescribed.

6   Disposal of disputed claims

(1)   The Commons Commissioner to whom any matter has been referred under section 5 of this Act shall inquire into it and shall either confirm the registration, with or without modifications, or refuse to confirm it; and the registration shall, if it is confirmed, become final, and, if the confirmation is refused, become void –

(a)   if no appeal is brought against the confirmation or refusal, at the end of the period during which such an appeal could have been brought;

(b)   if such an appeal is brought, when it is finally disposed of.

(2)   On being informed in the prescribed manner that a registration has become final (with or without modifications) or has become void a registration authority shall indicate that fact in the prescribed manner in the register and, if it has become void, cancel the registration.

(3)   Where the registration of any land as common land or as a town or village green is cancelled (whether under this section or under section 5(5) of this Act) the registration authority shall also cancel the registration of any person as the owner thereof.

7   Finality of undisputed registrations

(1)   If no objection is made to a registration under section 4 of this Act or if all objections made to such a registration are withdrawn the registration shall become final at the end of the period during which such objections could have been made under section 5 of this Act or, if an objection made during that period is withdrawn after the end thereof, at the date of the withdrawal.

(2)   Where by virtue of this section a registration has become final the registration authority shall indicate that fact in the prescribed manner in the register.

8   Vesting of unclaimed land

...

Amendment – Repealed by the Commons Act 2006, s 53, Sch 6, Pt 1, with effect from 1 October 2006.

9   Protection of unclaimed common land

...

Amendment – Repealed by the Commons Act 2006, s 53, Sch 6, Pt 1, with effect from 1 October 2006.

10   Effect of registration

The registration under this Act of any land as common land or as a town or village green, or of any rights of common over any such land, shall be conclusive evidence of the matters registered, as at the date of registration, except where the registration is provisional only.

11   Exemption from registration

(1)   The foregoing provisions of this Act shall not apply to the New Forest or Epping Forest nor to any land exempted from those provisions by an order of the Minister, and shall not be taken to apply to the Forest of Dean.

(2)   The Minister shall not make an order under this section except on an application made to him before such date as may be prescribed.

(3)   The Minister shall not make an order under this section with respect to any land unless it appears to him –

(a)   that the land is regulated by a scheme under the Commons Act 1899 or the Metropolitan Commons Acts 1866 to 1898 or is regulated under a local Act or under an Act confirming a provisional order made under the Commons Act 1876; and

(b)   that no rights of common have been exercised over the land for at least thirty years and that the owner of the land is known.

(4)   The Minister shall, before dealing with any application under this section, send copies thereof to the registration authority and to such other local authorities as may be prescribed, and shall inform those authorities whether he has granted or refused the application; and those authorities shall take such steps as may be prescribed for informing the public of the application and its grant or refusal.

(5)   If any question arises under this Act whether any land is part of the forests mentioned in subsection (1) of this section it shall be referred to and decided by the Minister.

12   Subsequent registration under Land Registration Acts 1925 and 1936

The following provisions shall have effect with respect to the registration [in the register of title] of any land after the ownership of the land has been registered under this Act, that is to say –

(a)   . . .

(b)   if the registration authority is notified by the Chief Land Registrar that the land has been registered [in the register of title] the authority shall delete the registration of the ownership under this Act and indicate in the register in the prescribed manner that it has been registered under those Acts.

Amendment – Land Registration Act 2002, s 133, Sch 11, (4); Land Registration Act 1997, s 4(2), Sch 2, Pt I.

13   Amendment of registers

Regulations under this Act shall provide for the amendment of the registers maintained under this Act where –

(a)   ... (b)   any land becomes common land or a town or village green; or

(c)   any rights registered under this Act are apportioned, extinguished or released, or are varied or transferred in such circumstances as may be prescribed;

...

Amendment – Commons Act 2006, s 53, Sch 6, Pt 1, with effect from 1 October 2006.

14   Rectification of registers

The High Court may order a register maintained under this Act to be amended if –

(a)   the registration under this Act of any land or rights of common has become final and the court is satisfied that any person was induced by fraud to withdraw an objection to the registration or to refrain from making such an objection; or

(b)   the register has been amended in pursuance of section 13 of this Act and it appears to the court that no amendment or a different amendment ought to have been made and that the error cannot be corrected in pursuance of regulations made under this Act;

and, in either case, the court deems it just to rectify the register.

15   Quantification of certain grazing rights

(1)   Where a right of common consists of or includes a right, not limited by number, to graze animals or animals of any class, it shall for the purposes of registration under this Act be treated as exercisable in relation to no more animals, or animals of that class, than a definite number.

(2)   Any application for the registration of such a right shall state the number of animals to be entered in the register or, as the case may be, the numbers of animals of different classes to be so entered.

(3)   When the registration of such a right has become final the right shall accordingly be exercisable in relation to animals not exceeding the number or numbers registered or such other number or numbers as Parliament may hereafter determine.

16   Disregard of certain interruptions in prescriptive claims to rights of common

(1)   Where during any period a right of common claimed over any land was not exercised, but during the whole or part of that period either –

(a)   the land was requisitioned; or
(b)   where the right claimed is a right to graze animals, the right could not be or was not exercised for reasons of animal health;

that period or part shall be left out of account, both –

(i) in determining for the purposes of the Prescription Act 1832 whether there was an interruption within the meaning of that Act of the actual enjoyment of the right; and

(ii) in computing the period of thirty or sixty years mentioned in section 1 of that Act.

(2) For the purposes of the said Act any objection under this Act to the registration of a right of common shall be deemed to be such a suit or action as is referred to in section 4 of that Act.

(3) In this section 'requisitioned' means in the possession of a Government department in the exercise or purported exercise of powers conferred by regulations made under the Emergency Powers (Defence) Act 1939 or by Part VI of the Requisitioned Land and War Works Act 1945; and in determining in any proceedings any question arising under this section whether any land was requisitioned during any period a document purporting to be a certificate to that effect issued by a Government department shall be admissible in evidence.

(4) Where it is necessary for the purposes of this section to establish that a right to graze animals on any land could not be or was not exercised for reasons of animal health it shall be sufficient to prove either –

(a) that the movement of the animals to that land was prohibited or restricted by or under the Diseases of Animals Act 1950 or any enactment repealed by that Act; or

(b) that the land was not, but some other land was, approved for grazing under any scheme in force under that Act or any such enactment and the animals were registered, or were undergoing tests with a view to registration, under the scheme.

17 Commons Commissioners and assessors

(1) The Lord Chancellor shall –

(a) appoint to be Commons Commissioners such number of [persons who have a 7 year general qualification, within the meaning of section 71 of the Courts and Legal Services Act 1990,] as he may determine; and

(b) draw up and from time to time revise a panel of assessors to assist the Commons Commissioners in dealing with cases calling for special knowledge;

and shall appoint one of the Commons Commissioners to be Chief Commons Commissioner.

[(1A) A Commons Commissioner shall vacate his office on the day on which he attains the age of seventy years; but this subsection is subject to section 26(4) to (6) of the Judicial Pensions and Retirement Act 1993 (power of Lord Chancellor to authorise continuance in office up to the age of seventy-five years).]

(2) Any matter referred under this Act to a Commons Commissioner shall be dealt with by such one of the Commissioners as the Chief Commons Commissioner may determine, and that Commissioner may sit with an assessor selected by the Chief Commons Commissioner from the panel appointed under this section.

(3)   If at any time the Chief Commons Commissioner is for any reason unable to act, the Lord Chancellor may appoint another Commons Commissioner to act in his stead.

(4)   A Commons Commissioner may order any party to any proceedings before him to pay to any other party to the proceedings any costs incurred by that party in respect of the proceedings; and any costs so awarded shall be taxed in the county court according to such of the scales prescribed by county court rules for proceedings in the county court as may be directed by the order, but subject to any modifications specified in the direction, or, if the order gives no direction, by the county court, and shall be recoverable in like manner as costs awarded in the county court.

(5)   The Minister shall pay to the Commons Commissioners and assessors appointed under this section such fees and such travelling and other allowances as the Minister may, with the approval of the Treasury, determine, and shall provide the Commons Commissioners with such services and facilities as appear to him required for the discharge of their functions.

Amendment – Courts and Legal Services Act 1990, s 71(2), Sch 10; Judicial Pensions and Retirement Act 1993, s 26, Sch 6 (for savings see s 27, Sch 7 thereof).

18   Appeals from Commons Commissioners

(1)   Any person aggrieved by the decision of a Commons Commissioner as being erroneous in point of law may, within such time as may be limited by rules of court, require the Commissioner to state a case for the decision of the High Court.

(2)   So much of section 63(1) of the Supreme Court of Judicature (Consolidation) Act 1925 as requires appeals to the High Court to be heard and determined by a Divisional Court shall not apply to an appeal by way of case stated under this section, but no appeal to the Court of Appeal shall be brought against the decision of the High Court in such a case except with the leave of that Court or the Court of Appeal.

19   Regulations

(1)   The Minister may make regulations –

(a)   for prescribing the form of the registers to be maintained under this Act and of any applications and objections to be made and notices and certificates to be given thereunder;

(b)   for regulating the procedure of registration authorities in dealing with applications for registration and with objections;

(c)   for prescribing the steps to be taken by registration authorities for the information of other local authorities and of the public in cases where registrations are cancelled or modified;

(d)   for requiring registration authorities to supply by post, on payment of such fee as may be prescribed, such information relating to the entries in the registers kept by them as may be prescribed;

(e)   for regulating the procedure of the Commons Commissioners and, in particular, for providing for the summoning of persons to attend and give evidence and produce documents and for authorising the administration of oaths, and for enabling any inquiry or proceedings begun by or before one Commons Commissioner to be continued by or before another;

(f)   for enabling an application for the registration of rights of common attached to any land to be made either by the landlord or by the tenant and for regulating the procedure where such an application is made by both;

(g)   for enabling the Church Commissioners to act with respect to any land or rights belonging to an ecclesiastical benefice of the Church of England which is vacant;

(h)   for treating any registration conflicting with another registration as an objection to the other registration;

(i)   for requiring, before applications for registration are entertained, the taking of such steps as may be specified in the regulations for the information of persons having interests in any land affected by the registration;

(j)   for the correction of errors and omissions in the registers;

(k)   for prescribing anything required or authorised to be prescribed by this Act.

(2)   The regulations may make provision for the preparation of maps to accompany applications for registration and the preparation, as part of the registers, of maps showing any land registered therein and any land to which rights of common registered therein are attached, and for requiring registration authorities to deposit copies of such maps with such Government departments and other authorities as may be prescribed.

(3)   The regulations may prescribe the payment of a fee not exceeding five pounds on an application made after the end of such period as may be specified in the regulations.

(4)   The regulations may make different provision with respect to different circumstances.

(5)   Regulations under this Act shall be made by statutory instrument which shall be subject to annulment in pursuance of a resolution of either House of Parliament.

20   Orders

(1)   Any order made by the Minister under any provision of this Act may be varied or revoked by subsequent order made thereunder.

(2)   Any such order, other than an order made under section 11 of this Act, shall be made by statutory instrument.

(3)   Any statutory instrument made under this section shall be subject to annulment in pursuance of a resolution of either House of Parliament.

21   Savings

(1)   Section 1(2) of this Act shall not affect the application to any land registered under this Act of section 193 or section 194 of the Law of Property Act 1925 (rights of access to, and restriction on inclosure of, land over which rights of common are exercisable).

(2)   Section 10 of this Act shall not apply for the purpose of deciding whether any land forms part of a highway.

22   Interpretation

(1)   In this Act, unless the context otherwise requires –

'common land' means –

(a)   land subject to rights of common (as defined in this Act) whether those rights are exercisable at all times or only during limited periods;

(b)   waste land of a manor not subject to rights of common;

but does not include a town or village green or any land which forms part of a highway;

'land' includes land covered with water;

'local authority' means . . . the council of a county, . . . London borough or county district, the council of a parish . . . ;

'the Minister' means the Minister of Land and Natural Resources;

'prescribed' means prescribed by regulations under this Act;

['register of title' means the register kept under section 1 of the Land Registration Act 2002;]

'registration' includes an entry in the register made in pursuance of section 13 of this Act;

'rights of common' includes cattlegates or beastgates (by whatever name known) and rights of sole or several vesture or herbage or of sole or several pasture, but does not include rights held for a term of years or from year to year;

'town or village green' means land which has been allotted by or under any Act for the exercise or recreation of the inhabitants of any locality or on which the inhabitants of any locality have a customary right to indulge in lawful sports and pastimes [or which falls within subsection (1A) of this section].

[(1A)Land falls within this subsection if it is land on which for not less than twenty years a significant number of the inhabitants of any locality, or of any neighbourhood within a locality, have indulged in lawful sports and pastimes as of right, and either –

(a)   continue to do so, or

(b)   have ceased to do so for not more than such period as may be prescribed, or determined in accordance with prescribed provisions.

(1B) If regulations made for the purposes of paragraph (b) of subsection (1A) of this section provide for the period mentioned in that paragraph to come to an end unless prescribed steps are taken, the regulations may also require registration authorities to make available in accordance with the regulations, on payment of any prescribed fee, information relating to the taking of any such steps.]

(2) References in this Act to the ownership and the owner of any land are references to the ownership of a legal estate in fee simple in any land and to the person holding that estate, and references to land registered [in the register of title] are references to land the fee simple of which is so registered.

Amendment – Local Government Act 1985, s 102(2), Sch 17; Local Government Act 1972, s 272(1), Sch 30; Land Registration Act 2002, s 133, Sch 11; Countryside and Rights of Way Act 2000, s 98(1), (2); Countryside and Rights of Way Act 2000, s 98(1), (3); Land Registration Act 2002, s 133, Sch 11, para 7(1), (6).

23 Application to Crown

(1) This Act shall apply in relation to land in which there is a Crown or Duchy interest as it applies in relation to land in which there is no such interest.

(2) In this section 'Crown or Duchy interest' means an interest belonging to Her Majesty in right of the Crown or of the Duchy of Lancaster, or belonging to the Duchy of Cornwall, or belonging to a Government department, or held in trust for Her Majesty for the purposes of a Government department.

24 Expenses

There shall be defrayed out of moneys provided by Parliament any expenses of the Minister under this Act and any increase attributable to this Act in the sums payable under any other Act out of moneys so provided.

25 Short title, commencement and extent

(1) This Act may be cited as the Commons Registration Act 1965.

(2) This Act shall come into force on such day as the Minister may by order appoint, and different days may be so appointed for different purposes; and any reference in any provision to the commencement of this Act is a reference to the date on which that provision comes into force.

(3) This Act does not extend to Scotland or to Northern Ireland.

LAW OF PROPERTY ACT 1925

(1925 c 20)

PART XI

MISCELLANEOUS

Commons and Waste Lands

193   Rights of the public over commons and waste lands

(1)   Members of the public shall, subject as hereinafter provided, have rights of access for air and exercise to any land which is a metropolitan common within the meaning of the Metropolitan Commons Acts, 1866 to 1898, or manorial waste, or a common, which is wholly or partly situated within [an area which immediately before 1st April 1974 was] a borough or urban district, and to any land which at the commencement of this Act is subject to rights of common and to which this section may from time to time be applied in manner hereinafter provided:

Provided that –

(a)   such rights of access shall be subject to any Act, scheme, or provisional order for the regulation of the land, and to any byelaw, regulation or order made thereunder or under any other statutory authority; and

(b)   the Minister shall, on the application of any person entitled as lord of the manor or otherwise to the soil of the land, or entitled to any commonable rights affecting the land, impose such limitations on and conditions as to the exercise of the rights of access or as to the extent of the land to be affected as, in the opinion of the Minister, are necessary or desirable for preventing any estate, right or interest of a profitable or beneficial nature in, over, or affecting the land from being injuriously affected, [for conserving flora, fauna or geological or physiographical features of the land,] or for protecting any object of historical interest and, where any such limitations or conditions are so imposed, the rights of access shall be subject thereto; and

(c)   such rights of access shall not include any right to draw or drive upon the land a carriage, cart, caravan, truck, or other vehicle, or to camp or light any fire thereon; and

(d)   the rights of access shall cease to apply –

(i)   to any land over which the commonable rights are extinguished under any statutory provision;

(ii)   to any land over which the commonable rights are otherwise extinguished if the council of the county[, county borough] [or metropolitan district] . . . in which the land is situated by resolution assent to its exclusion from the operation of this section, and the resolution is approved by the Minister.

(2)   The lord of the manor or other person entitled to the soil of any land subject to rights of common may by deed, revocable or irrevocable, declare that this section shall apply to the land, and upon such deed being deposited with the Minister the land shall, so long as the deed remains operative, be land to which this section applies.

(3)   Where limitations or conditions are imposed by the Minister under this section, they shall be published by such person and in such manner as the Minister may direct.

(4)   Any person who, without lawful authority, draws or drives upon any land to which this section applies any carriage, cart, caravan, truck, or other vehicle, or camps or lights any fire thereon, or who fails to observe any limitation or condition imposed by the Minister under this section in respect of any such land, shall be liable on summary conviction to a fine not exceeding [level 1 on the standard scale] for each offence.

(5)   Nothing in this section shall prejudice or affect the right of any person to get and remove mines or minerals or to let down the surface of the manorial waste or common.

(6)   This section does not apply to any common or manorial waste which is for the time being held for Naval, Military or Air Force purposes and in respect of which rights of common have been extinguished or cannot be exercised.

Amendment – Local Government Act 1972, s 189(4); Countryside and Rights of Way Act 2000, s 46(3), Sch 4; Local Government (Wales) Act 1994, s 66(6), Sch 16; Local Government Act 1985, s 16, Sch 8; Local Government Act 1972, s 272(1), Sch 30; Countryside and Rights of Way Act 2000, ss 46(1)(a), 102, Sch 16, Pt I; maximum fine increased and converted to a level on the standard scale by the Criminal Justice Act 1982, ss 37, 38, 46.

194   *Restrictions on inclosure of commons*

(1)   The erection of any building or fence, or the construction of any other work, whereby access to land to which this section applies is prevented or impeded, shall not be lawful unless the consent of the Minister thereto is obtained, and in giving or withholding his consent the Minister shall have regard to the same considerations and shall, if necessary, hold the same inquiries as are directed by the Commons Act 1876 to be taken into consideration and held by the Minister before forming an opinion whether an application under the Inclosure Acts 1845 to 1882 shall be acceded to or not.

(2)   Where any building or fence is erected, or any other work constructed without such consent as is required by this section, the county court within whose jurisdiction the land is situated, shall, on an application being made by the council of any county [or county borough] . . . or district concerned, or by the lord of the manor or any other person interested in the common, have power to make an order for the removal of the work, and the restoration of the land to the condition in which it was before the work was erected or constructed, but any such order shall be subject to the like appeal as an order made under section thirty of the Commons Act 1876.

(3)   This section applies to any land which at the commencement of this Act is subject to rights of common:

Provided that this section shall cease to apply –

(a) to any land over which the rights of common are extinguished under any statutory provision;

(b) to any land over which the rights of common are otherwise extinguished, if the council of the county[, county borough] [or metropolitan district] . . . in which the land is situated by resolution assent to its exclusion from the operation of this section and the resolution is approved by the Minister.

(4) This section does not apply to any building or fence erected or work constructed if specially authorised by Act of Parliament, or in pursuance of an Act of Parliament or Order having the force of an Act, or if lawfully erected or constructed in connexion with the taking or working of minerals in or under any land to which the section is otherwise applicable, or to any [telecommunication apparatus installed for the purposes of a telecommunications code system] [electronic communications apparatus installed for the purposes of an electronic communications code network].

Amendment – Local Government (Wales) Act 1994, s 66(6), Sch 16; Local Government Act 1972, s 272(1); Sch 30; Local Government Act 1985, s 16, Sch 8; Telecommunications Act 1984, s 109, Sch 4; Communications Act 2003, s 406(1), Sch 17.

Modification –Environment Act 1995, s 70, Sch 9.

Prospective Repeal – Commons Act 2006, Sch 6 as from a date to be appointed.

INCLOSURE ACT 1857

(1857 c 31)

12 Proceedings for prevention of nuisances in town and village greens and allotments for exercise and recreation

And whereas it is expedient to provide summary means of preventing nuisances in town greens and village greens, and on land allotted and awarded upon any inclosure under the said Acts as a place for exercise and recreation: If any person wilfully cause any injury or damage to any fence of any such town or village green or land, or wilfully and without lawful authority lead or drive any cattle or animal thereon, or wilfully lay any manure, soil, ashes, or rubbish, or other matter or thing thereon, or do any other act whatsoever to the injury of such town or village green or land, or to the interruption of the use or enjoyment thereof as a place for exercise and recreation, such person shall for every such offence, upon a summary conviction thereof before two justices, upon the information of any churchwarden or overseer of the parish in which such town or village green or land is situate, or of the person in whom the soil of such town or village green or land may be vested, forfeit and pay, in any of the cases aforesaid, and for each and every such offence, over and above the damages occasioned thereby, any sum not exceeding [level 1 on the standard scale] and it shall be lawful for any such churchwarden or overseer or other person as aforesaid to sell and dispose of any such manure, soil, ashes, and rubbish, or other matter or thing as aforesaid; and the proceeds arising from the sale thereof, and every such penalty as aforesaid, shall, as regards any such town, or village green not awarded under the said Acts or any of them to be used as a place for exercise and recreation, be applied in aid of the rates for the repair of the public highways in the parish, and shall, as regards the land so awarded, be applied by the persons or person in whom the soil thereof may be vested in the due maintenance of such land as a place for exercise and recreation; and if any manure, soil, ashes, or rubbish be not of sufficient value to defray the expense of removing the same, the person who laid or deposited such manure, soil, ashes, or rubbish shall repay to such churchwarden or overseer or other person as aforesaid the money necessarily expended in the removal thereof; and every such penalty as aforesaid shall be recovered in manner provided by the Summary Jurisdiction Act 1848; and the amount of damage occasioned by any such offence as aforesaid shall, in case of dispute, be determined by the justices by whom the offender is convicted; and the payment of the amount of such damage, and the repayments of the money necessarily expended in the removal of any manure, soil, ashes, or rubbish, shall be enforced in like manner as any such penalty.

Amendment – Maximum fine increased and converted to a level on the standard scale by the Criminal Justice Act 1982, ss 37, 38, 46.

COMMONS ACT 1876

(1876 c 56)

PART II

AMENDMENT OF THE INCLOSURE ACTS

Field Gardens and Recreation Grounds

29 Town and village greens

An encroachment on or inclosure of a town or village green, also any erection thereon or disturbance or interference with or occupation of the soil thereof which is made otherwise than with a view to the better enjoyment of such town or village green or recreation ground, shall be deemed to be a public nuisance, and if any person does any act in respect of which he is liable to pay damages or a penalty under section twelve of the Inclosure Act 1857, he may be summarily convicted thereof upon the information of any inhabitant of the parish in which such town or village green or recreation ground is situate, as well as upon the information of such persons as in the said section mentioned.

This section shall apply only in cases where a town or village green or recreation ground has a known and defined boundary.

Amendment – Statute Law Revision Act 1894.

COUNTRYSIDE AND RIGHTS OF WAY ACT 2000

(2000 c 37)

Part I, Part II, s 68 and Schedules 1–4

ARRANGEMENT OF SECTIONS

PART I

ACCESS TO THE COUNTRYSIDE

CHAPTER I

RIGHT OF ACCESS

General

Schedules:

Schedule 1—Excepted land for the purposes of Part I

Schedule 2—Restrictions to be observed by persons exercising rights of access

Schedule 3—Delegation of appellate functions

Schedule 4—Minor and consequential amendments relating to Part I

An Act to make new provision for public access to the countryside; to amend the law relating to public rights of way; to enable traffic regulation orders to be made for the purpose of conserving an area's natural beauty; to make provision with respect to the driving of mechanically propelled vehicles elsewhere than on roads; to amend the law relating to nature conservation and the protection of wildlife; to make further provision with respect to areas of outstanding natural beauty; and for connected purposes.

[30 November 2000]

PART I
ACCESS TO THE COUNTRYSIDE

CHAPTER I
RIGHT OF ACCESS

General

1   Principal definitions for Part I

(1)   In this Part 'access land' means any land which –

(a)   is shown as open country on a map in conclusive form issued by the appropriate countryside body for the purposes of this Part,

(b)   is shown on such a map as registered common land,

(c)   is registered common land in any area outside Inner London for which no such map relating to registered common land has been issued,

(d)   is situated more than 600 metres above sea level in any area for which no such map relating to open country has been issued, or

(e)   is dedicated for the purposes of this Part under section 16,

but does not (in any of those cases) include excepted land or land which is treated by section 15(1) as being accessible to the public apart from this Act.

(2)   In this Part –

'access authority' –

(a)   in relation to land in a National Park, means the National Park authority, and

(b)   in relation to any other land, means the local highway authority in whose area the land is situated;

'the appropriate countryside body' means –

(a)   in relation to England, the [*Countryside Agency*][Natural England], and
(b)   in relation to Wales, the Countryside Council for Wales;

'excepted land' means land which is for the time being of any of the descriptions specified in Part I of Schedule 1, those descriptions having effect subject to Part II of that Schedule;

'mountain' includes, subject to the following definition, any land situated more than 600 metres above sea level;

'mountain, moor, heath or down' does not include land which appears to the appropriate countryside body to consist of improved or semi-improved grassland;

'open country' means land which –

(a)   appears to the appropriate countryside body to consist wholly or predominantly of mountain, moor, heath or down, and
(b)   is not registered common land.

(3)   In this Part 'registered common land' means –

(a)   land which is registered as common land under the Commons Registration Act 1965 (in this section referred to as 'the 1965 Act') and whose registration under that Act has become final, or
(b)   subject to subsection (4), land which fell within paragraph (a) on the day on which this Act is passed or at any time after that day but has subsequently ceased to be registered as common land under the 1965 Act on the register of common land in which it was included being amended by reason of the land having ceased to be common land within the meaning of that Act.

(4)   Subsection (3)(b) does not apply where –

(a)   the amendment of the register of common land was made in pursuance of an application made before the day on which this Act is passed, or
(b)   the land ceased to be common land by reason of the exercise of –

(i)   any power of compulsory purchase, of appropriation or of sale which is conferred by an enactment,
(ii)   any power so conferred under which land may be made common land within the meaning of the 1965 Act in substitution for other land.

Prospective amendment – Words substituted: Natural Environment and Rural Communities Act 2006, s 105(1), Sch 11, Pt 1, para 154, as from a date to be appointed.

2   Rights of public in relation to access land

(1)   Any person is entitled by virtue of this subsection to enter and remain on any access land for the purposes of open-air recreation, if and so long as –

(a) he does so without breaking or damaging any wall, fence, hedge, stile or gate, and

(b) he observes the general restrictions in Schedule 2 and any other restrictions imposed in relation to the land under Chapter II.

(2) Subsection (1) has effect subject to subsections (3) and (4) and to the provisions of Chapter II.

(3) Subsection (1) does not entitle a person to enter or be on any land, or do anything on any land, in contravention of any prohibition contained in or having effect under any enactment, other than an enactment contained in a local or private Act.

(4) If a person becomes a trespasser on any access land by failing to comply with –

(a) subsection (1)(a),

(b) the general restrictions in Schedule 2, or

(c) any other restrictions imposed in relation to the land under Chapter II,

he may not, within 72 hours after leaving that land, exercise his right under subsection (1) to enter that land again or to enter other land in the same ownership.

(5) In this section 'owner', in relation to any land which is subject to a farm business tenancy within the meaning of the Agricultural Tenancies Act 1995 or a tenancy to which the Agricultural Holdings Act 1986 applies, means the tenant under that tenancy, and 'ownership' shall be construed accordingly.

3 Power to extend to coastal land

(1) The Secretary of State (as respects England) or the National Assembly for Wales (as respects Wales) may by order amend the definition of 'open country' in section 1(2) so as to include a reference to coastal land or to coastal land of any description.

(2) An order under this section may –

(a) make consequential amendments of other provisions of this Part, and

(b) modify the provisions of this Part in their application to land which is open country merely because it is coastal land.

(3) In this section 'coastal land' means –

(a) the foreshore, and

(b) land adjacent to the foreshore (including in particular any cliff, bank, barrier, dune, beach or flat which is adjacent to the foreshore).

Maps

4 Duty to prepare maps

(1) It shall be the duty of the [*Countryside Agency*][Natural England] to prepare, in respect of England outside Inner London, maps which together show –

(a) all registered common land, and

(b)   all open country.

(2)   It shall be the duty of the Countryside Council for Wales to prepare, in respect of Wales, maps which together show –

(a)   all registered common land, and
(b)   all open country.

(3)   Subsections (1) and (2) have effect subject to the following provisions of this section and to the provisions of sections 5 to 9.

(4)   A map prepared under this section must distinguish between open country and registered common land, but need not distinguish between different categories of open country.

(5)   In preparing a map under this section, the appropriate countryside body –

(a)   may determine not to show as open country areas of open country which are so small that the body consider that their inclusion would serve no useful purpose, and
(b)   may determine that any boundary of an area of open country is to be treated as coinciding with a particular physical feature (whether the effect is to include other land as open country or to exclude part of an area of open country).

Prospective amendment – Words substituted: Natural Environment and Rural Communities Act 2006, s 105(1), Sch 11, Pt 1, para 155, as from a date to be appointed.

5   Publication of draft maps

The appropriate countryside body shall –

(a)   issue in draft form any map prepared by them under section 4,
(b)   consider any representations received by them within the prescribed period with respect to the showing of, or the failure to show, any area of land on the map as registered common land or as open country,
(c)   confirm the map with or without modifications,
(d)   if the map has been confirmed without modifications, issue it in provisional form, and
(e)   if the map has been confirmed with modifications, prepare a map incorporating the modifications, and issue that map in provisional form.

6   Appeal against map after confirmation

(1)   Any person having an interest in any land may appeal –

(a)   in the case of land in England, to the Secretary of State, or
(b)   in the case of land in Wales, to the National Assembly for Wales,

against the showing of that land on a map in provisional form as registered common land or as open country.

(2)   An appeal relating to the showing of any land as registered common land may be brought only on the ground that the land is not registered common land.

(3) An appeal relating to the showing of any land as open country may be brought only on the ground that –

    (a) the land does not consist wholly or predominantly of mountain, moor, heath or down, and

    (b) to the extent that the appropriate countryside body have exercised their discretion under section 4(5)(b) to treat land which is not open country as forming part of an area of open country, the body ought not to have done so.

(4) On an appeal under this section, the Secretary of State or the National Assembly for Wales may –

    (a) approve the whole or part of the map which is the subject of the appeal, with or without modifications, or

    (b) require the appropriate countryside body to prepare under section 4 a new map relating to all or part of the area covered by the map which is the subject of the appeal.

7 Appeal procedure

(1) Before determining an appeal under section 6, the Secretary of State or the National Assembly for Wales may, if he or it thinks fit –

    (a) cause the appeal to take, or continue in, the form of a hearing, or

    (b) cause a local inquiry to be held;

and the appeal authority shall act as mentioned in paragraph (a) or (b) if a request is made by either party to the appeal to be heard with respect to the appeal.

(2) Subsections (2) to (5) of section 250 of the Local Government Act 1972 (local inquiries: evidence and costs) apply to a hearing or local inquiry held under this section as they apply to a local inquiry held under that section, but as if –

    (a) references in that section to the person appointed to hold the inquiry were references to the Secretary of State or the National Assembly for Wales, and

    (b) references in that section to the Minister causing an inquiry to be held were references to the Secretary of State or the Assembly.

(3) Where –

    (a) for the purposes of an appeal under section 6, the Secretary of State or the National Assembly for Wales is required by subsection (1) –

        (i) to cause the appeal to take, or continue in, the form of a hearing, or

        (ii) to cause a local inquiry to be held, and

    (b) the inquiry or hearing does not take place, and

    (c) if it had taken place, the Secretary of State or the Assembly or a person appointed by the Secretary of State or the Assembly would have had power to make an order under section 250(5) of the Local Government Act 1972 requiring any party to pay the costs of the other party, the power to make such an order may be exercised, in relation to costs incurred for the purposes of the inquiry or hearing, as if it had taken place.

(4)   This section has effect subject to section 8.

8   Power of Secretary of State or Assembly to delegate functions relating to appeals

(1)   The Secretary of State or the National Assembly for Wales may –

(a)   appoint any person to exercise on his or its behalf, with or without payment, the function of determining –

(i)   an appeal under section 6, or
(ii)   any matter involved in such an appeal, or

(b)   refer any matter involved in such an appeal to such person as the Secretary of State or the Assembly may appoint for the purpose, with or without payment.

(2)   Schedule 3 has effect with respect to appointments under subsection (1)(a).

9   Maps in conclusive form

(1)   Where –

(a)   the time within which any appeal under section 6 may be brought in relation to a map in provisional form has expired and no appeal has been brought, or
(b)   every appeal brought under that section in relation to a map has –

(i)   been determined by the map or part of it being approved without modifications, or
(ii)   been withdrawn,

the appropriate countryside body shall issue the map (or the part or parts of it that have been approved without modifications) as a map in conclusive form.

(2)   Where –

(a)   every appeal brought under section 6 in relation to a map in provisional form has been determined or withdrawn, and
(b)   on one or more appeals, the map or any part of it has been approved with modifications,

the appropriate countryside body shall prepare a map which covers the area covered by the map in provisional form (or the part or parts of the map in provisional form that have been approved with or without modifications) and incorporates the modifications, and shall issue it as a map in conclusive form.

(3)   Where either of the conditions in subsection (1)(a) and (b) is satisfied in relation to any part of a map in provisional form, the Secretary of State (as respects England) or the National Assembly for Wales (as respects Wales) may direct the relevant countryside body to issue that part of the map as a map in conclusive form.

(4)   Where on an appeal under section 6 part of a map in provisional form has been approved with modifications but the condition in subsection (2)(a) is not yet satisfied, the Secretary of State (as respects England) or the National Assembly for Wales (as respects Wales) may direct the relevant countryside body to issue a map which covers the area covered by that part of the map in provisional form and incorporates the modifications, and to issue it as a map in conclusive form.

(5)   Where a map in conclusive form has been issued in compliance with a direction under subsection (3) or (4), subsections(1) and (2) shall have effect as if any reference to the map in provisional form were a reference to the part not affected by the direction.

(6)   A document purporting to be certified on behalf of the appropriate countryside body to be a copy of or of any part of a map in conclusive form issued by that body for the purposes of this Part shall be receivable in evidence and shall be deemed, unless the contrary is shown, to be such a copy.

10   Review of maps

(1)   Where the appropriate countryside body have issued a map in conclusive form in respect of any area, it shall be the duty of the body from time to time, on a review under this section, to consider –

(a)   whether any land shown on that map as open country or registered common land is open country or registered common land at the time of the review, and

(b)   whether any land in that area which is not so shown ought to be so shown.

(2)   A review under this section must be undertaken –

(a)   in the case of the first review, not more than ten years after the issue of the map in conclusive form, and

(b)   in the case of subsequent reviews, not more than ten years after the previous review.

(3)   Regulations may amend paragraphs (a) and (b) of subsection (2) by substituting for the period for the time being specified in either of those paragraphs such other period as may be specified in the regulations.

11   Regulations relating to maps

(1)   Regulations may make provision supplementing the provisions of sections 4 to 10.

(2)   Regulations under this section may in particular make provision with respect to –

(a)   the scale on which maps are to be prepared,

(b)   the manner and form in which they are to be prepared and issued,

(c)   consultation with access authorities, local access forums and other persons on maps in draft form,

(d)   the steps to be taken for informing the public of the issue of maps in draft form, provisional form or conclusive form,

(e)   the manner in which maps in draft form, provisional form or conclusive form are to be published or to be made available for inspection,

(f)   the period within which and the manner in which representations on a map in draft form may be made to the appropriate countryside body,

(g)   the confirmation of a map under section 5(c),

(h)   the period within which and manner in which appeals under section 6 are to be brought,

(i)   the advertising of such an appeal,

(j)   the manner in which such appeals are to be considered,

(k)   the procedure to be followed on a review under section 10, including the issue of maps in draft form, provisional form and conclusive form on a review, and

(l)   the correction by the appropriate countryside body of minor errors or omissions in maps.

(3)   Regulations made by virtue of subsection (2)(b) or (e) may authorise or require a map to be prepared, issued, published or made available for inspection in electronic form, but must require any map in electronic form to be capable of being reproduced in printed form.

(4)   Regulations made by virtue of subsection (2)(k) may provide for any of the provisions of this Chapter relating to appeals to apply (with or without modifications) in relation to an appeal against a map issued in provisional form on a review.

Rights and liabilities of owners and occupiers

12   Effect of right of access on rights and liabilities of owners

(1)   The operation of section 2(1) in relation to any access land does not increase the liability, under any enactment not contained in this Act or under any rule of law, of a person interested in the access land or any adjoining land in respect of the state of the land or of things done or omitted to be done on the land.

(2)   Any restriction arising under a covenant or otherwise as to the use of any access land shall have effect subject to the provisions of this Part, and any liability of a person interested in any access land in respect of such a restriction is limited accordingly.

(3)   For the purposes of any enactment or rule of law as to the circumstances in which the dedication of a highway or the grant of an easement may be presumed, or may be established by prescription, the use by the public or by any person of a way across land in the exercise of the right conferred by section 2(1) is to be disregarded.

(4)   The use of any land by the inhabitants of any locality for the purposes of open-air recreation in the exercise of the right conferred by section 2(1) is to be disregarded in determining whether the land has become a town or village green.

13 Occupiers' liability

(1) In section 1 of the Occupiers' Liability Act 1957 (liability in tort: preliminary), for subsection (4) there is substituted –

'(4) A person entering any premises in exercise of rights conferred by virtue of –

(a) section 2(1) of the Countryside and Rights of Way Act 2000, or
(b) an access agreement or order under the National Parks and Access to the Countryside Act 1949,

is not, for the purposes of this Act, a visitor of the occupier of the premises.'

(2) In section 1 of the Occupiers' Liability Act 1984 (duty of occupier to persons other than his visitors), after subsection (6) there is inserted –

'(6A) At any time when the right conferred by section 2(1) of the Countryside and Rights of Way Act 2000 is exercisable in relation to land which is access land for the purposes of Part I of that Act, an occupier of the land owes (subject to subsection (6C) below) no duty by virtue of this section to any person in respect of –

(a) a risk resulting from the existence of any natural feature of the landscape, or any river, stream, ditch or pond whether or not a natural feature, or
(b) a risk of that person suffering injury when passing over, under or through any wall, fence or gate, except by proper use of the gate or of a stile.

(6B) For the purposes of subsection (6A) above, any plant, shrub or tree, of whatever origin, is to be regarded as a natural feature of the landscape.

(6C) Subsection (6A) does not prevent an occupier from owing a duty by virtue of this section in respect of any risk where the danger concerned is due to anything done by the occupier –

(a) with the intention of creating that risk, or
(b) being reckless as to whether that risk is created.'

(3) After section 1 of that Act there is inserted –

'1A Special considerations relating to access land

In determining whether any, and if so what, duty is owed by virtue of section 1 by an occupier of land at any time when the right conferred by section 2(1) of the Countryside and Rights of Way Act 2000 is exercisable in relation to the land, regard is to be had, in particular, to –

(a) the fact that the existence of that right ought not to place an undue burden (whether financial or otherwise) on the occupier,
(b) the importance of maintaining the character of the countryside, including features of historic, traditional or archaeological interest, and
(c) any relevant guidance given under section 20 of that Act.'

14 Offence of displaying on access land notices deterring public use

(1) If any person places or maintains –

(a)   on or near any access land, or

(b)   on or near a way leading to any access land,

a notice containing any false or misleading information likely to deter the public from exercising the right conferred by section 2(1), he is liable on summary conviction to a fine not exceeding level 1 on the standard scale.

(2)   The court before whom a person is convicted of an offence under subsection (1) may, in addition to or in substitution for the imposition of a fine, order him to remove the notice in respect of which he is convicted within such period, not being less than four days, as may be specified in the order.

(3)   A person who fails to comply with an order under subsection (2) is guilty of a further offence and liable on summary conviction to a fine not exceeding level 3 on the standard scale.

Access under other enactments or by dedication

15   Rights of access under other enactments

(1)   For the purposes of section 1(1), land is to be treated as being accessible to the public apart from this Act at any time if, but only if, at that time –

(a)   section 193 of the Law of Property Act 1925 (rights of the public over commons and waste lands) applies to it,

(b)   by virtue of a local or private Act or a scheme made under Part I of the Commons Act 1899 (as read with subsection (2)), members of the public have a right of access to it at all times for the purposes of open-air recreation (however described),

(c)   an access agreement or access order under Part V of the National Parks and Access to the Countryside Act 1949 is in force with respect to it, or

(d)   the public have access to it under subsection (1) of section 19 of the Ancient Monuments and Archaeological Areas Act 1979 (public access to monuments under public control) or would have access to it under that subsection but for any provision of subsections (2) to (9) of that section.

(2)   Where a local or private Act or a scheme made under Part I of the Commons Act 1899 confers on the inhabitants of a particular district or neighbourhood (however described) a right of access to any land for the purposes of open-air recreation (however described), the right of access exercisable by those inhabitants in relation to that land is by virtue of this subsection exercisable by members of the public generally.

16   Dedication of land as access land

(1)   Subject to the provisions of this section, a person who, in respect of any land, holds –

(a)   the fee simple absolute in possession, or

(b)   a legal term of years absolute of which not less than 90 years remain unexpired, may, by taking such steps as may be prescribed, dedicate the land for the purposes of this Part, whether or not it would be access land apart from this section.

(2) Where any person other than the person making the dedication holds –

(a) any leasehold interest in any of the land to be dedicated, or
(b) such other interest in any of that land as may be prescribed,

the dedication must be made jointly with that other person, in such manner as may be prescribed, or with his consent, given in such manner as may be prescribed.

(3) In relation to a dedication under this section by virtue of subsection (1)(b), the reference in subsection (2)(a) to a leasehold interest does not include a reference to a leasehold interest superior to that of the person making the dedication.

(4) A dedication made under this section by virtue of subsection (1)(b) shall have effect only for the remainder of the term held by the person making the dedication.

(5) Schedule 2 to the Forestry Act 1967 (power for tenant for life and others to enter into forestry dedication covenants) applies to dedications under this section as it applies to forestry dedication covenants.

(6) Regulations may –

(a) prescribe the form of any instrument to be used for the purposes of this section,
(b) enable a dedication under this section to include provision removing or relaxing any of the general restrictions in Schedule 2 in relation to any of the land to which the dedication relates,
(c) enable a dedication previously made under this section to be amended by the persons by whom a dedication could be made, so as to remove or relax any of those restrictions in relation to any of the land to which the dedication relates, and
(d) require any dedication under this section, or any amendment of such a dedication by virtue of paragraph (c), to be notified to the appropriate countryside body and to the access authority.

(7) A dedication under this section is irrevocable and, subject to subsection (4), binds successive owners and occupiers of, and other persons interested in, the land to which it relates, but nothing in this section prevents any land from becoming excepted land.

(8) A dedication under this section is a local land charge.

Miscellaneous provisions relating to right of access

17 Byelaws

(1) An access authority may, as respects access land in their area, make byelaws –

(a) for the preservation of order,
(b) for the prevention of damage to the land or anything on or in it, and

(c)   for securing that persons exercising the right conferred by section 2(1) so behave themselves as to avoid undue interference with the enjoyment of the land by other persons.

(2)   Byelaws under this section may relate to all the access land in the area of the access authority or only to particular land.

(3)   Before making byelaws under this section, the access authority shall consult –

(a)   the appropriate countryside body, and
(b)   any local access forum established for an area to which the byelaws relate.

(4)   Byelaws under this section shall not interfere –

(a)   with the exercise of any public right of way,
(b)   with any authority having under any enactment functions relating to the land to which the byelaws apply, or(c) with the running of a telecommunications code system or the exercise of any right conferred by or in accordance with the telecommunications code on the running of any such system
[(c)   with the provision of an electronic communications code network or the exercise of any right conferred by or in accordance with the electronic communications code on the operator of any such network].

(5)   Sections 236 to 238 of the Local Government Act 1972 (which relate to the procedure for making byelaws, authorise byelaws to impose fines not exceeding level 2 on the standard scale, and provide for the proof of byelaws in legal proceedings) apply to all byelaws under this section whether or not the authority making them is a local authority within the meaning of that Act.

(6)   The confirming authority in relation to byelaws made under this section is –

(a)   as respects England, the Secretary of State, and
(b)   as respects Wales, the National Assembly for Wales.

(7)   Byelaws under this section relating to any land –

(a)   may not be made unless the land is access land or the access authority are satisfied that it is likely to become access land, and
(b)   may not be confirmed unless the land is access land.

(8)   Any access authority having power under this section to make byelaws also have power to enforce byelaws made by them; and any county council or district or parish council may enforce byelaws made under this section by another authority as respects land in the area of the council.

18   Wardens

(1)   An access authority or a district council may appoint such number of persons as may appear to the authority making the appointment to be necessary or expedient, to act as wardens as respects access land in their area.

(2)   As respects access land in an area for which there is a local access forum, an access authority shall, before they first exercise the power under subsection (1)

and thereafter from time to time, consult the local access forum about the exercise of that power.

(3) Wardens may be appointed under subsection (1) for the following purposes –

(a) to secure compliance with byelaws under section 17 and with the general restrictions in Schedule 2 and any other restrictions imposed under Chapter II,

(b) to enforce any exclusion imposed under Chapter II,

(c) in relation to the right conferred by section 2(1), to advise and assist the public and persons interested in access land,

(d) to perform such other duties (if any) in relation to access land as the authority appointing them may determine.

(4) For the purpose of exercising any function conferred on him by or under this section, a warden appointed under subsection (1) may enter upon any access land.

(5) A warden appointed under subsection (1) shall, if so required, produce evidence of his authority before entering any access land in the exercise of the power conferred by subsection (4), and shall also produce evidence of his authority while he remains on the access land, if so required by any person.

(6) Except as provided by subsection (4), this section does not authorise a warden appointed under subsection (1), on land in which any person other than the authority who appointed him has an interest, to do anything which apart from this section would be actionable at that person's suit by virtue of that interest.

19 Notices indicating boundaries, etc

(1) An access authority may erect and maintain –

(a) notices indicating the boundaries of access land and excepted land, and

(b) notices informing the public of –

(i) the effect of the general restrictions in Schedule 2,

(ii) the exclusion or restriction under Chapter II of access by virtue of section 2(1) to any land, and

(iii) any other matters relating to access land or to access by virtue of section 2(1) which the access authority consider appropriate.

(2) In subsection (1)(b)(ii), the reference to the exclusion or restriction of access by virtue of section 2(1) is to be interpreted in accordance with section 21(2) and (3).

(3) Before erecting a notice on any land under subsection (1) the access authority shall, if reasonably practicable, consult the owner or occupier of the land.

(4) An access authority may also, as respects any access land in their area, defray or contribute towards, or undertake to defray or contribute towards, expenditure incurred or to be incurred in relation to the land by any person in displaying such notices as are mentioned in subsection (1)(a) and (b).

20   Codes of conduct and other information

(1)   In relation to England, it shall be the duty of the [*Countryside Agency*][Natural England] to issue, and from time to time revise, a code of conduct for the guidance of persons exercising the right conferred by section 2(1) and of persons interested in access land, and to take such other steps as appear to them expedient for securing –

  (a)   that the public are informed of the situation and extent of, and means of access to, access land, and

  (b)   that the public and persons interested in access land are informed of their respective rights and obligations –

  (i)   under this Part, and

  (ii)   with regard to public rights of way on, and nature conservation in relation to, access land.

(2)   In relation to Wales, it shall be the duty of the Countryside Council for Wales to issue, and from time to time revise, a code of conduct for the guidance of persons exercising the right conferred by section 2(1) and of persons interested in access land, and to take such other steps as appear to them expedient for securing the results mentioned in paragraphs (a) and (b) of subsection (1).

(3)   A code of conduct issued by the [*Countryside Agency*][Natural England] or the Countryside Council for Wales may include provisions in pursuance of subsection (1) or (2) and in pursuance of section 86(1) of the National Parks and Access to the Countryside Act 1949.

(4)   The powers conferred by subsections (1) and (2) include power to contribute towards expenses incurred by other persons.

Prospective amendment – Words substituted: Natural Environment and Rural Communities Act 2006, s 105(1), Sch 11, Pt 1, para 156, as from a date to be appointed.

CHAPTER II

EXCLUSION OR RESTRICTION OF ACCESS

21   Interpretation of Chapter II

(1)   References in this Chapter to the exclusion or restriction of access to any land by virtue of section 2(1) are to be interpreted in accordance with subsections (2) and (3).

(2)   A person excludes access by virtue of subsection (1) of section 2 to any land where he excludes the application of that subsection in relation to that land.

(3)   A person restricts access by virtue of subsection (1) of section 2 to any land where he provides that the right conferred by that subsection –

  (a)   is exercisable only along specified routes or ways,

  (b)   is exercisable only after entering the land at a specified place or places,

  (c)   is exercisable only by persons who do not take dogs on the land, or

(d)   is exercisable only by persons who satisfy any other specified conditions.

(4)   In this Chapter, except section 23(1), 'owner', in relation to land which is subject to a farm business tenancy within the meaning of the Agricultural Tenancies Act 1995 or a tenancy to which the Agricultural Holdings Act 1986 applies, means the tenant under that tenancy.

(5)   Subject to subsection (6), in this Chapter 'the relevant authority' –

(a)   in relation to any land in a National Park, means the National Park authority, and

(b)   in relation to any other land, means the appropriate countryside body.

(6)   Where –

(a)   it appears to the Forestry Commissioners that any land which is dedicated for the purposes of this Part under section 16 consists wholly or predominantly of woodland, and

(b)   the Forestry Commissioners give to the body who are apart from this subsection the relevant authority for the purposes of this Chapter in relation to the land a notice stating that the Forestry Commissioners are to be the relevant authority for those purposes as from a date specified in the notice,

the Forestry Commissioners shall as from that date become the relevant authority in relation to that land for those purposes, but subject to subsection (7).

(7)   Where it appears to the Forestry Commissioners that any land in relation to which they are by virtue of subsection (6) the relevant authority for the purposes of this Chapter has ceased to consist wholly or predominantly of woodland, the Forestry Commissioners may, by giving notice to the body who would apart from subsection (6) be the relevant authority, revoke the notice under subsection (6) as from a date specified in the notice under this subsection.

22   Exclusion or restriction at discretion of owner and others

(1)   Subject to subsections (2) and (6), an entitled person may, by giving notice to the relevant authority in accordance with regulations under section 32(1)(a), exclude or restrict access by virtue of section 2(1) to any land on one or more days specified in the notice.

(2)   The number of days on which any entitled person excludes or restricts under this section access by virtue of section 2(1) to any land must not in any calendar year exceed the relevant maximum.

(3)   In this section 'entitled person', in relation to any land, means –

(a)   the owner of the land, and

(b)   any other person having an interest in the land and falling within a prescribed description.

(4)   Subject to subsection (5), in this section 'the relevant maximum' means twenty-eight.

(5)   If regulations are made under subsection (3)(b), the regulations must provide that, in cases where there are two or more entitled persons having different interests in the land, the relevant maximum in relation to each of them is to be determined in accordance with the regulations, but so that the number of days on which access by virtue of section 2(1) to any land may be excluded or restricted under this section in any calendar year does not exceed twenty-eight.

(6)   An entitled person may not under this section exclude or restrict access by virtue of section 2(1) to any land on –

   (a)   Christmas Day or Good Friday, or
   (b)   any day which is a bank holiday under the Banking and Financial Dealings Act 1971 in England and Wales.

(7)   An entitled person may not under this section exclude or restrict access by virtue of section 2(1) to any land –

   (a)   on more than four days in any calendar year which are either Saturday or Sunday,
   (b)   on any Saturday in the period beginning with 1st June and ending with 11th August in any year,
   (c)   on any Sunday in the period beginning with 1st June and ending with 30th September in any year.

(8)   Regulations may provide that any exclusion or restriction under subsection (1) of access by virtue of section 2(1) to any land must relate to an area of land the boundaries of which are determined in accordance with the regulations.

23   Restrictions on dogs at discretion of owner

(1)   The owner of any land consisting of moor managed for the breeding and shooting of grouse may, so far as appears to him to be necessary in connection with the management of the land for that purpose, by taking such steps as may be prescribed, provide that, during a specified period, the right conferred by section 2(1) is exercisable only by persons who do not take dogs on the land.

(2)   The owner of any land may, so far as appears to him to be necessary in connection with lambing, by taking such steps as may be prescribed, provide that during a specified period the right conferred by section 2(1) is exercisable only by persons who do not take dogs into any field or enclosure on the land in which there are sheep.

(3)   In subsection (2) 'field or enclosure' means a field or enclosure of not more than 15 hectares.

(4)   As respects any land –

   (a)   any period specified under subsection (1) may not be more than five years,
   (b)   not more than one period may be specified under subsection (2) in any calendar year, and that period may not be more than six weeks.

(5) A restriction imposed under subsection (1) or (2) does not prevent a blind person from taking with him a trained guide dog, or a deaf person from taking with him a trained hearing dog.

24 Land management

(1) The relevant authority may by direction, on an application made by a person interested in any land, exclude or restrict access to that land by virtue of section 2(1) during a specified period, if the authority are satisfied that the exclusion or restriction under this section of access by virtue of section 2(1) to the extent provided by the direction is necessary for the purposes of the management of the land by the applicant.

(2) The reference in subsection (1) to a specified period includes a reference to –

    (a) a specified period in every calendar year, or

    (b) a period which is to be –

        (i) determined by the applicant in accordance with the direction, and

        (ii) notified by him to the relevant authority in accordance with regulations under section 32(1)(d).

(3) In determining whether to any extent the exclusion or restriction under this section of access by virtue of section 2(1) during any period is necessary for the purposes of land management, the relevant authority shall have regard to –

    (a) the existence of the right conferred by section 22,

    (b) the extent to which the applicant has exercised or proposes to exercise that right, and

    (c) the purposes for which he has exercised or proposes to exercise it.

(4) Where an application under this section relates to land which is not access land at the time when the application is made, the relevant authority shall not give a direction under this section unless they are satisfied that it is likely that the land will be access land during all or part of the period to which the application relates.

25 Avoidance of risk of fire or of danger to the public

(1) The relevant authority may by direction exclude or restrict access by virtue of section 2(1) in relation to any land during a specified period if the authority are satisfied –

    (a) that, by reason of any exceptional conditions of weather or any exceptional change in the condition of the land, the exclusion or restriction under this section of access to the land by virtue of section 2(1) to the extent provided by the direction is necessary for the purpose of fire prevention, or

    (b) that, by reason of anything done, or proposed to be done, on the land or on adjacent land, the exclusion or restriction under this section of access to the land by virtue of section 2(1) to the extent provided by the direction is necessary for the purpose of avoiding danger to the public.

(2) The reference in subsection (1) to a specified period includes a reference to –

(a) a specified period in every calendar year, and

(b) a period which is to be –

(i) determined by a specified person in accordance with the direction, and

(ii) notified by him to the relevant authority in accordance with regulations under section 32(1)(d).

(3) The relevant authority may exercise their powers under subsection (1) on the application of any person interested in the land, or without any such application having been made.

(4) In determining on an application made by a person interested in the land whether the condition in subsection (1)(a) or (b) is satisfied, the relevant authority shall have regard to –

(a) the existence of the right conferred by section 22,

(b) the extent to which the applicant has exercised or proposes to exercise that right, and

(c) the purposes for which he has exercised or proposes to exercise it.

(5) Where an application under this section relates to land which is not access land at the time when the application is made, the relevant authority shall not give a direction under this section unless they are satisfied that it is likely that the land will be access land during all or part of the period to which the application relates.

26 Nature conservation and heritage preservation

(1) The relevant authority may by direction exclude or restrict access by virtue of section 2(1) to any land during any period if they are satisfied that the exclusion or restriction of access by virtue of section 2(1) to the extent provided by the direction is necessary for either of the purposes specified in subsection (3).

(2) A direction under subsection (1) may be expressed to have effect –

(a) during a period specified in the direction,

(b) during a specified period in every calendar year, or

(c) during a period which is to be –

(i) determined by a specified person in accordance with the direction, and

(ii) notified by him to the relevant authority in accordance with regulations under section 32(1)(d), or

(d) indefinitely.

(3) The purposes referred to in subsection (1) are –

(a) the purpose of conserving flora, fauna or geological or physiographical features of the land in question;

(b) the purpose of preserving –

(i) any scheduled monument as defined by section 1(11) of the Ancient Monuments and Archaeological Areas Act 1979, or

(ii) any other structure, work, site, garden or area which is of historic, architectural, traditional, artistic or archaeological interest.

(4) In considering whether to give a direction under this section, the relevant authority shall have regard to any advice given to them by the relevant advisory body.

(5) Subsection (4) does not apply where the direction is given by the Countryside Council for Wales for the purpose specified in subsection (3)(a) or revokes a direction given by them for that purpose.

(6) In this section 'the relevant advisory body' –

(a) in relation to a direction which is to be given for the purpose specified in subsection (3)(a) or which revokes a direction given for that purpose, means –

(i) in the case of land in England, [*English Nature*] [in respect of which Natural England is not the relevant authority, Natural England], and

(ii) in the case of land in Wales in respect of which the Countryside Council for Wales are not the relevant authority, the Countryside Council for Wales, and

(b) in relation to a direction which is to be given for the purpose specified in subsection (3)(b) or which revokes a direction given for that purpose, means –

(i) in the case of land in England, the Historic Buildings and Monuments Commission for England, and

(ii) in the case of land in Wales, the National Assembly for Wales.

Prospective amendment – Words substituted: Natural Environment and Rural Communities Act 2006, s 105(1), Sch 11, Pt 1, para 157, as from a date to be appointed.

27 Directions by relevant authority: general

(1) Before giving a direction under section 24, 25 or 26 in relation to land in an area for which there is a local access forum so as to exclude or restrict access to the land –

(a) indefinitely, or
(b) during a period which exceeds, or may exceed, six months,

the relevant authority shall consult the local access forum.

(2) Any direction under section 24, 25 or 26 may be revoked or varied by a subsequent direction under that provision.

(3) Where a direction given under section 24, 25 or 26 in relation to any land by the relevant authority excludes or restricts access to the land –

(a) indefinitely,
(b) for part of every year or of each of six or more consecutive calendar years, or
(c) for a specified period of more than five years,

the authority shall review the direction not later than the fifth anniversary of the relevant date.

(4)   In subsection (3) 'the relevant date', in relation to a direction, means –

(a)   the day on which the direction was given, or
(b)   where it has already been reviewed, the day on which it was last reviewed.

(5)   Before revoking or varying a direction under section 24 or 25 which was given on the application of a person interested in the land to which the direction relates ('the original applicant'), the relevant authority shall –

(a)   where the original applicant still holds the interest in the land which he held when he applied for the direction and it is reasonably practicable to consult him, consult the original applicant, and
(b)   where the original applicant does not hold that interest, consult any person who holds that interest and with whom consultation is reasonably practicable.

(6)   Before revoking or varying a direction under section 26, the relevant authority shall consult the relevant advisory body as defined by section 26(6), unless the direction falls within section 26(5).

28   Defence or national security

(1)   The Secretary of State may by direction exclude or restrict access by virtue of section 2(1)to any land during any period if he is satisfied that the exclusion or restriction of such access to the extent provided by the direction is necessary for the purposes of defence or national security.

(2)   A direction under subsection (1) may be expressed to have effect –

(a)   during a period specified in the direction,
(b)   during a specified period in every calendar year,
(c)   during a period which is to be –

(i)   determined in accordance with the direction by a person authorised by the Secretary of State, and
(ii)   notified by that person to the relevant authority in accordance with regulations under section 32(1)(c), or

(d)   indefinitely.

(3)   Any direction given by the Secretary of State under this section may be revoked or varied by a subsequent direction.

(4)   Where a direction given under this section in relation to any land excludes or restricts access to the land –

(a)   indefinitely,
(b)   for part of every year or of each of six or more consecutive calendar years, or
(c)   for a specified period of more than five years,

the Secretary of State shall review the direction not later than the fifth anniversary of the relevant date.

(5) In subsection (4) 'the relevant date', in relation to a direction, means –

(a) the day on which the direction was given, or

(b) where it has previously been reviewed, the day on which it was last reviewed.

(6) If in any calendar year the Secretary of State reviews a defence direction, he shall –

(a) prepare a report on all reviews of defence directions which he has undertaken during that year, and

(b) lay a copy of the report before each House of Parliament.

(7) In subsection (6) 'defence direction' means a direction given under this section for the purposes of defence.

29 Reference by relevant advisory body

(1) Subsections (2) and (3) apply where –

(a) the relevant advisory body has given advice under section 26(4) or on being consulted under section 27(6), but

(b) in any respect, the relevant authority decide not to act in accordance with that advice.

(2) The relevant advisory body may refer the decision –

(a) in the case of land in England, to the [Secretary of State], or

(b) in the case of land in Wales, to the National Assembly for Wales.

(3) On a reference under this section the [Secretary of State] or the National Assembly for Wales may, if he or it thinks fit –

(a) cancel any direction given by the relevant authority, or

(b) require the relevant authority to give such direction under section 26 as the [Secretary of State] or, as the case may be, the Assembly, think fit.

(4) Sections 7 and 8 (and Schedule 3) have effect in relation to a reference under this section as they have effect in relation to an appeal under section 6 . . ..

(5) In this section –

. . .

'the relevant advisory body' has the same meaning as in section 26, except that it does not include the National Assembly for Wales.

Amendment – SI 2002/794, art 5(1), Schs 1 and 2.

30 Appeal by person interested in land

(1) Subsections (2) and (3) apply where –

(a) a person interested in any land (in this section referred to as 'the applicant') –

> (i)   has applied for a direction under section 24 or 25, or
> (ii) has made representations on being consulted under section 27(5), but

(b)   in any respect, the relevant authority decide not to act in accordance with the application or the representations.

(2)   The relevant authority shall inform the applicant of their reasons for not acting in accordance with the application or representations.

(3)   The applicant may appeal against the decision –

(a)   in the case of land in England, to the [Secretary of State], or
(b)   in the case of land in Wales, to the National Assembly for Wales.

(4)   On appeal under this section the [Secretary of State] or the National Assembly for Wales may, if he or it thinks fit –

(a)   cancel any direction given by the relevant authority, or
(b)   require the relevant authority to give such direction under section 24 or 25 as the [Secretary of State] or, as the case may be, the Assembly, think fit.

(5)   Sections 7 and 8 (and Schedule 3) have effect in relation to an appeal under this section as they have effect in relation to an appeal under section 6 . . ..

(6)   . . .

Amendment – SI 2002/794, art 5(1), Schs 1 and 2.

31   Exclusion or restriction of access in case of emergency

(1)   Regulations may make provision enabling the relevant authority, where the authority are satisfied that an emergency has arisen which makes the exclusion or restriction of access by virtue of section 2(1) necessary for any of the purposes specified in section 24(1), 25(1) or 26(3), by direction to exclude or restrict such access in respect of any land for a period not exceeding three months.

(2)   Regulations under this section may provide for any of the preceding provisions of this Chapter to apply in relation to a direction given under the regulations with such modifications as may be prescribed.

32   Regulations relating to exclusion or restriction of access

(1)   Regulations may make provision –

(a)   as to the giving of notice under section 22(1),
(b)   as to the steps to be taken under section 23(1) and (2),
(c)   as to the procedure on any application to the relevant authority under section 24 or 25, including the period within which any such application must be made,
(d)   as to the giving of notice for the purposes of section 24(2)(b)(ii), 25(2)(b)(ii), 26(2)(c)(ii) or 28(2)(c)(ii),
(e)   prescribing the form of any notice or application referred to in paragraphs (a) to (d),

(f) restricting the cases in which a person who is interested in any land only as the holder of rights of common may make an application under section 24 or 25 in respect of the land,

(g) as to requirements to be met by relevant authorities or the Secretary of State in relation to consultation (whether or not required by the preceding provisions of this Chapter),

(h) as to the giving of directions by relevant authorities or the Secretary of State,

(i) as to notification by relevant authorities or the Secretary of State of decisions under this Chapter,

(j) as to steps to be taken by persons interested in land, by relevant authorities, by the bodies specified in section 26(6) or by the Secretary of State for informing the public about the exclusion or restriction under this Chapter of access by virtue of section 2(1), including the display of notices on or near the land to which the exclusion or restriction relates,

(k) as to the carrying out of reviews by relevant authorities under section 27(3) or by the Secretary of State under section 28(4),

(l) as to the period within which and manner in which appeals under section 30 are to be brought,

(m) as to the advertising of such an appeal, and

(n) as to the manner in which such appeals are to be considered.

(2) Regulations made under subsection (1)(k) may provide for any of the provisions of this Chapter relating to appeals to apply (with or without modifications) on a review under section 27.

33 Guidance by countryside bodies to National Park authorities

(1) Subject to subsection (3), the [*Countryside Agency*] [Natural England]may issue guidance –

(a) to National Park authorities in England with respect to the discharge by National Park authorities of their functions under this Chapter, and

(b) to the Forestry Commissioners with respect to the discharge by the Forestry Commissioners of any functions conferred on them by virtue of section 21(6) in relation to land in England.

(2) Subject to subsection (3), the Countryside Council for Wales may issue guidance –

(a) to National Park authorities in Wales with respect to the discharge by National Park authorities of their functions under this Chapter, and

(b) to the Forestry Commissioners with respect to the discharge by the Forestry Commissioners of any functions conferred on them by virtue of section 21(6) in relation to land in Wales.

(3) The [*Countryside Agency*] [Natural England]or the Countryside Council for Wales may not issue any guidance under this section unless the guidance has been approved –

(a) in the case of the [*Countryside Agency*] [Natural England], by the Secretary of State, and

(b)   in the case of the Countryside Council for Wales, by the National Assembly for Wales.

(4)   Where the [*Countryside Agency*] [Natural England]or the Countryside Council for Wales issue any guidance under this section, they shall arrange for the guidance to be published in such manner as they consider appropriate.

(5)   A National Park authority or the Forestry Commissioners shall have regard to any guidance issued to them under this section. **Prospective amendment** – Words substituted: Natural Environment and Rural Communities Act 2006, s 105(1), Sch 11, Pt 1, para 158, as from a date to be appointed.

CHAPTER III

MEANS OF ACCESS

34   Interpretation of Chapter III

In this Chapter –

'access land' does not include any land in relation to which the application of section 2(1) has been excluded under any provision of Chapter II either indefinitely or for a specified period of which at least six months remain unexpired;

'means of access', in relation to land, means –

(a)   any opening in a wall, fence or hedge bounding the land (or part of the land), with or without a gate, stile or other works for regulating passage through the opening,

(b)   any stairs or steps for enabling persons to enter on the land (or part of the land), or

(c)   any bridge, stepping stone or other works for crossing a watercourse, ditch or bog on the land or adjoining the boundary of the land.

35   Agreements with respect to means of access

(1)   Where, in respect of any access land, it appears to the access authority that –

(a)   the opening-up, improvement or repair of any means of access to the land,

(b)   the construction of any new means of access to the land,

(c)   the maintenance of any means of access to the land, or

(d)   the imposition of restrictions –

(i)   on the destruction, removal, alteration or stopping-up of any means of access to the land, or

(ii)   on the doing of any thing whereby the use of any such means of access to the land by the public would be impeded,

is necessary for giving the public reasonable access to that land in exercise of the right conferred by section 2(1), the access authority may enter into an agreement with the owner or occupier of the land as to the carrying out of the works or the imposition of the restrictions.

(2)   An agreement under this section may provide –

(a)   for the carrying out of works by the owner or occupier or by the access authority, and

(b)   for the making of payments by the access authority –

    (i)   as a contribution towards, or for the purpose of defraying, costs incurred by the owner or occupier in carrying out any works for which the agreement provides, or

    (ii)   in consideration of the imposition of any restriction.

36   Failure to comply with agreement

(1)   If the owner or occupier of any access land fails to carry out within the required time any works which he is required by an agreement under section 35 to carry out, the access authority, after giving not less than twenty-one days' notice of their intention to do so, may take all necessary steps for carrying out those works.

(2)   In subsection (1) 'the required time' means the time specified in, or determined in accordance with, the agreement as that within which the works must be carried out or, if there is no such time, means a reasonable time.

(3)   If the owner or occupier of any access land fails to observe any restriction which he is required by an agreement under section 35 to observe, the access authority may give him a notice requiring him within a specified period of not less than twenty-one days to carry out such works as may be specified in the notice, for the purpose of remedying the failure to observe the restriction.

(4)   A notice under subsection (3) must contain particulars of the right of appeal conferred by section 38.

(5)   If the person to whom a notice under subsection (3) is given fails to comply with the notice, the access authority may take all necessary steps for carrying out any works specified in the notice.

(6)   Where the access authority carry out any works by virtue of subsection (1), the authority may recover the amount of any expenses reasonably incurred by them in carrying out the works, reduced by their contribution under the agreement, from the person by whom under the agreement the cost (apart from the authority's contribution) of carrying out the works would fall to be borne.

(7)   Where the access authority carry out any works by virtue of subsection (5), the authority may recover the amount of any expenses reasonably incurred by them in carrying out the works from the person to whom the notice under subsection (3) was given.

37   Provision of access by access authority in absence of agreement

(1)   Where, in respect of any access land –

(a)   it appears to the access authority that –

    (i)   the opening-up, improvement or repair of any means of access to the land,

    (ii)   the construction of any new means of access to the land, or

(iii)   the maintenance of any means of access to the land,

is necessary for giving the public reasonable access to that land, or to other access land, in pursuance of the right conferred by section 2(1), and

(b)   the access authority are satisfied that they are unable to conclude on reasonable terms an agreement under section 35 with the owner or occupier of the land for the carrying out of the works,

the access authority may, subject to subsection (3), give the owner or occupier a notice stating that, after the end of a specified period of not less than twenty-one days, the authority intend to take all necessary steps for carrying out the works specified in the notice for the opening-up, improvement, repair, construction or maintenance of the means of access.

(2)   A notice under subsection (1) must contain particulars of the right of appeal conferred by section 38.

(3)   Where a notice under subsection (1) is given to any person as the owner or occupier of any land, the access authority shall give a copy of the notice to every other owner or occupier of the land.

(4)   An access authority exercising the power conferred by subsection (1) in relation to the provision of a means of access shall have regard to the requirements of efficient management of the land in deciding where the means of access is to be provided.

(5)   If, at the end of the period specified in a notice under subsection (1), any of the works specified in the notice have not been carried out, the access authority may take all necessary steps for carrying out those works.

38   Appeals relating to notices

(1)   Where a notice under section 36(3) or 37(1) has been given to a person in respect of any land, he or any other owner or occupier of the land may appeal against the notice –

(a)   in the case of land in England, to the Secretary of State, and
(b)   in the case of land in Wales, to the National Assembly for Wales.

(2)   An appeal against a notice under section 36(3) may be brought on any of the following grounds –

(a)   that the notice requires the carrying out of any works which are not necessary for remedying a breach of the agreement,
(b)   that any of the works have already been carried out, and
(c)   that the period specified in the notice as that before the end of which the works must be carried out is too short.

(3)   An appeal against a notice under section 37(1) may be brought on any of the following grounds –

(a)   that the notice requires the carrying out of any works which are not necessary for giving the public reasonable access to the access land in question,

(b) in the case of works to provide a means of access, that the means of access should be provided elsewhere, or that a different means of access should be provided, and

(c) that any of the works have already been carried out.

(4) On an appeal under this section, the Secretary of State or the National Assembly for Wales may –

(a) confirm the notice with or without modifications, or

(b) cancel the notice.

(5) Sections 7 and 8 (and Schedule 3) have effect in relation to an appeal under this section as they have effect in relation to an appeal under section 6.

(6) Regulations may make provision as to –

(a) the period within which and manner in which appeals under this section are to be brought,

(b) the advertising of such an appeal, and

(c) the manner in which such appeals are to be considered.

(7) Where an appeal has been brought under this section against a notice under section 36(3) or 37(1), the access authority may not exercise their powers under section 36(5) or section 37(5) (as the case may be) pending the determination or withdrawal of the appeal.

39 Order to remove obstruction

(1) Where at any time two or more access notices relating to a means of access have been given to any person within the preceding thirty-six months, a magistrates' court may, on the application of the access authority, order that person –

(a) within such time as may be specified in the order, to take such steps as may be so specified to remove any obstruction of that means of access, and

(b) not to obstruct that means of access at any time when the right conferred by section 2(1) is exercisable.

(2) If a person ('the person in default') fails to comply with an order under this section –

(a) he is liable on summary conviction to a fine not exceeding level 3 on the standard scale, and

(b) the access authority may remove any obstruction of the means of access and recover from the person in default the costs reasonably incurred by them in doing so.

(3) In this section 'access notice' means a notice under section 36(3) or 37(1) in respect of which the period specified in the notice has expired, other than a notice in respect of which an appeal is pending or which has been cancelled on appeal.

CHAPTER IV

GENERAL

40   Powers of entry for purposes of Part I

(1)   A person who is authorised by the appropriate countryside body to do so may enter any land –

(a)   for the purpose of surveying it in connection with the preparation of any map under this Part or the review of any map issued under this Part,

(b)   for the purpose of determining whether any power conferred on the appropriate countryside body by Chapter II should be exercised in relation to the land,

(c)   for the purpose of ascertaining whether members of the public are being permitted to exercise the right conferred by section 2(1),

(d)   in connection with an appeal under any provision of this Part, or

(e)   for the purpose of determining whether to apply to the Secretary of State or the National Assembly for Wales under section 58.

(2)   A person who is authorised by a local highway authority to do so may enter any land –

(a)   for the purpose of determining whether the local highway authority should enter into an agreement under section 35, give a notice under section 36(1) or (3) or section 37(1) or carry out works under section 36(1) or (5), section 37(5) or section 39(2)(b),

(b)   for the purpose of ascertaining whether an offence under section 14 or 39 has been or is being committed, or

(c)   for the purposes of erecting or maintaining notices under section 19(1).

(3)   A person who is authorised by a National Park authority to do so may enter any land –

(a)   for the purpose of enabling the authority to determine whether to exercise any power under Chapter II of this Act in relation to the land,

(b)   for the purpose of determining whether members of the public are being permitted to exercise the right conferred by section 2(1),

(c)   in connection with an appeal under any provision of this Part,

(d)   for the purpose of determining whether the authority should enter into an agreement under section 35, give a notice under section 36(1) or (3) or section 37(1) or carry out works under section 36(1) or (5), section 37(5) or section 39(2)(b),

(e)   for the purpose of ascertaining whether an offence under section 14 or 39 has been or is being committed, or

(f)   for the purposes of erecting or maintaining notices under section 19(1).

(4)   A person who is authorised by the Forestry Commissioners to do so may enter any land –

(a)   for the purpose of determining whether any power conferred on the Forestry Commissioners by Chapter II should be exercised in relation to the land, or

(b)   in connection with an appeal under any provision of this Part.

(5)   A person acting in the exercise of a power conferred by this section may –

(a)   use a vehicle to enter the land;

(b)   take a constable with him if he reasonably believes he is likely to be obstructed;

(c)   take with him equipment and materials needed for the purpose for which he is exercising the power of entry;

(d)   take samples of the land and of anything on it.

(6)   If in the exercise of a power conferred by this section a person enters land which is unoccupied or from which the occupier is temporarily absent, he must on his departure leave it as effectively secured against unauthorised entry as he found it.

(7)   A person authorised under this section to enter upon any land –

(a)   shall, if so required, produce evidence of his authority before entering, and

(b)   shall produce such evidence if required to do so at any time while he remains on the land.

(8)   A person shall not under this section demand admission as of right to any occupied land, other than access land, unless –

(a)   at least twenty-four hours' notice of the intended entry has been given to the occupier, or

(b)   it is not reasonably practicable to give such notice, or

(c)   the entry is for the purpose specified in subsection (2)(b) and (3)(e).

(9)   The rights conferred by this section are not exercisable in relation to a dwelling.

(10) A person who intentionally obstructs a person acting in the exercise of his powers under this section is guilty of an offence and liable on summary conviction to a fine not exceeding level 2 on the standard scale.

41   Compensation relating to powers under s 40

(1)   It is the duty of a body by which an authorisation may be given under section 40 to compensate any person who has sustained damage as a result of –

(a)   the exercise of a power conferred by that section by a person authorised by that body to do so, or

(b)   the failure of a person so authorised to perform the duty imposed on him by subsection (6) of that section,

except where the damage is attributable to the fault of the person who sustained it.

(2)   Any dispute as to a person's entitlement to compensation under this section or as to its amount shall be referred to an arbitrator to be appointed, in default of agreement –

(a)   as respects entry on land in England, by the Secretary of State, and

(b)   as respects entry on land in Wales, by the National Assembly for Wales.

42 References to public places in existing enactments

(1) This section applies to any enactment which –

    (a)   is contained in an Act passed before or in the same Session as this Act, and

    (b)   relates to things done, or omitted to be done, in public places or places to which the public have access.

(2) Regulations may provide that, in determining for the purposes of any specified enactment to which this section applies whether a place is a public place or a place to which the public have access, the right conferred by section 2(1), or access by virtue of that right, is to be disregarded, either generally or in prescribed cases.

43 Crown application of Part I

(1) This Part binds the Crown.

(2) No contravention by the Crown of any provision of this Part shall make the Crown criminally liable; but the High Court may declare unlawful any act or omission of the Crown which constitutes such a contravention.

(3) The provisions of this Part apply to persons in the public service of the Crown as they apply to other persons.

44 Orders and regulations under Part I

(1) Any power to make an order or regulations which is conferred by this Part on the Secretary of State or the National Assembly for Wales is exercisable by statutory instrument.

(2) Any power to make an order or regulations which is conferred by this Part on the Secretary of State or the National Assembly for Wales includes power –

    (a)   to make different provision for different cases, and

    (b)   to make such incidental, supplementary, consequential or transitional provision as the person making the order or regulations considers necessary or expedient.

(3) No order under section 3 or regulations under paragraph 3 of Schedule 2 shall be made by the Secretary of State unless a draft has been laid before, and approved by a resolution of, each House of Parliament.

(4) Any statutory instrument containing regulations made by the Secretary of State under any other provision of this Part shall be subject to annulment in pursuance of a resolution of either House of Parliament.

45 Interpretation of Part I

(1) In this Part, unless a contrary intention appears –

'access authority' has the meaning given by section 1(2);

'access land' has the meaning given by section 1(1);

'the appropriate countryside body' has the meaning given by section 1(2);

'excepted land' has the meaning given by section 1(2);

'Inner London' means the area comprising the inner London boroughs, the City of London, the Inner Temple and the Middle Temple;

'interest', in relation to land, includes any estate in land and any right over land, whether the right is exercisable by virtue of the ownership of an estate or interest in land or by virtue of a licence or agreement, and in particular includes rights of common and sporting rights, and references to a person interested in land shall be construed accordingly;

'livestock' means cattle, sheep, goats, swine, horses or poultry, and for the purposes of this definition 'cattle' means bulls, cows, oxen, heifers or calves, 'horses' include asses and mules, and 'poultry' means domestic fowls, turkeys, geese or ducks;

'local highway authority' has the same meaning as in the Highways Act 1980;

'local or private Act' includes an Act confirming a provisional order;

'mountain' has the meaning given by section 1(2);

'open country' has the meaning given by section 1(2);

'owner', in relation to any land, means, subject to subsection (2), any person, other than a mortgagee not in possession, who, whether in his own right or as trustee for another person, is entitled to receive the rack rent of the land, or, where the land is not let at a rack rent, would be so entitled if it were so let;

'prescribed' means prescribed by regulations;

'registered common land' has the meaning given by section 1(3);

'regulations' means regulations made by the Secretary of State (as respects England) or by the National Assembly for Wales (as respects Wales);

'rights of common' has the same meaning as in the Commons Registration Act 1965;

'telecommunications code' and 'telecommunications code system' have the same meaning as in Schedule 4 to the Telecommunications Act 1984.

(2) In relation to any land which is subject to a farm business tenancy within the meaning of the Agricultural Tenancies Act 1995 or a tenancy to which the Agricultural Holdings Act 1986 applies, the definition of 'owner' in subsection (1) does not apply where it is excluded by section 2(5) or 21(4) or by paragraph 7(4) of Schedule 2.

(3) For the purposes of this Part, the Broads are to be treated as a National Park and the Broads Authority as a National Park authority.

(4) In subsection (3) 'the Broads' has the same meaning as in the Norfolk and Suffolk Broads Act 1988.

46 Repeal of previous legislation, and amendments relating to Part I

(1) ...

(2)   No access agreement or access order under Part V of the National Parks and Access to the Countryside Act 1949 (access to open country) may be made after the commencement of this section in relation to land which is open country or registered common land for the purposes of this Part.

(3)   Schedule 4 (which contains minor and consequential amendments relating to access to the countryside) has effect.

Amendment – Repealed by Commons Act 2006, Sch 6, Pt 1 with effect from 1 October 2006.

PART II

PUBLIC RIGHTS OF WAY AND ROAD TRAFFIC

. . .

Miscellaneous

. . .

[68   *Vehicular access across common land etc*

(1)   This section applies to a way which the owner or occupier (from time to time) of any premises has used as a means of access for vehicles to the premises, if that use of the way –

    (a)   was an offence under an enactment applying to the land crossed by the way, but

    (b)   would otherwise have been sufficient to create on or after the prescribed date, and to keep in existence, an easement giving a right of way for vehicles.

(2)   Regulations may provide, as respects a way to which this section applies, for the creation in accordance with the regulations, on the application of the owner of the premises concerned and on compliance by him with prescribed requirements, of an easement subsisting at law for the benefit of the premises and giving a right of way for vehicles over that way.

(3)   An easement created in accordance with the regulations is subject to any enactment or rule of law which would apply to such an easement granted by the owner of the land.

(4)   The regulations may in particular –

    (a)   require that, where an application is made after the relevant use of the way has ceased, it is to be made within a specified time,

    (b)   specify grounds on which objections may be made and the procedure to apply to the making of objections,

    (c)   require any matter to be referred to and determined by the Lands Tribunal, and make provision as to procedure and costs,

    (d)   make provision as to the payment of any amount by the owner of the premises concerned to any person or into court and as to the time when any payment is to be made,

    (e)   provide for the determination of any such amount,

    (f)   make provision as to the date on which any easement is created,

(g)   *specify any limitation to which the easement is subject,*

(h)   *provide for the easement to include any specified right incidental to the right of way,*

(i)   *make different provision for different circumstances.*

(5)   *In this section –*

'enactment' includes an enactment in a local or private Act and a byelaw, regulation or other provision having effect under an enactment;

'owner', in relation to any premises, means –

(a)   *a person, other than a mortgagee not in possession, who is for the time being entitled to dispose of the fee simple of the premises, whether in possession or in reversion, or*

(b)   *a tenant under a long lease, within the meaning of the Landlord and Tenant Act 1987;*

'prescribed' means prescribed by regulations;

'regulations' means regulations made, as respects England, by the Secretary of State and, as respects Wales, by the National Assembly for Wales.

(6)   *Regulations under this section shall be made by statutory instrument, and no such regulations shall be made by the Secretary of State unless a draft has been laid before, and approved by a resolution of, each House of Parliament.*]

Prospective Repeal – Commons Act 2006, Sch 6, Pt 5 as from a date to be appointed.

SCHEDULES

SCHEDULE 1

EXCEPTED LAND FOR PURPOSES OF PART I

PART I

EXCEPTED LAND

1   Land on which the soil is being, or has at any time within the previous twelve months been, disturbed by any ploughing or drilling undertaken for the purposes of planting or sowing crops or trees.

2   Land covered by buildings or the curtilage of such land.

3   Land within 20 metres of a dwelling.

4   Land used as a park or garden.

5   Land used for the getting of minerals by surface working (including quarrying).

6   Land used for the purposes of a railway (including a light railway) or tramway.

7   Land used for the purposes of a golf course, racecourse or aerodrome.

8 Land which does not fall within any of the preceding paragraphs and is covered by works used for the purposes of a statutory undertaking or a telecommunications code system [an electronic communications code network], or the curtilage of any such land.

9 Land as respects which development which will result in the land becoming land falling within any of paragraphs 2 to 8 is in the course of being carried out.

10 Land within 20 metres of a building which is used for housing livestock, not being a temporary or moveable structure.

11 Land covered by pens in use for the temporary reception or detention of livestock.

12 Land habitually used for the training of racehorses.

13 Land the use of which is regulated by byelaws under section 14 of the Military Lands Act 1892 or section 2 of the Military Lands Act 1900.

Amendment – Communications Act 2003, s 406(1), Sch 17.

PART II

SUPPLEMENTARY PROVISIONS

14 In this Schedule –

'building' includes any structure or erection and any part of a building as so defined, but does not include any fence or wall, or anything which is a means of access as defined by section 34; and for this purpose 'structure' includes any tent, caravan or other temporary or moveable structure;

'development' and 'minerals' have the same meaning as in the Town and Country Planning Act 1990;

'ploughing' and 'drilling' include respectively agricultural or forestry operations similar to ploughing and agricultural or forestry operations similar to drilling;

'statutory undertaker' means –

(a) a person authorised by any enactment to carry on any railway, light railway, tramway, road transport, water transport, canal, inland navigation, dock, harbour, pier or lighthouse undertaking or any undertaking for the supply of hydraulic power,

(b) any public gas transporter, within the meaning of Part I of the Gas Act 1986,

(c) any water or sewerage undertaker,

(d) any holder of a licence under section 6(1) of the Electricity Act 1989, or

(e) the Environment Agency, [a universal service provider (within the meaning of the Postal Services Act 2000) in connection with the provision of a universal postal service (within the meaning of that Act)][, the Civil Aviation Authority or a person who holds a licence under Chapter I of Part I of the Transport Act 2000 (to the extent that the person is carrying out activities authorised by the licence)];

'statutory undertaking' means –

(a) the undertaking of a statutory undertaker [(which, in the case of a universal service provider (within the meaning of the Postal Services Act 2000), means his undertaking so far as relating to the provision of a universal postal service (within the meaning of that Act) [and, in the case of a person who holds a licence under Chapter I of Part I of the Transport Act 2000, means that person's undertaking as licence holder])], or

(b) an airport to which Part V of the Airports Act 1986 applies.

15 (1) Land is not to be treated as excepted land by reason of any development carried out on the land, if the carrying out of the development requires planning permission under Part III of the Town and Country Planning Act 1990 and that permission has not been granted.

(2) Sub-paragraph (1) does not apply where the development is treated by section 191(2) of the Town and Country Planning Act 1990 as being lawful for the purposes of that Act.

16 The land which is excepted land by virtue of paragraph 10 does not include –

(a) any means of access, as defined by section 34, or
(b) any way leading to such a means of access,

if the means of access is necessary for giving the public reasonable access to access land.

17 Land which is habitually used for the training of racehorses is not to be treated by virtue of paragraph 11 as excepted land except –

(a) between dawn and midday on any day, and
(b) at any other time when it is in use for that purpose.

Amendment – SI 2001/1149; SI 2001/4050.

Modification – in relation to a public gas transporter: the Utilities Act 2000, s 76(7).

SCHEDULE 2

RESTRICTIONS TO BE OBSERVED BY PERSONS EXERCISING RIGHT OF ACCESS
General restrictions

1 Section 2(1) does not entitle a person to be on any land if, in or on that land, he –

(a) drives or rides any vehicle other than an invalid carriage as defined by section 20(2) of the Chronically Sick and Disabled Persons Act 1970,
(b) uses a vessel or sailboard on any non-tidal water,
(c) has with him any animal other than a dog,
(d) commits any criminal offence,
(e) lights or tends a fire or does any act which is likely to cause a fire,
(f) intentionally or recklessly takes, kills, injures or disturbs any animal, bird or fish,

(g)   intentionally or recklessly takes, damages or destroys any eggs or nests,

(h)   feeds any livestock,

(i)   bathes in any non-tidal water,

(j)   engages in any operations of or connected with hunting, shooting, fishing, trapping, snaring, taking or destroying of animals, birds or fish or has with him any engine, instrument or apparatus used for hunting, shooting, fishing, trapping, snaring, taking or destroying animals, birds or fish,

(k)   uses or has with him any metal detector,

(l)   intentionally removes, damages or destroys any plant, shrub, tree or root or any part of a plant, shrub, tree or root,

(m)   obstructs the flow of any drain or watercourse, or opens, shuts or otherwise interferes with any sluice-gate or other apparatus,

(n)   without reasonable excuse, interferes with any fence, barrier or other device designed to prevent accidents to people or to enclose livestock,

(o)   neglects to shut any gate or to fasten it where any means of doing so is provided, except where it is reasonable to assume that a gate is intended to be left open,

(p)   affixes or writes any advertisement, bill, placard or notice,

(q)   in relation to any lawful activity which persons are engaging in or are about to engage in on that or adjoining land, does anything which is intended by him to have the effect –

    (i)   of intimidating those persons so as to deter them or any of them from engaging in that activity,

    (ii)   of obstructing that activity, or

    (iii)   of disrupting that activity,

(r)   without reasonable excuse, does anything which (whether or not intended by him to have the effect mentioned in paragraph (q)) disturbs, annoys or obstructs any persons engaged in a lawful activity on the land,

(s)   engages in any organised games, or in camping, hang-gliding or para-gliding, or

(t)   engages in any activity which is organised or undertaken (whether by him or another) for any commercial purpose.

2   (1) In paragraph 1(k), 'metal detector' means any device designed or adapted for detecting or locating any metal or mineral in the ground.

    (2) For the purposes of paragraph 1(q) and (r), activity on any occasion on the part of a person or persons on land is 'lawful' if he or they may engage in the activity on the land on that occasion without committing an offence or trespassing on the land.

3   Regulations may amend paragraphs 1 and 2.

4   During the period beginning with 1st March and ending with 31st July in each year, section 2(1) does not entitle a person to be on any land if he takes, or allows to enter or remain, any dog which is not on a short lead.

5   Whatever the time of year, section 2(1) does not entitle a person to be on any land if he takes, or allows to enter or remain, any dog which is not on a short lead and which is in the vicinity of livestock.

6 In paragraphs 4 and 5, 'short lead' means a lead of fixed length and of not more than two metres.

Removal or relaxation of restrictions

7 (1) The relevant authority may by direction, with the consent of the owner of any land, remove or relax any of the restrictions imposed by paragraphs 1, 4 and 5 in relation to that land, either indefinitely or during a specified period.

(2) In sub-paragraph (1), the reference to a specified period includes references –

(a) to a specified period in every calendar year, or

(b) to a period which is to be determined by the owner of the land in accordance with the direction and notified by him to the relevant authority in accordance with regulations.

(3) Regulations may make provision as to –

(a) the giving or revocation of directions under this paragraph,

(b) the variation of any direction given under this paragraph by a subsequent direction so given,

(c) the giving or revocation of consent for the purposes of sub-paragraph (1), and

(d) the steps to be taken by the relevant authority or the owner for informing the public about any direction under this paragraph or its revocation.

(4) In this paragraph –

'the relevant authority' has the meaning given by section 21;

'owner', in relation to any land which is subject to a farm business tenancy within the meaning of the Agricultural Tenancies Act 1995 or a tenancy to which the Agricultural Holdings Act 1986 applies, means the tenant under that tenancy.

Dedicated land

8 In relation to land to which a dedication under section 16 relates (whether or not it would be access land apart from the dedication), the provisions of this Schedule have effect subject to the terms of the dedication.

SCHEDULE 3

DELEGATION OF APPELLATE FUNCTIONS

Interpretation

1 In this Schedule –

'appointed person' means a person appointed under section 8(1)(a);

'the appointing authority' means –

(a)   the Secretary of State, in relation to an appointment made by him, or

(b)   the National Assembly for Wales, in relation to an appointment made by it;

'appointment', in the case of any appointed person, means appointment under section 8(1)(a).

Appointments

2   An appointment under section 8(1)(a) must be in writing and –

(a)   may relate to any particular appeal or matter specified in the appointment or to appeals or matters of a description so specified,

(b)   may provide for any function to which it relates to be exercisable by the appointed person either unconditionally or subject to the fulfilment of such conditions as may be specified in the appointment, and

(c)   may, by notice in writing given to the appointed person, be revoked at any time by the appointing authority in respect of any appeal or matter which has not been determined by the appointed person before that time.

Powers of appointed person

3   Subject to the provisions of this Schedule, an appointed person shall, in relation to any appeal or matter to which his appointment relates, have the same powers and duties as the appointing authority, other than –

(a)   any function of making regulations;

(b)   any function of holding an inquiry or other hearing or of causing an inquiry or other hearing to be held; or

(c)   any function of appointing a person for the purpose –

    (i)   of enabling persons to appear before and be heard by the person so appointed; or

    (ii)   of referring any question or matter to that person.

Holding of local inquiries and other hearings by appointed persons

4   (1) If either of the parties to an appeal or matter expresses a wish to appear before and be heard by the appointed person, the appointed person shall give both of them an opportunity of appearing and being heard.

(2) Whether or not a party to an appeal or matter has asked for an opportunity to appear and be heard, the appointed person –

    (a)   may hold a local inquiry or other hearing in connection with the appeal or matter, and

    (b)   shall, if the appointing authority so directs, hold a local inquiry in connection with the appeal or matter.

(3) Where an appointed person holds a local inquiry or other hearing by virtue of this Schedule, an assessor may be appointed by the appointing authority to sit with the appointed person at the inquiry or hearing and advise him on

any matters arising, notwithstanding that the appointed person is to determine the appeal or matter.

(4) Subject to paragraph 5, the costs of a local inquiry held under this Schedule shall be defrayed by the appointing authority.

Local inquiries under this Schedule: evidence and costs

5   Subsections (2) to (5) of section 250 of the Local Government Act 1972 (local inquiries: evidence and costs) shall apply to local inquiries or other hearings held under this Schedule by an appointed person as they apply to inquiries caused to be held under that section by a Minister, but as if –

(a)   in subsection (2) (evidence) the reference to the person appointed to hold the inquiry were a reference to the appointed person,

(b)   in subsection (4) (recovery of costs of holding the inquiry) –

(i)   references to the Minister causing the inquiry to be held were references to the appointing authority, and
(ii)   references to a local authority included references to the appropriate countryside body, and

(c)   in subsection (5) (orders as to the costs of the parties) the reference to the Minister causing the inquiry to be held were a reference to the appointed person or the appointing authority.

Revocation of appointments and making of new appointments

6   (1) Where under paragraph 2(c) the appointment of the appointed person is revoked in respect of any appeal or matter, the appointing authority shall, unless he proposes to determine the appeal or matter himself, appoint another person under section 8(1)(a) to determine the appeal or matter instead.

(2) Where such a new appointment is made, the consideration of the appeal or matter, or any hearing in connection with it, shall be begun afresh.

(3) Nothing in sub-paragraph (2) shall require any person to be given an opportunity of making fresh representations or modifying or withdrawing any representations already made.

Certain acts and omissions of appointed person to be treated as those of appointing authority

7   (1) Anything done or omitted to be done by an appointed person in, or in connection with, the exercise or purported exercise of any function to which the appointment relates shall be treated for all purposes as done or omitted to be done by the appointing authority.

(2) Sub-paragraph (1) does not apply –

(a)   for the purposes of so much of any contract made between the appointing authority and the appointed person as relates to the exercise of the function, or

(b) for the purposes of any criminal proceedings brought in respect of anything done or omitted to be done as mentioned in that sub-paragraph.

SCHEDULE 4

MINOR AND CONSEQUENTIAL AMENDMENTS RELATING TO PART I

Law of Property Act 1925 (c 20)

1   In section 193(1) of the Law of Property Act 1925 (rights of public over commons and waste lands), in paragraph (b) of the proviso, after 'injuriously affected,' there is inserted 'for conserving flora, fauna or geological or physiographical features of the land,'.

Forestry Act 1967 (c 10)

2   In section 9 of the Forestry Act 1967 (requirement of licence for felling), in the definition of 'public open space' in subsection (6), after '1949' there is inserted 'or Part I of the Countryside and Rights of Way Act 2000)'.

Agriculture Act 1967 (c 22)

3   In section 52 of the Agriculture Act 1967 (control of afforestation), in the definition of 'public open space' in subsection (15), after '1949' there is inserted 'or Part I of the Countryside and Rights of Way Act 2000)'.

Countryside Act 1968 (c 41)

4   In section 2(6) of the Countryside Act 1968 (Countryside Agency and Countryside Council for Wales to make recommendations to public bodies in relation to byelaws) for 'and the Act of 1949' there is substituted ', the Act of 1949 and Part I of the Countryside and Rights of Way Act 2000'.

Local Government Act 1974 (c 7)

[5   *In section 9 of the Local Government Act 1974 (grants and loans by Countryside Agency and Countryside Council for Wales), for 'or the National Parks and Access to the Countryside Act 1949' there is substituted ', the National Parks and Access to the Countryside Act 1949 or the Countryside and Rights of Way Act 2000'.*]

Prospective repeal –Natural Environment and Rural Communities Act 2006, s 105(2), Sch 12, as from a date to be appointed.

Wildlife and Countryside Act 1981 (c 69)

6   In paragraph 13(1) of Schedule 13 to the Wildlife and Countryside Act 1981 (Countryside Agency's annual report on the discharge of their functions) after '1968 Act' there is inserted ', the Countryside and Rights of Way Act 2000'.

COMMONS REGISTRATION (GENERAL) REGULATIONS 1966

SI 1966 No 1471

PART I

PRELIMINARY

1   Title and commencement

These Regulations may be cited as the Commons Registration (General) Regulations 1966 and shall come into operation on 2nd January 1967.

2   Interpretation

(1)   The Interpretation Act 1889 applies for the interpretation of these Regulations as it applies for the interpretation of an Act of Parliament.

(2)   In these Regulations, unless the context otherwise requires –

'the Act' means the Commons Registration Act 1965;

'charity' bears the meaning assigned to that expression in section 45 of the Charities Act 1960, and 'charitable purposes' and 'charity trustees' bear the meanings assigned to those expressions in section 46 of that Act;

'concerned authority', in relation to a registration, means a local authority (other than the registration authority) in whose area any part of the land affected by the registration lies;

'Form' means one of the forms in Schedule 1 to these Regulations, or a form to substantially the same effect;

'Model Entry' means one of the specimen entries provided as examples in Part 1 of Schedule 2 to these Regulations, and 'Standard Entry' one of the specimen entries in Part 2 of that Schedule, or an entry to substantially the same effect;

'parcel of land', in relation to a search under Part VI of these Regulations, means a piece of land in separate occupation or separately rated at the time of the requisition for search; and for the purpose of this definition any land which is neither occupied nor rated shall be deemed to be occupied by the person who receives the rackrent therefor, whether on his own account or as agent or trustee for any other person, or who would so receive it if the land were let at a rackrent;

'provisional registration' means a registration under section 4 of the Act which has not become final;

'register map' means any map, other than a supplemental map, which, by virtue of any regulation made under the Act, for the time being forms part of a register;

'register unit' bears the meaning assigned to that expression in regulation 10 below;

'registration area' means the land in relation to which a local authority is the registration authority;

'supplemental map' bears the meaning assigned to that expression in regulation 20 below.

(3)   A requirement or permission to publish a document in any area is a requirement or permission to cause it to be published in a newspaper circulating in that area, with, in the case of a requirement or permission to publish more than once, an interval of at least seven days between each publication.

(4)   A requirement to display a document or copies thereof is a requirement to treat it, for the purposes of section 287 of the Local Government Act 1933 (public notices), as if it were a public notice within that section.

(5)   Where the day or the last day on which anything is required or permitted by or in pursuance of these regulations to be done is a Sunday, Christmas Day, Good Friday, bank holiday or a day appointed for public thanksgiving or mourning, the requirement or permission shall be deemed to relate to the first day thereafter which is not one of the days before-mentioned.

3   Official stamp of registration authority

(1)   Every registration authority shall have an official stamp for the purposes of the Act, as follows:–

COMMONS REGISTRATION ACT 1965

(Name of registration authority)

REGISTRATION AUTHORITY

(Date)

(2)   A requirement upon a registration authority to stamp any document is a requirement to cause an impression of the said official stamp to be affixed to it, and that the impression shall bear the date mentioned in the requirement or (where no date is mentioned) the date when it was affixed.

(3)   An indication in any form in Schedule 1 to these Regulations that the form shall bear the official stamp of a registration authority is a requirement upon the authority to stamp it.

PART II

THE REGISTERS AND PROVISIONAL REGISTRATION

4   The registers

(1)   Every register, whether of common land or of town or village greens, shall consist of –

(a)   a general part,
(b)   a register map,
(c)   as many register units as there are registrations of land in the register, and
(d)   such supplemental maps (if any) as may be necessary.

(2)   The general part of each register shall be in Form 1, and shall contain –

(a)   particulars of any agreement under section 2 of the Act to which the registration authority is a party;
(b)   particulars of any land situated in the area of the registration authority to which, by virtue of section 11 of the Act or of an order made thereunder, the registration provisions of the Act do not apply;
(c)   particulars of any transfer, to or from the registration authority, of responsibility for maintaining any register or register unit, otherwise than under section 2 of the Act;
(d)   such other information as may by any regulation made under the Act be required or authorized to be entered therein.

(3)   Model Entries 1, 2 and 3 are provided for general guidance in complying with sub-paragraphs (a), (b) and (c) respectively of paragraph (2) above.

(4)   The register map to be prepared under these Regulations shall be a provisional register map and shall be prepared in accordance with Part III thereof.

(5)   The register units shall be prepared in accordance with regulation 10 below, and each register unit shall consist of three sections, called the land section, the rights section and the ownership section.

(6)   The land section of each register unit shall be in Form 2, and shall contain the registrations of the common land, or of the town or village green, as the case may be, comprised therein, with a reference to the register map, and such other information as may by any regulation made under the Act be required or authorized to be entered therein.

(7)   The rights section of each register unit shall be in Form 3, and shall contain the registrations of the rights of common registered as exercisable over the land comprised in the land section of the register unit, or any part thereof, particulars of the persons on whose applications the rights were registered and the capacities in which they applied, descriptions of the land (if any) to which the rights are attached, and such other information as may by any regulation made under the Act be required or authorized to be entered therein.

(8)   The ownership section of each register unit shall be in Form 4, and shall contain the registration of every person registered as owner of any part of the land

comprised in the register unit, and such other information as may by any regulation made under the Act be required or authorized to be entered therein.

(9) Supplemental maps, where necessary, shall be prepared in accordance with Part III of these Regulations.

(10) Every register shall be bound, or otherwise held together and protected, in such manner as the Minister may approve.

5   Registration periods

(1) There shall be two periods during which applications for registration may be made, called the first registration period and the second registration period.

(2) The first registration period shall begin on 2nd January 1967 and end on 30th June 1968, and the second shall begin on 1st July 1968 and end on 2nd January 1970.

6   Notice of intention to make application

(1) Any person may, during the first registration period, give a registration authority notice in Form 5 of his intention to apply to the authority for registration during the second registration period, and the authority shall send him a written acknowledgment for that notice, and shall retain it until after the end of the second registration period.

(2) Form 6, if used for the purpose of an acknowledgment under this regulation, shall be sufficient.

[7   Applications in special cases]

[(1) Where a right of common is attached to any land, and is comprised in a tenancy of the land, an application for the registration of that right may be made by the landlord, the tenant, or both of them jointly.

(2) Where a right of common belongs to an ecclesiastical benefice of the Church of England which is vacant an application for the registration of that right may be made by the Church Commissioners.

(3) Where any land registered under the Act belongs to an ecclesiastical benefice of the Church of England which is vacant an application for the registration of a claim to the ownership of that land may be made by the Church Commissioners.

(4) The foregoing provisions of this regulation do not affect the right of any person entitled, apart from those provisions, to make any application under the Act.]

Amendment – SI 1968/658.

8   Applications, declarations and fees

(1) An application for registration must be –

    (a)   in Form 7, 8, 9 or 10 as appropriate;

    (b)   signed by [or on behalf of] every applicant who is an individual, and by the secretary or some other duly authorized officer of every applicant which is a body corporate or unincorporate; and

(c)   supported by a statutory declaration made by [every applicant].

(2)   Every application for registration made during the second registration period must be accompanied by a fee of five pounds, unless either –

(a)   during the first registration period the applicant gave the registration authority notice in Form 5 of his intention to make that application; or

(b)   the application is for the registration of land as common land or as a town or village green, and the land did not become so registrable until after 30th April 1968; or

(c)   the application is for the registration of a right of common and the right did not become registrable until after 30th April 1968; or

(d)   the application is for the registration of a claim to ownership and the land to which it relates was not registered until after 30th April 1968.

[(3)   An application for the registration of a right of common, or of a claim to the ownership of any land, made by a person who is not the owner of the right or, as the case may be, of the land, shall, unless that person is entitled by virtue of any provision of regulation 7 above to make the application, be supported by such further evidence (if any) of his right to make it as, after considering the application and the declaration in support, the registration authority may reasonably require.]

Amendment – SI 1968/658.

9   Disposal of applications

(1)   On receiving an application for registration, a registration authority shall allot a distinguishing number to it, and shall mark the application form with that number. The number so allotted shall be from a single series, whatever the type of application.

(2)   . . .

(3)   The registration authority shall send to the applicant for registration a receipt for his application containing a statement of the number allotted thereto; and Form 6, if used for that purpose, shall be sufficient.

(4)   Where a registration authority rejects an application for registration, it shall so inform the applicant in writing, giving the reasons for the rejection.

(5)   Where an application is made for the registration of a right of common attached to any land, but the right has already been registered in such manner that, if the application were acceded to, no conflict would arise between the two registrations, the registration authority shall not register the right again but (unless it determines to reject the application) shall note the application in the register.

(6)   Where a registration authority accepts an application for registration it shall make a registration in respect thereof, or as the case may require, shall note the application, in the appropriate register in accordance with regulation 10 below, and shall inform the applicant of the disposal of the application, using Form 11,

12 or 13, as appropriate, with such omissions and adaptations as may be necessary, and shall file the application form and any plan thereto which is not required for the purposes of regulation 20 below (supplemental maps).

(7)   References in this regulation to 'the applicant' shall, where two or more persons are concerned together in an application, be construed as references to that one of them whose name appears first in the application form.

Amendment – SI 1994/2567.

10   Method of registration

(1)   A registration authority shall, in making any registration, or in noting an application in a register pursuant either to section 4(4) of the Act or to regulation 9(5) above, follow as closely as possible such of the Model Entries 4 to 12 as may be applicable, with such variations and adaptations as the circumstances may require, and shall mark every registration as provisional.

(2)   The registration authority shall, when registering any land, enter the particulars on a fresh register sheet in Form 2, and shall place register sheets in Forms 3 and 4 immediately below that sheet in its place on the register.

(3)   The register sheets referred to in paragraphs (2) above and (6) below shall constitute a register unit, and shall be kept on the register in sequence with other register units.

(4)   Where a registration of land falls to be made in pursuance of an application which relates to two or more pieces of land, the registration authority may, if it thinks fit, prepare two or more register units, each comprising one or more of those pieces of land, and there shall then be deemed to be a separate registration in respect of the land comprised in each such unit; and in this paragraph 'piece of land' means an area of land comprised, with other land, in an application, and having no common boundary with any of that other land.

(5)   The registration authority shall allot a distinguishing number to each register unit from a separate series for each register. Every register unit number for the Register of Common Land shall bear the prefix CL, and every such number for the Register of Town or Village Greens shall bear the prefix VG.

(6)   The registration authority shall from time to time as necessary add fresh register sheets to a register unit, and every sheet forming part of a register unit shall be marked with the number of that unit.

(7)   Where a right of common affecting any minerals is registered, there shall be included in, or, as the case may require, added to, the registration of the land over which the right is exercised an entry in accordance with Standard Entry 1.

(8)   Every entry relating to any land, to rights thereover or to ownership thereof, which is required or authorized by the Act or any regulation made thereunder to be made in any section of a register shall be made in the appropriate section of the register unit relating to that land, and no entry forming part of a registration or of an amendment made pursuant to section 13 of the Act shall be

made in the general part of a register or in any space on a register sheet headed 'Notes'.

11 Information to public about registrations

(1) Not later than four weeks after the date of any registration the registration authority shall send a copy thereof to every concerned authority.

(2) Where a registration is of land, or, being of rights or ownership, has necessitated the preparation of a supplemental map or the insertion of fresh particulars on the provisional register map, every copy of the registration sent out under this regulation shall be accompanied by a plan showing the relevant particulars.

(3) Every authority to whom such a copy or plan is sent under this regulation shall keep it available for public inspection at all reasonable times.

12 Conflicting registrations

(1) A registration authority shall, on making any registration (in this regulation referred to as the new registration) ascertain whether the new registration conflicts with any other registration in its registers (in this regulation referred to as the old registration) and, where it appears to the authority to do so, the following provisions of this regulation shall apply.

(2) After making the new registration the registration authority shall add to each registration a note about the conflict in accordance with Standard Entry 2.

(3) The registration authority shall, where the new registration was made on the application of any person, give that person notice of the conflict by means of Form 11, 12 or 13, as appropriate, and shall give the person (if any) on whose application the old registration was made, and any person whose application is noted (whether under section 4(4) of the Act or under regulation 9(5) above) notice thereof in Form 14.

(4) Every copy of the entry of the new registration prepared in accordance with regulation 11 above shall include the note added under paragraph (2) above, and where regulation 14 below applies, the note added under that regulation.

(5) The registration authority shall prepare fresh copies of the entry of the old registration, including the note added under paragraph (2) above, and, where regulation 14 below applies, the note added under that regulation, and shall send one such copy, marked 'Replacement Copy', to every concerned authority.

(6) Every authority receiving a replacement copy under paragraph (5) above shall destroy any earlier copy of the old registration in its possession and shall keep the replacement copy available for public inspection at all reasonable times.

(7) A registration authority may, if it thinks fit, cancel or modify a registration to which this regulation applies if either –

    (a) the person (if any) on whose application it was made, or any person whose application is noted (whether under section 4(4) of the Act or under regulation 9(5) above) so requests, and the persons, or, as the case may be, the other persons (if any) whose applications have been noted under regulation 9(5) above consent in writing, or

(b)   the registration was made otherwise than on the application of any person;

and, where the authority cancels any registration under this paragraph, it shall also cancel any note under paragraph (2) above.

(8)   Where the registration of any land as common land or as a town or village green is cancelled under this regulation the registration authority shall also cancel the registration of any person as the owner thereof.

Amendment – SI 1994/256.

14   Double registration of land

(1)   Where any land is registered both as common land and as a town or village green, entries relating to that land of the classes mentioned in paragraph (2) below made in one register shall be deemed also to be made in the other, adapted, where applicable, as in paragraph 4(b) below, and the registration authority shall note the land, rights and ownership section of each register as indicated in Standard Entry 3.

(2)   The entries referred to in paragraph (1) above are –

(a)   in the land section, an entry under regulation 10(7) (as to inclusion of minerals);
(b)   in the rights and ownership sections, every entry.

(3)   The cancellation in one register, under regulation 12(8) above, of the registration of any person as owner of the land consequent upon the cancellation of the registration of the land in that register shall not affect the registration of the ownership of that person deemed, under this regulation, to have been made in the other register.

(4)   Where the registration in one register of any land registered in both registers is cancelled ... the registration authority shall cancel in each register the note made under paragraph (1) above, and shall transfer from the register wherein the registration of that land has been cancelled to the other register every entry deemed, under this regulation, to have been made therein, in the following manner:–

(a)   every entry shall be allotted a fresh number and shall be dated as of the date when so transferred, but in the left-hand column of the register sheet, below such number and date, shall appear '(Formerly No .. .. dated .... in Register Unit No ......)';
(b)   references to land in column 4 of the rights and ownership sections of the original register containing expressions valid only in relation to that register shall be adapted as necessary; and
(c)   the register map shall be amended as necessary.

Amendment – SI 1968/989.

15   Interpretation of regulations 5 to 14

In regulations 5 to 14 above 'registration' means registration under section 4 of the Act and 'registered' shall be construed accordingly.

PART III

MAPS

16   Provisional register map

(1)   Every registration authority shall prepare and keep up to date a provisional register map for each of its registers.

(2)   Every such map shall be based on the ordnance map and shall be on a scale of not less, or not substantially less, than six inches to one mile, but where the registration authority considers it expedient to show any particulars on a larger scale, it may insert an inset map for that purpose.

(3)   A provisional register map may consist of one sheet or of more than one, and further sheets may be added from time to time as necessary.

(4)   Where such a map consists of more than one sheet, each sheet shall bear a distinguishing number, and the sheets shall be bound together bookwise, but so that sheets can be added or removed without damage.

(5)   Every provisional register map shall show:–

(a)   by black lines verged yellow inside the boundary, and the word EXEMPTED, the boundaries of any land situated in the area of the registration authority to which, by virtue of an order under section 11 of the Act, the provisions of sections 1 to 10 thereof do not apply;

(b)   by black lines verged green inside the boundary, and the appropriate register unit number, the boundaries of the land comprised in each register unit;

(c)   by red line suitably lettered, or by lettering alone, the limits of any land over which a registered right of common is exercisable, or to which a registration of ownership applies, so far as those limits do not coincide with the boundaries of the land comprised in a register unit, and cannot conveniently be described by reference to any feature appearing on the said map;

(d)   by black hatching, and if necessary by lettering as well, land which has been removed from the register under section 13 of the Act [or by virtue of the Common Land (Rectification of Registers) Act 1989], or of which the registration has been cancelled;

(e)   by black interrupted lines, any boundaries of the registration area falling within the said map;

(f)   by such other colours and symbols as the registration authority may think fit, other particulars mentioned in the general part of the register, or in any registration (not being particulars of land to which rights of common are attached), which it is necessary or convenient to show on the said map.

(6)   There shall be kept annexed to every provisional register map a table headed 'Key to Colouring and Symbols' containing a description or representation of every colour or symbol used in the said map (except such of those used under paragraph (5)(f) above as are not of general application) with a statement of the meaning of each such colour or symbol.

17   Overlays

(1)   Where it appears to a registration authority that the inclusion on one surface of all the particulars required to be shown on a provisional register map or any sheet thereof would be impracticable or confusing, the authority may prepare one or more transparent overlays for the map or sheet, and may show thereon, instead of on the map or sheet itself, the particulars, or some of the particulars, required to be shown by virtue of sub-paragraphs (c), (d) and (f) of regulation 16(5) above.

(2)   Every such overlay shall be fastened to the original map or sheet so that the details thereon coincide with those on the original, but so that it may be lifted away to enable either the original alone, or the original and any other overlay fastened thereto, to be inspected.

(3)   Every overlay prepared under this regulation shall form part of the provisional register map.

18   Fresh editions

A registration authority may, whenever it deems it expedient to do so, prepare a fresh edition of a provisional register map or of any sheet thereof, showing only particulars of subsisting entries in the register. A fresh edition of a sheet forming part of a provisional register map shall bear the same number as the sheet it is to replace.

19   Indorsement

Every provisional register map consisting of one sheet, and every sheet of such a map consisting of more than one sheet, shall be indorsed as follows:–

'Provisional Register Map of (Common Land) (Town or Village Greens). (Sheet No …..). This is the ………. edition of this (map) (sheet)'

and shall be stamped by, and signed on behalf of, the registration authority, and shall then form part of the register and (in the case of a fresh edition) the map or sheet which is replaced shall be marked on its face 'This (map) (sheet) was replaced by a fresh edition on (date)', but shall not cease to be part of the register.

20   Supplemental maps

(1)   Where a right of common attached to any land falls to be registered, and that land or any part thereof is described in the application for registration by means of a plan, the registration authority shall describe that land or part in the register by means of a map to be called a supplemental map in accordance with this regulation.

(2)   The registration authority may adopt as the supplemental map the plan referred to in paragraph (1) above, or may itself prepare a map showing the necessary particulars; and where the authority so adopts a plan it shall not mark it otherwise than as mentioned in paragraph (4) below.

(3)   The land to be described by means of a supplemental map (not being an adopted plan) shall be coloured, tinted, verged or hatched thereon in such manner as may seem to the registration authority most convenient for identifying it, and the means of identification used in any supplemental map shall be referred to in column 5 of the rights section of the register, as in the following example:–

'The land at &c as shown verged red within the boundary on the supplemental map bearing the number of this registration.'

(4)   The supplemental map shall be stamped by the registration authority as of the date of the entry of registration, and shall be indorsed as follows:–

'Supplemental map referred to in column 5 of entry No ..... in the rights section of register unit No ..... in the Register of (Common Land) (Town or Village Greens)'

and shall then form part of the register.

(5)   Supplemental maps shall be kept separately for each register, in register unit order, and within that order in entry number order.

PART IV

OTHER ENTRIES IN THE REGISTERS

21   Registration under Land Registration Acts 1925 and 1936

Where any land is registered under the Act, and the registration authority is notified by the Chief Land Registrar that the land has been registered under the Land Registration Acts 1925 and 1936, then –

(a)   if the ownership of the land has not been registered under the Act, the authority shall note the ownership section of the register in accordance with Standard Entry 4;

(b)   if the ownership of the land has been so registered, the authority shall, after deleting the registration of the ownership pursuant to section 12(b) of the Act, note the ownership section of the register in accordance with Standard Entry 5.

22   Matters affecting the public

(1)   Where any of the matters to which this regulation applies affects land registered under the Act, the registration authority may enter a note thereof in the land section of the register notwithstanding that no application in that behalf has been made, and, where it has not done so, it shall do so upon application made in accordance with the following provisions of this regulation.

(2)   This regulation applies to the following matters:–

    (a)   schemes under Part I of the Commons Act 1899 or under the Metropolitan Commons Acts 1866 to 1898;

    (b)   local Acts regulating the land;

    (c)   Acts confirming provisional orders made under the Commons Act 1876;

    (d)   limitations and conditions imposed under proviso (b) to section 193(1) of the Law of Property Act 1925.

(3)   Applications under this regulation must be in writing and may be made by any local authority in whose area any part of the land lies, by any person charged by law with the management or regulation of the land or (in the case of the said limitations and conditions) by –

    (a)   the owner of any part of the land;

    (b)   any person appearing from the register to be interested in a right of common registered as exercisable thereover; or

    (c)   where any part of the land, or any such right, belongs to an ecclesiastical benefice of the Church of England which is vacant, by the Church Commissioners.

(4)   Any note entered in a register under this regulation shall be in accordance with Model Entry 13 or 14 as applicable, and, where the entry is made pursuant to an application, the registration authority shall send the applicant a copy of the entry.

24   Private rights and interests

(1)   Where any land is registered under the Act, the registration authority shall, upon application made in accordance with the following provisions of this regulation, enter a note in the land section of the register of the existence, in relation to that land, of a claim to any right or interest to which this regulation applies, unless it appears to the authority that the right or interest is of a trivial, obvious or transitory nature, or that an entry relating to it would be likely to cause confusion or inconvenience or unlikely to add substantially to the information obtainable from an inspection of the land.

(2)   This regulation applies to the following rights and interests:–

    (a)   easements;

    (b)   profits à prendre other than rights of common;

    (c)   franchises;

    (d)   rights and interests of the lord of the manor (in that capacity) other than the ownership of the land;

    (e)   where the ownership of any minerals in or under the land is severed from the ownership of the surface, the ownership of those minerals and all rights incident thereto;

    (f)   rights of the lessee or licensee under any mineral lease or licence;

    (g)   rights acquired by statutory undertakers for the purposes of their undertakings.

(3)   Every application under this regulation must be in Form 16 and be made by the person claiming to be entitled to the right or interest, or, where the right or

interest belongs to an ecclesiastical benefice of the Church of England which is vacant, by the Church Commissioners.

(4)   Where a registration authority accepts an application under this regulation, it shall make a note in the register in accordance with Model Entries 16 to 19 as applicable, and shall send written notice to the applicant of the making of the note together with a copy of the note as entered.

(5)   No marking shall be made on the register map or any supplemental map in connexion with any note under this regulation.

(6)   Where a registration authority rejects an application under this regulation it shall so inform the applicant in writing, giving the reasons for the rejection.

25   Cancellation of certain entries

A registration authority may cancel an entry under regulation 22, 23 or 24 above if it is satisfied on reasonable grounds that the matter to which the entry relates is no longer subsisting.

26   New addresses

(1)   Any person to whom this regulation applies, having changed his address, may apply in writing to the registration authority to note the new address on the register, and the registration authority shall note the appropriate section of the register accordingly.

(2)   This regulation applies to the following persons:–

(a)   where land is registered under the Act, any person registered as owner thereof and, where the registration of the land is provisional, the person (if any) on whose application it was made, and any person whose application has been noted under section 4(4) of the Act;

(b)   where a right of common is so registered, any person appearing from the register to be interested therein, and, where the registration is provisional, the person on whose application it was made and any person whose application is noted under regulation 9(5) above.

27   Land ceasing to be common land or a town or village green

(1)   Where any land registered under the Act has ceased to be common land or a town or village green, application may be made to the registration authority, in accordance with the following provisions of this regulation, for the amendment of the register.

[(2)   An application under this regulation may be made by the person who, at the date of the application, would have been entitled (whether or not by virtue of any provision of these Regulations) to apply under section 4 of the Act for the registration of a claim to the ownership of the land if at that date such an application could have been made.]

(3)   Every such application must be –

(a)   in Form 17;

(b)   signed by [or on behalf of] every applicant who is an individual, and by the secretary or other duly authorized officer of every applicant which is a body corporate; and

(c)   supported by a statutory declaration made by every person who has signed the application, and by such further evidence (if any) as, after considering the application and declaration, the registration authority may reasonably require.

(4)   Applications under this regulation shall be numbered in order of receipt by the registration authority, and shall be entitled, unless rejected, to be given effect to on the register in that order.

(5)   The registration authority shall, on receipt of any application under this regulation which it does not, after preliminary consideration, determine to reject, publish in the concerned area, and shall display, a notice in Form 18, and shall send the notice to –

(a)   every concerned authority;

(b)   any person other than the applicant who is registered as owner of the land;

(c)   where a right of common is registered as exercisable over the land, any person appearing from the register to be interested therein, and, where the registration is provisional, the person on whose application it was made and any person whose application is noted under regulation 9(5) above.

(6)   Every authority receiving a Form 18 notice under this regulation shall display copies thereof.

(7)   Upon the expiration of forty days from the date on which paragraph (5) above is complied with, the registration authority shall further consider the application and shall consider any written representations which it has received, and, if it deems the application well-founded, shall amend the register as shown in Standard Entry 6.

(8)   In this regulation 'concerned area' means, in the case of a registration authority which is the council of a county borough, an area including the area of the county borough and the areas of every concerned authority, and, in any other case, an area including the areas of every concerned authority.

Amendment – SI 1968/658.

PART V

AMENDMENT OF REGISTERS UNDER SECTION 13 OF ACT

28   Substituted land

(1)   Where –

(a)   application is made to a registration authority under regulation 27 above with respect to any land registered under the Act, and

(b)   it appears to the authority that, under or by virtue of any of the enactments mentioned in paragraph (2) below, the said land (in this regulation referred to as the taken land) has ceased to be common land or a town or village green, and that certain other land not registered under the Act (in this regulation referred to as the substituted land) has become common land or a town or village green in substitution therefor,

the authority shall not give effect to the application until the substituted land has been registered under the Act, unless it is exempt from registration under section 11 thereof.

(2) The enactments referred to in paragraph (1) above are the following:–

(a) sections 147 and 148 of the Inclosure Act 1845;

(b) paragraph 11 of the First Schedule to the Acquisition of Land (Authorisation Procedure) Act 1946;

(c) any other enactment providing, on the exchange of land, for the transfer of rights trusts or incidents attaching to the land given in exchange from that land to the land taken in exchange and vice versa.

(3) Substituted land in the same registration area as the taken land shall be registered in the register unit containing the registration of the taken land, with a statement as in Standard Entry 7, and both the taken and the substituted land shall be identified by lettering in the register unit and on the register map.

29 Amendment in regard to registered rights

(1) Where a right of common registered under the Act has been apportioned, varied, extinguished or released, or, being or having become a right in gross, has been transferred, application may be made to the registration authority, in accordance with the following provisions of this regulation, for the amendment of the register.

[(2) (a) An application under this regulation may be made by any person having an interest under the apportionment, variation, extinguishment, release or transfer.

(b) For the purposes of this regulation the following are included in the expression 'person having an interest', but without prejudice to the generality of that expression:–

(i) in the case of an apportionment, variation or transfer, any person who, at the date of the application under this regulation, would have been entitled (whether or not by virtue of any provision of these Regulations) to apply under section 4 of the Act for the registration of the right as apportioned, varied or transferred, if at that date such an application could have been made;

(ii) in the case of an extinguishment or release, any person who, at the date of the application under this regulation, would have been entitled (whether or not by virtue of any provision of these Regulations) to apply under the said section 4 for the registration of a claim to the ownership of any part of the land over which the right extinguished or released was formerly exercisable, if at that date such an application could have been made.]

(3) Every such application must be –

(a) in Form 19;

(b) signed by [or on behalf of] every applicant who is an individual, and by the secretary or other duly authorized officer of every applicant which is a body corporate; and

(c) supported by a statutory declaration made by every person who has signed the application, and by such further evidence (if any) as, after considering the application and declaration, the registration authority may reasonably require.

(4) Applications under this regulation shall be numbered in order of receipt by the registration authority and shall be entitled, unless rejected, to be given effect to on the register in that order.

(5) The registration authority shall, on receipt of any application under this regulation which it does not after preliminary consideration determine to reject, serve notice in Form 20 upon every person (other than the applicant) appearing, either from the register or from any prior pending application under this regulation, to be interested in the right of common referred to in the application, and, where the registration is provisional, upon the person on whose application it was made and any person whose application is noted under regulation 9(5) above.

(6) Upon the expiration of forty days from the date on which paragraph (5) above is complied with, the registration authority shall further consider the application and shall consider any written representations which it has received, and, if it deems the application well-founded, shall make the necessary amendment to the register in accordance with Model Entry 20 or 21 as appropriate.

(7) Where an assurance entitled to be registered under the Yorkshire Registries Act 1884 effects any such apportionment, variation, extinguishment, release or transfer as is mentioned in paragraph (1) above, section 14 of that Act shall not apply to that assurance so far as it relates to that apportionment, variation, extinguishment, release or transfer.

Amendment – SI 1968/658.

30   Information about disposal of applications

(1) Where a registration authority has accepted an application under regulation 27 or 29 above, and has made the necessary amendment in the register, it shall give written notice thereof, with particulars of the amendment, to every concerned authority, to the applicant and to every person served with notice of the application, and, where the authority has rejected such an application, it shall give written notice of the rejection to the applicant and to every such person as aforesaid, giving the reasons for the rejection.

(2) An authority to whom a notice is sent under paragraph (1) above shall annex it to the copy of the registration to which it relates and keep it available for public inspection at all reasonable times.

PART VI

MISCELLANEOUS

31   Land descriptions

(1)   Land must be described for the purposes of any application, other than an application under Part IV of these Regulations –

(a)   by a plan accompanying the application and referred to therein; or

(b)   in the case of land already registered under the Act, by a reference to the register sufficient to enable the land to be identified; or

(c)   in the case of land to which rights of common are attached, by reference to the numbered parcels on the most recent edition of the ordnance map (quoting the edition).

(2)   Any plan accompanying an application must –

(a)   be drawn to scale;

(b)   be in ink or other permanent medium;

(c)   be on a scale of not less, or not substantially less, than six inches to one mile;

(d)   show the land to be described by means of distinctive colouring; and

(e)   be marked as an exhibit to the statutory declaration in support of the application.

[31A   Applications signed by agents]

[Any application signed by an agent on behalf of an individual applicant shall be supported by such evidence (if any) of the agent's authority as, after considering the application, the registration authority may reasonably require.]

Amendment – 1968/658.

32   Official searches and certificates

(1)   Where any person requires a search to be made in [the registers], he may on payment of the prescribed fee lodge with the registration authority a requisition in that behalf.

(2)   A requisition for a search must be in Form 21, signed by the person making the same or by his solicitor, and must define the land in respect of which the search is to be made by means of a plan drawn to scale and (except where the applicant does not require a plan to be returned) furnished in duplicate.

(3)   The registration authority shall thereupon make the search required, and shall issue a certificate setting forth the results of the search by completing the appropriate portion of Form 21 and returning one copy of the form to the person who required the search or his solicitor.

(4)   A separate requisition for search shall be made in respect of each parcel of land against which a search is requested, except where for the purpose of a single registration or of a single transaction a certificate is required in respect of two or

more parcels of land which have a common boundary or are separated only by a road, railway, river, stream or canal.

(5)   Every registration authority shall close its registers for entries at a fixed time each working day, and shall make no entries therein after that time until the next working day.

(6)   An official certificate of the result of the search shall extend to registrations effected during the day of the date of the certificate and shall be issued only when the registers have been closed for entries on that day.

Amendment – SI 1980/1195.

Modification – SI 1991/2684.

33   Certified copies and extracts

Any person may, on payment of the prescribed fee, bespeak from a registration authority, and the registration authority shall thereupon issue, a copy of, or extract from, the general part of any register maintained by it under the Act, or any map or register unit forming part of such a register, certified on behalf of the registration authority as a true copy or extract as at the date of issue thereof.

34   Fees for searches, etc

(1)   The fees payable for searches and official certificates of search, and for certified copies and extracts, shall be those specified in Schedule 3 to these regulations.

(2)   All fees payable by virtue of this regulation shall be paid in advance.

35   Supply of certain forms

Forms 1 to 4, 7 to 10, 16, 17, 19 and 21 shall be supplied to registration authorities under arrangements to be made by HM Stationery Office . . .

Amendment – SI 1982/210.

36   Errors and omissions

Where any clerical error or omission, or error or omission of a like nature, is discovered in a register, and can be corrected without either –

(a)   increasing or diminishing the area of any land registered therein, or

(b)   increasing the burden on any such land of any right of common so registered, or

(c)   increasing the area of any land subject to any such right, or

(d)   causing any registration to conflict with another registration, or

(e)   affecting any provisional registration which falls to be referred to a Commons Commissioner, or any registration under section 4 of the Act which has become final,

the registration authority shall make the necessary correction, and, where the correction affects any provisional registration, shall inform every concerned authority in writing, and every such authority shall make a corresponding correction in the copy of the registration held by it.

[SCHEDULES 1, 2 and 3 ARE NOT REPRODUCED IN THIS BOOK]

COMMONS REGISTRATION (NEW LAND) REGULATIONS 1969

SI 1969 No 1843

1 Title and commencement

These Regulations may be cited as the Commons Registration (New Land) Regulations 1969, and shall come into operation on 3rd January 1970.

2 Interpretation

(1) The Interpretation Act 1889 applies for the interpretation of these Regulations as it applies for the interpretation of an Act of Parliament.

(2) In these Regulations, unless the context otherwise requires –

'the Act' means the Commons Registration Act 1965;

'application' means an application under these Regulations;

'concerned authority', in relation to an application to a registration authority, means a local authority (other than the registration authority) in whose area any part of the land affected by the application lies;

'Form 6' means the form so numbered in the General Regulations or a form to substantially the same effect, and 'Form' followed by a number above 28 means the form so numbered in the Schedule to these Regulations, or a form to substantially the same effect;

'the General Regulations' means the Commons Registration (General) Regulations 1966 as amended, and 'General Regulation' followed by a number means the regulation so numbered in the General Regulations;

'Model Entry' followed by a number means the specimen entry so numbered in Part I of Schedule 2 to the General Regulations, and 'Standard Entry' followed by a number means the specimen entry so numbered in Part 2 of that Schedule, or an entry to substantially the same effect;

'provisional registration' means a registration under section 4 of the Act which has not become final;

'substituted land' and, in relation to any substituted land, 'the taken land', bear the same meanings as in General Regulation 28.

(3) A requirement upon a registration authority to publish a document in any area is a requirement to cause the document to be published in such one or more newspapers circulating in that area as shall appear to the authority sufficient to secure adequate publicity for it.

(4) A requirement to display a document or copies thereof is a requirement to treat it, for the purposes of section 287 of the Local Government Act 1933 (public notices), as if it were a public notice within that section.

(5)   Where the day or the last day on which anything is required or permitted by or in pursuance of these Regulations to be done is a Sunday, Christmas Day, Good Friday, bank holiday or a day appointed for public thanksgiving or mourning, the requirement or permission shall be deemed to relate to the first day thereafter which is not one of the days before-mentioned.

(6)   Any requirement (however expressed) that a registration authority shall send anything to 'the applicant' shall, where a solicitor has been instructed for the purposes of an application, be deemed to be satisfied by sending it to the solicitor, or, where two or more persons are concerned together in an application and no solicitor has been instructed, to that one of them whose name appears first in the application form.

(7)   A requirement upon a registration authority to stamp any document is a requirement to cause an impression of its official stamp as described in General Regulation 3 to be affixed to it, and that the impression shall bear the date mentioned in the requirement or (where no date is mentioned) the date when it was affixed.

(8)   An indication in any form in the Schedule to these Regulations that the form shall bear the official stamp of a registration authority is a requirement upon the authority to stamp it.

Modification – in relation to solicitors: SI 1991/2684.

3   Land becoming common land or a town or village green

(1)   Where, after 2nd January 1970, any land becomes common land or a town or village green, application may be made subject to and in accordance with the provisions of these Regulations for the inclusion of that land in the appropriate register and for the registration of rights of common thereover and of persons claiming to be owners thereof.

(2)   Where any land is for the time being registered under the Act, no application shall be entertained for its registration under these Regulations, and, where any land is for the time being registered under section 4 of the Act (whether or not the registration has become final) no application shall be entertained for the registration of rights of common over it.

(3)   No person shall be registered under these Regulations as the owner of any land which is registered under the Land Registration Acts 1925 to 1966 and no person shall be registered under these Regulations as the owner of any other land unless the land itself is registered under these Regulations.

(4)   An application for the registration of any land as common land or as a town or village green may be made by any person, and a registration authority shall so register any land in any case where it registers rights over it under these Regulations.

(5)   An application for the registration of a right of common over land which is registered, or which is capable of being registered, under these Regulations, may be made by the owner of the right, or by any person entitled by law to act, in relation to the right, on the owner's behalf or in his stead, or, where the right

belongs to an ecclesiastical benefice of the Church of England which is vacant, by the Church Commissioners.

(6) An application for the registration of a claim to the ownership of any land registered under these Regulations may be made by the owner of the land, or by any person entitled by law to act, in relation to the land, on the owner's behalf or in his stead, or, where the land belongs to an ecclesiastical benefice of the Church of England which is vacant, by the Church Commissioners.

(7) An application must be –

    (a)   in Form 29, 30, 31 or 32 as appropriate;

    (b)   signed by or on behalf of every applicant who is an individual, and by the secretary or some other duly authorised officer of every applicant which is a body corporate or unincorporate;

    (c)   accompanied by such documents (if any) as may be requisite under regulation 4 below;

    (d)   supported –

        (i)   by a statutory declaration as set out in the appropriate form of application, with such adaptations as the case may require, to be made by the applicant, or by one of the applicants if there is more than one, or by his or their solicitor, or, if the applicant is a body corporate or unincorporate, or charity trustees, by its or their solicitor or by the person who signed the application; and

        (ii)   by such further evidence, if any, as, at any time before finally disposing of the application, the registration authority may reasonably require.

Modification – in relation to solicitors: SI 1991/2684.

4   Documents to accompany applications

(1) Subject to paragraph (2) below, every application must be accompanied by, or by a copy or sufficient abstract of, every document relating to the matter which the applicant has in his possession or under his control, or of which he has a right to the production.

(2) In the case of an application for the registration of any rights of common, or of a claim to the ownership of any land, the applicant shall not be obliged to furnish to the registration authority, or to disclose the existence of, any document which he would not be obliged to abstract or produce to a purchaser under a contract for the sale by the applicant of the rights or the land made otherwise than by correspondence and containing no stipulations as to title.

Modification – in relation to solicitors: SI 1991/2684.

5   Disposal of applications

(1) On receiving an application, the registration authority shall allot a distinguishing number to it, and shall mark the application form with that number.

(2)   Where a registration authority receives an application for the registration of a right of common affecting any coal or anthracite it shall, before entertaining the application, serve notice in writing to that effect upon [the Coal Authority], giving the name and address of the applicant and particulars of the right of common, of the land over which it is exercisable and of the land (if any) to which it is attached.

(3)   the registration authority shall send the applicant a receipt for his application containing a statement of the number allotted thereto; and Form 6, if used for that purpose, shall be sufficient.

(4)   Subject to paragraph (7) below, a registration authority shall, on receipt of an application –

   (a)   send a notice in Form 33, 34 or 35, as appropriate, to every person (other than the applicant) whom the registration authority has reason to believe (whether from information supplied by the applicant or otherwise) to be an owner, lessee, tenant or occupier of any part of the land affected by the application, or to be likely to wish to object to the application;

   (b)   publish in the concerned area, and display, such a notice as aforesaid, and send the notice and a copy of the application to every concerned authority;

   (c)   affix such a notice to some conspicuous object on any part of the land which is open, unenclosed and unoccupied, unless it appears to the registration authority that such a course would not be reasonably practicable.

(5)   The date to be inserted in any notice under paragraph (4) above by which statements in objection to an application must be submitted to the registration authority shall be such as to allow an interval of not less than six weeks from the latest of the following dates, that is to say, the date on which the notice is displayed by the registration authority, or is published, or may reasonably be expected to be delivered in due course of post or to be displayed under paragraph (6) below.

(6)   Every concerned authority receiving, under this regulation, a notice and a copy of an application shall forthwith display copies of the notice, and shall keep the copy of the application available for public inspection at all reasonable times until informed by the registration authority of the disposal of the application.

(7)   Where an application appears to a registration authority after preliminary consideration not to be duly made, the authority may reject it without complying with paragraph (4) above, but where it appears to the authority that any action by the applicant might put the application in order, the authority shall not reject the application under this paragraph without first giving the applicant a reasonable opportunity of taking that action.

(8)   In this regulation 'concerned area' means, in the case of a registration authority which is the council of a county borough, an area including the area of the county borough and the area of every concerned authority, and in any other case, an area including the area of every concerned authority.

Amendment – SI 1994/2567.

6   Consideration of objections

(1)   As soon as possible after the date by which statements in objection to an application have been required to be submitted, the registration authority shall proceed to the further consideration of the application, and the consideration of statements (if any) in objection thereto, in accordance with the following provisions of this regulation.

(2)   The registration authority shall not consider any statement in objection to an application unless it is in writing and signed by or on behalf of the person making it, but, subject as aforesaid, the authority shall consider every statement in objection to an application which it receives before the date on which it proceeds to the further consideration of the application under paragraph (1) above, and may consider any such statement which it receives on or after that date and before the authority finally disposes of the application.

(3)   The registration authority shall send the applicant a copy of every statement which it is required under paragraph (2) above to consider, and of every statement which it is permitted under that paragraph to consider and intends to consider, and shall not reject the application without giving the applicant a reasonable opportunity of dealing with the matters contained in the statement of which copies are sent to him under this paragraph and with any other matter in relation to the application which appears to the authority to afford prima facie grounds for rejecting the application.

Amendment – SI 1994/2567.

7   Method of registration

(1)   Where a registration authority accepts an application, it shall make the necessary registration, following as closely as possible whichever of the Model Entries 4 and 7 to 12 may be applicable, with such variations and adaptations as the circumstances may require, but with the substitution, for the words '(Registration provisional.)', of the words '(Registration under section 13 of the Act.)'.

(2)   The provisions of paragraphs (2) to (7) of General Regulation 10 shall apply to registrations under these Regulations as they apply to provisional registrations.

(3)   The provisions of regulation 9 of the Commons Registration (Objections and Maps) Regulations 1968 (Changes as to provisional maps) shall apply for the purposes of section 13 of the Act as they apply for the purposes of section 4 thereof …

(4)   Where a registration authority has made a registration under this regulation, it shall file the application form and any plan thereto which is not required for the purpose of General Regulation 20 (supplemental maps) and shall return all other documents which accompanied the application form to the applicant.

Amendment – Words omitted amend SI 1968/989.

8   Information about disposal of applications, and procedure on rejection

(1)   When a registration authority has disposed of an application and, if it has accepted the application, has made the necessary registration, it shall give written notice of the fact to every concerned authority, to the applicant and to every person whose address is known to the registration authority and who objected to the application, and such notice shall include, where the registration authority has accepted the application, details of the registration, and, where it has rejected the application, the reasons for the rejection.

(2)   A person shall be taken to have objected to an application for the purposes of paragraph (1) above if he submitted a statement in objection to the application which the registration authority was required to consider under paragraph (2) of regulation 6 above or which it did consider under that paragraph.

(3)   Where a registration authority has rejected an application, it shall return the application form and all accompanying documents to the applicant.

9   Substituted land

(1)   Where under these Regulations a registration authority registers any substituted land in a register, and the taken land is registered in that register, then –

(a)   if no application has been duly made under General Regulation 27 for the removal of the taken land from the register, the authority shall nevertheless amend the register in relation to the taken land as shown in Standard Entry 6;

(b)   if such an application has been duly made, the registration authority shall not be required to comply with paragraphs (5) to (8) of General Regulation 27 (except so much of paragraph (7) thereof as requires the register to be amended in accordance with Standard Entry 6).

(2)   In General Regulation 28(1) (which prohibits the removal of any taken land from a register until the substituted land has been registered under the Act, unless the substituted land is exempt from registration under section 11 of the Act) the words 'unless it is exempt from registration under section 11 thereof' are hereby revoked, but without prejudice to their effect in relation to applications and registrations under section 4 of the Act.

10   Land descriptions

(1)   Land must be described for the purposes of any application –

(a)   by a plan accompanying the application and referred to therein; or
(b)   in the case of land already registered under the Act, by a reference to the register sufficient to enable the land to be identified; or
(c)   in the case of land to which rights of common are attached, by reference to the numbered parcels on the most recent edition of the ordnance map (quoting the edition).

(2)   Any plan accompanying an application must –

(a)   be drawn to scale;

(b) be in ink or other permanent medium;

(c) be on a scale of not less, or not substantially less, than six inches to one mile;

(d) show the land to be described by means of distinctive colouring; and

(e) be marked as an exhibit to the statutory declaration in support of the application.

SCHEDULE

FORMS

Form 29

This section for official use only
Official stamp of registration authority indicating date of receipt

Application No

Register unit No(s):

CL

CL

COMMONS REGISTRATION ACT 1965, SECTION 13

APPLICATION FOR THE REGISTRATION OF LAND WHICH BECAME COMMON LAND AFTER 2nd JANUARY 1970 IMPORTANT NOTE:– Before filling in this form, read carefully the notes at the end. An incorrectly completed application form may have to be rejected.

To the (1)

(1) Insert name of registration authority

Application is hereby made for the registration as common land of the land described below, which became so registrable after 2nd January 1970.

Part 1.

Name and address of the applicant or (if more than one) of every applicant.

(Give Christian names or forenames and surnames or, in the case of a body corporate or unincorporate, the full title of the body. If part 2 is not completed all correspondence and notices will be sent to the first-named applicant.)

Part 2.

Name and address of solicitor, if any.

(This part should be completed only if a solicitor has been instructed for the purposes of the application. If it is completed, all correspondence and notices will be sent to the solicitor.)

Part 3.

Particulars of the land to be registered, i.e. the land claimed to have become common land.

Name by which usually known

Locality

Colour on plan herewith

Part 4.

On what date did the land become common land?

Part 5.

How did the land become common land?

Part 6.

Name and address of every person whom the applicant believes to be an owner, lessee, tenant or occupier of any part of the land claimed to have become common land. (If none are known, write 'none'.)

Part 7.

Applications to register substituted land (see Note 5); to be disregarded in other cases.

Particulars of the 'taken land', ie the land which ceased to be common land when the land described in part 3 became common land.

Name by which usually known

Locality

Colour on plan herewith (if any)

If registered under the 1965 Act, register unit No(s).

Part 8.

List of supporting documents sent herewith, if any. (If none are sent, write 'none'.)

Part 9.

If there are any other facts relating to the application which ought to be brought to the attention of the registration authority (in particular if any person interested in the land is believed to dispute the claim that it has become common land) full particulars should be given here.

Date ....19 .....

Signatures (2) ....

> (2) The application must be signed by or on behalf of each individual applicant, and by the secretary of some other duly authorised officer of any applicant which is a body corporate or unincorporate.

STATUTORY DECLARATION IN SUPPORT

(See Note 10) To be made by the applicant, or by one of the applicants, or by his or their solicitor, or, if the applicant is a body corporate or unincorporate, by its solicitor or by the person who signed the application.

I   .... solemnly and sincerely declare as follows:–

1.   I am ((the person) (one of the persons) who (has) (have) signed the foregoing application)) ((the solicitor to (the applicant) ((3) .... one of the applicants)).

2.   I have read the Notes to the application form.

3.   The facts set out in the application form are to be the best of my knowledge and belief fully and truly stated and I am not aware of any other fact which should be brought to the attention of the registration authority as likely to affect its decision on this application, nor of any document relating to the matter other than those (if any) mentioned in parts 8 and 9 of the application.

4.   The plan now produced and shown to me marked(4) ' ' is the plan referred to in part 3 of the application.

5.   The plan now produced and shown to me marked (4) ' ' is the plan referred to in part 7 of the application.

And I make this solemn declaration, conscientiously believing the same to be true, and by virtue of the Statutory Declarations Act 1835.

(1)   Insert full name (and address if not given in application form).

(2)   Delete and adapt as necessary.

(3)   Insert name if applicable.

(4)   Insert 'marking' as on plan.

(5)   Delete this paragraph if there is no plan referred to in part 7.

Declared by the said .... at .... in the .... of .... this .... day of .... 19 .....

Signature of Declarant

Before me,

Signature ....

Address ....

Qualification ....

REMINDER TO OFFICER TAKING DECLARATION: Please initial all alterations and mark any plan as an exhibit.

NOTES

1   Registration authorities

The applicant should take care to submit his application to the correct registration authority. This depends on the situation of the land which is claimed to have become common land. The registration authority for land in an administrative county is the county council; for land in a county borough, it is the county borough council, and for land in Greater London, it is the Greater London Council. However, if the land in question is partly in the area of one registration authority and partly in that of another, the authorities may by agreement have provided for one of them to be the registration authority for the whole of the land. An applicant concerned with the land lying close to the boundary of an administrative area, or partly in one area and partly in another, should therefore enquire whether such an agreement has been made and, if so, which authority is responsible for the land.

2   Who may apply for registration

An application for the registration of any land which has become common land after 2nd January 1970 may be made by any person, but a person who wishes to apply for the registration of rights of common over land which became common land after 2nd January 1970 should use C.R. Form 31 and not this form, whether or not the land itself has been registered under the Act.

3   No double registration

If the land is already registered under the Act, whether in the Register of Common Land or in the separate Register of Town or Village Greens, and whether the registration is provisional, final, or under section 13 of the Act (which relates to land becoming common land or a town or village green after 2nd January 1970), an application for registration cannot be entertained, but this does not prevent the submission of an application later on, should the existing registration cease for any reason to be effective (as, for example, by the land being removed from the register under section 13 or by a provisional registration being cancelled or failing to achieve finality). If an earlier registration is believed to exist a search of the register may be obtained by means of C.R. Form 21 (a separate form must be used for each register).

4   Meaning of 'common land'

For the purpose of an application after 2nd January 1970, common land may be taken to mean either –

(a)   land which, after 2nd January 1970, became subject to rights of common (see Note 6 below) whether those rights are exercisable at all times or only during limited periods; or

(b)   land which, after 2nd January 1970, became 'substituted land', whether or not subject to rights of common (this category is explained in Note 5 below).

It does not include a town or village green or any land forming part of a highway. (There is a separate form available for applying for the registration under the Act of land which became a town or village green after 2nd January 1970). 'Land' includes land covered with water, so that common land can, for instance, include ponds and lakes.

5 How land can become common land

Land can become common land after 2nd January 1970 in any of the following ways:–

(1) By or under an Act of Parliament otherwise than as substituted land (as to substituted land, see category (4) below).

(2) By a grant by the owner of the land of rights of common over it.

(3) By rights of common being acquired over it by prescription.

(4) By substitution or exchange for other land which has ceased to be common land under –

    (a) sections 147 and 148 of the Inclosure Act 1845; or

    (b) paragraph 11 of Schedule 1 to the Acquisition of Land (Authorisation Procedure) Act 1946; or

    (c) any other enactment providing, on the exchange of land, for the transfer of rights, trusts or incidents attaching to the land given in exchange from that land to the land taken in exchange and vice versa.

Land in category (4) is referred to in this form as 'substituted land', and the land for which it is substituted, and which has ceased to be common land, is referred to as 'the taken land'. If this application is accepted for registration, and the taken land is registered in the Register of Common Land maintained by the same registration authority, the taken land will be removed from the register automatically provided the registration authority is satisfied as to the exact areas of both the substituted and the taken land. No separate application in regard to the latter is necessary in such a case.

6 Meaning of 'rights of common'

There are many different kinds of rights of common, some existing only in particular areas. This is why there is no exhaustive list or definition of rights of common in the Act. However, it may be said that a right of common is a right which a person has (generally in common with others including the owner of the soil) to take part of the natural produce of another man's land. Examples are: a right to turn out sheep or other animals to graze (common of pasture, called in the Act a right to graze animals); a right to turn out pigs to eat acorns and beechmast (pannage); a right to take tree loppings, gorse, furze, bushes or underwood (estovers); a right to take turf or peat (turbary); a right to take fish (piscary). There is also a right of common in the soil, as it is called, which consists of the right of taking sand, gravel, etc. from another man's land. These are only a few of the most frequently encountered rights of common; there are many others, and any person in doubt should seek legal advice. On the other hand, many rights connected with land are not rights of common and are not subject to the Act; for example, rights of way (public or private), and rights to water cattle, horses or other animals on the land of another.

The Act provides that cattlegates or beastgates (by whatever name known) and rights of sole or several vesture or herbage or of sole or several pasture are to be considered as rights of common. These are in essence various kinds of rights of pasture normally enjoyed to the exclusion of the owner of the land.

Rights held for a term of years or from year to year are not registrable under the Act, and, accordingly, land subject to such rights does not qualify for registration on that account, although it may do so in some other way, e.g. as substituted land.

7   Land descriptions

In addition to the particulars asked for at part 3 of the form, a plan of the land claimed to have become common land must accompany the application. The particulars in part 3 are necessary to enable the registration authority to identify the land concerned, but the main description of the land will be by means of the plan. This must be drawn to scale, in ink or other permanent medium, and be on a scale of not less, or not substantially less, than six inches to one mile. It must show the land by means of distinctive colouring (a coloured edging inside the boundary will usually suffice) and it must be marked as an exhibit to the statutory declaration (see Note 10 below). If the land to be registered is substituted land (see Note 5 above), then a description of the taken land must be given in part 7, and a plan of this area, too, may have to be provided. If the taken land has already been registered under the Act (as it will have been in most cases) and comprises the whole of the land in one or more register units, a plan is unnecessary provided the register unit number(s) are quoted. If the taken land comprises only part of the land in a register unit a plan may be dispensed with if the land can be described by reference to some physical feature such as a road, river or railway; the description might, for example, read: 'The land in register unit No ..... lying to the south of the road from A to B'. Where this method is not practicable, or the taken land is not registered under the Act, it must be described by a plan which must conform to the requirements mentioned above. Where two plans accompany the application, a different colour should be used in each.

8   Grounds of application: evidence

In part 5 should be set out, as concisely as possible, a statement of the facts relied on to show that the land became common land on the date stated in part 4; this date must be after 2nd January 1970, otherwise the application cannot be entertained. The statement should include particulars of every Act of Parliament, statutory order, order of court, deed or other instrument, and of every act or event, which is material for the purpose. The registration authority has power to call for such further evidence in support of the application as it may reasonably require. If the land is substituted land (see Note 5 above) there should be included in part 5 particulars of the enactment and of the compulsory purchase order, order of exchange or other instrument authorising the exchange or substitution, and of the instrument (if any) under which the exchange or substitution actually took place.

9   Supporting documents

The application must be accompanied by the original or (preferably) by a copy or sufficient abstract of every document relating to the matter which the applicant has in his possession or under his control, or of which he has a right to the production.

The following are examples of documents which, under this rule, may normally be expected to be among the documents accompanying applications in the particular cases mentioned:–

(1) Where the land is stated to have become common land by virtue of a private or local Act or of a statutory instrument, the award or other instrument of allotment (if any) made thereunder.

(2) Where the land is stated to have become common land by a grant of rights of common, a copy of the deed of grant.

(3) Where the land is stated to have become common land by the acquisition of rights of common over it by prescription, and there is a declaration by a court of competent jurisdiction to that effect, an office copy of the order embodying that declaration. (In the absence of such a declaration, a claim based solely on the Prescription Act 1832 cannot be admitted, and the claim based on prescription otherwise than under that Act is unlikely to be admitted if any objection is received by the registration authority.)

(4) Where the land is stated to be substituted land (see Note 5 above), the original or a duly authenticated copy (a) of the compulsory purchase order, order of exchange or other instrument authorising the exchange or substitution, and (b) of the instrument (if any) under which the exchange or substitution actually took place.

The foregoing list is not exhaustive and in special cases the applicant may need to consult the registration authority. Applicants are strongly recommended NOT to forward the original of any deed or other private document. Instead, a copy should be supplied, preferably indorsed with a certificate signed by a solicitor that it has been examined against the original. The applicant should indicate, either on the copy itself or in part 8 of the application, as convenient, who has the original and where it maybe inspected. If any document relating to the matter is believed to exist, but neither the original nor a copy can be produced, the fact should be mentioned in part 9 of the application, where particulars of the missing document should be given and its non-production accounted for.

The registration authority has power to call for such further evidence as it may reasonably require.

10 Statutory Declaration

The statutory declaration must be made before a justice of the peace, commissioner for oaths or notary public. The plan (or each plan) accompanying the application and referred to in the statutory declaration must be marked as an exhibit and signed by the officer taking the declaration (initialling is insufficient). A plan is marked by writing on the face in ink an identifying symbol such as the letter 'A'. If there is more than one plan a different identifying letter must be used for each. On the back of the plan should appear these words:

This is the exhibit marked 'A' referred to in the statutory declaration of (name of declarant) made this (date) .... 19 ..... before me,

(Signature and qualification)

11   Action by registration authority

The registration authority will on receipt of the application send an acknowledgement. If this is not received within 10 days the applicant should communicate with the authority. Unless the application has to be rejected after preliminary consideration, the registration authority will give publicity to it and will consider it further in the light of any objections which may be received. The applicant will be supplied with copies of all objections which fall to be considered and will have an opportunity of answering them. Later, the applicant will be informed whether the application has been accepted or rejected. If it is accepted, the land will be registered as common land, and the applicant will be supplied with particulars of the registration. If it is rejected, the applicant will be notified of the reasons for the rejection.

12   False statements

The making of a false statement for the purposes of this application may render the maker liable to prosecution.

Form 30

This section for official use only

Official stamp of registration authority indicating date of receipt

Application No

Register unit No(s):

VG

VG

COMMONS REGISTRATION ACT 1965, SECTION 13

APPLICATION FOR THE REGISTRATION OF LAND WHICH BECAME A TOWN OR VILLAGE GREEN AFTER 2nd JANUARY 1970I

IMPORTANT NOTE:– Before filling in this form, read carefully the notes at the end. An incorrectly completed application form may have to be rejected.

To the(1)

    (1) Insert name of registration authority

Application is hereby made for the registration as a town or village green of the land described below, which became so registrable after 2nd January 1970.

Part 1

Name and address of the applicant or (if more than one) of every applicant.

(Give Christian names or forenames and surname or, in the case of a body corporate or unincorporate, the full title of the body. If part 2 is not completed all correspondence and notices will be sent to the first named applicant.)

Part 2

Name and address of solicitor, if any.

(This part should be completed only if a solicitor has been instructed for the purposes of the application. If it is completed, all correspondence and notices will be sent to the solicitor.)

Part 3

Particulars of the land to be registered, ie the land claimed to have become a town or village green.

Name by which usually known

Locality

Colour on plan herewith

Part 4

On what date did the land become a town or village green?

Part 5

How did the land become a town or village green?

Part 6

Name and address of every person whom the applicant believes to bean owner, lessee, tenant or occupier of any part of the land claimed to have become a town or village green. (If none are known, write 'none'.)

Part 7

For applications to register substituted land (see Note 5); to be disregarded in other cases.

Particulars of the 'taken land', ie the land which ceased to be a town or village green (or part thereof) when the land described in part 3 became a town or village green (or part).

Name by which usually known

Locality

Colour on plan herewith (if any)

If registered under the 1965 Act, register unit No(s).

Part 8

List of supporting documents sent herewith, if any. (If none are sent, write 'none'.)

Part 9

If there are any other facts relating to the application which ought to be brought to the attention of the registration authority (in particular if any person interested in the land is believed to dispute the claim that it has become a town or village green) full particulars should be given here.

Date .... 19 .....

Signatures(2) ....

> (2) The application must be signed by or on behalf of each individual applicant, and by the secretary or some other duly authorised officer of any applicant which is a body corporate or unincorporate.

STATUTORY DECLARATION IN SUPPORT

(See Note 9) To be made by the applicant, or by one of the applicants, or by his or their solicitor, or, if the applicant is a body corporate or unincorporate, by its solicitor or by the person who signed the application.

I solemnly and sincerely declare as follows:–

1.   I am ((the person) (one of the persons) who (has) (have) signed the foregoing application)) ((the solicitor to (the applicant) ((3) .... one of the applicants)).

2.   I have read the Notes to the application form.

3.   The facts set out in the application form are to the best of my knowledge and belief fully and truly stated and I am not aware of any other fact which should be brought to the attention of the registration authority as likely to affect its decision on this application, nor of any document relating to the matter other than those (if any) mentioned in parts 8 and 9 of the application.

4.   The plan now produced and shown to me marked (4) ' ' is the plan referred to in part 3 of the application.

5.   The plan now produced and shown to me marked(4) ' ' is the plan referred to in part 7 of the application.

And I make this solemn declaration, conscientiously believing the same to be true, and by virtue of the Statutory Declarations Act 1835.

> (1)   Insert full name (and address if not given in the application form).
> (2)   Delete and adapt as necessary.
> (3)   Insert name if applicable.
> (4)   Insert 'marking' as on plan
> (5)   Delete this paragraph if there is no plan referred to in part 7

Declared by the said .... at .... in the .... of .... this .... day of .... 19 .....

Signature of Declarant

Before me,

Signature ....

Address ....

Qualification ....…...

REMINDER TO OFFICER TAKING DECLARATION: Please initial all alterations and mark any plan as an exhibit.

NOTES

1 Registration authorities

The applicant should take care to submit his application to the correct registration authority. This depends on the situation of the land which is claimed to have become a town or village green. The registration authority for land in an administrative county is the county council; for land in a county borough, it is the county borough council, and for land in Greater London, it is the Greater London Council. However if the land in question is partly in the area of one registration authority and partly in that of another, the authorities may by agreement have provided for one of them to be the registration authority for the whole of the land. An applicant concerned with land lying close to the boundary of an administrative area, or partly in one area and partly in another, should therefore enquire whether such an agreement has been made and, if so, which authority is responsible for the land.

2 Who may apply for registration

An application for the registration of any land which has become a town or village green after 2nd January 1970 may be made by any person.

3 No double registration

If the land is already registered under the Act, whether in the Register of Town or Village Greens or in the separate Register of Common Land, and whether the registration is provisional, final, or under section 13 of the Act (which relates to land becoming common land or a town or village green after 2nd January 1970), an application for registration cannot be entertained, but this does not prevent the submission of an application later on, should the existing registration cease for any reason to be effective (as, for example, by the land being removed from the register under section 13 or by a provisional registration being cancelled or failing to achieve finality). If an earlier registration is believed to exist a search of the register may be obtained by means of C.R. Form 21 (a separate form must be used for each register).

4 Meaning of 'town or village green'

'Town or village green' is defined in the Commons Registration Act 1965 as land –

(a) which has been allotted by or under any Act for the exercise or recreation of the inhabitants of any locality, or

(b) on which the inhabitants of any locality have a customary right to indulge in lawful sports and pastimes, or

(c)   on which the inhabitants of any locality have indulged in such sports and pastimes as of right for not less than twenty years.

While a town or village green can be subject to rights of common, it does not include land which is registered as common land in the separate Register of Common Land maintained under the Act. (There is a separate form available for applying for the registration under the Act of land which became common land after 2nd January 1970.) 'Land' includes land covered with water so that a town or village green can, for instance, include a pond.

5   How land can become a town or village green

Land can become a town or village green after 2nd January 1970 in one of the following ways:–

(1)   By or under an Act of Parliament otherwise than as substituted land (as to substituted land, see category (4) below).

(2)   By customary right established by judicial decision.

(3)   By the actual use of the land by the local inhabitants for lawful sports and pastimes as of right for not less than 20 years.

(4)   By substitution or exchange for other land which has ceased to be a town or village green under –

    (a)   sections 147 and 148 of the Inclosure Act 1845; or

    (b)   paragraph 11 or Schedule 1 to the Acquisition of Land (Authorisation Procedure) Act 1946; or

    (c)   any other enactment providing, on the exchange of land, for the transfer of rights, trusts or incidents attaching to the land given in exchange from that land to the land taken in exchange and vice versa.

Land in category (4) is referred to in this form as 'substituted land', and the land for which it is substituted, and which has ceased to be a town or village green, is referred to as 'the taken land'. If this application is accepted for registration, and the taken land is registered in the Register of Town or Village Greens maintained by the same registration authority, the taken land will be removed from the register automatically provided the registration authority is satisfied as to the exact areas of both the substituted and the taken land. No separate application in regard to the latter is necessary in such a case.

6   Land descriptions

In addition to the particulars asked for at part 3 of the form, a plan of the land claimed to have become a town or village green must accompany the application. The particulars in part 3 are necessary to enable the registration authority to identify the land concerned, but the main description of the land will be by means of the plan. This must be drawn to scale, in ink or other permanent medium, and be on a scale of not less, or not substantially less, than six inches to one mile. It must show the land by means of distinctive colouring (a coloured edging inside the boundary will usually suffice) and it must be marked as an exhibit to the statutory declaration (see Note 9 below). If the land to be registered is substituted land (see Note 5 above), then a description of the taken land must be given in part 7, and a plan of this area, too, may have to be provided. If the taken land has already been registered under the Act (as it will have been in most cases) and comprises the whole of the land in one or more register units, a plan is unnecessary provided the register unit number(s) are quoted. If the taken land comprises only part of the land in a register unit a plan may be dispensed with if the land can be described by reference to some physical feature such as a road, river or railway; the description might, for example, read 'The land in register unit No ..... lying to the south of the road from A to B'. Where this method is not practicable, or the taken land is not registered under the Act, it must be described by a plan which must conform to the requirements mentioned above. Where two plans accompany the application, a different colour should be used in each.

7   Grounds of application: evidence

In part 5 should be set out, as concisely as possible, a statement of the facts relied on to show that the land became a town or village green on the date stated in part 4; this date must be after 2nd January 1970, otherwise the application cannot be entertained. The statement should include particulars of every Act of Parliament, statutory order, order of court, deed or other instrument, and of every act or event, which is material for the purpose. The registration authority has power to call for such further evidence in support of the application as it may reasonably require. If the land is substituted land (see Note 5 above) there should be included in part 5 particulars of the enactment and of the compulsory purchase order, order of exchange or other instrument authorising the exchange or substitution, and of the instrument (if any) under which the exchange or substitution actually took place.

8   Supporting documents

The application must be accompanied by the original or (preferably) by a copy or sufficient abstract of every document relating to the matter which the applicant has in his possession or under his control, or of which he has a right to the production. The following are examples of documents which, under this rule, may normally be expected to be among the documents accompanying applications in the particular cases mentioned:–

(1)   Where the land is stated to have become a town or village green by virtue of a private or local Act or of a statutory instrument, the award or other instrument of allotment (if any) made thereunder.

(2)   Where the land is stated to have become a town or village green by customary right, an office copy of an order of a court of competent jurisdiction embodying a declaration to that effect.

(3)   Where the land is stated to have become a town or village green by the actual use of the land by the local inhabitants for lawful sports and pastimes as of right for not less than 20 years, and there is a declaration by a court of competent jurisdiction to that effect, an office copy of the order embodying that declaration.

(4)   Where the land is stated to be substituted land (see Note 5 above), the original or a duly authenticated copy (a) of the compulsory purchase order, order of exchange or other instrument authorising the exchange or substitution, and (b)

of the instrument (if any) under which the exchange or substitution actually took place.

The foregoing list is not exhaustive and in special cases the applicant may need to consult the registration authority. Applicants are strongly recommended NOT to forward the original of any deed or other private document. Instead, a copy should be supplied, preferably indorsed with a certificate signed by a solicitor that it has been examined against the original. The applicant should indicate, either on the copy itself or in part 8 of the application, as convenient, who has the original and where it may be inspected. If any document relating to the matter is believed to exist but, neither the original nor a copy can be produced, the fact should be mentioned in part 9 of the application, where particulars of the missing document should be given and its non-production accounted for.

The registration authority has power to call for such further evidence as it may reasonably require.

9   Statutory Declaration

The statutory declaration must be made before a justice of the peace, commissioner for oaths or notary public. The plan (or each plan) accompanying the application and referred to in the statutory declaration must be marked as an exhibit and signed by the officer taking the declaration (initialling is insufficient). A plan is marked by writing on the face in ink an identifying symbol such as the letter 'A'. If there is more than one plan a different identifying letter must be used for each. On the back of the plan should appear these words:

This is the exhibit marked 'A' referred to in the statutory declaration of (name of declarant) made this (date) .... 19..... before me,

....

(Signature and qualification)

10   Action by registration authority

The registration authority will on receipt of the application send an acknowledgement. If this is not received within 10 days the applicant should communicate with the authority. Unless the application has to be rejected after preliminary consideration, the registration authority will give publicity to it and will consider it further in the light of any objections which may be received. The applicant will be supplied with copies of all objections which fall to be considered and will have an opportunity of answering them. Later, the applicant will be informed whether the application has been accepted or rejected. If it is accepted, the land will be registered as a town or village green, and the applicant will be supplied with particulars of the registration. If it is rejected, the applicant will be notified of the reasons for the rejection.

11   False statements

The making of a false statement for the purposes of this application may render the maker liable to prosecution.

Form 31

This section for official use only

Official stamp of registration authority indicating date of receipt

Application No

Register Unit No(s):

COMMONS REGISTRATION ACT 1965, SECTION 13

APPLICATION FOR THE REGISTRATION OF A RIGHT OF COMMON OVER LAND, WHERE BOTH THE RIGHT AND THE LAND BECAME REGISTRABLE AFTER 2nd JANUARY 1970. IMPORTANT NOTE:– Before filling in this form, read carefully the notes at the end. An incorrectly completed application may have to be rejected.

To the(1)

 (1) Insert name of registration authority.

Application is hereby made for the registration of the right of common of which particulars are set out below.

Part 1.

Name and address of the applicant or (if more than one) of every applicant, and the capacity in which he applies.

(Give Christian names or forenames and surname or, in the case of a body corporate, the full title of the body. If part 2 is not completed all correspondence and notices will be sent to the first-named applicant.)

Part 2.

Name and address of solicitor, if any.

(This part should be completed only if a solicitor has been instructed for the purposes of the application. If it is completed, all correspondence and notices will be sent to the solicitor.)

Part 3.

Particulars of the land over which the right of common is exercisable.

(a) Name by which usually known

(b) Locality

(c) Colour on plan herewith (if any)

If the land is registered under the 1965 Act, registration particulars –

(d) Register(2)

 (2) Insert 'Common Land' or 'Town or Village Greens'.

(e)   Register unit No(s).

Part 4.

Description of the right of common, including, if it is exercisable only during limited periods, full particulars of the periods, and, if it is a right to graze animals, details of the number(s) and kind(s) of animals.

Part 5.

Description of the farm, holding or other land to which the right is attached, if any. (If the right is not attached to any land, the fact should be stated here.)

Name by which usually known

Locality, OS Nos and reference to ordnance map (if given), and any further description

Colour on plan herewith (if any)

Part 6.

On what date did the right first become exercisable over the land described in part 3 above?

Part 7.

How did the right first become exercisable over the land described in part 3 above?

Part 8.

Name and address of every person whom the applicant believes to be an owner, lessee, tenant or occupier of any part of the land described in part 3 above. (If none are known, write 'none'.)

Part 9.

List of supporting documents sent herewith, if any. (If none are sent, write 'none'.)

Part 10.

If there are any other facts relating to the application which ought to be brought to the attention of the registration authority (in particular if any person interested in the land described in part 3 above is believed to dispute the claim that it is subject to rights of common) full particulars should be given here.

Date .... 19 .....

Signatures (3) ....

> (3) The application must be signed by or on behalf of each individual applicant, and by the secretary or some other duly authorised officer of any applicant

which is a body corporate or charity trustees. STATUTORY DECLARATION IN SUPPORT

(See Note 12) To be made by the applicant, or by one of the applicants, or by his or their solicitor, or, if the applicant is a body corporate or charity trustees, by its or their solicitor or by the person who signed the application.

I solemnly and sincerely declare as follows:–

1.   I am ((the person) (one of the persons) who (has) (have) signed the foregoing application)) ((the solicitor to (the applicant) ((3) .... one of the applicants)).

2.   I have read the Notes to the application form.

3.   The facts set out in the application form are to the best of my knowledge and belief fully and truly stated and I am not aware of any other fact which should be brought to the attention of the registration authority as likely to affect its decision on this application, nor of any document which ought to be submitted or disclosed to the authority other than those (if any) mentioned in parts 9 and 10 of the application.

4.   The plan now produced and shown to me marked(4) ' ' is the plan referred to in part 3 of the application.

5.   The plan now produced and shown to me marked (4) ' ' is the plan referred to in part 5 of the application.

And I make this solemn declaration, conscientiously believing the same to be true, and by virtue of the Statutory Declarations Act 1835.

(1)   Insert full name (and address if not given in the application form).

(2)   Delete and adapt as necessary.

(3)   Insert name if applicable.

(4)   Insert 'marking' as on plan.

(5)   Delete this paragraph if there is no plan referred to in part 5.

Declared by the said .... at .... in the .... of............ this .... day of .... 19 ..... Signature of Declarant

Before me,

Signature ....…....

Address ....

Qualification ....

REMINDER TO OFFICER TAKING DECLARATION: Please initial all alterations and mark any plan as an exhibit.

NOTES

1　Registration authorities

The applicant should take care to submit his application to the correct registration authority. This depends on the situation of the land over which the right of common is claimed. The registration authority for land in an administrative county is the county council; for land in a county borough, it is the county borough council, and for land in Greater London, it is the Greater London Council. However, if the land over which the right is claimed is partly in the area of one registration authority and partly in that of another, the authorities may by agreement have provided for one of them to be the registration authority for the whole of the land. An applicant concerned with land lying close to the boundary of an administrative area, or partly in one area and partly in another, should therefore enquire whether an agreement has been made and, if so, which authority is responsible for the land.

2　When to use this form

This form should not be used in cases where a right of common has been shifted from one piece of land to another in the circumstances mentioned in category (4) of Note 5 below, and both pieces of land are in the area of one registration authority. In such cases, re-registration of the right of common is automatic on registration of the substituted land. The matter is fully explained in Note 5. Nor should it be used where a right of common which has already been registered has been apportioned or varied, or, in the case of a registered right in gross (that is, not attached to any land), has been transferred. In such cases amendment of the register should be applied for on CR Form 19. In all other cases within Note 9 below this form should be used to apply to register a right of common whether or not the land over which the right is claimed to be exercisable has itself been registered, since it is not necessary for the land over which a right of common is exercisable to be registered before an application for the registration of the right itself is made: see Note 13 below.

3　Who may apply for registration

An application for the registration of a right of common may be made by the owner of the right or, where the right belongs to an ecclesiastical benefice of the Church of England which is vacant, by the Church Commissioners.

In certain cases a person may be entitled by law to apply on behalf of the owner of the right or in his stead. Examples are:

(a)　a receiver appointed under section 105 of the Mental Health Act 1959;

(b)　charity trustees where the right of common is vested in the Official Custodian for Charities;

(c)　trustees for the purposes of the Settled Land Act 1925 authorised by order under section 24 of that Act.

In all cases the applicant should state in part 1 the capacity in which he applies (e.g. as owner of the right). If he applies on behalf of, or instead of, another person he should also state in part I:–

(a)   the Act of Parliament, statutory instrument, order of court or other authority under which he claims to be entitled to apply;

(b)   the name and address of the person on whose behalf or in whose stead the application is made; and

(c)   the capacity of that person (who will normally be the owner of the right).

Where the Church Commissioners apply with respect to a right of common belonging to a vacant benefice, the fact should be stated, and the name of the benefice given, in part 1. Where charity trustees apply the fact should be stated, and the name of the charity given, in part 1.

4   Meaning of 'rights of common'

There are many different kinds of rights of common, some existing only in particular areas. This is why there is no exhaustive list or definition of rights of common in the Act. However, it may be said that a right of common is a right which a person has (generally in common with others including the owner of the soil) to take part of the natural produce of another man's land. Examples are: a right to turn out sheep or other animals to graze (common of pasture, called in the Act a right to graze animals); a right to turn out pigs to eat acorns and beechmast (pannage); a right to take tree loppings, gorse, furze, bushes or underwood (estovers); a right to take turf or peat (turbary); a right to take fish (piscary). There is also a right of common in the soil, as it is called, which consists of the right of taking sand, gravel, stone, etc from another man's land. These are only a few of the most frequently encountered rights of common; there are many others, and any person in doubt should seek legal advice. On the other hand, many rights connected with land are not rights of common and are not subject to the Act; for example, rights of way (public or private), and rights to water cattle, horses or other animals on the land of another.

The Act provides that cattlegates or beastgates (by whatever name known) and rights of sole or several vesture or herbage or of sole or several pasture are to be considered as rights of common. These are in essence various kinds of rights of pasture normally enjoyed to the exclusion of the owner of the land.

Rights held for a term of years or from year to year are not registrable under the Act.

5   How land can become subject to rights of common

Land can become subject to rights of common after 2nd January 1970 in one of the following ways:–

(1)   By or under an Act of Parliament, otherwise than as substituted land (as to substituted land, see category (4) below).

(2)   By a grant by the owner of the land of rights of common over it.

(3)   By rights of common being acquired over it by prescription.

(4)   By substitution or exchange for other land which has ceased to be common land under –

       (a)   sections 147 and 148 of the Inclosure Act 1845; or
       (b)   paragraph 11 of Schedule 1 to the Acquisition of Land (Authorisation

Procedure) Act 1946; or

(c)   any other enactment providing, on the exchange of land, for the transfer of rights trusts or incidents attaching to the land given in exchange from that land to the land taken in exchange and vice versa.

Land in category (4) is referred to in this form as 'substituted land', and the land for which it is substituted, and which has ceased to be subject to rights of common, is referred to as 'the taken land'. If both the taken and the substituted land are in the area of one registration authority, then when the substituted land is registered under the Act, a note will appear in the register to the effect that rights of common (if any) which subsisted over the taken land at the date of the substitution or exchange have shifted over to the substituted land, and no application for the re-registration of these rights will be necessary. Inquiry should be made of the registration authority whether the substituted land has been registered, and whether a note about the shifting of the rights appears in the register.

6   Land descriptions

(a)   For purposes of part 3. Except where the land has already been registered under the Act (see Note 7 below), the particulars asked for at (a), (b) and (c) of part 3 of the form must be given, and a plan must accompany the application. The particulars at (a) and (b) of part 3 are necessary to enable the registration authority to identify the land concerned, but the main description of the land will be by means of the plan. This must be drawn to scale, in ink or other permanent medium, and be on a scale of not less, or not substantially less, than six inches to one mile. It must show the land to be described by means of distinctive colouring (a coloured edging inside the boundary will usually suffice), and it must be marked as an exhibit to the statutory declaration (see Note 12 below).

Where the land has already been registered (see Note 7 below) and comprises the whole of the land in one or more register units, a plan is unnecessary provided the register and register unit number(s) are quoted at (d) and (e) of part 3 of the form. If the application concerns only part of the land in a register unit a plan may be dispensed with if the land can be described by reference to some physical feature such as a road, river or railway; the description might, for example, read 'The land in register unit No ..... lying to the south of the road from A to B'. Where this method is not practicable the land must be described by a plan prepared as mentioned above. Where the procedure of reference to an existing register unit is adopted, part 3 of the form should be adapted accordingly.

(b)   For purposes of part 5. If the right is attached to any farm, holding or other land, that land must be described in part 5. This may be done either by a plan prepared as explained in (a) above, or, alternatively, by reference to the numbered parcels on the most recent edition of the ordnance map (quoting the edition), supplemented, where necessary to describe part of a parcel, or any land not numbered on the ordnance map, by a plan prepared in accordance with (a) above. Sufficient particulars of the locality must in any case be given to enable the land to be identified on the ordnance map. Where two plans accompany the application, a different colour should be used in each.

If the right is held in gross, that is, not attached to any land, that fact should be stated in part 5.

7 Inspection and search of registers

To ascertain whether land has been registered under the Act, anyone may inspect the registers free of charge at the office of the registration authority. Alternatively, an official certificate of search may be obtained from the registration authority. A requisition for such search must be made in writing on CR Form No 21, a separate requisition being required for each register. If the land is registered, the certificate will reveal the register unit number(s) and whether any rights of common and claims to ownership are registered.

8 Rights for limited periods: grazing rights

Certain rights of common (usually grazing rights) are not exercisable at all times but only during limited periods. In the case of a right of common to which this applies, full particulars must be given in part 4 of the period or periods during which the right is exercisable. Further, if the right (by whatever name it may be known) consists of or includes a right to graze animals, or animals of any class, the applicant must state at part 4 the number of animals, or the numbers of animals of different classes, to be entered in the register.

9 Date for part 6

The date to be entered in part 6 is the date on which the right of common first came into existence and became registrable as exercisable over the land described in part 3. If this date is before 3rd January 1970 the application cannot be entertained by the registration authority. Moreover, the land over which the right is exercisable must have become registrable under the Act after 2nd January 1970, whether it has in fact been so registered or not. If either the right or the land was registrable under the Act before 3rd January 1970 it is now too late to apply for the registration of either.

10 Grounds of application: evidence

In part 7 should beset out, as concisely as possible, a statement of the facts relied on to show that the right of common came into existence and became registrable on the date stated in part 6 (as to this date, see Note 9 above). The statement should include particulars of every Act of Parliament, statutory order, order of court, deed or other instrument, and of every act or event, which is material for the purpose. The registration authority has power to call for such further evidence in support of the application as it may reasonably require.

11 Supporting documents

The application must be accompanied by the original or (preferably) by a copy or sufficient abstract of every document relating to the matter which the applicant has in his possession or under his control, or of which he has a right to the production, with the exception of documents which he would not be obliged to abstract or produce to a purchaser under a contract for the sale of the right of common made otherwise than by correspondence and containing no stipulations as to title. The following are examples of documents which, under this rule, may normally be expected to be among the documents accompanying applications in the particular cases mentioned:–

(1)   Where the right is stated to have become exercisable by virtue of a private or local Act or of a statutory instrument, the award or other instrument of allotment (if any) made thereunder.

(2)   Where the right is stated to have become exercisable by a grant of rights of common, a copy of the deed of grant.

(3)   Where the right is stated to have become exercisable by prescription, and there is a declaration by a court of competent jurisdiction to that effect, an office copy of the order embodying that declaration. (In the absence of such a declaration, a claim based solely on the Prescription Act 1832 cannot be admitted, and a claim based on prescription otherwise than under that Act is unlikely to be admitted if any objection is received by the registration authority.

The foregoing list is not exhaustive and in special cases the applicant may need to consult the registration authority. Applicants are strongly recommended NOT to forward the original of any deed or other private document. Instead, a copy should be supplied, preferably indorsed with certificate signed by a solicitor that it has been examined against the original. The applicant should indicate, either on the copy itself or in part 9 of the application, as convenient, who has the original and where it may be inspected.

If for any reason a document cannot be produced, the fact should be mentioned in part 10 of the application, where particulars of the missing document should be given and its non-production accounted for.

The registration authority has power to call for such further evidence as it may reasonably require.

12   Statutory declaration

The statutory declaration must be made before a justice of the peace, commissioner for oaths or notary public. Any plan referred to in the statutory declaration must be marked as an exhibit and signed by the officer taking the declaration (initialling is insufficient). A plan is marked by writing on the face in ink an identifying symbol such as the letter 'A'. On the back of the plan should appear these words:–

This is the exhibit marked 'A' referred to in the statutory declaration of (name of declarant) made this (date) ……………….. 19 ….. before me,

(Signature and qualification)

If there is more than one plan care should be taken to choose a different letter for each.

13   Action by registration authority

The registration authority will on receipt of the application send an acknowledgement. If this is not received within 10 days the applicant should communicate with the authority. Unless the application has to be rejected after preliminary consideration, the registration authority will give publicity to it and will consider it further in the right of any objections which may be received. The applicant will be supplied with copies of all objections which fall to be considered and will have an opportunity of answering them. Later, the applicant will be informed whether the application has been accepted or rejected. If the application is accepted, and the land over which the right is exercisable is not already registered under the Act, this will be done, and, whether or not the land is already registered, the right of common will be registered and the applicant will be supplied with particulars of the registration. If the application is rejected, the applicant will be notified of the reasons for the rejection.

14   False statements

The making of a false statement for the purposes of this application may render the maker liable to prosecution.

Form 33

(Name of registration authority)

COMMONS REGISTRATION ACT 1965

Notice of application for registration of land claimed to have become

(common land) (a town or village green)(1) after 2nd January 1970

To every reputed owner, lessee, tenant or occupier of any part of the land described below, and to all others whom it may concern.

Application has been made to the registration authority, the (name and address of registration authority) by (name and address of applicant) under section 13 of the Commons Registration Act 1965 for the inclusion in the Register of (Common Land) (Town or Village Greens)(1) of the land described (at Annex A)(2) below, which it is claimed became (common land) (a town or village green)(1) on (date given in part 4 of Form 29 or 30) (in substitution for the land described at Annex B below, which, it is claimed, ceased to be (common land) (a town or village green)(1) on that date)(2), under and by virtue of (account of circumstances, etc., summarised from part 5 of Form 29 or 30).

The application, which includes a plan of ( ),(3) may be inspected at (address where application available) (and copies of the application and plan(s) may be inspected at the following local authority offices (insert names and addresses of concerned local authorities, if any)).(1)

If the registration authority is satisfied that the land described (at Annex A)(2) below has become (common land) (a town or village green)(1) as claimed, it will so register the land, and such registration will be conclusive evidence of the status of the land as at the date of registration. (The land described at Annex B below will then be removed from the register).(2)

Any person wishing to object to the registration of the land as (common land) (a town or village green)(1) (or to the removal from the register of the land described at Annex B below)(2) should send a written and signed statement of the facts on which he bases his objection to (name and address of registration authority) so as to arrive not later than(4)

Dated .... 19 .....

(Signature on behalf of registration authority) .

(ANNEX A)(2)

Description of the land claimed to have become (common land) (a town or village .... green)(1)

(ANNEX B)(2)

(Description of the land claimed to have ceased to be (common land) (a town or village green) (1) including a reference to the register unit number if the land is registered)(2)

    (1)   Delete as necessary.
    (2)   For substituted land cases only.
    (3)   Insert 'the land proposed for registration' or, in a substituted land case where a plan of the taken land is also provided, 'both areas'.
    (4)   Insert date in accordance with regulation 5(5).

Form 34

(Name of registration authority)

COMMONS REGISTRATION ACT 1965 Notice of application for registration of rights of common over land (registered) (claimed to be registrable) (under section 13 of the Act

To every reputed owner, lessee, tenant or occupier of any part of the land lastly described below, and to all others whom it may concern.

Application has been made to the registration authority, the (name of registration authority) for the registration under section 13 of the Commons Registration Act 1965 of the right(s) of common specified in Annex A below which (is)(are)(1) claimed by the (person) (persons respectively)(1named in the said Annex to be exercisable over the land described in Annex B below. The alleged origin of the right(s) is as stated in Annex A.

The application, (which includes a plan of) (and register unit No ..... in the Register of (Common Land) (Town or Village Greens) (1) which (comprises) (includes)(1)) (1) the land over which the right(s) (is)(are) claimed to be exercisable (and a plan or other description of the land to which they are attached)(1) may be inspected at (insert address where application etc. available) (and copies of the application and plan(s) may be inspected at the following local authority offices (insert names and addresses of concerned local authorities, if any))(1).

If the registration under the Act of (any of)(1) the said right(s) of common is effected, it will be conclusive evidence of the matters registered as at the date of registration.

(If any of the said rights are registered, the land over which the rights are exercisable will be registered also, and such registration will be conclusive evidence of the matters registered as at the date of registration.)(2)

Any person wishing to object to the registration of (any of)(2) the said right(s) of common (or to the registration of the said land)(1) should send a written and signed statement of the facts on which he bases his objection to (name and address of registration authority) so as to arrive not later than(3)

Dated .... 19 .....

(Signature on behalf of registration authority)

ANNEX A

Description of the claimed right(s) of common

Name and address of claimant	Particulars of the claimed right of common	Particulars of the land (if any) to which the right is alleged to be attached	Alleged origin of the right

(1)   Delete or adapt as necessary.
(2)   For use only where the land has not yet been registered under section 13.
(3)   Insert date in accordance with regulation 5(5).

ANNEX B

Description of the land over which the claimed rights are alleged to be exercisable

Form 35

(Name of registration authority)

COMMONS REGISTRATION ACT 1965

Notice of application for registration of a claim to the ownership of land registered under section 13 of the Act

To every reputed owner, lessee, tenant or occupier of any part of the land described below, and to all others whom it may concern.

Application has been made to the registration authority, the (name of registration authority) for the registration in the Register of (Common Land) (Town or Village Greens)(1) of (name and address) as owner of the land described below, which was registered as (common land) (a town or village green)(1) under Register unit No .....
on (date of registration) under section 13 of the Act.

The application, and the register unit affected, may be inspected at (insert address where register maintained) (and copies of the application alone may be inspected at the following local authority offices (insert names and addresses of concerned local authorities, if any))(1).

Any person wishing to object to the application should send a written and signed statement of the facts upon which he bases his objection to (name and address of registration authority) so as to arrive not later than(2)

Dated .... 19 .....

(Signature on behalf of registration authority)

DESCRIPTION OF THE LAND referred to above

    (1)   Delete as necessary.

    (2)   Insert date in accordance with regulation 5(5).

VEHICULAR ACCESS ACROSS COMMON AND OTHER LAND (ENGLAND) REGULATIONS 2002

SI 2002 No 1711

1 Title, commencement and extent

(1) These Regulations may be cited as the Vehicular Access Across Common and Other Land (England) Regulations 2002 and shall come into force on the day after the date on which they are made.

(2) These Regulations shall apply to land in England only.

(3) For the purposes of paragraph (2), 'land' means any land which is crossed by a way used as a means of access for vehicles to premises.

2 Interpretation

(1) In these Regulations –

'the Act' means the Countryside and Rights of Way Act 2000;

'the applicant', 'the land' and 'the land owner' have the meanings given in regulation 3(2);

'compensation sum' means the amount of compensation payable by the applicant;

'easement' means an easement subsisting at law for the benefit of the premises and giving a right of way for vehicles;

'the parties' means the applicant and the land owner and 'party' shall be construed accordingly;

'the premises' means the premises served by the way in respect of which an application for an easement is made;

'the value of the premises' has the meaning given in regulation 11(4).

(2) Any reference in these Regulations to a numbered regulation shall be construed as a reference to the regulation so numbered in these Regulations.

3 Entitlement to make an application

(1) An owner of any premises may, as respects a way to which section 68 of the Act applies, apply for the creation of an easement in accordance with these Regulations.

(2) For the purposes of these Regulations, the owner who makes an application shall be referred to as 'the applicant', the land crossed by the way shall be referred to as 'the land' and the person who, for the time being, has the freehold title to the land, shall be referred to as 'the land owner'.

4   Prescribed date

The prescribed date for the purpose of section 68(1)(b) of the Act is 5th May 1993.

5   Nature of easement

An easement created in accordance with these Regulations shall –

(a)   be subject to any limitation agreed by the parties or determined by the Lands Tribunal;

(b)   include any right incidental to the right of way agreed by the parties or determined by the Lands Tribunal; and

(c)   be subject to any rule of law which would apply to the easement had it been acquired by prescription.

6   Procedure for making an application

(1)   An application for the easement shall be made by the applicant serving a notice on the land owner.

(2)   The application must be served within 12 months of the date on which these Regulations come into force or, if later, the date on which the relevant use of the way has ceased.

(3)   The application shall contain the information specified in paragraph 1, and be accompanied by the information specified in paragraph 2, of the Schedule to these Regulations.

7   Unopposed applications

(1)   Where the land owner does not object to the application he shall, within three months of receipt of the application, serve a notice on the applicant, agreeing to the application.

(2)   The notice shall contain the following information –

(a)   the name and address of the land owner and a description of his interest in the land; and

(b)   a statement confirming that upon payment of the compensation sum he will provide a written receipt.

(3)   The notice shall be accompanied by evidence of the land owner's title to the land.

8   Opposed applications

(1)   Where the land owner has objections to the application, he shall, within three months of receipt of the application, serve a notice (a 'counter notice') on the applicant, objecting to the application.

(2)   Objections to the application may be made on the following grounds –

(a)   the applicant has served the application after the expiry of the period for service;

(b) the applicant has not provided the information required by regulation 6(3);

(c) information provided by the applicant is not correct;

(d) the easement should be subject to limitations other than those (if any) described in the application;

(e) any rights incidental to the right of way, which are described in the application as being rights which should be included in the easement, are not agreed;

(f) the value of the premises is not agreed.

(3) The counter notice shall contain the following information–

(a) the name and address of the land owner and a description of his interest in the land;

(b) the objections to the application; and

(c) any alternative proposals.

(4) The counter notice shall be accompanied by –

(a) any evidence relevant to the objections and alternative proposals; and

(b) evidence of the land owner's title to the land.

9   Amended application and amended counter notice

(1) Within two months of receipt of a counter notice, the applicant may serve on the land owner an amended application addressing the objections and any alternative proposals set out in the counter notice.

(2) An amended application shall contain the information specified in paragraph 1 of the Schedule to these Regulations and shall be accompanied by any evidence relevant to the applicant's response to the objections and any alternative proposals set out in the counter notice.

(3) Where the applicant has served an amended application on the land owner, the land owner shall, within two months of receipt of the amended application –

(a) serve a notice on the applicant agreeing to the amended application and confirming that upon payment of the compensation sum he will provide a written receipt, or

(b) serve an amended counter notice on the applicant objecting to the amended application.

(4) An amended counter notice shall comply with regulation 8(2), (3) and (4)(a) and, for this purpose –

(a) references in regulation 8(2) and (3) to the application, except for the reference in sub-paragraph (a) of regulation 8(2), shall be treated as references to the amended application; and

(b) an objection may also be made on the ground that the applicant has served the amended application after the expiry of the period for service or has not provided the information required by paragraph (2) of this regulation.

(5)   Where the land owner has served an amended counter notice on the applicant, the applicant may, within two months of receipt of the amended counter notice, serve a notice on the land owner agreeing to the amended counter notice.

10   Lands Tribunal

(1)   Where a counter notice has been served, either party may, where there is a dispute relating to any matter other than the value of the premises, request the Lands Tribunal to determine the matter in dispute by sending a notice of reference to the Lands Tribunal in accordance with the Lands Tribunal Rules 1996.

(2)   The notice of reference shall have annexed to it –

    (a)   the application;

    (b)   the counter notice; and

    (c)   if applicable, the amended application and amended counter notice.

11   Calculation of the compensation sum

(1)   Subject to paragraph (2), the compensation sum shall be 2 per cent of the value of the premises.

(2)   Where the premises were in existence on –

    (a)   31st December 1905; or

    (b)   30th November 1930,

the compensation sum shall be 0.25 per cent. or 0.5 per cent. of the value of the premises respectively.

(3)   Where the premises are in residential use and replaced other premises on the same site which were also in residential use ('the former premises'), the compensation sum shall be calculated in accordance with paragraph (2) by reference to the date on which the former premises were in existence.

(4)   For the purposes of these Regulations, the value of the premises shall be calculated as at the valuation date on the basis of the open market value of the premises with the benefit of the easement.

(5)   In paragraph (4), the 'valuation date' means the date as at which the premises are valued for the purposes of the application, being a date no more than 3 months before the date on which the application is served.

12   Determination of the compensation sum in default of agreement

(1)   Where no agreement can be reached on the value of the premises, either party may serve on the other a notice (the 'valuation notice') requiring the amount to be determined by a chartered surveyor.

(2)   Where a valuation notice has been served, the appointment of a chartered surveyor shall be agreed by the parties within one month of the service of the valuation notice and, where agreement on such appointment cannot be reached, either party may request the President of the Royal Institution of Chartered Surveyors to appoint a chartered surveyor.

(3) Where a chartered surveyor has been appointed in accordance with paragraph (2), the following provisions shall apply as appropriate –

    (a) where the appointment has been made by the President of the Royal Institution of Chartered Surveyors, the parties shall be equally liable for the costs of that appointment;

    (b) unless the parties agree that the chartered surveyor shall act as an independent expert, he shall act as an arbitrator and the provisions of the Arbitration Act 1996 shall apply; and

    (c) where the chartered surveyor acts as an independent expert, the parties shall –

        (i) be bound by his final decision; and

        (ii) each party shall bear their own costs and shall be equally liable for the fees and costs of the chartered surveyor.

13 Payment of the compensation sum

(1) Where –

    (a) the land owner has notified the applicant in accordance with regulation 7 or 9(3)(a);

    (b) the applicant has notified the land owner in accordance with regulation 9(5); or

    (c) any matters in dispute have been determined in accordance with regulation 10 or 12,

the applicant shall pay the compensation sum to the land owner.

(2) The compensation sum shall be paid within two months of –

    (a) the date of notification under regulation 7 or paragraph (3)(a) or (5) of regulation 9, as the case may be; or

    (b) where a determination is made under regulation 10 or 12, the date of the determination or, if more than one such determination is made, the date of the last determination.

(3) The land owner shall, within one month from the date of receipt of the compensation sum, provide the applicant with a written receipt for that sum.

14 Payment into court

Where –

(a) the land owner does not serve a notice in accordance with either regulation 7 or 8; or

(b) the applicant has served an amended application on the land owner and the land owner fails to act in accordance with regulation 9(3),

the applicant may, within two months of the expiry of the period for service of a notice under regulation 7, 8 or 9(3), as the case may be, pay the compensation sum into a county court in accordance with the Court Funds Rules 1987.

15   Creation of the easement

Upon payment of the compensation sum either –

(a)   to the land owner in accordance with regulation 13; or

(b)   into court in accordance with regulation 14,

the easement shall be created.

16   Notices

(1)   A notice under these Regulations shall be in writing and may be served by sending it by post.

(2)   Where any notice is required by these Regulations to be served within a specified period, the parties may, except in the case of an application, agree in writing to extend or further extend that period.

17   Abandonment etc by applicant

Where the applicant withdraws or otherwise fails to continue with the application at any stage, he shall be liable for the reasonable costs incurred by the land owner.

SCHEDULE

INFORMATION TO BE PROVIDED BY THE APPLICANT

1   The application shall contain the following information –

(a)   the name and address of the applicant;

(b)   a description of the premises;

(c)   a description of the applicant's interest in the premises;

(d)   details of the current use of the premises and the use during the period giving rise to the entitlement to apply for the easement;

(e)   where the relevant use of the way has ceased, the date of the cessation;

(f)   where the premises, or, where regulation 11(3) applies, the former premises, were in existence on 31st December 1905 or 30th November 1930, a statement confirming those facts;

(g)   the nature of the use of the access, including any limitation or incidental right to which the easement should be subject or which should be included in the easement;

(h)   the dimensions of the width of the way; and

(i)   the proposed compensation sum to be paid to the land owner in respect of the easement, together with the basis on which it is calculated.

2   The application shall be accompanied by –

(a)   a map of an appropriate scale (1:1250 or 1:2500) showing the premises (marked in blue), the way (marked in red) and sufficient other land to establish the exact location of the premises and the way in relation to the surrounding area;

(b)   evidence (which may include a statutory declaration) that –

   (i)   the way is a way to which section 68 of the Act applies; and
   (ii)   where the application is served after 12 months of the date on which these Regulations come into force, either that the relevant use of the way has not ceased or that such use ceased no more than 12 months before the date on which the application is served; and

(c)   an estimate prepared by a chartered surveyor of the value of the premises as at the valuation date, and 'valuation date' has the same meaning for this purpose as in regulation 11(4).

INDEX

References are to paragraph numbers.